Aelbert Cuyp

Thames & Hudson

Edited by Arthur K. Wheelock Jr.

Aelbert Cuyp

Shell Oil Company Foundation, on behalf of the employees of Shell Oil Company, is proud to make possible this presentation to the American people.

The exhibition is organized by the National Gallery of Art, Washington, in cooperation with the National Gallery, London, and the Rijksmuseum, Amsterdam.

The exhibition in Washington is supported by an indemnity from the Federal Council on the Arts and the Humanities.

This book is published in association with the exhibition *Aelbert Cuyp*.

Exhibition dates

National Gallery of Art, Washington
7 October 2001 – 13 January 2002

National Gallery, London
13 February – 12 May 2002

Rijksmuseum, Amsterdam
7 June – 1 September 2002

Library of Congress Cataloging-in-Publication Data

Cuyp, Aelbert, 1620 – 1691. Aelbert Cuyp / edited by Arthur K. Wheelock, Jr.

p.   cm.

Catalog of an exhibition held at the National Gallery of Art, Washington, 7 Oct. 2001 – 13 Jan. 2002, National Gallery, London, 13 Feb. – 12 May 2002, Rijksmuseum, Amsterdam, 7 June – 1 Sept. 2002. Includes bibliographical references.

ISBN 0-89468-286-5 (softcover)
ISBN 0-500-51057-1 (hardcover)

1. Cuyp, Aelbert, 1620 – 1691 — Exhibitions.
I. Wheelock, Arthur K. II. National Gallery of Art (U.S.)
III. National Gallery (Great Britain) IV. Rijksmuseum (Netherlands)

ND653.C8 A4 2001
759.9492 — dc21   2001030757

British Library Cataloging-in-Publication Data

A catalogue record for this book is available from the British Library.
Library of Congress Catalog Card Number 2001088625

First published in hardcover in the United States of America in 2001 by Thames & Hudson Inc., 500 Fifth Avenue, New York, New York 10110.

First published in the United Kingdom in 2001 by Thames & Hudson Ltd, 181A High Holborn, London WC1V 7QX.

Produced by the National Gallery of Art
Editor-in-chief, Judy Metro
Editor, Julie Warnement
Designer, Wendy Schleicher Smith

Typeset in Adobe Jenson and Officina Serif by Duke & Company, Devon, Pennsylvania, and printed on Lumisilk matte by Arnoldo Mondadori Editore, Verona, Italy

Details

cover: cat. 28; pages 2 – 3: cat. 8;
pages 12 – 13: cat. 19; page 14: cat. 35;
page 34: cat. 29; page 52: cat. 39;
page 64: cat. 45; page 74: cat. 49;
pages 86 – 87: cat. 35; page 91: cat. 1;
page 108: cat. 9; page 117: cat. 12;
page 137: cat. 22; page 175: cat. 40;
pages 212 – 213: cat. 36; pages 292 – 293: cat. 12

Lenders to the Exhibition

Maida and George Abrams

Amsterdams Historisch Museum

Anglesey Abbey (The National Trust)

Ascott (The National Trust)

The British Museum, London

Hannah L. Carter

The Cleveland Museum of Art

Collection Frits Lugt, Institut Néerlandais, Paris

Colnaghi, London

The Corcoran Gallery of Art, Washington

Dordrechts Museum

The Trustees of Dulwich Picture Gallery, London

École Nationale Supérieure des Beaux Arts, Paris

English Heritage (The Iveagh Bequest, Kenwood)

Fogg Art Museum, Harvard University
   Art Museums, Cambridge

Graphische Sammlung Albertina, Vienna

Groninger Museum, The Netherlands

Indianapolis Museum of Art

The Israel Museum, Jerusalem

The J. Paul Getty Museum, Los Angeles

Mr. and Mrs. George M. Kaufman

Kunstsammlungen zu Weimar

Los Angeles County Museum of Art

The Menil Collection, Houston

The Metropolitan Museum of Art, New York

Musées Royaux des Beaux-Arts de Belgique, Brussels

Museum Boijmans Van Beuningen, Rotterdam

The National Gallery, London

National Gallery of Art, Washington

National Gallery of Scotland, Edinburgh

Private Collections

Her Majesty Queen Elizabeth II

Residenzgalerie Salzburg, Salzburg

Rijksmuseum, Amsterdam

Mrs. Edward Speelman

Staatliche Museen zu Berlin, Kupferstichkabinet

Städelsches Kunstinstitut, Frankfurt am Main

Statens Museum for Kunst, Copenhagen

Stichting Collection P. en N. de Boer, Amsterdam

Szépmüvészeti Múzeum, Budapest

Teylers Museum, Haarlem

The Toledo Museum of Art

Wadsworth Atheneum Museum of Art, Hartford

Wallraf-Richartz-Museum, Cologne

Note to the Reader

The painting entries are written by Alan Chong (AC), Axel Rüger (AR), and Arthur K. Wheelock Jr. (AKW).

The drawing entries, written by Wouter Kloek (WK), are based on material generously supplied by Egbert Haverkamp-Begemann, which incorporates the pioneering work of the late Jan van Gelder and his wife Ingrid van Gelder-Jost.

Dimensions are cited in centimeters, followed by inches in parentheses.

Directors' Foreword

Aelbert Cuyp (1620–1691) was a visual poet. His light-filled depictions of the Dutch landscape — views of shepherds and herds of cattle resting in verdant pastures, travelers wending past picturesque ruins, or stately sailing ships anchored on the inland waterways near his native Dordrecht — have entranced viewers ever since the seventeenth century. Not only did he draw the inspiration for his images from the land itself, for he made numerous drawings, both refined and expressive, documenting motifs he found in nature, but he also turned to Dutch literary and pictorial traditions that celebrated arcadian ideals.

Despite his fame, the magnitude of Cuyp's creative achievement has never been fully understood. Until now, no international loan exhibition has ever brought together a full range of his paintings and drawings. But with this exhibition, a careful selection of Cuyp's works surveys the breadth of this remarkable artist's achievement and provides an overview of his career, from his early drawings of the late 1630s to the fully realized paintings he created in the 1660s.

The exhibition and catalogue are the result of a close collaboration between the National Gallery of Art, Washington, the National Gallery, London, and the Rijksmuseum, Amsterdam. Arthur K. Wheelock Jr., curator of northern baroque painting at the National Gallery of Art, Axel Rüger, curator of Dutch paintings at the National Gallery, London, and Wouter Kloek, curator at the Rijksmuseum, all contributed to the catalogue and guided the project at their respective institutions.

The catalogue, which benefits from the contributions of a number of scholars, contains essays that help expand our understanding of Cuyp's work and its historical significance. Arthur Wheelock, with contributions from Jacob de Groot, provides an overview of Cuyp's artistic career, paying special attention to the historical, literary, and pictorial ideals that underlie Cuyp's distinctive choice of subject matter and manner of painting; Alan Chong discusses Cuyp's patrons and the history of Cuyp's artistic reputation; Emilie Gordenker examines the costumes in Cuyp's paintings; Marika Spring writes about the pigments and materials Cuyp used; and Egbert Haverkamp-Begemann surveys Cuyp's drawings, describing their distinctive character and their place in Dutch art.

Aelbert Cuyp is made possible in Washington by the enthusiastic support of Shell Oil Company Foundation. We owe particular thanks to Steven Miller, chairman, president, and chief executive officer of Shell Oil Company, for Shell's ongoing commitment to the National Gallery of Art. Indeed, Shell has sponsored a range of exhibitions at the Gallery over the course of fifteen years: with *Aelbert Cuyp*, we celebrate the fifth exhibition of Dutch art to benefit from Shell's support. The exhibition in Washington is also supported by an indemnity from the Federal Council on the Arts and the Humanities. In London, Océ N.V.'s longstanding support for the National Gallery has been extended by their generous agreement to sponsor the exhibition. In Amsterdam, we owe many thanks to Royal Philips Electronics, founder of the New Rijksmuseum, who made the exhibition and catalogue possible there with their generous support. Together, the Rijksmuseum and Philips, two Dutch multinational partners, look forward to presenting in the near future impressive exhibitions at the renovated national museum in Amsterdam.

Earl A. Powell III	Neil MacGregor	Ronald de Leeuw
Director	*Director*	*Director General*
National Gallery of Art	*National Gallery*	*Rijksmuseum*
Washington	*London*	*Amsterdam*

Acknowledgments

This exhibition has been a shared enterprise between the National Gallery of Art, Washington, the National Gallery, London, and the Rijksmuseum, Amsterdam. The enthusiasm of my colleagues from these institutions, particularly Axel Rüger at the National Gallery and Wouter Kloek at the Rijksmuseum, has greatly enhanced the character of the exhibition. These colleagues also share with me enormous appreciation for the many contributions of other experts on the artist, in particular Alan Chong, Norma Jean Calderwood Curator of the Collection, Isabella Stewart Gardner Museum, Boston, and Egbert Haverkamp-Begemann, professor emeritus, New York University, both of whom helped advise on the selection of the works. Chong's 1992 dissertation on Cuyp, which is the standard work on the artist's paintings, served as the basis for many of the observations and much of the provenance information contained in this catalogue. Professor Haverkamp-Begemann, who is preparing a book on Cuyp's drawings, generously shared the unpublished manuscript with Wouter Kloek for his use in writing the entries on the drawings in this catalogue. This manuscript, which also includes information about the provenances of the drawings, is, in itself, indebted to the extensive research on Cuyp's drawings undertaken in the 1960s by Jan van Gelder and his wife Ingrid van Gelder-Jost.

Each of us would like to extend our deepest gratitude to the many institutions and private collectors that have generously lent their precious works to this celebration of Aelbert Cuyp's artistic genius. The enthusiasm with which this project has been greeted has meant that the exhibition includes many of Cuyp's finest paintings and drawings, works that demonstrate both the extraordinary quality and surprising range of his subject matter. Many of the drawings, moreover, relate specifically to the paintings, thus revealing much about Cuyp's working methods.

Among the many colleagues who kindly advised or assisted on various aspects of the exhibition, I would particularly like to acknowledge Frits Duparc for his important role in the genesis of the show: it was he who first suggested to me that an Aelbert Cuyp exhibition would be a fascinating and fruitful project. Another individual who helped guide me in the beginning stages of this project was Peter Schatborn, who spent many hours with me looking at the remarkable collection of Cuyp drawings in the Rijksprentenkabinet in Amsterdam. My initial discussion about sharing the exhibition with the National Gallery, London, was with Christopher Brown, formerly chief curator at that institution. In planning this exhibition, I also had extremely useful discussions with Jacob de Groot, former director of the Dordrechts Museum and a contributor to this catalogue.

Numerous other colleagues have assisted and advised us on this project, or have supported our requests for loans of valuable and fragile works of art; we thank Ronni Baer, Suzanne Benfield, Martin Bijl, Mária van Berge-Gerbaud, Holm Bevers, Peter and Hilde de Boer, Julius Bryant, Emanuelle Brugerolles, Edwin Buijsen, Jill Capobianco, Michael Clarke, Laura Coyle, Anthony Crichton-Stuart, Marguerite Glass, Diane De Grazia, Ian Dejardin, Frederik J. Duparc, Ildikó Ember, Jan Piet Filedt Kok, Jeroen Giltaij, Dare Hartwell, Jo Hedley, Guido Jansen, Lorraine Karasel, Ronda Kasl, Alison McNeil Kettering, Fritz Koreny, Alastair Laing, Friso Lammertse, Catherine Levesque, Walter Liedtke, Richard Lingner, Christopher Lloyd, Julia Lloyd Williams, John Loughman, Michael Maek-Gerard, Ekkehard Mai, Volker Manuth, Patrice Marandel, Bram Meij, Norbert Middelkoop, Miklós Mojzer, Otto Naumann, Larry Nichols, Robert Noortman, Gill Pessach, Michiel Plomp, Willem de Ridder, Ned Rifkin, Bill Robinson, Martin Royalton-Kisch, Francis

Russell, Marijn Schapelhouman, Peter Schoon, Desmond Shawe-Taylor, Anthony Speelman, Margret Stuffmann, Peter Sutton, C. van Tuyl van Serooskerken, Sarah Walden, Lavinia Wellicome, Adele de Werff Stevens, Marieke de Winkel, James A. Welu, and Eric Zafran. Finally, we are indebted to Jennifer Kilian and Katy Kist for their excellent translations of the Dutch text into English.

We would also like to acknowledge the importance of various centers for scholarly research, whose staff and resources were essential to the success of our project, including the British Library, London; the National Art Library, London; the National Gallery Library, London; the Frick Art Reference Library, New York; the National Gallery of Art Library, Washington; and the Netherlands Institute for Art History, The Hague.

In each of the three participating institutions many individuals worked tirelessly to ensure the exhibition's success. We thank our colleagues at the National Gallery in London and at the Rijksmuseum in Amsterdam.

In Washington, Carol Christensen skillfully conserved the four paintings in the exhibition from the National Gallery of Art's collection, recapturing pictorial subtleties that had been diminished because of old, discolored varnish. Melanie Gifford and Michael Palmer undertook scientific examinations of these paintings that helped answer intriguing questions about Cuyp's painting techniques. Richard Ford ably constructed a number of frames for paintings to enhance their appearance, while Hugh Phibbs helped frame a large number of the drawings. D. Dodge Thompson, Ann Bigley Robertson, and Jennifer Bumba-Kongo in the department of exhibitions handled the organization of the exhibition and administration of the loan requests. In the department of imaging and visual services, Sara Sanders-Buell gathered color transparencies from lenders. In the registrar's office Michelle Fondas and Sally Freitag coordinated the transportation of the works of art, while Mervin Richard of the department of loans and exhibitions conservation supervised the packing and safe transport of the panel paintings. Mark Leithauser, and his outstanding department of installation and design, developed the handsome installation of the exhibition. Finally, many people in the editors office contributed to the production of this catalogue: Judy Metro and Tam Curry Bryfogle supervised the project; Julie Warnement, with great care and patience, worked with the various authors to prepare and edit the manuscripts; and Wendy Schleicher Smith created its especially elegant design.

Finally, to the staff of the department of northern baroque painting at the National Gallery of Art, I am extremely grateful. Quint Gregory and Phoebe Avery helped develop the exhibition concept. Anna Tummers offered a number of keen insights on Cuyp and his paintings, and oversaw many of the complexities presented by this show. Aneta Georgievska-Shine helped prepare the bibliography for the catalogue. Michelle Naimo Bird, our staff assistant, diligently handled the many administrative demands connected with this project.

To all of those who have helped bring our project to its successful conclusion, we extend our deepest gratitude.

Arthur K. Wheelock Jr.

Essays

Aelbert Cuyp and the Depiction of the Dutch Arcadia   *Arthur K. Wheelock Jr., with contributions by Jacob M. de Groot*

The Netherlands that Aelbert Cuyp portrayed was a peaceful world, a verdant, sun-filled arcadia blessed with gentle breezes and billowing clouds.[1] Shepherds tend herds of cattle and sheep graze contentedly in pastoral landscapes, travelers wend their way along well-beaten paths to enjoy beautiful vistas and marvel at picturesque ruins, and sailing ships find steady winds to guide them along inland waterways. Farm buildings, protectively nestled amongst stands of tall, gracefully bending trees, and well-maintained fences and footbridges indicate the harmonious coexistence of man and nature in the young Dutch Republic. Even in Cuyp's rare depictions of contemporary events, such as the massing of the Dutch fleet near his native Dordrecht (cat. 28), nature complements the drama of the unfolding scene: the great ships are visually joined to the imposing cloud formations and enhanced by sunlight streaming across the expansive sky.

Aelbert Cuyp is one of the Netherlands' greatest artists, a visual poet whose idyllic scenes of the Dutch countryside have entranced collectors and connoisseurs ever since the seventeenth century. The appeal of his paintings and drawings, however, lies not only in their subject matter but also in their distinctive style, for Cuyp infused his arcadian subjects and river views with a sensitivity to light, color, and clarity of form that is firmly grounded in reality. Despite Cuyp's substantial fame, surprisingly little is known about the specifics of the artist's career or the motivations that drove his distinctive approach to the representation of nature. These concerns, however, can be addressed by tracing the broad evolution of the artist's life and career — from his early,

monochromatic depictions of the native Dutch landscape to his later, light-filled pastoral scenes — and by examining his work in relation to broader intellectual and artistic currents within the Dutch Republic, primarily contemporary ideals of arcadia and the golden age.

Cuyp spent his entire artistic career in Dordrecht. Though not an important artistic center, it was a wealthy city proud of its heritage as the oldest city in Holland (fig. 1).[2] Joan Blaeu, in his topographic atlas of Dutch cities of 1649, described Dordrecht as "the principal [city], and the capital of Holland: therefore some call it Mother and Queen of the cities in this lovely landscape."[3] John Ray, an English traveler who visited the Netherlands in the late 1660s, remarked that the elegantly paved streets of this large, well-built city were so clean "that a man may walk them in Slippers without wetting his foot in the midst of Winter."[4] Dordrecht's mercantile importance largely resulted from its favorable geographic situation at the confluence of a number of major inland waterways, including the Rhine, the Maas, and the Merwede (fig. 2). From this location ships could easily sail to Rotterdam and the North Sea, or inland to Nijmegen and beyond. As an old, established city, Dordrecht had important economic advantages, among them the privilege of staple

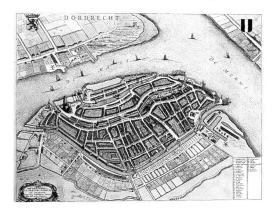

1 **Dordrecht** from Joan Blaeu, **Toonneel der steden van de Vereenighde Nederlanden** (Amsterdam, 1649), private collection, Washington

2 Aelbert Cuyp, **A View of the Maas at Dordrecht,** c. 1644, The J. Paul Getty Museum, Los Angeles

right (gained in 1299), whereby shipments of wine, grain, wood, and certain other goods were unloaded in Dordrecht and assessed for duties before being allowed to travel further.[5]

While its well-protected inner harbor was lined with stately homes, Dordrecht's distinctive skyline was best viewed from the Maas or from the villages of Papendrecht or Zwijndrecht, which were situated on the far banks of this broad and busy river. From these vantage points, one could admire both the elegant Groothoofdspoort, the city's major port of entry, and the massive Grote Kerk, the city's real and symbolic center of power. Indeed, the formidable presence of the Dutch Reformed Church in the city was instrumental in its being chosen for the site of the important Synod of Dordrecht in 1618–1619. This synod codified Reformed Church worship and instigated the translation of the Bible into the Dutch language (the Statenbijbel was published in 1637). The Synod of Dordrecht was also historically important for siding with the Counter-Remonstrants, who preached predestination, rather than with the Remonstrants, who believed in free will as a means to achieve grace.[6]

The results of the Synod of Dordrecht reinforced the conservative character of Dordrecht's rich patrician class. Aelbert Jacobsz Cuyp, who was baptized in the Reformed Church in October 1620, must have fit comfortably within this ambiance as he grew and matured as a painter in his native city.[7] His father, the painter Jacob Gerritsz Cuyp (1594–1652), numbered several wealthy Dordrecht patrician families among his patrons and served as a deacon in the Walloon, or French-speaking Reformed Church.[8] Jacob had joined this church in 1618, shortly after his marriage to Aertken Cornelisdr van Cooten, and seems to have raised his son to value religion and to live an upright life. Arnold Houbraken, a native of Dordrecht, noted in his early eighteenth-century commentary on

the artist that Aelbert was a man of *onbesproken leven* (irreproachable character).[9]

When Aelbert eventually married at the age of thirty-eight, he chose as his wife Cornelia Boschman (1617–1689), the widow of a wealthy Dordrecht regent, Johan van den Corput (1609–1650).[10] Cornelia, who had three children from her previous marriage, was the granddaughter of Franciscus Gomarus, a Leiden theologian who had led the Counter-Remonstrants at the Synod of Dordrecht.[11] During his later life, Aelbert became extremely active in religious and social activities, serving as a deacon and elder of the Reformed Church, a regent of a major charity associated with the Grote Kerk (Heilig Geest-en Peesthuis der Groter Kerk), and a member of the tribunal of Zuid Holland.[12] Both his marriage and his life pursuits proved financially rewarding, for at his death in November 1691, he was one of the wealthiest men in Dordrecht.

Houbraken, whose sparse account is the earliest commentary on the artist's life and work, related that Aelbert received his basic artistic training from his father.[13] Although nothing more is known about the nature of his training, Aelbert was certainly raised in an artistic ambiance. His grandfather Gerrit Gerritsz Cuyp (c. 1565–1644) was Dordrecht's most important glass painter. His uncle, Jacob Gerritsz Cuyp's half brother, was Benjamin Gerritsz Cuyp (1612–1652), a prolific painter of religious subjects and peasant and inn scenes, which he executed in a distinctively expressive, monochromatic style.[14] By the early-to-mid 1630s, when Aelbert probably entered his father's workshop, Jacob had developed a successful career as a specialist in portraiture, although he was also known for his depictions of animals (see cat. 2, fig. 1).[15] Jacob occasionally combined these two interests in his pastoral portraits, a genre that he probably learned from his teacher, the famed Utrecht artist and teacher Abraham Bloemaert (1564 – 1651), or from Bloemaert's colleague Paulus Moreelse (1571 – 1638).[16] These delightful pastoral portraits focused upon aristocratic patrons, often women and children in the guise of shepherds or shepherdesses, situated within a landscape setting (fig. 3).

Jacob Cuyp's pastoral portraits reflect attitudes found in contemporary literature that eulogized a serene, idyllic life in the country, where the human spirit could be refreshed and gladdened.[17] Although these portraits were generally painted for aristocratic patrons, the ideals underlying such pastoral imagery were broadly shared in Dutch society during the early years of the seventeenth century. Indeed, religious traditions, sociological developments, and political circumstances had coalesced to reinforce a widely held belief that the newly formed Dutch Republic was entering into a golden age, one guided and protected by the munificence of God's blessing. The character of this belief held important implications for Cuyp's artistic approach.

3 Jacob Cuyp, **The Shepherdess**, 1628, Rijksmuseum, Amsterdam

Seventeenth-Century Views of the Golden Age and the Dutch Arcadia

Today, when we use the term the golden age to describe the Dutch Republic in the seventeenth century, we refer not only to the extraordinary achievements of its artists, poets, playwrights, and scientists, but also to its admirable political structure, tolerant attitudes toward different religious sects, maritime fleet, economic power, and prosperous way of life. But even before all of this came to pass, before Aelbert Cuyp first picked up his brushes, the concepts of a Dutch arcadia and golden age had already entered into the popular consciousness of the Dutch.

Jacob Cuyp's pastoral portraits were only one facet of this popular fascination with these concepts. Comparable attitudes also underlay the positive view of the Netherlands presented by artists who portrayed the specific characteristics of the Dutch countryside. The most significant of these images can be found in a series of landscape prints that were published in Haarlem and Amsterdam by Esaias van de Velde (1587 – 1630), Jan van de Velde (1593 – 1641), Claes Jansz Visscher (1587 – 1652), and Willem Buytewech (1591 / 1592 – 1624) in the second decade of the century. Their views of "pleasant places" in the vicinity of Haarlem captured the freshness of the Dutch countryside in appealing and inviting images (see fig. 14).

Most early seventeenth-century Dutch landscapists and marine painters, including Aelbert Cuyp, similarly captured the essential harmony of humanity and nature, whether depicting farmers or shepherds in their fields, skaters enjoying the ice on a cold winter's day (cat. 32), or sailors caring for the hulls of ships that were the backbone of the Dutch maritime empire (fig. 4). These artists, seemingly following Karel van Mander's advice in his 1604 treatise on painting, reveled in their opportunities to travel into the countryside, leaving the city at dawn "to see

the beauty outside, / where beaked musicians sing in the open."[18]
Van Mander's treatise opens with a poem by P.C. Ketel that contains
similar advice:

Take charcoal and chalk, pen, ink, paper
and draw what you see, whatever pleases your eye
. . . .
Return to the town…
when the trees' leaves, which gave you shade
serve you no longer.
The landscapes that you have seen outside
and recorded in your book,
you must now paint at home,
and bring to life in colours
which you have ground yourself.[19]

4 Simon de Vlieger, **Estuary at Dawn**, c. 1645, National Gallery of Art, Washington, Patrons' Permanent Fund and Gift in memory of Kathrine Dulin Folger

Cuyp, no less than any of his contemporaries, gained much of his
inspiration for his paintings from his drawings after nature. He not only
depicted landscapes with distant towns and cities (cat. 75), but also
focused on the picturesque beauty of rugged, weatherworn trees (cat. 55),
the broad, leafy shapes of woodland plants (cat. 96), or the simple dignity of a reclining cow (cat. 103). However, Cuyp's interest in landscape
elements was not all inclusive. One looks in vain for depictions of dilapidated barns, broken fences, and untended fields, subjects that appealed
to many of his contemporaries. The selectivity with which he approached
his subject matter and the manner in which he depicted those choices
indicate that he brought to his work an underlying framework. Understanding the character of that framework and its relationship to the contemporary political and social environment of the Netherlands as well
as to ideas with roots deep in antiquity is essential for assessing the artist's
unique interpretation of the Dutch landscape.

The literary precedents for Dutch ideals of the golden age and arcadia
hearken back to ancient Greece and Rome. The poet Hesiod (c. 800 B.C.)
was probably the first to describe the five ages — Gold, Silver, Bronze,
Heroic, and Iron — although Ovid's *Metamorphoses* was the main source
of such myths for the Dutch. Ovid was particularly expressive in describing a golden age of peace and prosperity when Saturn reigned and man
lived in easy communion with nature "untroubled by any fears." It was, as
Ovid wrote, "a season of everlasting spring, when peaceful zephyrs, with
their warm breath, caressed the flowers that sprang up without having
been planted."[20] The closely related concept of arcadia as a pastoral paradise ruled by Pan, with shepherds, shepherdesses, nymphs, and satyrs
dwelling in a world revolving around romantic love, stems from the writings of the Greek poet Theocritus (c. 310 – 250 B.C.).[21] These arcadian

5 Jan Krul, **Pastoral Scene** from **Eerlycke tytkorting** (Haarlem, 1634)

ideas were enormously popular in sixteenth-century courtly literature in France and Italy, literary traditions that, in turn, influenced Dutch writers and poets. A harmonious country existence was also glorified in Horace's widely read lyrical poem "Beatus ille" and in Virgil's *Georgics* and *Eclogues*.[22]

Descriptions of an idyllic and peaceful world from Greek antiquity fueled the imagination of the Dutch.[23] Playwrights, poets, and songwriters described the new political, cultural, and even physical reality evolving around them in comparable terms, although the images they created of a Dutch arcadia were extremely varied. A number of writers alluded to the joys of pastoral existence in evocative tales of shepherds and shepherdesses living in exotic, foreign lands.[24] Some romantic adventures set Greek or Roman shepherds and shepherdesses in the Dutch landscape[25] or Dutch shepherds and shepherdesses in a specific Dutch locale (fig. 5).[26] Other writers excluded their presence entirely and emphasized the pastoral beauty of the Dutch countryside itself. This setting was seen as no less appealing than the Greek Arcadia, as Hendrick Laurensz Spieghel demonstrated in his description of the onset of spring:

Thalia lead us out by Amsterlandic streams
To see the novel robe of the wet fields and orchards
Whose gaily light-green leaves all of a sudden burst
From swelling, gravid buds out of the dry-skinned branches.
The grass that in the autumn sank under layers of ice

Now raises pointed heads that pierce the water's surface.
The field, a while ago still an abounding lake,
Shows its rough edges now, its colors are returning.
Where long the darting fish played to their hearts' content
Soon cattle full of milk will daily be sent grazing.[27]

Early seventeenth-century references to the Dutch golden age not only commented upon the romantic appeal of pastoral life, but also stressed the social, political, and economic benefits resulting from the new political circumstances brought about by the Twelve-Year Truce (1609–1621). After the years of war and strife, hunger and hardship suffered during the Dutch revolt against Spanish control, the freedom to travel without fear of military encounter, as well as an influx of talented artists and craftsmen from the Southern Netherlands, gave new promise and hope to the Dutch people. The sense of wealth was enhanced by the untold riches that Dutch traders brought from distant shores — spices, exotic flowers and plants, rare shells, and even unknown types of animals and birds. The construction of dikes and windmills added new lands for crops and grazing, while improved waterways allowed commerce to pass easily from city to city, from town to town.[28]

The celebration of the new land and the benefits of peace were the focus of a number of images. Many Dutch maps had decorative borders depicting major cities, the diverse populace, historical curiosities, and the industrious ways in which careful nurturing of the land and its resources promised to bring prosperity (fig. 6).[29] The various print series published in Haarlem and Amsterdam shortly after the signing of the Twelve-Year Truce also reflect these ideas. For example, while Buytewech depicted the ruins of Brederode and Huis ter Kleef in his landscape series of 1616,

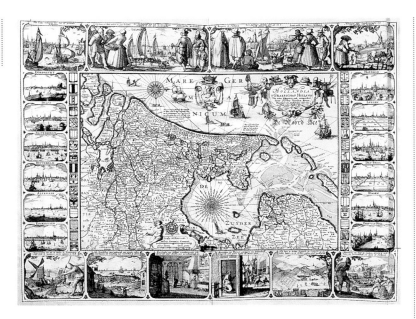

6 Claes Jansz Visscher, **Comitatus Hollandia**, Pieter van den Keere, ed. (1610), Palacio Royal, Madrid

reminding viewers of the destruction caused by Spanish aggression, he also included laborers working to reinvigorate the land by clearing and tending woodland and cultivating the soil. Buytewech, who infused his landscape prints with the ideals of Virgil's *Georgics*, also included scenes of prosperous farms in order to indicate the visual rewards of a virtuous life. Cuyp's early landscapes depicting well-maintained farms (cat. 6), hard-working peat laborers (cat. 4), and boats ferrying passengers across the river Merwede (cat. 8) share a comparable ideal of a promised land made more prosperous through the careful husbandry and cultivation of its resources by industrious inhabitants.

With peace, prosperity, and ease of travel also came the opportunity to build country houses, pleasant respites situated in garden settings away from the pressures of city or courtly life. The homes built outside urban centers such as Middelburg, The Hague, Utrecht, Amsterdam, and Dordrecht were not grand by European standards. Nevertheless, in a society that increasingly valued the associations of the pastoral, they came to represent the attainment of a fulfilling existence, one quite apart from economic or social status. The ideals of life spent on or near private estates were celebrated in country house poems *(hofdicht)*, a literary genre that parallels the type of imagery in Jacob Cuyp's pastoral portraits. Although international in origin and related in spirit to the writings of Horace and Virgil, these celebratory poems, which appeared as early as 1613 and flourished throughout the remainder of the decade, had a specifically Dutch character. Largely autobiographical, they stressed the enjoyment of gardens and horticulture, the nurturing of friendships, and the enhancement of family virtue.[30]

Country house poetry was but one of the many indications that the Twelve-Year Truce inspired an enormous confidence that peace would help usher in a new era, a new golden age for the Dutch Republic. For example, the anthology *Nederduytschen helicon* (Haarlem, 1610) organized poetry and prose into a narrative that contrasted the blessings of a peaceful Netherlands with the sufferings of the past. After describing the beauty of a number of Dutch cities, the text concludes: "Remain in pleasant peace in each city and village / free within Holland's garden / …Who denies / that this here is Saturn's golden time?"[31] Only one year later, the historian Johannes Pontanus wrote that Amsterdam was embarking on its golden age.[32] And in 1615, another historian, Jean Le Petit, similarly noted that, with the many military and social improvements enacted in recent years, the Dutch Republic had the potential to enter into a golden age.[33]

Such associations are not surprising since the Dutch were at that time in the midst of transforming their land and defining their own mythology. Reclamation projects had done much to change the "dunes, bogs, and lakes…as well as other barren districts, unfit for crops or pastures," into a landscape that was fertile and productive.[34] Nevertheless, the transformation of the Dutch landscape from an inhospitable region into an arcadian paradise was as much mental as physical. Well into the seventeenth century, foreigners described the land in terms far different from the evocative terms favored by Dutch writers. For example, in 1600 one French observer caustically remarked that Holland in "the winter is an immense layer of ice and in the summer an endless swamp."[35] Some fifty years later Andrew Marvell's poem *The Character of Holland* colorfully describes Holland as "indigested vomit of the sea."[36]

Arcadia, however, was how the Dutch viewed their own land. This notion took hold in large part because of the allegorical nature of contemporary Dutch thought, which underlay the mythologies the Dutch devised to explain their own history and character. For example, the Dutch firmly believed that they, like the ancient Israelites, were a chosen people, favored and blessed by God's protection. This analogy, based on the fact that the Dutch, like the Israelites, had fought for their existence against a powerful oppressor, not only lent their struggle against Spain a legitimacy based on historic and heroic precedent, but also allowed the Dutch the assurance that their "promised" land would be one of peace and prosperity. They even used the term fatherland (*vaderland*) to designate their own land, at a time in which this term was otherwise exclusively used to indicate the "home of our Father," the destination of every Christian pilgrim.[37]

Thus, the Dutch, who saw themselves as the modern-day Israelites, brought to the classical concept of a golden age a theological and moral component. The bounty they so richly deserved had been provided by God, and every celebration of nature, be it a drawing, a painting, or a

discovery through a telescope or microscope, was an act of homage to his greatness.[38]

The Dutch were also in the process of establishing a new society built upon a political structure radically different from those of other European nations. They associated their republic with Rome's,[39] often using Roman consuls as models of decorum and equanimity for Dutch burgomasters, magistrates, and judges, who were drawn from the wealthiest and most respected families.[40] This comparison became another component of their national myth, as did the successful revolt of their ancient forefathers, the Batavians, against the Romans.[41] As one political pamphlet expressed it in a dialogue between Batavia and a Friend of the Fatherland: "I [Batavia] was in olden times in a free state, thereafter very unfree and now I am returned to my first state…named now…the 'Hollandtsche Republijc.'"[42]

For the Dutch, the fiercely proud, bold Batavians epitomized all of their finest qualities, and they frequently invoked their name in the literature of the period. The most important expression of the link between the Batavians and Dutch pastoral life is, without question, J. van Heemskerk's *Batavische arcadia* (Amsterdam, 1647).[43] Heemskerk, who stressed this connection in his introduction, dedicated his book to the Dutch aristocracy in hopes of educating readers about his homeland while entertaining them with amorous stories of young lovers who take pleasure rides through the Dutch countryside. Describing his homeland or *vaderland* as an arcadia, Heemskerk interspersed his narrative journey with descriptions of the landscape and reflections upon the historical events that had made it possible for the Dutch to enjoy a golden age.[44] At one point in the story the fashionably dressed group even visits a country house, where Heemskerk's description of its productive dairy with well-fed cows, its orchards bursting with produce, and its fertile lands is comparable to a *hofdicht* or to a painting by Cuyp.[45]

The underlying sense of well-being and security that accompanies Heemskerk's fashionably dressed aristocrats as they partake of the pleasures of a homeland was a theme frequently found in later seventeenth-century pastoral literature. The most relevant of these works for our discussion of Cuyp's approach to the depiction of landscape is Lambert van den Bos' 1662 publication *Dordrechtsche arcadia*. Van den Bos not only expressed similar pride in the fatherland, but also localized its arcadian imagery in the landscape and riverscape near Dordrecht.[46] Most important, his descriptive passages of the landscape evoke atmospheric effects comparable to those in Aelbert Cuyp's finest works. His narrative, for example, opens at sunset as two foreign travelers and their horses cross the river Merwede on a ferry going from Dordrecht to Zwijndrecht: "The sun had begun to set in the late afternoon, and its [fire] heat begun to weaken, when ... [a] carriage with two horses, in an ordinary ferry, crossed the Dortsche Stroom [Merwede] to Swijndrecht."[47] Later, the protagonists of his story sit outside an enclosed garden on an idyllic green, where they enjoy "the pleasantness of the day, that was not one of the hottest, while a sweet wind was tempering the rays of sunlight."[48]

Despite the similarities between the pictorial characteristics of pastoral literature and the arcadian imagery of Cuyp's mature paintings, the two worlds are quite different. Cuyp never required such an extensive narrative thread to give interest to his landscapes, which, enhanced by the poetic beauty of atmospheric effects created by the setting sun and passing clouds, are there for us to quietly behold and enjoy. Although in Cuyp's mature works travelers frequently pass through the landscape, most of them are incidental figures, ones who demonstrate through ges-

ture and demeanor both the freedom to move through the countryside and the pleasure of viewing the pastoral beauty of the land (fig. 7). Occasionally, Cuyp portrayed aristocratic families riding out to enjoy the countryside or to hunt (cat. 29), but even in such paintings (often done in the manner of a *hofdicht*), he avoided anecdotal incidents that would freeze the moment in time and place. While some of Cuyp's landscapes do form a setting for religious or mythological scenes, such works are in the minority.

The underlying basis of Cuyp's distinctive pictorial language remained remarkably consistent throughout his career, whether he was painting his native Dutch countryside or an evocative vision of an idealized Dutch landscape seen through an overlay of pastoral beauty. The most important shift of emphasis may well be in the range of human activities that he depicted, for unlike his early paintings, his mature works rarely suggest that human endeavor is fundamental to the benefit of society.

In these works, arcadia is an accepted, enduring state of being. Shepherds, huntsmen, and travelers alike partake of its benefits without laboring to maintain and improve it.

The Cuyp Family[49]

Aelbert's choice of career was largely determined by his family's importance among the artists and artisans of Dordrecht. When Cuyp's grandfather, the glazier Gerrit Gerritsz Cuyp, arrived in Dordrecht in the early-to-mid 1580s from Venlo in the Southern Netherlands, Dordrecht was without a significant artistic heritage.[50] Nevertheless, one painting he certainly would have admired was a late fifteenth-century altarpiece commemorating the Saint Elizabeth Flood of 1421.[51] On the outer wings of the altarpiece was the earliest painted view of the city's distinctive profile, a depiction of the destruction this terrible tidal deluge caused to Dordrecht and its nearby villages and hamlets.

During the mid-sixteenth century a few minor artists were active in the city, but most of the important commissions were awarded to painters from other centers, among them Willem Key (1529–1568) from Antwerp, Jan van Scorel (1495–1562) from Utrecht, and Maarten van Heemskerk (1498–1574) from Haarlem.[52] Even as late as 1621, town officials awarded a prestigious commission to paint for the town hall a representation of the 1618–1619 meeting of the Synod of Dordrecht to the Delft artist Pouwel Weyts (d. 1629).[53] Indeed, the 1629 commission for a panoramic view of the city and its surrounding waterways (fig. 8) was awarded to the Utrecht artist Adam Willaerts (1577–1664), indicating that well into the seventeenth century the city fathers continued to lack confidence in the ability of local painters to create works that celebrated Dordrecht's appearance and historical significance. Nevertheless, this imposing work would eventually serve as an inspiration for Aelbert Cuyp's panoramic views of his native city (see cats. 35, 36).

8 Adam Willaerts, **View of Dordrecht**, 1629, Dordrechts Museum

Gerrit Gerritsz Cuyp joined the Saint Luke's Guild in Dordrecht in 1585, the same year that he married the Dordrecht widow Geerten Matthijsdr. Within ten years he had established a prosperous business primarily focused upon glazing and decorative painting. His artistic abilities are manifest in his only extant work: a glass window in the Sint Janskerk in Gouda (1596) that depicts the Dordrecht maiden in the Dutch garden surrounded by the four cardinal virtues. The cartoon for this window also demonstrates the artist's not insignificant merits as a draftsman.[54]

Gerrit's son, Jacob Gerritsz Cuyp, was a versatile artist who joined the Saint Luke's Guild in 1617. He not only dominated the city's artistic life for almost half a century, but also taught an entire generation of Dordrecht painters, including his half brother Benjamin and his son Aelbert. Other pupils include Paulus Lesire (1611 – after 1656) and Ferdinand Bol (1616 – 1680).[55] As a pupil of Abraham Bloemaert, a Utrecht master of Dordrecht descent, Jacob Cuyp depicted history scenes, religious subjects, still lifes, and poultry. He even painted a signboard. Nevertheless, Jacob was primarily a portraitist and the good citizens of Dordrecht were highly taken with his sober, skillful manner of painting.[56] Aside from his pastoral portraits (fig. 3), he also depicted pendant portraits, in which he portrayed sitters in conservative clothing against a gray-green background (figs. 9, 10).

Aelbert's uncle, Benjamin Cuyp, was an inventive artist who joined the Saint Luke's Guild in 1631. He produced inn scenes and religious subjects, making numerous variations of favorite themes, among them the Nativity, the Adoration of the Shepherds, and the Conversion of Saul (fig. 11). Although little is

known about his artistic contacts, he was apparently familiar with the work of Rembrandt, perhaps through the encouragement of Jacob Cuyp.[57]

Aelbert Cuyp's Artistic Training and Stylistic Evolution

Assessing the precise stages of Aelbert Cuyp's stylistic and thematic evolution is difficult because of the lack of documentation and of dated works of art. Nevertheless, a general view of Cuyp's training and artistic development has evolved through the years based on the research of a number of scholars.[58] Although no documents describe Aelbert's role within his father's active workshop, he almost certainly painted landscape backgrounds, and even animals, in a few of Jacob's figurative compositions. Interestingly, Aelbert continued to assist his father's artistic production in the early 1640s (see cat. 3) after he had begun to paint independent compositions (fig. 12). During this same period, he incorpo-

9 Jacob Gerritsz Cuyp, **Portrait of Anthonis Repelaer**, 1647, Dordrechts Museum

10 Jacob Gerritsz Cuyp, **Portrait of Emerantia van Driel**, 1647, Gemäldegalerie der Akademie der Bildenden Künste, Vienna

11 Benjamin Gerritsz Cuyp, **The Conversion of Saul**, 1640–1650, Gemäldegalerie der Akademie der Bildenden Künste, Vienna

12 Aelbert Cuyp, **The Melk-poortje on the Dordrecht Harbor,** 1639, private collection

13 Jan van Goyen, **Cottage by a River,** c. 1627/1629, National Gallery of Art, Washington, Ailsa Mellon Bruce Fund

14 Willem Buytewech, Plate 8 from the series **Verscheyden Lantschapjes (The Charcoal-Burner),** 1621, National Gallery of Art, Washington, Rosenwald Collection

rated animal motifs related to his father's etched series *Diversa animalia* into his naturalistic views of the Dutch countryside (cat. 2).[59] Unfortunately, because the records of the Saint Luke's Guild in Dordrecht are missing during the early 1640s, the exact year when Aelbert became an independent master is not certain.[60] It is entirely possible that he worked in his father's studio until the latter's death in 1652.

Despite the close, ongoing associations Aelbert had with Jacob's workshop, it seems unlikely that he received his entire artistic training with his father. There is little artistic precedent in Dordrecht for the views of the native Dutch landscape that so characterize Cuyp's early drawings and paintings.[61] Stylistically and thematically these works relate broadly to the tonal landscapes painted in various artistic centers in the Netherlands during the 1630s and early 1640s, most notably by Jan van Goyen (1596–1656). Van Goyen — who was born in Leiden, trained in Haarlem, and lived in The Hague after the mid-1630s — traveled extensively throughout the Netherlands with sketchbook in hand. He used these rapid sketches, which depict dilapidated farmhouses, river views, and vistas of distant towns and cities (fig. 13), as the basis for paintings that he executed with a quick, unerring hand. One of Van Goyen's favorite subjects was Dordrecht viewed across the Dortse Kil (see cat 18, fig. 2).[62]

Cuyp certainly knew Van Goyen's paintings and drawings, and, perhaps inspired by the latter's interest in traveling to distant reaches of the Dutch Republic, he literally followed in the older artist's footsteps to Amersfoort, Nijmegen, Rhenen, and beyond. Nevertheless, it seems improbable that he was ever Van Goyen's student.[63] While Cuyp's early painted landscapes are also monochromatic, they are executed with dense paint and vigorous brushstrokes that differ from the loose brushwork characteristic of Van Goyen's style. The elegantly rendered trees in Cuyp's drawings (cat. 51), moreover, are more comparable to those in drawings and etchings by the Rotterdam artist Willem Buytewech (fig. 14) than to those in Van Goyen's work.

While this stylistic association hardly identifies Buytewech as Cuyp's teacher (Buytewech died when Cuyp was but four years old), it indicates that Cuyp was familiar with artistic traditions in Rotterdam. Cuyp's

stylistic and thematic connections with other Rotterdam artists, including Herman Saftleven the Younger (1609–1685), his brother Cornelis (1607–1681), and Simon de Vlieger (c. 1601–1653), raise the possibility that he studied awhile in Rotterdam. Indeed, Dordrecht and Rotterdam had numerous artistic and commercial ties, not only because of their physical proximity but also because of Rotterdam's location on the trade route between Dordrecht and the North Sea.

While no documentary evidence specifically links Aelbert Cuyp with Rotterdam, drawings Cuyp made about 1640 of the Buurkerk and Maria-kerk in Utrecht (cats. 46–48) confirm that he visited that artistic center early in his career. Hence, it is entirely possible that Cuyp, following a path similar to the one trod by his father, developed his artistic sensitivities in Utrecht, which was, moreover, his mother's native city. Cuyp, however, probably did not study with his father's master, Abraham Bloemaert, even though Bloemaert had remained the most important teacher for young artists in Utrecht. Although extremely versatile, Bloemaert did not paint native landscapes or stall interiors, specialties Cuyp developed early in his career.[64]

15 Herman Saftleven, **Dune Rim under Stormy Sky**, c. 1630, Museum Boijmans Van Beuningen, Rotterdam

For a number of reasons, not least among them Cuyp's early interest in depicting monochromatic native landscapes and stall interiors, it seems that Cuyp came into contact with Herman Saftleven, who had moved from Rotterdam to Utrecht in 1632.[65] At the beginning of his career Saftleven had painted expressive native landscapes, ones that capture the drama of a stormy sky swirling over the flat, Dutch dunescape (fig. 15). Although broadly reflective of Jan van Goyen's tonal landscapes of the 1620s and 1630s, Saftleven's views have more pronounced contrasts of light and dark and more expressively brushed impastos. Cuyp similarly enlivened his dune landscapes from the early 1640s with strong chiaroscuro contrasts and restless brushwork in the impastos. Cuyp's landscapes, moreover, often include a small shepherd pointing into the distance (see cat. 2), a motif Saftleven also used in his paintings.[66]

In the mid-1630s Saftleven's talented brother Cornelis, a specialist in animal and genre scenes, joined him in Utrecht.[67] The two artists frequently collaborated in the late 1630s and 1640s, with Cornelis painting figures and animals in Herman's barn interiors and landscape compositions (fig. 16). Cornelis, who was an excellent draftsman, based his figures on life drawings executed in black chalk (fig. 17). These drawings are extremely close in style to those subsequently made by Cuyp (see cats. 104–106), further suggesting that the young Dordrecht artist was familiar with the artistic production of the Saftleven workshop. The example of the two artists' successful collaboration would have served Cuyp well as an assistant in his father's workshop (see cat. 3).

Utrecht must have been an exciting intellectual and artistic center during the 1630s and 1640s for an aspiring artist such as Cuyp. It was there, more than in any other city, that broader European literary and pictorial traditions infused and transformed the indigenous Dutch cul-

ture. Pastoral ideals in poetry, plays, and painting truly took hold in Utrecht because the city
was a melting pot for artists and writers who
had lived and trained abroad. For example,
Cuyp was certainly influenced by the fanciful
scenes of exotic birds and animals made by
Roelandt Savery (1578–1639), who had once
been court painter for Rudolf II in Prague.[68]
Savery often included a variety of animals in his
paintings, for example, his *Orpheus Charming
the Animals* (fig. 18), in order to suggest ideals of
harmony and abundance, themes that became
important for Cuyp as well (see cat. 1).

Even more important for determining the
character of painting in Utrecht were artists
who had traveled to Italy for inspiration. Some,
such as Hendrick ter Brugghen (1588–1629)
and Gerrit van Honthorst (1592–1656), had
discovered there the expressive drama of Cara-
vaggio's paintings. Others, such as Cornelis van Poelenburch (1594–1667),
had been inspired by the classical dignity of Raphael's mythological and
religious figures as well as by the idealized arcadian landscapes found in
small copper paintings by Adam Elsheimer (1578–1610). Still others,
in particular Jan Both (d. 1652), had become entranced by the golden
light that flooded the Italian *campagna*. The resultant artistic ambiance in
Utrecht was unlike that in any other city: the imaginative evocation of
an idealized world was valued above the realistic impulses so esteemed in
other Dutch artistic centers.

Cuyp, directly or indirectly, responded to this Italianate ideal. Like
Saftleven, he adapted the visual vocabulary of such artists as Cornelis
van Poelenburch and Jan Both to create a new vision of the native
Dutch countryside. Cuyp was particularly influenced by Both, who had
returned to Utrecht in 1642 just as the younger artist was embarking
upon his artistic career. Both's evocative images of peasant travelers
passing through hilly landscapes softly illuminated by early morning or
late evening light (fig. 19) emboldened Cuyp to infuse his paintings with
comparable effects. Eventually, however, Cuyp transformed Jan Both's
gracefully rendered wooded hillsides and diffused Italianate light into
his own idiom, one that emphasized the flat expansiveness of the Dutch
landscape and the atmospheric clarity of the Maas river valley. Cuyp
always maintained a tangible sense of weight and mass in his landscapes,

which differ fundamentally from Both's more ethereal images. In Cuyp's works, light does not quietly settle over the land, dissolving forms, but streaks across the sky, its dramatic shafts illuminating clouds, trees and buildings, ships and animals, shepherds and travelers; light takes on an active role, both compositionally and spiritually, enhancing the sense that the land has been blessed and protected by divine providence.

The optimism surrounding the conclusion of the Eighty Years' War in 1648 reinforced Cuyp's positive vision of the Dutch countryside at a crucial point in his career. His imposing paintings of the massing of the Dutch fleet near Dordrecht are filled with a sense of joy and expectation as well as with pride in the achievements of the fatherland at the time of the signing of the Treaty of Münster (cat. 28). Moreover, with peace at hand, travel to the lush river valleys near Cleves became easier, and

Cuyp, presumably eager to give his arcadian interests new visual stimuli, ventured forth again to record what was for him a distant landscape. The drawings he made on this extended trip served him well for numerous panoramic paintings he made during the 1650s (see cats. 38, 42), which reflect both the beauty of the landscape and a sense of peace and prosperity.

As Cuyp began infusing his native landscapes with Italianate atmospheric effects, his painting techniques evolved subtly. In his early paintings, most of which he executed on panel, Cuyp primarily used thin, opaque layers of paint that he occasionally applied wet in wet. His approach was quite painterly, with vigorous yellow brushstrokes indicating landscape elements, such as grassy knolls or reeds growing along riverbanks (see cat. 7). Occasionally he gave added texture to distant landscapes by dragging a brush through drying paint. About 1650 he began to be more suggestive and less descriptive in creating atmospheric effects or in modeling form. For example, he began joining the varied rhythms of quickly applied brushstrokes, a characteristic of his early style, with freely applied planes of color in order to suggest flickering reflections on water or clouds illuminated at sunrise or sunset (see cat. 28). Nevertheless, he continued to give weight and structure to his paintings through the thick application of paint, particularly on large forms, whether the hull of a sailing boat or the hide of a cow.

By the mid-to-late 1650s, Cuyp had begun to paint almost exclusively on canvas, particularly for his large, panoramic scenes. For these works, he simplified his painting techniques, devising new means that may have been inspired by Dutch Italianate painters. He suggestively indicated distant forms with broad strokes brushed over an exposed underlying imprimatura layer, allowing it to become an active design element (see cat. 38). He enlivened these late arcadian scenes with foreground plants whose elegant rhythms he articulated with flickering accents along their bark or on their leaves (fig. 20).

Cuyp seems to have stopped painting a number of years before his death in 1691, perhaps because of the civic and religious responsibilities he had assumed after his marriage in 1658. There is certainly no indication that his style went out of fashion: he was an extremely proficient artist who had a ready market for his works throughout his career. Whether or not he had an active workshop is a question that cannot be easily answered. Although his style was imitated by other artists during his lifetime, Houbraken identified only one student, Barent van Calraet (1649–1737). Houbraken wrote that Calraet went to Cuyp when he was fifteen years old, which would place his apprenticeship in the mid-1660s, about the time that Cuyp's production seems to have slowed down.[69] However, because the date of this apprenticeship seems unlikely and because Barent's older brother Abraham van Calraet (1642–1722) often painted in Cuyp's style (see Chong's essay), Houbraken may have confused which of the two brothers studied with the master.[70]

During the seventeenth century, Cuyp's fame remained almost entirely local: only a few documents indicate that his paintings were then col-

lected in other artistic centers. His large-scale paintings, many of which can be dated to the 1650s and 1660s, must have been acquired primarily by wealthy patricians in and around Dordrecht. But the nature of Cuyp's patronage, as well as the manner in which his reputation spread to foreign shores, is another question (see Chong's essay).

1. I would like to thank Anna Tummers for her help and advice in writing this essay. I would also like to thank Emilie Gordenker, Joaneath Spicer, Shirley Bennett, and Meredith Hale for their thoughtful comments on the text.

2. Dordrecht received its municipal rights in 1220.

3. Blaeu 1649 (not paginated): "Dordrecht is d'eerst, en de Hooftstadt van Hollant: daerom noemen haer sommige een Moeder en Vorstin aller steden van dit heerlick Lantschap." The English translation is taken from Buijsen in Leiden 1993, 174.

4. Ray 1673, 23.

5. By the seventeenth century, Dordrecht's mercantile importance had diminished as shippers, searching for less costly ports, increasingly chose to go through Amsterdam and Dordrecht's neighbor, Rotterdam.

6. For a historical account of the Remonstrant / Counter-Remonstrant dispute, see Geyl 1966, 3, 177. For an interesting discussion of the international repercussions of the synod, see Van Deursen 1994, 31–41.

7. The most extensive biography of Cuyp is found in Chong 1992, particularly 83–102.

8. Dordrecht 1977, 16.

9. Houbraken 1718–1721, I: 249.

10. The marriage was celebrated on 30 July 1658.

11. The couple had one daughter, Arendina (b. 1659), who married Pieter Onderwater.

12. Dordrecht 1977, 19.

13. Houbraken 1718–1721, I: 248.

14. Gerrit Gerritsz Cuyp was probably Jacob Cuyp's first teacher. Houbraken indicated that Jacob taught Benjamin as well as Aelbert. Although Benjamin lived most of his life in Dordrecht, he was listed as a painter in The Hague in 1643 and in Utrecht in 1645. For Benjamin, see Dordrecht 1977, 17–18, 42–52; Chong 1992, 88.

15. Not only did Jacob Cuyp include animals in his paintings, he also made a number of animal drawings that were engraved by R. Persyn and published by Nicolaes Visscher in 1641 as *Diversa animalia quadrupedia ad vivum delineata a Iacobo Cupio*. See Hollstein 1949–, vol. 17, Reinier van Persijn nos. 11–23, 73–74.

16. Houbraken 1718–1721, I: 237. Houbraken noted that Jacob was one of the prime movers in establishing the painters' guild of Saint Luke in Dordrecht in 1642.

17. See, in particular, Kettering 1983, 63–82.

18. Van Mander 1604, folio 34: "En gaen sien de schoonheyt / die daer is buyten / Daer ghebeckte wilde musijckers fluyten." The text appears in Van Mander's chapter on landscape in his theoretical poem *Den grondt der edel vry schilderconst (The Foundations of the Noble and Liberal Art of Painting)*, which he published in *Het Schilder-boeck* (Haarlem, 1604), see Van Mander and Miedema 1973, I: 204–205. The English translation is taken from Buijsen in Leiden 1993, 47.

19. Van Mander 1604, folio 34:

Neemt kool en krijt,, [sic] pen, inckt, pampiere,
Om teeck'nen dat ghy siet ,, oft u de lust ghebiedt,
. . . .
Keert vveer naer Stadt…
Als t'lommer u begheeft ,, t'welck u beschaduvvt heeft,
Stelt t'huys al dat ,, ghy saeght hier buyten,
T'geen ghy in't Boeck beschreeft ,, sulcx lantschaps doen aencleeft,
Met vervven die ghy vvreeft ,, maekt dat het leeft.

See Van Mander and Miedema 1973, I: 64–65. Cambridge and Montreal 1988, 12–13. The English translation is taken from Buijsen in Leiden 1993, 47.

20. Ovid compresses Hesiod's five ages into four. For the description of the Golden Age, see Ovid, *Metamorphoses*, book 1, lines 89–112.

21. The actual source of Theocritus' idyllic world was an area called Arcadia on the central plateau of the Greek Peloponnese, populated by shepherds and hunters who worshiped Pan.

22. These texts were widely known in the Netherlands through contemporary translations by eminent Dutch scholars. Horace's text was translated into Dutch by Dirck Volkertsz Coornhert at the end of his treatise, *Recht Ghebruyck ende Misbruyck van tijdlicke have* (Amsterdam, 1610). Virgil's *Georgics* and *Eclogues* were translated by Karel van Mander: P. Vergilius Maro, *Bucolica en Georgica, dat is Ossen-stel en Landt-werck, Nu eerst in rijm-dict vertaelt, door K. V. Mander* (Haarlem, 1597). Crispijn van de Passe published an illustrated *Compendium operum Virgilianorum* in Utrecht in 1612. Joost van den Vondel also translated Horace and Virgil.

23. Mannerist painters delighted in depicting allegorical images of "The Golden Age," in which sensuous and evocative gods and goddesses lived in a world of peace, harmony, and prosperity as they lounged gracefully around banquet tables. See Sluijter 1986.

24. The most important play of this type is Pieter Cornelisz Hooft's *Granida* (1605), which focuses on the romantic adventures of Granida and Daifilo. Although the story unfolds in Persia, the landscape descriptions reflect an arcadian vision that Hooft derived from Giovanni Battista Guarini's popular play, *Il Pastor Fido* (Venice, 1589). For an excellent discussion of the differences between the two plays and their impact on Dutch society, see Kettering 1983, 102–113.

25. The most important of the numerous examples of this type of imagery is Karel van Mander's section on landscape in *Den grondt der edel vry schilder-const*, as quoted in Schenken-

30

veld 1991, 94–95, and Kettering 1983, 5; see also London 1986, 35–43, for an English translation of Van Mander's text. Jacob Cats also wrote extensively in this vein. See, for example, "Harders-klacht," which was first published in *Silenus Alcibiadis, sive Proteus* (Middelburg, 1618). This poem revolves around the romantic adventures of Daphnis and Galathea in the province of Zeeland. After Cats moved to Dordrecht in 1623 he republished it in expanded form as "Galathee ofte Harders-klachte," in *Proteus ofte Minnebeelden verandert in Sinnebeelden* (Rotterdam, 1627). At this time he eliminated many of the specific references to Zeeland; see Kettering 1983, 22.

26. Theodore Rodenburgh, in *Anna Rodenburgh's Trouwen Batavier* (Amsterdam, 1617), written 1601–1602, adapted Guarini's *Il Pastor Fido* by placing sixteenth-century Dutch burghers from Leiden and surrounding towns within the woods near The Hague. As Kettering 1983, 21, noted, Rodenburgh identified the hero as a Batavian, thus endowing him with physical and moral qualities that were considered "truly and admirably Dutch."

27. Hendrick Laurensz Spieghel's *Hart-spieghel* was first published in Amsterdam in 1614. The English translation of this text, which introduces his second book of this publication, is taken from Schenkenveld 1991, 95. Spieghel's original Dutch text, also cited by Schenkenveld 1991, 95–96, is as follows:

Taal-leye leid ons uyt, langs d'Amsterlandse stromen
t'Anschouwen t' nieuwe kleed, van t'natte veld en bomen:
Diens vrolik-bleke-lof, drong plotselijcken uyt
(Met swanger knoppen bol) der takken dorre huyd:
En tgras dat onder t'ijs in d'Heerefst was gheweken,
Begon zijn Spichtigh hoofd door twater op te steken:
Het veld dat korts noch scheen een water rijke Meer,
De ruighe kantten toond', en kreegh zijn verwe weer:
Daar lang de spertel-vis na lust had ghaan vermayen,
Daar zoumen alle daagh melkrijke besten wayen:
Dien walght het doffe hoy, en tochten zeer na tveld

Dat beter voedt: tot vett en grazich zuivel, smelt.

28. De Vries 1986, 79–86.

29. Claes Jansz Visscher's small vignettes surrounding this map of Holland, published by Pieter van den Keere in 1610, include images of a mermaid imprisoned in a Dutch jail and a man killing a horse by pushing it against a wall. These miraculous occurrences may have been intended to represent Dutch strength.

30. For *hofdicht* poems, see Van Veen 1960 and De Vries 1998. See also Kettering 1983, 26–27, who identifies Philibert van Borsselen's *Binckhorst*, written in 1613, as the earliest example of this genre.

31. *Helicon* 1610, 98:

Ja elcke Stadt en Dorp in vrede lustigh blijft
Bin Hollandts Thuyn bevrijdt
gelijck men nu siet blijcken
een soete stilt' al-om
en alle tweedracht wijcken:
Wie loochent
of 'tis hier Saturni gulden tijdt?

The English translation is taken from Levesque 1994, 60, who extensively used this important publication as a framework for her interpretation of early seventeenth-century print series.

32. Pontanus 1614, 105, noted that the city was entering "een guilden tijt." Pontanus also wrote about the expansion of Amsterdam that could occur during "die selve jaren als onder een gouden tijt stellen" (the same years as the period of the golden age). I would like to thank Professor Eco Haitsma Mulier from the Universiteit van Amsterdam for providing me with this reference.

33. Le Petit 1615, dedication, n.p., as noted by Levesque 1994, 71.

34. This description is from a petition written to the emperor Charles V in 1548 by the States of Holland. The quotation is taken from Boxer 1990, 6. For a discussion of the reclamation of the Dutch land, see De Vries 1986, 79–86.

35. This quotation, taken from Henri, Count of Rohan, is found in Gibson 2000, xxi.

36. This quotation is taken from Haitsma Mulier 1994, 133.

37. See Gibson 2000, 60.

38. See Amsterdam 1993b–1994, 22–25.

39. The idea that liberty, virtue, and prosperity are best preserved within government that is consultative and reserved to a close oligarchy, as in ancient Rome, was articulated by Hugo Grotius in his *Parallela Rerumpublicarum* (survives partially, 1602), and in his *De Antiquitate Reipublicae Batavicae* (see Grotius 1610).

40. The most visible manifestation of the associations with ancient Rome is the Amsterdam town hall. See Goossens 1996, particularly 10–11.

41. See, for example, Grotius 1610. For further parallels drawn between the story of the Batavians and the foundation of the Dutch Republic, see Van de Waal 1974, 28–43.

42. *Merckt de Wysheyt vermaert vant Hollantsche huyshouwen*, fol. Aii. The Dutch text reads: "Ick was in ouden tijden in een vrijen staet, daer na zeer onvrij / ende ben nu wederom in myn eersten staet...nu ter tijt de Hollandtsche Republijc ghenaemt." The English translation is taken from Levesque 1994, 79, who discusses the broader implications of this text for contemporary ideas of the Dutch landscape.

43. Heemskerk's 1647 publication is a greatly expanded version of his 1637 publication of this romance. For further discussion of the history of the publication, with bibliographic documentation, see Kettering 1983, 71–73.

44. Heemskerk 1647, 558–559, cites a poem written at the occasion of the conquest of Maastricht (1632), praising the stadtholder Frederik Hendrik (1584–1647) and his family for having made possible a golden age: "Uv Vader heeft de grond van 't groote werck gheleydt / En ons een gulden eeuw standvastigh voorberydt." In the epilogue of Van Heemskerk's *Batavische arcadia*, the editor suggests that Van Heemskerk chose to name his book "Arcadia" in order to give Holland an arcadia comparable to that claimed by any other land: "Wat de naam van Arcadia aangaet, die geloof ick dat hy uyt-gekosen heeft op dat ons Hollandt mede sijn Arcadia soude hebben so wel als d'Italianen, de Spangjaarden, d'Engelsche, en mogelijck andere volkeren, de haere hebben."

45. See Kettering 1983, 73.

46. Van den Bos' 1662 publication was reprinted in Amsterdam in 1701, which is the edition used for this essay.

47. Van den Bos 1701, 17: "De Son begost in het langen der dagen den Middaghlijn te naerderen, en sijn brant te met meerder en meerder aan te steken, wanneer een aansienlijcke Karos met twee paerden, in de gewoonlycke Ponten, de Dordtsche Stroom na Swindrecht overgevaren is."

48. Van den Bos 1701, 24: "Aengenaemheydt van den dagh, die als doe geen van de heetste was, en door een soet windeken de stralen van de Sonne vry matighde."

49. I would like to thank Jacob M. de Groot, former director of the Dordrechts Museum, for providing me with the information included in this section of the essay.

50. He probably left the Southern Netherlands because of the political unrest in that region and because of his Protestant beliefs.

51. The altarpiece was commissioned by the villagers of nearby Wieldrecht for the Grote Kerk in Dordrecht, and completed about 1490–1495. After 1572 the wings were kept in the refectory of the Augustinian cloister along with

several other paintings. See Balen 1677, 666. For a discussion of the altarpiece, see Helmus 1991.

52. A.M. Kolderen et al., "Kunst en Cultuur in Dordrecht tot Alteratie," *Projectgroep Middeleeuwen* (1993–1994), 171.

53. Illustrated in Dordrecht 1992, 280, fig. 77.

54. Illustrated in Dordrecht 1977, 102–103, no. 36.

55. For students of Jacob listed in the register of the Dordrecht Saint Luke's Guild, see Dordrecht 1977, 16.

56. Jacob, the only member of the Cuyp family of painters to execute a self-portrait, portrayed himself at the age of twenty-five holding a palette and maulstick in the upper left of the 1617 *Keepers, Functionaries and Mint-Masters of the Mint of Holland* (Museum Mr. Simon van Gijn, Dordrecht). Although no portrait of Aelbert Cuyp exists, Jacob de Groot believes that Jacob Cuyp may have used his father Gerrit Cuyp as the model for *Apostle Paul* in the Dordrechts Museum. This picture and its pendant *Apostle Peter* are dated 1627. See Chong 1988, 19–23.

57. Chong in the introduction of Dordrecht 1992, 18, noted that a number of Jacob Cuyp's students, including Benjamin Cuyp, Paulus Lesire, and Ferdinand Bol, eventually came under the sway of Rembrandt.

58. Primary among them are J.G. van Gelder and Ingrid van Gelder-Jost, Stephen Reiss, Jacob de Groot, and Alan Chong. See Van Gelder and Jost 1969, Reiss 1975, Dordrecht 1977, and Chong 1992.

59. *Diversa animalia quadrupedia ad vivum delineata a Iacobo Cupio*, see Hollstein 1949–, vol. 17, Reinier van Persijn nos. 11–23, 73–74 (see note 15). Although Reiss 1975, 31, 43, points to a number of instances in which Aelbert used these prints as models, Chong 1992, 255, plausibly suggests that Aelbert may have made some of the drawings used as models for this print series.

60. Houbraken 1718–1721, 1: 237, notes that in 1642 Jacob was one of the prime movers in the establishment in Dordrecht of a Saint Luke's Guild. This guild would have focused more exclusively on the needs of painters than had the organization from which they split, the Guild of the Five Trades (Gild van de vyf Nerigen).

61. For the possible influence of Jacob Cuyp on Aelbert's manner of depicting landscape, see the essay by Haverkamp-Begemann. The Middelburg artist François Ryckhals (1600–1647), who was active in Dordrecht in 1633–1634, painted stall interiors similar to those Cuyp later executed (see cat. 15): See Bol 1982, 21–29.

62. Chong 1992, 157–158, notes that Van Goyen's first depiction of this site is dated 1633.

63. Chong 1992, 88, raises the possibility that Cuyp and Jan van Goyen knew each other through the intermediary of Cuyp's neighbor, the still-life painter Jacques de Grief (called Klauw), who married Van Goyen's daughter in 1649.

64. Bloemaert, moreover, was a devout Catholic, and Cuyp's family was devoutly Protestant. Jacob Gerritsz Cuyp's strong religious convictions, which he developed subsequent to his own student days, may have deterred him from sending his son to study with a Catholic, even such an esteemed master. However, Kaplan in Baltimore and San Francisco 1997–1998, 71, stressed that religious beliefs did not separate Utrecht artists from each other. Indeed, as he rightly noted, Abraham Bloemaert taught together with the Counter-Remonstrant artist Paulus Moreelse at the Utrecht drawing academy.

65. It is possible that Cuyp's family had contact with the Saftlevens in Rotterdam, where Herman had joined the painter's guild in 1627. For example, stylistic and thematic similarities exist between the broadly executed, monochromatic peasant scenes painted by Aelbert Cuyp's uncle, Benjamin Gerritsz Cuyp, and those made by Herman Saftleven's brother, Cornelis. For Chong's discussion of Cuyp's relationship to Saftleven, see Chong 1992, 255, and for an overview of Rotterdam as an artistic center, see Rotterdam 1994–1995.

66. By 1635 Saftleven had begun to paint in a broad, generalized style of landscape influenced by the Utrecht painter Cornelis van Poelenburch. In that year he executed *The Wounding of Dorinda*, which he painted in collaboration with Hendrick Bloemaert (Gemäldegalerie, Staatliche Museen zu Berlin-Preussischer Kulturbesitz, 958). This work was part of an important commission from the prince of Orange, Frederik Hendrik, for a series of paintings illustrating scenes from Guarini's play *Il Pastor Fido*. For an excellent discussion of this series, see The Hague 1997–1998, 216–225.

67. As Marten Jan Bok has noted in Baltimore and San Francisco 1997–1998, 389, Herman Saftleven did not become a citizen of Utrecht until 1654. Thus, one may assume that he did not register as a master painter in the Utrecht Saint Luke's Guild until that time, and would not have had to register students working with him during that period. Cornelis Saftleven appears to have worked closely with his brother in Utrecht between 1634–1637, when he returned to Rotterdam.

68. Another important animal painter in Utrecht was Gijsbert Gillisz de Hondecoeter (1604–1653).

69. Houbraken 1718–1721, 3: 292.

70. See Chong 1992, 95. For a catalogue of Calraet's paintings (whose monogram, A.C., has often been confused with that of Cuyp), see Chong 1992, 502–529.

Aristocratic Imaginings: Aelbert Cuyp's Patrons and Collectors   *Alan Chong*

I n 1829, Thomas Emmerson sold a painting in London attributed to Aelbert Cuyp — the imposing equestrian scene now in the Metropolitan Museum of Art (see detail, page 34). The auction catalogue described the picture as a "Departure for the Hunt of the Prince of Orange; a clear and sunny Landscape, with the Prince of Orange mounted on a Grey Horse giving directions to a Garde de Chasse; his two sons richly habited, are also mounted; near them are several dogs, and figures in the distance." Coincidentally, four days earlier, a very similar equestrian scene by Cuyp had also appeared at auction: "Morning — Preparing for the Chase. This picture was probably painted for the Stadtholder's Family, as on the left is an accurate portrait of Maurice Prince of Orange, drawing on his boots; near him is a Moor holding two Horses…in the distance is the Castle of Nassau" (Gordenker essay, fig. 7).[1]

1 Aelbert Cuyp, **Avenue of Trees at Meerdervoort**, c. 1652, The Wallace Collection, London

While we might expect eighteenth- and nineteenth-century auction catalogues to describe paintings in fanciful and romanticized ways, these attempts to identify the figures and patrons of paintings by Aelbert Cuyp are not at all implausible. The artist crafted convincing images of wealth, sophistication, and power completely appropriate to a royal or princely court. Attired in exotic dress and surrounded by servants (including an African page), proud horsemen hunt in sun-drenched, Italianate landscapes. All of these features could be encountered in seventeenth-century portraits of rulers and courtiers, especially those by Peter Paul Rubens and Anthony van Dyck, as well as in portraits commissioned by the Dutch court.

In reality Aelbert Cuyp's apparently courtly images of riders on horseback were produced for far less exalted customers. An inventory taken in 1680 of a collection in Dordrecht identifies Cuyp's painting in New York as "Mr. Caulier on horseback with the two young gentlemen and Willem the coachman."[2] Another document of 1749 states that the work "depicts

Michiel and Cornelis Pompe van Meerdervoort departing for the hunt with their teacher, servant, etc."[3] The father of the two boys had died in 1639, therefore the portrait shows them receiving instruction from their tutor Mr. Caulier. The inventories also indicate that the painting hung over the mantel in the children's room of the Huis te Meerdervoort, a small manor just across the river from Dordrecht. This house can be glimpsed on the left edge of Cuyp's *Avenue of Trees at Meerdervoort* (fig. 1), which shows how close the residence was to Dordrecht. This painting must have also been commissioned by the Pompe van Meerdervoort family because the woman with two young boys at the end of the avenue of trees is almost certainly Adriana de Beveren and her sons Michiel and Cornelis Pompe van Meerdervoort.[4]

The significance of Aelbert Cuyp's images was intimately connected to the social circle of his clientele. This dependence of meaning on patronage is all the more important since almost nothing is known about Cuyp when he was active as a painter. The isolation of Dordrecht's art market relative to other towns in the Dutch Republic suggests a tradition of close connections between Dordrecht's artists and patrons. The Pompe van Meerdervoort family was characteristic of Cuyp's patrons: well-to-do Dordrecht burghers who identified themselves with the aristocratic values suggested by Cuyp's pictures. At the time Cuyp portrayed Michiel and Cornelis Pompe van Meerdervoort, the family was wealthy and socially prominent, but had not yet been admitted to the ruling faction of Dordrecht's government.[5] The boys' grandfather Michiel Pompe had made his mark as a successful merchant and minor town official. He purchased Huis te Meerdervoort and added the estate's name to his own. Since the Dutch Republic did not grant titles and the remnants of the old nobility were gradually dying off, rich city dwellers often acquired "titles" by purchasing estates connected to a noble name — a practice that became especially common in Amsterdam in the later 1600s. Michiel Pompe's younger son similarly acquired the estate and suffix "Slingeland." Equally important for social climbing was strategic marriage. Michiel Pompe's two sons married daughters of the most powerful man in Dordrecht, Cornelis de Beveren, five times burgomaster, representative to the Staten-Generaal, ambassador to England, and a French knight (De Beveren proudly added a fleur-de-lis to his arms).[6]

Equestrian hunting had long been associated with the courts of Europe, its status visually confirmed by well-established modes of portraiture and by illustrated equestrian manuals. Cuyp provided an image for the Pompe van Meerdervoort family that asserted not only their wealth and sophistication, but more specifically their right to hunt on horseback, an activity long reserved for the court and the aristocracy.

For example, Hugo Grotius in 1631 noted that hunting was one of the only privileges retained by the nobility under the Dutch Republic.[7] However, with the demise of the old nobility, new groups — including government officials, bearers of foreign titles, and new owners of country estates — claimed the right to hunt. On several occasions, the Staten-Generaal felt the need to expressly forbid from the hunt those who had acquired new titles.[8] The region of Zuid Holland, which governed the environs of Dordrecht, revised its hunting regulations in 1623. One crucial new provision, which differed from national and provincial laws, expanded hunting privileges to owners of estates and to citizens who had an annual income of 100 guilders.[9] While it has been suspected that hunting had expanded into the upper classes, this provision is firm evidence that a less restrictive policy had been legally adopted by Dordrecht.[10]

Cuyp's painting asserts the Pompe van Meerdervoort family's claim to aristocratic hunting rights. The painting sets two young seigneurs (accompanied by their servants) in front of their manor, surveying their estate — vast tracts of land on which they will hunt game on horseback. They are being carefully tutored in hunting and the equestrian arts, as would be appropriate for youthful princes or lords. These would-be aristocrats are presented to the viewer as controllers of land and people. However, the family surely realized how new and tentative these claims were: the Pompe clan was only slowly being admitted to local regency, their hunting privileges had just recently been sanctioned, and even their exalted name had been bought a generation ago. There is no proof that they ever hunted large game on horseback. The glamorous, exotic costumes — mere artist's props — and the fictive castle Cuyp added to the landscape further indicate the audacity of the family's pretensions.

and elaborate buttons, while the swords depicted in each appear nearly identical. These accoutrements seem to have come from a shared stock of costumes in the Cuyp family studio. About 1655 Matthijs ordered another hunting portrait, this time from the fashionable portraitist Jan Mijtens, who had worked at the court in The Hague. Depicted as a hunter returning with his dogs, Matthijs appears with his second wife and eldest daughter (fig. 2).

How demanding Aelbert Cuyp's patrons were in determining the themes, costumes, and other details seen in the artist's commissioned portraits is not certain. Many of the features found in the portrait of the Pompe van Meerdervoort boys — the exotic attire, the equestrian hunt, the Italianate landscape filled with ruins, the topography based on Cuyp's landscape sketches made around Elten — occur in nearly all Cuyp's equestrian portraits (see cat. 37). And since several different patrons commissioned these portraits, they most likely did not determine the inclusion of more than one or two relevant details. Rather, Aelbert Cuyp invented a complete mode of portraiture suited to an entire class of patrons. Because his equestrian portraits are derived only generally from the earlier aristocratic examples of Daniel Mijtens and Anthony van Dyck, Cuyp's role in devising this new model for this group of clients must have been especially strong. This newly minted imagery also filtered from Cuyp's commissioned portraits into his pure landscapes. It is especially significant that specific aspects of Cuyp's art reinforced the basic theme of aristocratic hunters. The exotic costumes and the golden, sun-drenched scenery, derived from the work of Jan Both, evoke a luxurious, elegant way of life, far away from the quotidian existence in Dordrecht.

This complex process of invention seems to have partially involved Aelbert's father. Jacob Cuyp must have introduced some of his clients

Hunting was one of the surest means of asserting status, and images of the hunt seem to have been in considerable demand in Dordrecht. The Pompe family in particular ordered several elegant hunting portraits. At about the same time the large equestrian portrait was made, the boys' uncle Matthijs Pompe van Slingeland commissioned a portrait from Jacob Cuyp, Aelbert's father, showing his son hunting with a falcon (Gordenker essay, fig. 5). Both portraits depict exotically attired boys at the hunt. The costumes in each picture share similar brocade trims

imperiously toward a fish as if he were a lord exacting tribute from a serf. The cannon salute and the manor house in the distance confirm the sitter's patrician authority. Although Pieter de Roovere had no official function as a fishing inspector, fishing was a major source of revenue for his estate at Hardinxveld,[12] as well as a prime commercial attribute of such long-standing importance in Dordrecht that it often appeared in maps and printed views of the city's waterways. However, compared to the stately images of Titian and Van Dyck, and even to Cuyp's later paintings of elegant hunters, the De Roovere portrait is awkward, and its subject, the supervision of fishing, is not an especially fashionable activity. Indeed, the portrait cannot have been much of a hit with Cuyp's patrons since the artist undertook nothing comparable afterward.

Pieter de Roovere occupied almost exactly the same social position as did the Pompe family.[13] His father had bought an estate just outside Dordrecht and with it certain agricultural rights. Pieter de Roovere succeeded his father as the regional bailiff, a minor post with few real duties. De Roovere, like the Pompe brothers, married into the powerful De Beveren family. Pieter de Roovere amassed considerable wealth and his widow owned the largest recorded collection of paintings in Dordrecht.[14] Significantly, the couple had five other works by Aelbert Cuyp, including paintings of cattle in a barn, a horse, two horses on a bridge, and the Valkhof at Nijmegen.[15] Although no other specific details of these paintings are known, the De Roovere family seems to have favored works by Cuyp with cattle and horses — even his depictions of Nijmegen usually contain elegantly dressed horsemen (see cat. 33). The De Roovere pictures also illustrate activities of the Hardinxveld estate such as farming, fishing, and cattle breeding, thus indicating the family's role as managers of their property. This preoccupation with agriculture was

to this son. Their collaborative group portrait of 1641 (cat. 3) has a hunting theme, as do Jacob Cuyp's portrait dated 1649 and Aelbert's portrait of a family of about the same year (Gordenker essay, figs. 5, 9).[11] In this last painting, some family members are attired in fancy velvet caps, jackets with slit sleeves, Moorish turbans, and silk robes — just the kind of costuming found in the Pompe van Meerdervoort portrait. Although these earlier hunting portraits lack an equestrian element, they indicate the taste for hunting portraits in Dordrecht.

Aelbert Cuyp's first equestrian portrait, created for Pieter de Roovere about 1650 (fig. 3), lies surprisingly outside the tradition of equestrian portraits. As is the case with many of Cuyp's paintings, the interaction between an upper-class horseman and a peasant or servant is central to the image. Dressed in a rich velvet costume, Pieter de Roovere gestures

as essential a component of aristocratic country life in seventeenth-century Holland as it would become in eighteenth-century England.

Among Jacob Cuyp's best clients were the Berk family, who also commissioned Aelbert Cuyp to produce a major equestrian portrait. Erkenraad Berk and her husband Adriaen Snouck were painted by Aelbert Cuyp (cat. 40) shortly after 1654, when the couple were married.[16] Adriaen Stevensz Snouck (c. 1634–1671) was born in Rotterdam and lived in The Hague before he married Erkenraad Berk (1638–1712). Marriage into a powerful family gave Adriaen Snouck entry into Dordrecht's governing councils. Erkenraad's father was city secretary and briefly *pensionaris*; her mother was the sister of Pieter de Roovere.

Cuyp's equestrian portraits with hunting themes became popular in Dordrecht. However, as in a depiction of a cavalry officer tying ribbons

4 Aelbert Cuyp, **Man Seated behind a Horse**, mid-1650s, Museum Boijmans Van Beuningen, Rotterdam

on his horse (Gordenker essay, fig. 8), the identity of the sitter is usually not known. This figure wears a breastplate, a satin sash, and the sort of fancy dress (militaristic rather than authentically military) typical of Dutch civic militias.[17] Guard officers in Dordrecht were almost always city officials or members of regent families, and several are recorded patrons of the Cuyp family. Other landscapes by Cuyp depict upper-class horsemen in a manner nearly identical to commissioned portraits. Such paintings may have been destined for clients who could not afford specially commissioned portraits, or may have been meant to accompany such works. Many of Cuyp's landscapes have hunting themes. One example (fig. 4) shows a horseman at rest, his mount held by a groom, while the hunt continues in the distance. The contrived and rather peculiar anonymity of the picture — the hunter's face is hidden by the horse — creates a "portrait-in-kind" that allowed the owner to identify with the hunting scene. Related to this type are Cuyp's paintings of elegantly dressed horsemen traveling through the countryside. In an expansive landscape with travelers and peasants (cat. 38), riders wear exotic jackets trimmed with fur similar to those seen in Cuyp's portraits. One horseman points his riding whip toward nearby peasants, a gesture that closely echoes the haughty superiority depicted in Cuyp's equestrian portraits.

The juxtaposition of the classes, so crucial to the sense of authority generated in the equestrian portraits, is often found in Cuyp's landscapes. In scenes with horsemen (cats. 29, 40), Cuyp used lowly peasants, shepherds, or pages to delineate the prestige of the riders, who seem to need a supporting cast in order to have any status at all. Cuyp suggests that these horsemen possess estates with castles, own enough land for hunting, or control agricultural production. Indeed, some of Cuyp's patrons did, but many more hoped to. Even when the horseman is not evidently a feudal landlord, but merely a well-off traveler asking the way (cats. 25, 38) or an itinerant artist (dismounted) sketching the scene as shepherds doze (cat. 29, fig. 1), adjacent rustics amplify his rank.

Cuyp's painting of a riding school before a Romanesque church (cat. 39) also has obvious aristocratic connotations. The statues and the ancient ruined fragments lend a classical elegance to the scene. The sculptural and architectural motifs, as well as the framing buildings, are borrowed from the work of Cornelis van Poelenburch. The horseman has brought his mount into a levade, a position essential in dressage and ubiquitous in royal equestrian portraits. The richly dressed rider at the right gestures authoritatively with his whip. Cuyp apparently borrowed his image from Crispijn van de Passe's prints for Antoine de Pluvinel's dressage manual *Maneige royal* (published in Paris in 1623 and in Utrecht shortly afterward),[18] which shows Pluvinel instructing Louis XIII in the equestrian arts.

Although the evidence is limited, Cuyp's patrons seem to belong to the "striving classes"— families with newly acquired wealth who were only beginning to break into the most powerful circles in Dordrecht and were unafraid to lay visual claim to prestigious rights associated with the ancient nobility. Evidence also suggests that a majority of Cuyp's patrons, along with the artist himself, were connected to the Orange faction. During the Stadtholderless Period of 1650–1672, the government of the Dutch Republic was controlled by the Dordrecht brothers Cornelis and Johan de Witt. When political and economic crisis in 1672 brought about their overthrow and execution, a sweeping change in Dordrecht's town government was ordered by Willem III. An entirely new regency consisting of a "Hundred Men" was nominated; the group included

Aelbert Cuyp, who by this time had abandoned his career as a painter. From this body, the new governing councils were chosen. Cuyp himself joined a judicial tribunal. Many of the artist's patrons were part of the new regime, including the De Beveren clan, which, as rivals of the De Witts, had long been out of power. The son and son-in-law of Pieter de Roovere became, respectively, bailiff of Zuid Holland and burgomaster. Matthijs Pompe van Slingeland and his son received important posts, while Cornelis Pompe van Meerdervoort (cat. 29) was allowed to continue in office.

Several of Aelbert Cuyp's best clients, as well as the artist himself, were new members of the regency who had never before held office. Abraham Heyblom was a modestly successful apothecary who was elevated to the town council in 1672. He lived near Aelbert Cuyp, borrowed money from him, and owned six of his paintings.[19] The merchant Johannes Bladegom van Woenssel also joined the town council, later becoming burgomaster. He served on the Hoge Vierschaar (high court) of Zuid Holland with Cuyp; therefore the two must have known each other well. Johannes owned as many as five paintings by Cuyp.[20]

These men, some old regents, others new, all supported the new stadtholder, Willem III. Whether or not these alliances were operable in the 1650s when Cuyp was actively painting, Cuyp very likely worked within a close-knit group of patrons whose politics and aspirations he shared. In addition, Cuyp's family was closely associated with Dordrecht's Counter-Remonstrants, who strongly supported the prince of Orange. Jacob Cuyp had been an elder of Dordrecht's Waalse Kerk, a conservative participant at the 1618–1619 Synod of Dordrecht. Even more significant, Aelbert Cuyp's wife Cornelia Boschman was the granddaughter of the theologian Franciscus Gomarus, founder of the Counter-Remonstrant

5 Aelbert Cuyp, **The Fleet at Nijmegen**, mid-1650s, Duke of Sutherland Collection

Nijmegen (fig. 5).[24] Somewhat surprisingly, Benjamin Cuyp's hastily produced paintings were slightly higher in value and far more common in local collections. Works by artists such as David Vinckboons, Cornelis van Poelenburch, and Philips Wouwermans were much more highly valued in Cuyp's home town.

Aelbert Cuyp was a local painter in every sense. He painted exclusively in Dordrecht, sold all of his pictures to locals, and often painted familiar regional subjects. The painter himself was remarkably similar to his clients. The Cuyps were a respectable, church-going family of moderate wealth; they lived in a big house on a "good" street. If one can conceive of a middle class in seventeenth-century Dordrecht, the Cuyp family was positioned at the upper end of it. Aelbert Cuyp possessed about the same amount of property as the majority of his patrons did. The painter worked for his social equals (neighbors and political colleagues) as well as for a few very wealthy patrons who were anxious to insinuate themselves into the aristocracy and regency.

This is not to say that Cuyp lacked ambition, for his acquisition of property and, more important, the elegance of his paintings suggest otherwise. His elevation to the peripheries of the regency in 1672 depended not on his marriage but on his connections with the stadtholder's party, which seem to have developed during his career as a painter. Cuyp appears to have crafted an image for himself, just as he crafted images for his clients, whose status was enhanced by the landscapes and portraits he painted for them. Cuyp himself became something of a seigneur following his marriage in 1658, soon after which he seems to have given up painting in order to manage his estate and that of his wife's family. He administered vast tracts of agricultural land near Dordrecht, diligently collected rent from dozens of tenants, and at one point even received

movement itself. While these various connections are widely separated in time, a social network consisting of local factionalism, intermarriage, royalist sentiment, and theology connects Aelbert Cuyp with his group of patrons. Equally remarkable is the absence of Cuyp's work from the collections of powerful families in the rival faction: the De Witts, Van Blijenburghs, and Muys van Holys. Nor was the famed Trip family an important patron.[21]

Paintings by Aelbert Cuyp were also popular among wealthy merchants in Dordrecht, who bought several works by the artist, as well as some by his father and uncle.[22] Aert Teggers, an independent tax collector, owned the largest gathering of paintings attributed to Aelbert Cuyp in the seventeenth century. Teggers ran the first coffee house in Dordrecht and appears to have been an art dealer.[23] Cuyp's paintings, which averaged 21.4 guilders apiece, were not particularly expensive. The highest valuation recorded before 1750 is 80 guilders in 1673 for a view of the fleet at

fish as payment for rent, just as Pieter de Roovere does in the portrait Cuyp had painted years before (fig. 3). In an important sense, Cuyp painted his way into the upper echelons of Dordrecht society.

Afterlife: The Appreciation of Aelbert Cuyp

Aelbert Cuyp's landscapes were appreciated by collectors of the nineteenth century for reasons nearly identical to those that surrounded their creation. Images of aristocratic life and landed power, although carefully constructed in the 1650s for clients in Dordrecht, were readily understood by later collectors and critics — viewers who possessed little or no knowledge of seventeenth-century Dutch society. Britain in particular provided the ideal setting for the afterlife of Aelbert Cuyp. While loved for their gilded beauty and careful verisimilitude, Cuyp's landscapes also perfectly illustrated the aspirations of the British landed gentry and aristocracy. Horses, hunting, and husbandry were the common preoccupations of painter, patrons, and later collectors.

Aelbert Cuyp was almost totally unknown outside his native Dordrecht in the seventeenth century. Surprisingly enough, seventeenth-century sources do not refer to Cuyp as a painter.[25] Dordrecht alone preserved the memory of Aelbert Cuyp in the years following his death. The Dordrecht painter and writer Arnold Houbraken in 1718 provided the first and, for more than a century, only account of Cuyp's career. Houbraken stated that Aelbert was a pupil of his father and correctly listed some of his favored subjects, including moonlit scenes and Dordrecht's riding school.[26] The author also recognized that Cuyp sketched the environs of Dordrecht in black chalk and colored washes. Most important, Houbraken characterized the distinctive quality of Cuyp's landscapes: "Moreover, he paid attention to the time of day when he depicted subjects, so that one can distinguish in his pictures the misty sunrise from bright noontime, and these in turn from saffron-colored sunset."[27]

The most important collector of Cuyp's paintings, in any era, was Johan van der Linden van Slingeland, a Dordrecht iron dealer and mintmaster who owned ten major works by Cuyp by 1752 (including cats. 16, 24, 28, 32, 38, 39, 44) and as many as forty-one in 1785.[28] He probably bought most of his pictures from local families.[29] When the collection was sold in 1785, several works made extremely high sums that were not equaled for decades — the record was held by the equestrian landscape with ruins (cat. 39). Compared with works by his contemporaries, Cuyp's paintings were exceptionally slow to appear on the international art market. While London auctions are full of Dutch paintings from 1690 onward, Cuyp's name does not appear in London sale records until 1741 and a significant number of references do not appear until the 1760s.[30] Although none of the principal art writers of the early eighteenth century mention Cuyp at all, Richard Wilson certainly appreciated him. When asked who the best landscape painter was, Wilson replied, "Claude for air and Gaspard for composition and sentiment, but there are two painters whose merit the world does not yet know, who will not fail hereafter to be highly valued, Cuyp and Mompers."[31] Among the few paintings attributed to Cuyp that attracted any critical attention was the landscape that Sir Nathaniel Curzon purchased in 1759 (fig. 6). Although the painting can now, I believe, be attributed to Abraham van Calraet, Cuyp's principal student, it brought Cuyp's name to the attention of the many tourists who visited Kedleston Hall.[32]

In 1769, John Boydell compiled a volume of prints (fig. 7) etched after old master paintings; Cuyp's expansive river landscape (cat. 45), then owned by the third earl of Bute, was lovingly described:

The distant groupe of sheep and figures, which appear between the opening of the trees, are involved in the bright misty rays of the sun, which is exactly the character of nature, and is executed in a manner equal to any thing of the like kind ever painted by Claude Lorraine....Cuyp may, with great propriety, be styled the *Dutch Claude*. It does not appear that Cuyp ever quitted his native country: he was consequently a stranger to the romantic scene of the more southern climates, and, therefore it is no wonder that his genius was solely confined to the representation of...such objects as the country in which he lived afford.[33]

Remarkably, the author realized that Cuyp did not journey to Italy. The passage also introduces two commonplaces: Cuyp as the Dutch rival of Claude and as a master of misty sunlight. Criticism for the next century and a half did not significantly expand these perceptions. The Boydell commentary (like other eighteenth-century English accounts) also brags about the British discovery of Cuyp:

It is astonishing, that the works of so great a master as Cuyp should have been almost totally unknown, or disregarded, till within the last twenty years. That his merit should have been overlooked by his countrymen is not at all surprising. The boldness of his pencil, and the freedom of his touches were not calculated to please a people who have been accustomed to the exquisite finishings of the most laborious class of artists that the world has produced: but that pictures of such extraordinary merit should have so long escaped the attention of collectors of other nations...appears incredible....It is entirely owing to the taste of the British nation, that his pictures have been retrieved from obscurity, their value enhanced, and places allotted them in some of the first Collections in this kingdom.[34]

6 Attributed to Aelbert Cuyp, **Landscape with Peasants and Riders,** Kedleston Hall, The Scarsdale Collection (The National Trust)

7 William Elliott, **A View on the Maese near Maastricht,** from John Boydell, **A Collection of Prints, Engraved after the Most Capital Paintings in England** (London, 1769), National Gallery of Art, Washington, Library

Despite this testimony, it is not certain that Cuyp was as popular in 1769 as Boydell implies, since some decades passed before his paintings began to bring good prices at auction. The painting owned by the third earl of Bute was largely known through the reproduction in Boydell's volume.[35]

Paintings by Cuyp became especially popular during the English Regency. Noel Joseph Desenfans (1745–1807), the dealer whose collection became the basis of the Dulwich Picture Gallery, owned at least ten works by Aelbert Cuyp. Desenfans assembled a collection of paintings for Stanislaw Augustus, king of Poland, but after the fall of Poland in 1795, Desenfans was left with hundreds of paintings that he tried unsuccessfully to sell to the Russian czar and to the British government as a national gallery.[36] One of Desenfans' most precious paintings by Cuyp was sold to J.J. Martin for 350 guineas (cat. 42), and the remainder of the collection was put up for sale. In the face of much criticism, however, nearly all the paintings remained unsold.[37] The Prince Regent (later George IV) was one of the most important collectors of Cuyp's work (perhaps second only to Johan van der Linden van Slingeland). He owned at least five genuine landscapes (for example, cat. 44 and Gordenker essay, fig. 8), which were installed at Carlton House along with an impressive collection of Dutch pictures and more modern works by Joshua Reynolds, Thomas Gainsborough, George Stubbs, David Wilkie, and J.M.W. Turner. In the early decades of the 1800s, a new breed of English collectors began to buy Dutch pictures. These amateurs were usually untitled (at least at first), resident in London, active in banking or commerce, and often involved in politics as well. Sir Abraham Hume, Bt., caused a stir by paying the unheard of price of £1,200 for *The Maas at Dordrecht* (see cat. 28). Abraham Wildey Robarts, M.P., bought two notable pendant cattle pieces (cats. 22, 23) for his London residence.

Old Masters, Modern Painters

The escalating market for old masters engendered antagonisms between living artists and collectors of traditional paintings, who were often viewed as conservative and tasteless. These tensions came to a head with the foundation of the British Institution, which held the first of a series of old master exhibitions in London in 1815.[38] The institution's mission was to create a national gallery, and the avowed purpose of these exhibitions was to properly instruct modern painters through the example of old masters. Reaction from artists was swift and overwhelmingly negative. Thomas Lawrence muttered, "I suppose they think we want teaching," while Augustus Wall Callcott complained that the institution had "set up a body of amateurs as critics for the people."[39] Even William Hazlitt, who generally supported such exhibitions, considered most of the lenders shameless self-promoters.[40]

The British Institution's exhibition of 1815 assembled a notable group of Dutch and Flemish pictures, including twelve works attributed to Aelbert Cuyp (see cats. 25, 28, 35, 38, 43). While engendering controversy, the show (as the first in a line of annual shows that extended almost a hundred years) can be reckoned the forerunner of the modern museum loan exhibition. A parody of the exhibition, entitled *A Catalogue Raisonné of the British Institution Exhibition,* offered extensive commentaries on the exhibited pictures.[41] For example, one of the institution's directors, Sir Abraham Hume, was attacked for unethical behavior because his expensive seapiece by Cuyp (cat. 28) was placed on view. The quality of the exhibited pictures was found to be inferior to works by living British painters. Cuyp did not escape criticism: one work (cat. 43) was judged much too brown; another (cat. 25), muddy; the ice scene at Woburn Abbey, poorly drawn; and the fleet at Dordrecht (cat. 28), clumsy and in poor condition.

The most entertaining contribution to this debate was surely Henry Richter's pamphlet, *Day-light; A recent discovery in the art of painting: with hints on the philosophy of the fine arts, and on that of the human mind, as first dissected by Emanuel Kant*, which first appeared in 1816.[42] The text is based on the conceit that on the last day of the exhibition, the ghosts of the artists themselves suddenly appear. The old masters are taken to task for having failed to observe nature and record the effects of sunlight. Cuyp is asked what pigments he used for grass. "A mixture of *black* and *yellow*, to be sure, said Cuyp, at which we all burst out a-laughing." The ghost of Cuyp also states that the foregrounds of landscapes should always be black. The aerial perspective so often praised in Cuyp's art is also ridiculed. Finally, Cuyp is made to see the errors of his art and, being the old master most interested in sunlight, proposes a solution:

My plan is this: That THE DIRECTORS *of this very* INSTITUTION should form a COLLECTION of genuine *studies of light and colour*, taken faithfully from *Nature* itself, *out of doors*, under all its various aspects, forming a valuable SCHOOL for the study of COLOURING *in which the public as well as the artists, might educate themselves in the knowledge of Nature*. The works of *us ancients*, which, in their present dirty and doctored condition, I own I am not a little ashamed of.

"Bravo, Cuyp, bravo!" shouted every one.[43]

Artists and Apologists

Beginning with Richard Wilson (1713–1782), British landscape painters have had a special affection for Cuyp's work. Wilson not only praised Cuyp, but seems to have been influenced by his pictures as well; both artists brought the glow of Italian sunlight to their native lands. Other British artists, such as Thomas Gainsborough (1727–1788), borrowed occasionally

from Aelbert Cuyp's paintings. John Constable (1776–1837) was impressed by Cuyp's stormiest landscape (cat. 12, fig. 1), calling it "a truly sublime Cuyp, a tempest, still mild, & tranquil." Full of dark clouds and dramatic lightning, Cuyp's picture appealed to Constable's rather vague concept of the landscape chiaroscuro, which seemed to denote not just formal lighting schemes, but also the sense of morality and passion stirred by nature. Constable picked out Jacob van Ruisdael (1628/1629–1682) and Cuyp as having this special trait: "Chiaroscuro is by no means confined to dark pictures; the works of Cuyp, though generally light, are full of it…It is the power which creates space."[44] Cuyp escaped the attacks that Constable directed at other Dutch Italianate landscapists, like Jan Both (d. 1652) and Claes Berchem (1620–1683), "who by an incongruous mixture of Dutch and Italian taste, produced a bastard style of landscape, destitute of the real excellence of either."[45] Did Constable not see the hybrid nature of Cuyp's landscapes, or was he unfamiliar with Cuyp's later, more obviously Italian pictures? Others shared Constable's sentiments; Anna Jameson wrote "to come upon one of Cuyp's pictures after looking at Berghem and Both is like opening a door and stepping out into the fresh air — into heaven's own light and earth's own verdure."[46]

J. M. W. Turner (1775–1851) paid explicit homage to Cuyp in a painting entitled *The Dort Packet-Boat from Rotterdam Becalmed, or Dort*, which was exhibited at the Royal Academy in 1818 (fig. 8). The previous year, Turner had visited Dordrecht and made numerous sketches of the city, including one close in composition to the final painting. But Turner's *Dort* seems less dependent on topography than on Cuyp's art. Although Dordrecht had changed little from the seventeenth century, it was Cuyp's association with the town that stirred Turner's imagination. When Turner returned to Holland in 1825, he scribbled Cuyp's name on several sketches,

almost as a title or characterization of the composition or the coloring of the scene. On one drawing, Turner enthused, "Quite a Cyp."[47]

Turner's *Dort* emulates the light and compositional structure of Cuyp's paintings, particularly *The Maas at Dordrecht* (see cat. 28), which he had seen at the 1815 exhibition. Cuyp's picture had been such a controversial part of the British Institution exhibition that Turner must have been motivated both to rival it and to pay tribute to it. Ironically, John Ruskin, Turner's most fervent defender, complained that Turner's painting was little more than a pastiche: "Very fine in distant effect — but a mere amplification of Cuyp: the boat with figures almost copied from him. But the water, much more detailed, is not at all as like water as Cuyp's: there are far more streaks and spots on it than can properly be accounted for."[48]

Turner's close colleague, Augustus Wall Callcott, may have provided an intermediate step between Cuyp and Turner. Callcott's *Entrance to*

the Pool of London (fig. 9), exhibited at the Royal Academy in 1816, is even closer in composition to Cuyp's painting and appears in turn to have influenced Turner.[49] Callcott's painting was commissioned by the third marquess of Lansdowne, who also bought Cuyp's very similar view of Dordrecht now in Kenwood (cat. 36). Walter Fawkes of Farnley Hall in Yorkshire, a devoted patron of Turner, owned an equestrian landscape by Cuyp (cat. 17). That collectors who favored Aelbert Cuyp also acquired the gilded landscapes of Turner and Callcott is no coincidence.

Attacks on Cuyp's art frequently came from critics who had a special connection with Turner. John Ruskin's 1843 treatise *Modern Painters: Their Superiority in the Art of Landscape to all the Ancient Masters* is a lengthy encomium to Turner. Since much of his book is highly polemical and almost comically overstated, it is important to realize that Ruskin believed that Cuyp was a great painter, simply one inferior to Turner.

Of pastoral or Georgic landscape, one of the four orders of landscape, Ruskin wrote, "Its principal master is Cuyp."[50] Ruskin therefore ranked Cuyp alongside Titian, Claude Lorrain, and Nicolas Poussin, above other famous landscape painters, and far higher than the masters of genres Ruskin considered inferior (these included Canaletto, Berchem, and Wouwermans). Of course, for Ruskin, the supreme landscapist was Turner:

For the expression of effects of yellow sunlight, paints might be chosen out of the good pictures of Cuyp, which have never been equaled in art. But I much doubt if there be a single *bright* Cuyp in the world, which, taken as a whole, does not present many glaring solecisms in tone. I have seen many fine pictures of his, which were not utterly spoiled by the vermilion dress of some principal figure, a vermilion totally unaffected and unwarmed by the golden hue of the rest of the picture.[51]

American painters were occasionally influenced by Cuyp's work. The early landscapist Thomas Doughty (1793–1856) painted a copy of the river landscape then attributed to Cuyp (but probably by Abraham van Calraet) in the National Gallery, London.[52] Doughty's own pictures of cattle were compared to Cuyp's; a reviewer referred to Doughty's cattle pictures as containing "the Doughty-stock produced at Philadelphia by breeding in-and-in with the Cuyp-stock, and showing them off in a Cuyp-atmosphere."[53] Fitz Hugh Lane (1804–1865) appears to have been strongly affected by Cuyp's work, which he probably knew through copies and prints. In several of his early paintings, Lane borrowed compositions and motifs from Cuyp's early work.[54]

It is tempting to believe that American landscapists were attracted to Cuyp's paintings because their sweeping vistas, clear skies, and golden sunsets evoked the American countryside. American artists themselves left little testimony to this affinity, but Frances Trollope, that haughty English observer of American manners in the 1820s, was struck by how closely the American countryside resembled pictures by Cuyp. The clarity and brightness of the Ohio autumn were beyond anything she had encountered in England:

Cuyp's clearest landscapes have an atmosphere that approaches nearer to that of America than any I remember on canvas; but even Cuyp's *air* cannot reach the lungs, and, therefore, can only give an idea of half the enjoyment.[55]

A Country House Artist

The collecting of Cuyp's paintings is an essentially English phenomenon. More works by Cuyp are found in Britain than in any other country, and most of those found elsewhere have spent a considerable portion of their history in British collections. Cuyp is the quintessential country house artist. His elegant landscapes, so often filled with aristocratic riders (their status made clear by attending servants and nearby peasants), perfectly confirmed the self-importance of nineteenth-century British noblemen, who typically accumulated titles apace with wealth and land. As one critic claimed, Cuyp's paintings specifically "appealed to a stock-breeding nobility."[56]

The nineteenth-century landed gentry typically collected large equestrian paintings by Cuyp, as can be seen in the purchases of John Cator, who lived in Kent (cat. 37), the duke of Buckingham at Stowe (cat. 30), Edward Loyd (Gordenker essay, fig. 7), the earl of Hopetoun (cat. 39), and Edmund Higginson of Saltmarshe, who collected numerous Cuyp works with an equestrian theme. Ferdinand de Rothschild, a member of the Austrian branch of the family who settled in England, acquired five pictures attributed to Aelbert Cuyp within the space of a few years around 1890 in order to furnish his newly built country estate, Waddesdon Manor. The extravagant Alfred de Rothschild bought three fine late paintings by Cuyp. The French Rothschilds acquired most of their numerous paintings by Cuyp on the English art market. Alphonse de Rothschild installed several works (cats. 3, 34) in the mansion Ferrières outside Paris. His son Edouard inherited them and added an equestrian scene with ruins (cat. 39). Gustave de Rothschild purchased the *Baptism of the Eunuch* (cat. 30) and an impressive cattle picture.

The favor that American collectors and museums have shown for Cuyp in the twentieth century can be regarded as an extension of English taste. In general, the American collecting of old masters is closely bound up with British traditions. Genuine paintings by Cuyp do not seem to have entered the United States until the last decade of the nineteenth century, although several copies and school works are recorded.[57] The situation changed suddenly about 1900, as wealthy industrialists such as John G. Johnson, Peter Widener, Henry Clay Frick, and Andrew W. Mellon began to collect. While America's own landscapists of the nineteenth century approached the grandeur and tonality of Cuyp, the prestige of Cuyp as a collectible artist attracted the richest buyers. The imitation of the British aristocracy at the turn of the century is best exemplified by Peter Widener, whose Lynnewood Hall outside Philadelphia was an American version of the English country house. Widener purchased two late Cuyp paintings with very similar moods and almost identical backgrounds. And his double equestrian portrait (cat. 40),

purchased in 1894, was the first mature Cuyp to come to America. The Irish writer Shane Leslie, on viewing Widener's Cuyps, was struck by their appropriateness in an American collection.[58]

A few conclusions can be drawn concerning the collecting of Aelbert Cuyp's pictures. Compared to other Dutch painters, Cuyp was discovered rather late, but once his collectability was established, the flight of his paintings from Holland was immediate and total. By 1800, no significant works by Aelbert remained in his homeland, a record shared by no other major Dutch painter. Equally remarkable is the concentration of his major paintings in England. No other Dutch artist was represented so strongly there and so sparsely in other European nations otherwise enamored of Dutch pictures. Was it mere circumstance that brought so many Cuyp paintings to England? Or did his works simply find a well-timed marketing niche? Cuyp's popularity in England is best compared with the collecting of Claude, that essential ingredient in the English country house. And who is a more perfect country house artist than Cuyp? His unthreatening naturalism — polish without demanding intellectual fuss — provided a satisfying confirmation of status, property, and seigneurial authority. In the seventeenth century, Cuyp's landscapes and equestrian portraits were created for the newly wealthy in Dordrecht. Both artist and patron belonged to the conservative royalist faction aligned against the parliamentary forces in the Netherlands. How remarkable that this taste could have been translated almost unedited to Regency Britain and to American industrialist collectors around 1900.

1. Thomas Emmerson sale, London, Phillips, 2 May 1829 (lot 165), sold for £1,102 10s. Richard Mortimer sale, London, Fosters, 28 April 1829 (lot 54), bought in at 440 guineas.

2. The 1680 inventory of the Huis te Meerdervoort, Zwijndrecht, lists: "int kinder camertie: d'heer Caulier te peert met 2 Jonckhers en Willem de koetsier, voor de schoortsteen." The Hague 1933, 89.

3. The 1749 inventory of the estate of Johan Diederik Pompe van Meerdervoort: "Een stuk zijnde een Schoorsteenstuk verbeeldende de Heer Michiel en Cornelis Pompe van Meerdervoort op jacht gaande met haer praeceptor, knegts etc door A. Kuijp." The Hague 1933, 89.

4. The Pompe van Meerdervoort family also owned Cuyp's *Conversion of Saul* (cat. 16).

5. See Gemeente Archief Dordrecht, Veldhuijzen 1988, and Balen 1677.

6. Although De Beveren claimed noble status, foreign knighthoods did not confer title or privilege in the Netherlands, nor was the Dutch nobility inclined to recognize such honors (see Van Nierop 1993, 24 – 25). Stephen Reiss believed that the sons of Cornelis de Beveren might be depicted in the painting in the Barber Institute (Gordenker essay, fig. 7) because a fleur-de-lis appears on a saddle cloth (Reiss 1975, 113, 162). This is insufficient evidence since fleurs-de-lis were a common armorial symbol.

7. Hugo de Grotius, *Inleidinge tot de Hollandsche rechts-geleerdheid* (1631), 39.

8. Van Nierop 1993, 37; for the legislation of 1666 and 1674, see the manuscript *Het groot placaet-boek*, vol. 3, book 4, 608 – 609 and 614 – 622, in the Algemeen Rijksarchief, The Hague.

9. Jan van der Eyck, *Corte beschrijvinghe mitsgaders handvesten, priviligien, costumen ende ordonnantien vanden Lande van Zuyt-Hollandt* (Dordrecht, 1628), 426 – 430 ("Ordonnatie vande Jacht"), esp. 428: "te moghen vlieghen often jaghen, soo

sullen de *Edel-luyden, Ambrachts-Heeren*, ende goede Luyden, ofte Borgers binnen *Dordrecht*, ende in *Zuyt-Hollandt* geseten ende woonachtigh, die ghegoet sullen zijn ter somme van hondert Carolus Gulden s'Jaers vry incomende, en niemands anders" (allowed to hawk or hunt, so shall noblemen, estate owners, and good folk or citizens of Dordrecht and of Zuid Holland and living therein who have the income of a hundred Carolus guilders, and no one else).

10. Compare Sullivan 1984, 33 – 45; Haarlem 1986, 261; Van Nierop 1993, 37, 152.

11. Reiss (1975, 186, no. 141) attributed the work to Cuyp's studio, but there is no reason to doubt Cuyp's authorship.

12. There were three fish smokehouses at Hardinxveld, and fishing was important enough to involve Pieter de Roovere in litigation with the neighboring estate of Houweninge (see Dordrecht 1977, 78). Pieter de Roovere's son-in-law Samuel Everwijn later became salmon inspector (*opziender van de zalm*) in 1678; Matthijs Balen, *Dag-lyste* (Dordrecht, 1678).

13. See Veldhuijzen 1988, esp. 81 – 82; A. de Roever, *Een tak van het brabantsche geslacht de Roovere* (Helmond, 1893); Dordrecht 1977, 78.

14. The 1682 inventory of the possessions of Sophia van Beveren (c. 1610 – 1682) included 118 paintings; Hoge Raad van Adel, The Hague: Slingeland archive, fols. 56r – 77r.

15. The 1682 inventory of Sophia van Beveren lists in the *Voorsael* (front salon), "Een koestal, van Cuyp" (a cattle stall by Cuyp); in the *blau kantoor* (blue office), "Een bond paert, van Cuyp" (a spotted horse by Cuyp); in the *Boven aghter kamer* (upper back room), "een soldaet van Cuyp" (a soldier by Cuyp); and "een landschap van Cuyp" (a landscape by Cuyp).
    Most of the paintings were inherited by Pompejus de Roovere and are recorded again in a 1723 inventory: "Een koets stal door C:kuyp, ƒ20" (a cattle stall by C. Kuyp); "Een bont paart door kuyp en een bekertje door stillever, ƒ3"

(a spotted horse and a vase still life); "Een bond paard door kuyp ƒ7" [perhaps a repetition]; "Twee paarden op een brug door kuyp, ƒ1.10" (two horses on a bridge by Cuyp); "Het hoff van Nijmegen door kuyp, ƒ20" (the court of Nijmegen by Cuyp); "Een lanschappie door kuyp, ƒ10" (a small landscape by Cuyp). Hoge Raad van Adel, The Hague: Slingeland archive, fol. 57r – 57v. A Conversion of Saul is recorded in the Pompe van Meerdervoort auction of 1749 (cat. 16).

16. The identification of the sitters is based on a later portrait explicitly identified as Adriaen Snouck, which is clearly a copy of the man in Cuyp's portrait, with the facial features made somewhat older. This work is in the Snouck-Hurgronje collection, Zeeuws Museum, Middelburg. Its pendant portrait, identified as Erkenraad Berk, is also based on the Washington portrait. It was common practice to copy portraits so that family members could own images of ancestors. Snouck was appointed to the Veertig of Dordrecht in 1667 and later served on the Hoge Vierschaar of Zuid Holland.

17. A civic guard portrait made in Dordrecht, attributed to Cornelis Bisschop, and datable to about 1675, shows a council of eleven civic companies (Rijksdienst Beeldende Kunst, on loan to the Dordrechts Museum; Rijksmuseum 1976, repro. on 118). Other group portraits by Jacob Cuyp and Paulus Lesire once hung in the Kloveniers Doelen, but are now lost (Balen 1677, 666).

18. Antoine de Pluvinel, *Maneige royal…*(Paris, 1623). Revised editions, *L'Instruction du Roy en l'exercice de monter à cheval* (Paris and Utrecht, 1625).

19. A 1685 inventory: Gemeente Archief Dordrecht, ONA 198.

20. In a 1699 inventory, "2 groote stucke van kuyp / 2 idem lantschapies / 1 idem huys te merwede." These consecutive entries are the only occasions when "idem" is used, therefore they probably refer to paintings by Cuyp. Gemeente Archief Dordrecht, ONA 123, no. 11, f. 5v.

21. Aelbert Cuyp painted a portrait of Jacob Trip in 1652 (private collection, Amsterdam), finishing a commission for several pairs of portraits of Trip and his wife begun by Jacob Cuyp.

22. Dordrecht's wealthy merchants, who typically left estates of 10,000 to 50,000 guilders, seemed to have been especially fond of Cuyp. In 1674, Pieternella Palm and Jacob van der Radt owned five landscapes by Aelbert Cuyp and several others by the Cuyp family. In 1688, Abraham Sam, a wine merchant, had at least four landscapes by Aelbert Cuyp, plus two group portraits attributed variously to Jacob or Aelbert Cuyp.

23. A 1688 inventory: Gemeente Archief Dordrecht, ONA 561. See Loughman 1991a.

24. In a 1673 inventory of Anthonetta van Bouthem [also van Haerlem], widow of Arent Dichters (merchant), "een groote schilderije wtbeeldende een leger ofte Rendevou van schepen leggende voor Nummegen, gemaeckt door Aelbert Cuyp" (a large painting depicting a fleet or rendezvous of ships lying before Nijmegen by Aelbert Cuyp). Dordrechts Archives, ONA 157, f.195v; valued at 80 guilders. For further details on collectors in Dordrecht, see Chong 1992 and Loughman 1993.

25. Aelbert Cuyp's name appears in print only a handful of times in his own lifetime, namely in Matthijs Balen's *Dag-lyste* (a city almanac published annually after 1673) and in the same author's extensive history of Dordrecht (Balen 1677, 186, 909), which briefly lists Cuyp's civic positions. Although Balen described two paintings by Jacob Cuyp, he did not mention any works by Aelbert, nor indeed the younger Cuyp's profession as a painter. Only the will of Cuyp's wife refers to works that Aelbert Cuyp painted as part of her estate.

26. Houbraken 1718–1721 (1753 ed.), 1: 248–249: "de Pikeurbaan, daar hy dan de schilderagtigste Paerden die daar gewoonlyk kwamen, in te pas bragt, zoo dat men dezelve kost onderkennen." (the Pikeurbaan, in which he depicted the most picturesque horses that usually came there, so that one could recognize them).

27. Houbraken 1718–1721 (1753 ed.), 1:248, "Daarenboven heeft hy inzonderheid wel in agt genomen de tydstonden waar in hy de voorwerpen verbeelde, zoo dat men den benevelden morgenstond van de klaren middag, en dezen weer van den saffraanverwigen avondstond in zyn tafereelen kost onderscheiden."

28. Recorded by Hoet 1752, 2: 489–500; Descamps 1753–1765, 2: 80. See also the auction catalogue of 22 August 1785.

29. Except for the presence of so many paintings by Cuyp, the collector's favorite painter, the collection is typical of eighteenth-century tastes and includes no other Dordrecht artists active in the middle of the 1600s except for a single work by Samuel van Hoogstraten. Among the Dordrecht paintings from about 1700 are three by Arnold Houbraken, two by Godfried Schalcken, and one by Arent de Gelder.

30. London auctions in the 1690s contain numerous Dutch landscapes by Cornelis van Poelenburch, Claes Berchem, Anthonie Waterloo, Herman Saftleven, Paulus Bril, Egbert van der Poel, Pieter Lastman, Herman van Swanevelt, Roelandt Savery, Jan Porcellis, Simon de Vlieger, Philips Wouwermans, Esaias van de Velde, Jan Griffier, Pieter van Laer, and Jan van der Capelle.

The earliest sale references to Cuyp may be Edmund Glover sale, London, 16 March 1741 (58) "A Landskip and Cattle, by Coyp" £1.2; (day 3, lot 115) "A Sea-port, by Coyp" £1.19 (copy of catalogue in British Library). Maria Drolenvaux (widow of Thomas Parker) sale, Leiden 29 April 1743 (13) "Een Landschap met Beesjes en Beelden, door A. Kuyp" fl. 5-5.

An earlier reference might be in the Droste sale, The Hague, 21 July 1734 (47) "Een Pleyster-plaats, door Aelbert Knip, 48 x 67 duim." This may be a misspelling of "Kuip."

31. Sir William Beechey told Mr. Harvey of Catton of a conversation with Wilson; W. T. Whitley, *Artists and Their Friends in England, 1700–1799* (Cambridge, 1928), 1: 380–381 (no source given).

32. The duchess of Northumberland described it in 1766. Also mentioned in Arthur Young, *A Farmer's Tour through the East of England* (London, 1771), 1: 195; William Gilpin, *Observations, Relative Chiefly to Picturesque Beauty* (London, 1786), 2: 242.

33. Boydell 1769, 12 (plate 12 is the Cuyp painting). Benjamin Ralph and Edward Penny were probably the authors of the texts in the volume.

34. Boydell 1769, 11, pl. 12. About 1790, several other commentators described how Cuyp had been discovered, including Samuel Ireland, *A Picturesque Tour through Holland, Brabant, and Part of France (Autumn 1789)* (London, 1790), 44: "Valuable as this great artist's works are now held by the connoisseur, I am informed it is not more than thirty years since a room full of his best cabinet pictures were purchased by the late Mr. Blackwood, for seven or eight pounds a picture"; Desenfans 1801, 164: Cuyp's pictures were "in the private houses of the Hollanders, covered with filth, not considered as cabinet pictures, but merely fit to supply the place of furniture, 'till at length, sometime about 1740, a native of Switzerland called *Grand Jean*, who resided in London, but made frequent excursions to Holland, for the purpose of selling watches and scissars of English manufacture, returned with ten or twelve landscapes of Cuyp. His speculation was attended with every success….It was reserved to the English nation, to have the merit of bringing them to light, and to give his works the high reputation they are now held in."

35. An unpopular prime minister, Lord Bute was forced from public life because it was believed that he had had an affair with the king's mother, Princess Augusta, and had used public funds on his houses. As a result, very few connoisseurs were admitted to Luton Hoo.

36. Giles Waterfield, "'That white-faced man': Sir Francis Bourgeois, 1756–1811," *Turner Studies* 9, no. 2 (1989), 36–48; Washington and Los Angeles 1985; Waterfield 1988.

37. See Washington and Los Angeles 1985, 13 – 17. The catalogue of the exhibition sale is Desenfans 1802; the sale took place on 18 March 1802.

38. See Peter Fullerton, "Patronage and Pedagogy: The British Institution in the Early Nineteenth Century," *Art History* 5 (1982), 59 – 72; Gregory Martin, "Birth of the British Institution," *Country Life* 151 (1972), 186 – 188; Thomas Smith, *Recollections of the British Institution* (London, 1860). The institution's papers are now in the Victoria and Albert Museum library. Farington 1978 – 1984, vol. 12, provides an account of the setting up of the organization. Founded in 1805, the British Institution held annual exhibitions of British painting (as did the Royal Academy), and, from 1815, old master shows as well. The first old master exhibition in the British Isles was held in Dublin in 1814.

39. Lawrence's comment is reported by Benjamin Haydon (Whitley 1928, 1: 247), while Callcott's, made in 1813, is given in Farington 1978, 12: 4332.

40. Whitley 1928, 1: 254 – 255 (in the review *Champion*). Hazlitt also attacked the *Catalogue Raisonné* and what he saw as the Royal Academy conspiracy behind it: William Hazlitt, *Round Table* (Edinburgh, 1817), 2: 211 – 214.

41. The British Library attributes the *Catalogue Raisonné* to the artist Robert Smirke, based upon *Memoirs and Recollections of Abraham Raimbach*, ed. M. Raimbach (London, 1843), 35. However, Smirke, who thought it must be by a supporter of Lord Egremont, a patron of contemporary artists including Turner, suggested Thomas Philips. Farington approached Philips, who assigned it to Fawkes (Farington 1978 – 1984, 13: 4643, 4645, 4650 [June 1815]). Although the identity of the author is uncertain, it may have been Walter Fawkes of Farnley Hall, Yorkshire, a friend and patron of Turner.

Extracts of the pamphlet appeared in the *Morning Chronicle*. A pamphlet of similar tone had appeared earlier: *Declaration Issued in the Preface to the Catalogue of the British Institution, April, 1811* (London, 1815).

42. Richter 1817.

43. Richter 1817, 10.

44. John Constable, *John Constable's Discourses*, ed. R. B. Beckett (Ipswich, 1970), 62.

45. Constable 1970, 56, and note 6.

46. Jameson 1844, 17 – 18.

47. The closest sketch is in the 1817 sketchbook, no. CLIX, page 50; see London 1994, 42 – 43, fig. 9b. Joll connects it with sketchbook CLIVa, page 59; Butlin and Joll 1984, 103. There are several more drawings of Dordrecht in the 1817 sketchbook ("Dort") no. CLXII, pages 77, 77v, 85 – 88, 89v, 92, and inside the covers. The annotation "Cuyp" or "Cyp" appears in the 1825 sketchbook "Holland" no. CCXIV, pages 60v, 117a, 131. The sketchbooks are in the Turner Bequest, Tate Gallery, London, and are catalogued by A. J. Finberg, *A Complete Inventory of the Drawings of Turner Bequest*, 2 vols. (London, 1909).

48. Ruskin was writing in 1851; see Butlin and Joll 1984, no. 137. In *Modern Painters*, Ruskin found Cuyp inferior to Turner except in certain details: "Now, there is no instance in the works of Turner of anything so faithful and imitative of sunshine as the best parts of Cuyp; but, at the same time, there is not a single vestige of the same kind of solecism" (Ruskin 1903 – 1912, 3: 272 – 273).

49. See David B. Brown, *Augustus Wall Callcott* [exh. cat., Tate Gallery] (London, 1981), 29, 36 – 37, no. 15. Much of Callcott's work, including a lost marine of 1815, views of Rotterdam done in 1819, and several pastoral scenes, was directly dependent on Cuyp's compositions.

50. Ruskin 1903 – 1912, 7: 254.

51. Ruskin 1903 – 1912, 3: 271.

52. The painting Doughty copied at the National Gallery, London, is *Hilly River Landscape* (inv. 53). Doughty also produced copies after Van Ruisdael and Claude. His 1846 copy after Van Ruisdael's landscape in the Louvre is preserved in the Brooklyn Museum; F. Goodyear, *Thomas Doughty* [exh. cat., Pennsylvania Academy of Fine Arts] (Philadelphia, 1973 – 1974), no. 43, repro.

53. John Neal, "Three Days in Boston," *The Yankee and Boston Literary Gazette*, 10 December 1828, vol. 1, no. 50, page 398.

54. John Wilmerding, *Paintings by Fitz Hugh Lane* [exh. cat., National Gallery of Art] (Washington, 1988), nos. 1, 9, repro. A later work of 1852, *Entrance of Somes Sound*, is so close to Cuyp's view of Dordrecht then in the marquess of Lansdowne's collection that Lane must have seen a reproduction of the picture. Lane's overall composition is very similar to Cuyp's, as is Lane's depiction of the principal ship near a raft of timber.

55. Frances Trollope, *Domestic Manners of the Americans* (London, 1832), 146 (chapter 10).

56. Gerald Reitlinger, *The Economics of Taste* (London, 1961), 1: 13.

57. Paintings attributed to Cuyp were exhibited in America as early as 1817, when a painting described as "An Old Man, for sale" was shown at the American Academy of the Fine Arts, New York; the subject is more typical of Benjamin Cuyp than of Aelbert. At the same venue, works attributed to Cuyp appeared in 1821 ("Landscape, with Cattle"), 1822 ("Cattle"), and 1828 ("Landscape with Cow and Figure, lent by W. Hall"). In 1821, Doggett's Repository of Art exhibited a "Landscape and Cattle" and "The Cottage Door, with the painter in the character of a peasant," both for sale. The Peale Museum in Baltimore, about 1823, showed a "View on the banks of a river" that was owned by F. Cook. As early as 1817, Robert Gilmor Jr., the noted Baltimore collector, purchased a picture attributed to Cuyp at a London auction.

58. Shane Leslie, *American Wonderland: Memories of Four Tours in the United States of America* (London, 1936), 115: "Cuyp painted the brilliant atmosphere of the American landscape."

Cuyp's Horsemen: What Do Costumes Tell Us? *Emilie E. S. Gordenker*

Just as Aelbert Cuyp introduced golden, Mediterranean sunlight into recognizably Dutch landscapes to give them a dreamy, pastoral quality, he used exotic costumes to lend his figures a rich and foreign appearance, often combining Eastern and Western elements in a unique amalgam. In or about 1653, Cuyp painted two boys from the wealthy Pompe van Meerdervoort family with their tutor on horseback, accompanied by their coachman on foot (cat. 29). The portrait presents the group setting off for a day's sport. The figures in the foreground are luxuriously and colorfully dressed in garb that is by no means ordinary riding attire. The horsemen wear loose, knee-length garments of richly colored velvet, closed with gold braid and buttons at the front, and tied at the waist with a sash. The coachman sports a dark red coat of bulkier proportion, in a coarser fabric with broader braiding ending in fuzzy tufts. Three of the figures have identical swords at their sides, with a honeycomb pattern on the hilt, a pommel in the form of an animal head, a swept-back blade, and a scabbard ending in a square tip.

These costumes have variously been described as outlandish, of Persian influence, or arcadian,[1] but they have not been firmly identified to date. Nevertheless, they are certainly eastern European, most probably Hungarian, in origin. While similar in cut and construction to the clothing worn in other eastern European countries, particularly in Poland, a distinctly Hungarian male costume developed during the sixteenth and seventeenth centuries.[2] Hungarian dress combined Western with Oriental elements derived from Ottoman garments brought to Hungary by the Turks.[3] Contemporary Hungarian paintings and western European prints illustrating national costumes show how Hungarian dress looked and was worn (fig. 1).[4]

Hungarians wore two shirts, one under the other.[5] The under shirt, of undecorated linen, did not show. But the over shirt, short and cut

1 Hungarian, **Portrait of Prince Géza**, 17th century, Magyar Nemzeti Múzeum, Budapest, Történelmi Képcsarnok

53

square, with long, wide sleeves and silk and metal-thread embroidery decorating the hem, was intended to be seen from beneath the outer clothing. A garment called the *dolman* was worn over the shirts. This tightly fitting coat was cut straight to the waist, flaring at the side seams to form a full skirt, and overlapping right over left from waist to hemline. Winter *dolmans* were made of heavy silk, velvet, or broadcloth, while in the summer, lighter weight linens or silks were preferred. The *dolman* fastened down the front to the waist, sometimes with elaborate clasps or buttons. It varied in length, but in the seventeenth century was generally short, reaching halfway down the thigh. The fashion for the collar in the seventeenth century was narrow and upright. The sleeves varied in cut, but extended to the wrist. Belts were usually colorful silk net shawls, wrapped around the waist several times.[6] Over the *dolman*, Hungarians wore a *mente* (fig. 2). Similar in material, this was a loosely cut coat reaching to the calf. The front was fastened with large buttons (knit, metal, or precious stone) and often decorated further with braids made of metal thread or silk yarn. Hungarian trousers, usually made of broadcloth and relatively simple in style, were worn tight to the legs. Brightly colored boots with an arched front were pulled up over the kneecap. The most popular headgear was a high cap with a turned-back brim; made of felt or fur, the cap was often lined with fur and frequently adorned with feathers.

In Cuyp's portrait, the two boys and their tutor wear Hungarian *dolmans*, complete with net sashes and elaborate shirts underneath. The

2 Hungarian, **Mente**, 17th century, Iparművésti Múzeum, Budapest

3 Johann Wilhelm Baur, **Polish and Hungarian Horsemen**, 1636, The British Museum, London

coachman Willem, on the other hand, appears in a *mente*. The decoration, the shorter sleeves, and the fuller silhouette mark his coat as the outer garment that was intended to be worn over the *dolman*.

Why would Cuyp have chosen Hungarian dress? Perhaps he was not aware of the precise origin of the costume he used in the Pompe van Meerdervoort hunting portrait and simply considered it Eastern or Polish. Polish costume was well known in the Netherlands, and is frequently mentioned in literature, inventories, and in descriptions of paintings.[7] Since Hungarian dress was the dominant model for the fashions of other central European countries, the differences between it and Polish costume could be subtle and were often confused.[8] Even foreign travelers of the time noted the similarities between Hungarian and Polish dress.[9] Nevertheless, Western printmakers seem to have made some effort to distinguish the costumes. Johann Wilhelm Baur (1607–1641) showed the contrast between Polish and Hungarian national attire in one of a series of prints depicting national military costumes (fig. 3). While not without fanciful elements, the print distinguishes Polish garb (with its simpler decoration and longer silhouette) from Hungarian costume.[10]

rows of silver or gold braiding. Encountered exclusively in the possession of aristocratic military men, the Hungerline seems to have been a valuable garment with martial overtones.[13]

Hungarian dress suited Cuyp's hunting portraits for other reasons. The Dutch undoubtedly recognized the Hungarians for their equestrian prowess and for their cavalry.[14] As accomplished horsemen, Hungarians were also hunters of great skill. Indeed, Hungary had been a hunters' paradise in the Middle Ages and had played a definitive role in the development of hunting techniques.[15] Furthermore, Hungarians were known in the Netherlands as staunch fighters for the Protestant cause. Eastern Europe was engaged in a continuous battle to establish the fluid borders of its countries, and Hungary in particular was fighting fiercely against the Turks.[16] By the end of the sixteenth century, 90 percent of the Hungarian population was following the Protestant creed.[17] And Hungarian students were numerous in Dutch universities, where most of them studied theology.[18] These students would have brought to the Dutch an awareness of their bitter fight to defend the Protestant faith, as well as perhaps a taste for their clothing.[19]

In the Netherlands, heroic images of hunting on horseback with imposing figures in exotic or antiquated dress had a long and distinguished visual history. Fifteenth- and sixteenth-century tapestries such as those by Bernard van Orley (c. 1488–1541), engravings after designs by Jan van der Straet or Stradanus (1523–1605), prints by Antonio Tempesta (1555–1630), as well as Peter Paul Rubens' (1577–1640) muscular hunt scenes, all incorporate unusual dress.[20] Stradanus used Oriental dress, while Rubens, in his wolf and fox hunts, used antiquated costumes to evoke the courtly hunting scene and to underscore the continuity of the noble privilege of hunting.[21] In Dutch hunting portraits, too, exotic dress

4 Jacques Callot, **Man in Hungerline**, 1623, Bibliothèque Nationale de France, Paris, Cabinet des Estampes

5 Jacob Gerritsz Cuyp, **Portrait of Michiel Pompe van Slingeland**, 1649, Dordrechts Museum, on loan from the Rijksdienst Beeldenden Kunsten

Stefano della Bella (1610–1664), in his series of prints showing equestrians in exotic dress, brought out the same difference.[11]

While the various forms in eastern European costume were — and still are — confusing, Hungarian dress certainly had made its impact on western European fashions in Cuyp's day. The term Hungerline (*hongreline* in French; *hongerlijn* in Dutch), clearly derived from the name Hungary, was commonly used to describe a thigh-length overcoat. The man's version had a flared skirt and buttoned down the front from a high, turned-over collar to a shaped waist (fig. 4).[12] It was often made of colored velvet, almost always lined with fur, and frequently decorated on the chest with

was entirely appropriate. Cuyp's father, Jacob Gerritsz Cuyp (1594–1652), painted Michiel Pompe van Slingeland (1643–1685), the cousin of the Pompe van Meerdervoort boys, wearing a red velvet tunic, probably of Turkish origin, antique sandals, and a sixteenth-century bonnet (fig. 5). Entirely unsuited to hunting, this type of dress was chosen more for its exoticism and theatricality than for its accuracy.[22]

As one of the most prominent families in Dordrecht, the Pompe van Meerdervoorts must have sought an image that would emphasize their social status and link them to the aristocracy and royalty. While hunting imagery — from still lifes to scenes of peasant hunters — did not necessarily connote nobility in the Netherlands, the equestrian hunt was associated with the stadtholder and his court.[23] Portraits of the royal family on horseback setting out for a hunt are numerous.[24] By choosing a hunting image, the Pompe van Meerdervoorts made a reference to royal equestrian portraits. The colorful Hungarian dress increased the richness of the image and implied a link to exotic hunters in pursuit of large game, such as those painted by Rubens and Stradanus. Furthermore, the costumes (whether understood as Hungarian or Polish) may well have rung with the moral justice of the fight against the Turkish infidels and with the prowess of eastern European horsemen and hunters.

Variations on a Theme

The Pompe van Meerdervoort boys, their tutor, and coachman wore Hungarian garments but were not entirely dressed as Hungarians. Their boots with heels and spurs are typical for western Europe at this date. The headgear is incongruous with the *dolmans*. The youngest boy, Cornelis, has a cap with a distinctly Eastern flavor that resembles a Turkish turban. His older brother, Michiel, sports a sixteenth-century Euro-

pean bonnet adorned with a chain and feather.[25] The tutor Caulier's fur-trimmed cap more closely resembles those of the Hungarians, but is less sharply peaked in form and also comes close to the type worn by the Dutch in the winter.[26]

The sword, which appears three times in this portrait, is a fanciful hybrid. It was probably an actual object — a fanciful western European interpretation of Eastern or antique armor. The head-shaped pommel and horizontally placed quillons bear some resemblance to Hungarian cavalry swords (fig. 1).[27] The falcian (swept-back) blade and scabbard also lend the object an Eastern flavor. Yet the pommel and patterned grip are extremely similar to a hilt of circa 1630–1650 affixed to a German saber of circa 1540 (fig. 6). While not unlike a functional "hunting hanger," this object was probably more for show than actual use. Swords of this type were also looked on as typical of classical times. They appear in Netherlandish history paintings along with classical armor.[28] And Michiel Pompe van Slingeland appears to wear the same one in his portrait by Cuyp's father (fig. 5).

Cuyp did not, therefore, present his sitters in an accurate and complete national costume. More likely, he had two or three garments in his studio that he used as a basis for his exotic equestrian costumes and that he supplemented with fantastic additions (details derived from prints), and with various accessories, regardless of their age or origin. We know that Rembrandt (1606–1669), his pupils, and other Dutch artists collected old clothing and various exotic articles for use in their studios.[29] While these costumes frequently provided no more than a guide for the color and drape of a fabric, the recurrence of a specific motif or article of clothing is a good indicator that the artist owned and used a similar one in his studio.

Garments resembling the *dolmans* in the Pompe van Meerdervoort painting recur repeatedly, in various forms and variations, in almost all of Cuyp's hunting scenes. The artist altered the garments in detail and combined them with various accessories from one painting to the next. In Cuyp's other hunting scenes, such as *Equestrian Portrait of Pieter de Roovere* (see Chong essay, fig. 3), *Portrait of Two Men Hunting on Horseback* (private collection, Germany), *Horsemen Resting in a Landscape* (cat. 37), and *Horsemen and Herdsmen with Cattle* (cat. 38), similar knee-length garments of the same colors appear, sometimes fashioned with antiquated

slashing or trimmed with fur and gold braiding. The hats in these pictures vary, from fur-lined caps to bonnets, with or without feathers.

It is highly unlikely that all the men in Cuyp's hunting portraits, regardless of whether they are known subjects or unidentified hunters, would have owned such similar and costly garments. One constant in these hunting scenes is the color of the attire. A small range of hues — a bright red, blue, or a more muted dark red or brown — always appears. Almost all the garments are of a similar shape and construction. And while the decoration differs from one to the next, it always incorporates Eastern motifs, such as gold braiding and fur trim. The headgear, too, while varied, frequently has an antiquated or Eastern flavor. And the same sword appears constantly. This suggests that Cuyp was deliberately basing himself on a few garments in his studio, to which he added trim and decoration for variation. The Pompe van Meerdervoorts might have had luxurious clothing, but they almost certainly did not select these costumes from their own wardrobes.

Historicizing Dress

While eastern European costume must have appealed to Cuyp and his patrons for its richness and for its association with accomplished horsemen and huntsmen, it also melded well with seventeenth-century notions of historical dress. Like Rembrandt and his pupils, Cuyp introduced this type of Eastern and antiquated costume into his hunting scenes in order to lend his images the gravitas of a history painting and to avoid the pitfalls of current fashions, which could look dated in a few years.[30] In the pair of pendants showing a man and woman as hunters, Cuyp's use of dress closely resembles that of Rembrandt and of Ferdinand Bol (1616–1680, a native of Dordrecht) (cats. 26, 27).[31] The broad,

7 Aelbert Cuyp, **Huntsmen Halted**, c. 1655, The Barber Institute of Fine Arts, University of Birmingham

floppy bonnet with its edge cut into square sections is of sixteenth-century origin.[32] The gorget, accompanied both by sixteenth-century dress and by turbans and Eastern shawls, appeared frequently in *tronies* (bust-length figure studies, often featuring imaginative dress) by Rembrandt and his pupils. The slashed sleeves also derived from past styles. The pendant shows the hunter's wife in an adaptation of Eastern costume, which incorporates a low neckline decorated with a heavy brooch.[33] A similarly fanciful mixture of costumes, both exotic and archaic, appears in *Huntsmen Halted* (fig. 7) and in his history paintings as well. In the *Conversion of Saul* (cat. 16) and the *Baptism of the Eunuch* (cat. 9), for instance, Cuyp combined Turkish caftans and turbans with sixteenth-century bonnets and indeterminate draperies, in very much the same way that Rembrandt and his pupils did.

It is striking that almost all the costumes worn by Cuyp's hunters, no matter how embellished or simple, center around knee-length garments, frequently belted, and decorated around the hems. Probably seen as antique and associated with eastern Europe, these garments also evoke the costumes worn in pastoral scenes. The pastoral ideal, which comes to the fore in Cuyp's carefully selected light and construction of landscape, is therefore mirrored in his choice of dress. The knee-length garment he favored in his equestrian portraits is in many ways similar to the shepherd's tunic. Such costumes are represented in the frontispieces of popular pastoral plays and poetry.[34] Shepherds in comparable attire can be seen in illustrations to Dutch pastoral literature (see Wheelock essay, fig. 5)[35] and in many Netherlandish pastoral portraits.[36]

Riding Dress

While Cuyp's treatment of his hunters' costume was highly original, he represented more ordinary riding dress in other equestrian scenes. For riding, men wore doublets and breeches, as do the horsemen in most riding treatises.[37] Garments specifically intended for riding also existed. Breeches and boots were worn under either the *rock* or *rij-rock* (riding coat) or the *kabas* or *casaque* (cassock). Both were loose coats that widened toward the hem (frequently with a vent or short slit in the back for comfort on the saddle) and fastened down the front.[38] Such coats were made either of plain gray or red wool, which was sometimes decorated with braiding.[39] The thigh-length coat was also appropriate for hunting.[40]

In his *Landscape with Horse Trainers*, Cuyp depicted his horsemen in riding coats (cat. 39). In the right foreground, a man pointing his whip wears an elegant dark wool coat with large gold buttons at the sleeves and front opening. Combined with a short collar, riding boots, and a broad-brimmed hat with tall crown, his dress conforms perfectly to that of the 1650s. The other horsemen wear similar outfits, while the figures in *Horsemen with a Black Page* (Royal Collection, London) also wear clothes entirely fashionable for the date of the painting.[41]

The equestrian portrait of a couple, probably Adriaen Stevensz Snouck (c. 1634 – 1671) and Erkenraad Berk (1638 – 1712), is particularly interesting for changes made in the dress (cat. 40). The portrait was begun shortly after the couple's marriage in 1654. X-rays show that Snouck originally wore the tall hat typical for that date, as well as a cape with braid decoration along the edges (see cat. 40, fig. 1). Erkenraad Berk wore a dress with a low décolletage encircled with a *tours* (broad neckerchief). Cuyp must have been asked to alter the clothing at some point after 1660, because the second version of the costume

falls perfectly into line with the styles of the mid-1660s. Snouck now wears a *rock* in a rich brown wool. His *bef* (falling band), a collar in the form of a bib, is tied with tasseled band-strings. Over one shoulder is a bandoleer, a commonly worn decorative accessory embellished with gold fringe and a bunch of black ribbons at the shoulder. The biggest change occurred in his headgear and hairstyle: he wears not the broad-brimmed hat of the 1650s, but a full head of long curls, quite possibly a wig.[42] Erkenraad now has a sumptuous blue velvet bodice with slit sleeves and matching skirt. Such long, boned bodices were fashionable in the 1660s, and a surviving example of this date has very similar sleeves.[43] On her head is a small black cap decorated with blue ribbons and a luxuriant bunch of feathers.[44] The horsemen and the figure on horseback in the background remain, however, in their coats and broad-brimmed hats of the 1650s.

Military men, or equestrians wishing to appear as such, frequently wore buff leather jerkins or coats. Made of a strong material with a full skirt that reached over the thigh, these garments had a protective function like metal armor. Several examples have survived.[45] Cuyp did not depict the buff coat or jerkin in his portraits, but one does appear together with armor in a painting of a horseman standing with his gray dappled horse before a military encampment (fig. 8).

Historical and Geographical Accuracy in Dress

Although most of the costumes in Cuyp's equestrian pictures may be identified, being overly precise about the origin and dates of the garments is actually counterproductive. As clearly shown by the theoretical literature of the time[46] and by the bewildering combinations of garments that occur in the same image, historical and geographical accuracy in dress was not high on the list of an artist's priorities. Cuyp's portrait of a family before a Rhine town serves perfectly to illustrate this point (fig. 9). The figures, arranged in a stiff and uncomfortable grouping, are clad in a wide variety of costumes. Most of the adult men and women wear conservative and formal dress typical of the mid-1650s. The boy with the squirrel in the foreground is clad in an Orientalizing tunic with turban. The young girl next to him in the foreground wears a modified form of contemporary dress with sleeves slashed low on the arm and a waist dropped to hip level. The young boy with two dogs in the right foreground sports a riding coat. The boy standing next to him is attired in a velvet *dolman*. His older brother, at his side, has on a slashed tunic and a Rembrandtesque turban. The man only partly visible at the rear of the left group stands out for his round, Turkish turban, while the shepherds standing behind the cows on the riverbank carry crooks and wear tunics. Clearly, the intent was not to re-create an accurate impression of historical or

9 Aelbert Cuyp, **Portrait of a Family before a Rhine Town**, 1650s, Szépmüvészeti Múzeum, Budapest

regional dress. Rather, the artist spiced up the stodgy formal grouping with costumes that call to mind pastoral ideals and the glamour of hunting.

Cuyp chose a costume for his hunters that resonated with a variety of related associations. The knee-length garments were not unlike the riding coat and probably seemed familiar in cut and form, and appropriate for a huntsman. The richness and the exoticism of the eastern European costumes suited the social aspirations of Cuyp's sitters. The Hungarian origin of the hunters' costumes could have called to mind the skill of the eastern European horsemen, the fierceness of the cavalry, and perhaps even the fight for moral justice against the Turks. And it was an association that fell in line with traditional representations of the hunt. Also, the costumes' similarity to pastoral tunics accorded well with the glowing light and the landscape. As he did so well in his landscapes, Cuyp blended the familiar with the exotic to create a unique and yet entirely fitting costume for his hunters.

1. I would like to thank Marieke de Winkel for sharing invaluable research from inventories and for her help in clarifying terminology. I am also grateful to Irena Turnau, specialist in eastern European costumes, David Edge, arms and armor specialist at the Wallace Collection, and Bob Carroll, armor specialist at the Metropolitan Museum of Art, for their advice. For these descriptions of the costumes in the Pompe van Meerdervoort portrait, see Ben P. J. Broos, "Rembrandt's Portrait of a Pole and His Horse," *Simiolus* 7 (1974), 198, note 9; Barbara Burn, *Metropolitan Children* (New York, 1984), 58; Diana de Marly, "Undress in the Oeuvre of Peter Lely," *Burlington Magazine* 120 (November 1978), 750.

2. On eastern European dress, see Irena Turnau, *History of Dress in Central and Eastern Europe from the Sixteenth to the Eighteenth Century* (Warsaw, 1991). On Hungarian dress, see Emöke László, *Historic Hungarian Costume from Budapest* [exh. cat., Whitworth Art Gallery, University of Manchester] (Manchester, 1979), 7–9; Lilla Tompos, "Westerse en Oosterse invloeden op de kledij van de Hongaarse aristocratie," in *Hungaria Regia: Schittering en strijd 1000–1800* [exh. cat., Paleis voor Schone Kunsten] (Brussels, 1999), 62–65.

3. For the origin of Hungarian dress and the influence of Oriental textiles and costumes in Hungary, see Veronika Gervers, *The Influence of Ottoman Turkish Textiles and Costume in Eastern Europe with Particular Reference to Hungary*, Royal Ontario Museum, History Technology and Art Monograph 4 (Ontario, 1982); Turnau 1991, 14–16; Tompos in Brussels 1999, 62–65.

4. See also the print by Johann Christoph Weigel of a Hungarian nobleman, reproduced in Brussels 1999, 63.

5. Mentioned in seventeenth-century inventories. Manchester 1979, 7.

6. A spectacular example, worn by Miklós Esterházy (1582–1645) for his wedding, is still extant, but simpler ones survive as well. Turnau 1991, 19.

7. In a forthcoming publication about Rembrandt's *Polish Rider* (volume 4 of *A Corpus of Rembrandt Paintings*, 3 vols. [The Hague, Boston, and London, 1982–1989]), costume historian Marieke de Winkel lists extant examples and inventory entries of figures wearing Polish garments, as well as of actual Polish clothing. For a published discussion of dress in *The Polish Rider*, see also Julius S. Held, *Rembrandt's Aristotle and Other Rembrandt Studies* (Princeton, 1991), 73–78; Zdzisław Zygulski, "Rembrandt's 'Lisowczyk': A Study of Costume and Weapons," *Bulletin du Musée National de Varsovie* 6, no. 2/3 (1965), 43–67.

Hungarian garments per se have not been found in inventories; for Polish garments, see Joachim Wolfgang von Moltke, *Arent de Gelder (1645–1727), Rembrandts laatste leerling* [exh. cat., Dordrechts Museum] (Dordrecht, 1998), 170, note 3.

8. Held 1991, 73–78.

9. See citations in Turnau 1991, 127.

10. In particular, the Renaissance footwear and extreme shoulder rolls based on Spanish dress. Turnau 1991, 127.

11. See, for instance, the Polish and Hungarian horsemen, reproduced in the standard monograph on Della Bella's prints: Alexandre De Vesme, *Stefano della Bella: Catalogue Raisonné*, with introduction and additions by Phyllis Dearborn (New York, 1971), nos. 275, 277. Held noted correctly that the costumes are not to be distinguished by the presence or lack of braiding, but did not discuss the line of the dress. Held 1991, 73–74, note 57.

12. The women's Hungerline, fashionable in the 1630s and 1640s, usually made of silk and worn together with a skirt, was an overgarment derived from the men's version.

13. Marieke de Winkel, oral communication. For instance, it appears in the inventory of Floris II van Culemborg (RA Gelderland, Arch. Graven van Culemborg, 393), reprinted in A.J.M. Koenhein et al., *Johan Wolfert van Brederode 1599–1655: Een Hollands edelman tussen Nassau en Oranje* [exh. cat., Historische Vereniging Het land van Brederode] (Vianen, 1999), 90–95. Apparently, even at that time, there was some confusion between the cassock (*casaque* or *kabas*) and the Hungerline, since several entries cross out one term and replace it with the other.

14. Light horsemen played an important role in the defense of Hungary, and came to be known as hussars under Matthias Corvinus (1443–1490). We know little about the origins of the hussars, but the word *huszar* is said to derive from the Italian *corsare* (corsair or freebooter). The hussars wore coats of mail and armor that do not resemble that of Cuyp's horsemen. Ferenc Temesváry, *Arms and Armor* (Budapest, 1982), 24–25. Eastern European cavalry participated in the mercenary armies of western Europe, and Hungarian hussars fought in the Thirty Years' War, along with the Croats and Polish.

15. László Zolnay, "Game, Hunting and Hunters in Ancient Hungary," *Symposium of the History of Hunting* (Budapest, 1971), 6–7.

16. The name Hungary is something of a misnomer during the period in question, as it was made up of three separate political units.

17. Peter F. Sugar et al., eds., *A History of Hungary* (London and New York, 1990), 93–94.

18. Jonathan Israel, *The Dutch Republic: Its Rise, Greatness, and Fall 1477–1806* (Oxford, 1995), 900–902.

19. For more on relations between Hungary and the Netherlands, see Brussels 1999.

20. Tapestries by Bernard van Orley can be dated circa 1531–1533 (Musée du Louvre, Paris). See Sophie Schneebalg-Perelman, *Les Chasses de Maximilien: Les énigmes d'un chef d'oeuvre de la tapisserie* (Brussels, 1982); Arnout Balis et al., *Les Chasses de Maximilien* (Paris, 1993). On Stradanus' hunt scenes, see Welmoet Bok-van Kammen, "Stradanus and the Hunt," (Ph.D. diss., Johns Hopkins University, 1977). On Tempesta, see various lion hunts in Sebastian Buffa, ed., *The Illustrated Bartsch: Italian Masters of the Sixteenth Century: Antonio Tempesta*, vol. 38 (New York, 1985), especially no. 1123. On Rubens' hunt scenes, see Arnout Balis, *Corpus Rubenianum XVIII: Landscapes and Hunting Scenes*, vol. 2 (London, Oxford, New York, 1986).

21. Susan Koslow, "Law and Order in Rubens' Wolf and Fox Hunt," *Art Bulletin* 78 (December 1996), 697–700. For discussions of the iconography of Rubens' hunt scenes, see David Rosand, "Rubens's Munich *Lion Hunt*: Its Sources and Significance," *Art Bulletin* 51 (1969), 29–40; Balis 1986, esp. 50–69.

22. Even the hawk is an ordinary type that was never used for hunting. Peter Marijnissen et al., eds., *De Zichtbaere Werelt: schilderkunst uit de Gouden Eeuw in Hollands oudste stad* [exh. cat., Dordrechts Museum] (Dordrecht, 1992), 154.

23. In the Netherlands, hunting was traditionally the purview of the court. In the seventeenth century, restrictions were loosened somewhat to allow the nobility and eventually wealthy members of the regent class to participate in the sport. See Alan Chong's essay in this catalogue and Chong 1992, 138–139, 261–262; Eddy de Jongh, *Portretten van Echt en Trouw: Huwelijk en gezin in de Nederlandse kunst van de zeventiende eeuw* [exh. cat., Frans Halsmuseum] (Haarlem, 1986), 261–262.

24. For examples, Chong 1992, 143. On equestrian portraiture more generally, see Charles Dumas, *In het zadel: Het nederlands ruiterportret van 1550 tot 1900* [exh. cat., Fries Mu-seum] (Leeuwarden, Den Bosch, and Assen 1979) and Walter Liedtke, *The Royal Horse and Rider: Painting, Sculpture and Horsemanship 1500–1800* (New York, 1989).

25. Rembrandt and his pupils frequently introduced such caps into self-portraits and other fancy-dress pictures. Marieke de Winkel, "Costume in Rembrandt's Self-Portraits," in *Rembrandt by Himself*, eds. Christopher White and Quentin Buvelot [exh. cat., National Gallery] (London, 1999), 68–69.

26. Known as a *karpoes*, such a fur-lined cap can be seen, for instance, on the *kolf* player in Hendrick Avercamp's *Winter Landscape with Skaters* (c. 1609, Rijksmuseum, Amsterdam). The term *karpoes* occurs in inventories of eastern European clothing as well (see note 7).

27. Two examples, one from the end of the sixteenth century and the other from the seventeenth century, have these qualities (Magyar Nemzeti Múzeum, Fegyvertár, Budapest, inv. nos. 55.3331 and 55.3335). Reproduced in Brussels 1999, nos. 200, 201.

28. A. Vesey B. Norman, *Wallace Collection Catalogues: European Arms and Armour Supplement* (London, 1986), no. A711. A very similar one appears in Anthony van Dyck's *The Continence of Scipio*, 1620–1621 (Christ Church, Oxford).

29. Emilie E.S. Gordenker, "'En rafelkragen, die hy schilder-achtig vond': Was Rembrandt een voddenraper?" in *Kostuum verzamelingen in beweging: Twaalf studies over kostuumverzamelingen in Nederland & Inventarisatie van het kostuumbezit in Nederlandse openbare collecties, Nederlandse Kostuumvereeniging voor Mode en Streekdracht*, eds. H.M.A. Breukink-Peeze et al. (Zwolle, 1995), 21–32. Marieke de Winkel, "'Eene onbedenklyke vernadering van dragten, en vremde toestellingen omtrent de bekleedingen…': Het kostuum in het werk van Arent de Gelder," in Von Moltke 1998, 87–97.

30. Cuyp's primary point of reference would very likely have been artists from Rembrandt's circle who settled in Dordrecht, such as his uncle Benjamin Cuyp, Paulus Lesire, Nicolaes Maes, Samuel van Hoogstraten, and Aert de Gelder. See De Groot's essay in this catalogue.

31. A similar combination of bonnet with feather, metal gorget, and slashed sleeves occurs in Rembrandt's *Standardbearer* (1636, private collection, Paris), Ferdinand Bol's *The Falconer* (1647, Ranger's House, London), and Dirck Santvoort's *Portrait of Martinus Alewijn as a Hunter* (1644, Rijksmuseum, Amsterdam).

32. It can be seen in the first decades of the sixteenth century, for instance, in the work of Lucas van Leyden.

33. It resembles closely the one worn by Anna van Erckel as Rebecca in Ferdinand Bol's *portrait historié* of his future wife, a wealthy Amsterdammer, and her first husband, Erasmus Scharlaken (c. 1648, Dordrechts Museum).

34. The figure of Céladon on the title page of *L'Astrée* (Paris, 1615), the seminal pastoral play by Honoré d'Urfe, wears such a tunic.

35. See, for instance, Salomon Savery's illustration for J.H. Krul, *Pastorel Musyck-spel van Juliana en Claudiaen*; the engraving *Pastoral Scene*, in J.H. Krul, *Eerlycke tytkorting* (Haarlem, 1634); and the engraving in *Pastorel bly-eyndend-spel van Cloris en Philidia* (Amsterdam, 1634).

36. For examples, see Alison McNeil Kettering, *The Dutch Arcadia: Pastoral Art and Its Audience in the Golden Age* (Montclair, N.J., 1983), esp. 64–77; Peter van den Brink et al., *Het Gedroomde Land: Pastorale schilderkunst in de Gouden Eeuw* [exh. cat., Centraal Museum] (Utrecht, 1993); Alison McNeil Kettering, "Gender Issues in Seventeenth-Century Dutch Portraiture: A New Look," in *Rembrandt, Rubens, and the Art of Their Time*, Papers in Art History from The Pennsylvania State University, eds. Roland E. Fleischer and Susan Clare Scott, 11 (University Park, Pa., 1997), 145–175.

37. Riding treatises of the seventeenth century with plates showing horsemen in what can be considered daily attire include Antoine de Pluvinel with plates by Crispijn van de Passe, *Maneige royal ou l'on peut remarquer le defaut et la perfection du chevalier en tous les exercices de cet art, digne des princes…* (Paris, 1623); Antoine de Pluvinel, *L'Instruction du Roy en l'exercice de monter à cheval* (Paris, 1625); William Cavendish, the duke of Newcastle with plates by Lucas Vorsterman after Abraham van Diepenbeeck, *La Méthode nouvelle et invention extraordinaire de Dresser les Chevaux* (Antwerp, 1657–1658); Delcampe, *L'Art de Monter à Cheval* (Paris, 1658); Nicolas Chevalier, *Description de l'Academie à Monter à Cheval* (Utrecht, 1706).

38. The two garments can be distinguished by their sleeves, since the cassock had set-in sleeves that usually hung down the back of the arm.

39. They can be seen in many stable and riding scenes, such as the *Interior of a Smithy* (c. 1657, National Gallery, London, no. 2591) by Gabriel Metsu; Philips Wouwermans, a specialist in painting horses and equestrian scenes, represented the red coat with gold trim frequently as well, for instance, in his *The Outdoor Riding School* (Musée du Louvre, Paris, inv. no. 1956).

40. Jacques Callot depicted various coats, including a fur-lined one worn with broad-brimmed hats and feathers in his *The Large Hunt*, 1619–1628, etching (L 353).

41. Reiss dated the picture incorrectly in the late 1640s on the basis of costume. Stephen Reiss, *Aelbert Cuyp* (London, 1975), 9–11, 154.

42. In the 1650s, men began to wear their hair increasingly long, and the wig came into style for those who were not fortunate to have a head of full and long curls. Actual hair and wigs are not always distinguishable in paintings. On wigs in the Netherlands, see J. H. Der Kinderen-Besier, *Spelevaart der Mode: De kledij onzer voorouders in de zeventiende eeuw* (Amsterdam, 1950), 177–178, 215–217.

43. This dress (c. 1660–1665, National Trust, Claydon House) is reproduced in Jane Ashelford, *The Art of Dress: Clothes and Society 1500–1914* (London, 1996), 96, pl. 75.

44. Feathers are often seen on women in riding costumes: for instance, the rather masculine hats adorned with feathers worn in Adriaen Pietersz van de Venne, *Frederick of the Palatine and His Wife Elizabeth Stuart on Horseback* (1628, Rijksmuseum, Amsterdam) and the outrageous feather headdress in Jan Mijtens, *Maria, Princess of Orange with Her Horse and Two Pages* (Mauritshuis, The Hague). Similarly, the woman in Philips Wouwermans' *Departing for the Falcon Hunt* (Musée du Louvre, Paris, inv. no. 1954) wears a feather.

45. A buff jerkin, probably owned by Ernst Casimir of Nassau is in the Rijksmuseum, Amsterdam; another worn by King Gustavus Adolphus of Sweden at Lützen in 1632 is in the Livrustkammaren, Stockholm; an English one is at the Victoria and Albert Museum, London (inv. no. T34-1948).

46. Gordenker 1995.

Pigments and Color Change in the Paintings of Aelbert Cuyp *Marika Spring*

Aelbert Cuyp's landscapes have long been admired for their depiction of a soft golden sunlight, created with translucent yellow-green and soft gray-green colors. *River Landscape with Horseman and Peasants* (cat. 45), painted at the height of his career, is a prime example. The soft gray blue of the sky fades into pale yellow at the horizon. The distant sunlit mountains and landscape are a subtle yellowish green, and a strong yellow light falls onto the path in the foreground. Cuyp's earlier paintings, as has often been noted, have a more somber tonality, similar to the monochromatic landscapes of Jan van Goyen, while the later paintings have warmer, more yellow tones influenced by Dutch Italianate landscape painters such as Jan Both, who returned to Utrecht from Italy in 1642.[1]

This study of *River Landscape* and ten other paintings spanning the whole of his career looks at the pigments Cuyp used to achieve these effects and explores whether his materials changed along with his style. Cuyp's choice of pigments also had consequences for the conservation of his paintings. Looking more closely at *River Landscape*, the shadows of the burdock leaves in the bottom right corner are flat and formless, and the paint appears clouded by a grayish veil, the result of a pigment deterioration (fig. 1) that is quite common on paintings by Cuyp; a very similar deterioration can be seen in the burdock leaves in *Lady and Gentleman on Horseback* (cat. 40).

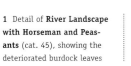

1 Detail of **River Landscape with Horseman and Peasants** (cat. 45), showing the deteriorated burdock leaves

Pigments

The wide variety of greens in the landscape and foliage of Cuyp's paintings comprise a complex mixture of pigments containing varying proportions of yellow lake, lead-tin yellow, yellow earth, the blue earth pigment vivianite, and green earth, modified with smaller amounts of umber, cassel earth, black, and red earth or vermilion.[2] Earth pigments are dominant in this list, as might be expected in the rather muddy tones of Cuyp's landscapes. The light and opaque lead-tin yellow (a manufactured lead-tin oxide) was used in significant amounts only in the lighter yellow shades, such as the touches of highlights on the leaves of trees and bushes and in the pale yellow-green middle landscape lit with sunlight depicted in many of Cuyp's compositions.

The major component of the mixtures in the darker shades of green is the translucent pigment yellow lake. The coloring matter in yellow lake pigments is a natural dyestuff extracted from plants, such as unripe buckthorn berries, weld, or dyer's broom, and precipitated or adsorbed onto a substrate such as alumina or chalk. The source of the dyestuff, the manufacturing method used, and the substrate determine the exact color, strength of hue, and permanence of the pigment.[3] A few recipes for yellow lake from the period have survived, for instance, those written down by Willem Pekstok, a painting materials manufacturer in Amsterdam who produced yellow lake pigments on an industrial scale. The ingredients for his recipe dated 1666 were a mixture of buckthorn berries, weld, yellow wood (old fustic), 100 pounds of chalk, and 20 pounds of alum.[4] This recipe is typical of those of the period in that it contains a great deal more chalk than alum, as does the yellow lake pigment used in these eleven paintings by Cuyp.[5] The product is a brighter yellow color than it would be if only alum had been used, but it is more prone to fading.[6] This deterioration usually makes it virtually impossible to determine the source of the dyestuff in the yellow lake pigment, but in three of the

paintings studied, the paint had been protected from light by the frame rebate. A minute sample taken from this area was analyzed using high-performance liquid chromatography (HPLC), which in every case found the dye-stuff to be derived from the weld plant.[7]

Yellow lake, particularly as a component of green paint mixtures, is mentioned very frequently in treatises of the period on painting technique, indicating the popularity of the pigment with seventeenth-century painters. One of a number of different mixtures for landscape painting listed by Théodore Turquet de Mayerne, from his conversations with artists, states that "all sorts of green can be made from diverse mixtures of yellow lake, yellow ochre, *cendre d'azur*, lead white and black earth."[8] Very little indication is given of the composition of *cendre d'azur* (blue ashes) in documentary sources. The name was used for artificial copper-containing pigments, but was also sometimes used for natural copper carbonate from the mineral azurite.[9] Samuel van Hoogstraten, in his book published in 1678, listed three types, "English, German and Haarlem ashes," among the blue pigments available to artists.[10] These may have all differed in composition, ashes being simply a color name referring to one of a number of different grayish blue pigments.

The grayish blue mineral pigment vivianite (hydrated iron phosphate), the blue component of the mixed greens in eight of the eleven paintings studied, may well have been classed as a type of ashes, but it has very rarely been found as a pigment in paintings. A few occurrences have been found on Romanesque and medieval wall paintings,[11] but none, as yet, have been reported on any other Dutch seventeenth-century paintings.[12]

Sometimes known as blue earth or blue ochre, vivianite has a color that seems perfectly suited to the grayish greens that are so typical of Cuyp's landscapes. Artists in this period usually did not prepare their own pigments but bought them from an apothecary or from the increasing number of grocers that specialized in painting supplies. Therefore, finding a pigment that apparently was not used by Cuyp's contemporaries is surprising.[13] Unfortunately, we do not know where Cuyp bought his pigments. Records show that a merchant sold artist's materials in Dordrecht, but we also know that painters would sometimes travel to buy them.[14] Pigments were traded across Europe and beyond, but vivianite was very rarely used as a pigment, possibly suggesting that it came from a local source. Deposits of the mineral exist in Cologne and Westphalia in Germany, and the Ardennes in the southern part of Belgium, none of which were too far away.[15] Deposits are also found in peat bog-iron ore, perhaps the most likely source for the vivianite used by Cuyp, since not only was peat abundant in the Netherlands, but a very active peat industry was located near Dordrecht (see cat. 4).[16] The blue color of the pulverant deposits found in peat bogs would probably have had more obvious potential as a pigment than the grayish black vivianite from sedimentary deposits, which only develops a blue color when crushed and ground (fig. 2).

A pigment that might be a blue earth, possibly vivianite, is mentioned in two documentary sources of the period.[17] Richard Symonds, who kept notebooks of his travels in Italy in the 1650s, recorded a conversation with a Mr. Remee, probably the French artist Remy van Leemput, about a pigment that he called "Harlems Oltramarin." Mr. Remee described the pigment as a "blew clay earth…not in any way produc'd from Lapis Lazzuli," making it clear that he was not talking about true ultramarine.[18] The only other pigment commonly used by seventeenth-century painters that might conceivably be called a blue earth is the mineral pigment azurite, but it is unlikely that azurite would be described as a clay. A mixture of "terra de Harlem pink lake" is suggested for "farthermost trees and dusky places" in some notes about the practice of a landscape painter referred to as Seigneur Otto, most likely the Dutch painter Otto Hoynck.

The context, in a mixture with pink lake (the English seventeenth-century term for yellow lake) that produced a green, suggests that "terra de Harlem" or Haarlem earth was a blue pigment, perhaps equivalent to the "Harlems Oltramarin" described in Symonds' notebooks.[19]

Cuyp also used vivianite for some of the figures in his paintings, such as the dress of the shepherdess in the background landscape of *River Landscape with Horseman and Peasants* (fig. 3), the trousers of the shepherd in *"The Small Dort"* (fig. 4), the skirt of the milkmaid in *"The Large Dort"* (The National Gallery, London) and the blue jacket of one of the horsemen in *Horsemen and Herdsmen with Cattle* (cat. 38).[20] However, he did use other blue pigments: the dress of the shepherdess in *A Hilly River Landscape* (The National Gallery, London) is painted with indigo, and the skies in all the paintings studied were painted with smalt (a blue glass) mixed with lead white. Smalt is not a particularly stable pigment, and it has often changed to a grayish hue, but it discolors less when mixed

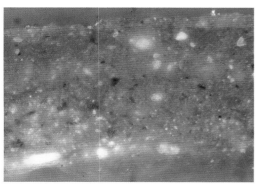

with lead white and has survived well on Cuyp's paintings. He seems to have used a particularly good quality of smalt, which in the brightest blue of some of the skies could almost be mistaken for ultramarine.

Cuyp's Early Period and Later Paintings

The change in style and tonality between Cuyp's early paintings and those painted after the middle of the 1640s, when the influence of Dutch Italianate painters began to appear in his work, is not reflected in his choice of materials — much the same pigments were used in the earliest and latest paintings studied. The most obvious change in technique is in the preparation of the support for painting. The influence of Van Goyen's paintings can perhaps be seen in the earliest painting examined, which has an off-white priming that is so thin that the texture of the wood grain is visible through the paint.[21] Most of the paintings have a beige preparatory layer, made from mixtures of white, yellow, black, and brown pigments.

A few of the late canvases have a rather different preparation — a gray layer applied over a red earth layer. This combination would have created a beige or flesh-colored surface to work on that was not much different in color from the grounds of the earlier paintings. A so-called double ground of gray over red earth was common in the seventeenth century in paintings from all over Europe, particularly later in the century, and several treatises on painting techniques of the period describe it. The few paintings by Jan Both that have undergone technical examination have this type of preparation, as do other paintings by Utrecht artists of the period and paintings by Rembrandt dating from as early as 1635.[22] Interestingly, though, a study of the preparatory layers on paintings by the Haarlem painter Frans Hals revealed a chronological pattern similar to the one found in Cuyp's work; Hals used a brownish ground until about

1660, when a few examples of gray-over-red earth grounds began to appear.[23] The significance of this similarity, however, is not clear. Our knowledge of the grounds used by seventeenth-century Dutch painters is too fragmentary to draw any firm conclusions.

Although Cuyp's later paintings show the influence of Dutch Italianate painters such as Jan Both, Cuyp's colors seem softer and more subtle. His skies were painted with gray-blue smalt rather than the brighter blue mixture of smalt and ultramarine that has been found on paintings by Jan Both. Jan also used different mixtures of pigments for his green paint: yellow earth, yellow lake, and lead-tin yellow mixed with ultramarine, azurite, and smalt rather than the softer blue of vivianite.[24] The influence of Jan Both seems to have been only superficial.

Color Change

Paintings by Aelbert Cuyp and Jan Both do have in common, however, a tendency to suffer from a type of paint defect known as blanching. This type of deterioration has occurred, to some extent, in nearly all the paintings in this study. As in the burdock leaves in *River Landscape with Horseman and Peasants* (fig. 1), the paint appears hazy and lighter than it originally was. Blanching has a number of different causes, but the type seen on paintings by some seventeenth-century artists appears to have a pigment-related cause because only certain colors are affected — darker translucent greens, yellow greens, and brownish greens.[25] Light and humidity also clearly play a role, since in several of the paintings in this study the paint has not deteriorated where it has been protected by the frame rebate (fig. 5).[26]

The major, and most unstable, component in the pigment mixture in blanched areas of paint is yellow lake.[27] Tests on yellow lake pigments made according to historical recipes have shown that the type of yellow lake used by Cuyp and prepared with a mainly chalk substrate for the dyestuff is more prone to fading than yellow lakes that have been prepared with alum.[28] This fading can be seen in cross sections of paint samples from deteriorated areas that all appear whitish at the surface — a white veil obscures the still-green paint beneath (fig. 6).

The process of deterioration is more complex than a simple loss of color from the yellow lake; it seems to involve some physical deterioration resulting in disruption of the paint film, creating an uneven surface and small voids that scatter light. The evidence for this is mostly indirect, coming from observations of cases in which the blanching is not too deep-seated. In these instances, applying a varnish of low viscosity or wetting with a solvent, which would reduce light scattering from the surface and from microvoids, improves the appearance of the deteriorated areas. Chalk, the substrate in the yellow lake pigment, is not a very satisfactory pigment in oil paint because it tends to adsorb water. Therefore, it is possible that the presence of chalk may have caused changes in the paint film beyond the simple fading of the yellow dyestuff adsorbed onto it.[29] Moisture could possibly have been introduced into the paint film by conservation treatments such as cleaning and relining, which have sometimes been implicated in studies of blanching. However, simple fluctuations in the humidity of the environment seem sufficiently disruptive to cause this effect, since blanching has occurred on both canvas and panel paintings by Cuyp with widely different conservation histories. This explanation of the cause of blanching rather simplifies what is a complex phenomenon, not yet completely understood, but in Cuyp's paintings, yellow lake does seem to be the principal culprit.

The two most distinctive features of Cuyp's palette that have emerged are the abundance of yellow lake in his green paint mixtures and the use of vivianite, a pigment not previously known to have been used on Dutch seventeenth-century paintings. Whether Cuyp sought out this pigment as an alternative to the more common blue pigments, or bought it as a type of blue ashes of unspecified composition we cannot know. Some of its characteristics could have made it appealing. The color seems very suitable for producing the muted tones of Cuyp's landscapes. The working properties of the fine-grained vivianite would also have been better than those of azurite and smalt, and vivianite would have been cheaper, of course, than ultramarine. Cuyp's use of large quantities of yellow lake might seem surprising because it already had a poor reputation for permanence in the seventeenth century. Abraham Latombé, whose comments were recorded by De Mayerne, stated that the pigment "endures neither the air nor the rain," suggesting that painters might even have been aware that moisture could play a part in the deterioration.[30] Yellow lake was, however, indispensable in creating the golden tones of Cuyp's atmospheric landscapes.

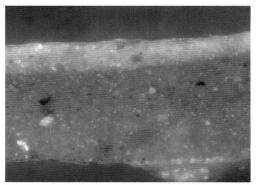

5 Detail of Aelbert Cuyp's **View on a Plain**, 1644, Dulwich Picture Gallery, London (after cleaning, before restoration), showing the edge that has been protected by the frame rebate. The paint is lighter where it has been exposed

6 Cross section of a paint sample from the grayish green landscape in Aelbert Cuyp's **View on a Plain**, 1644, Dulwich Picture Gallery, London. The major component of the paint layers is yellow lake. The uppermost layer has faded at the surface

1. Michael Palmer has carried out extensive analysis on samples from two paintings by Cuyp in the National Gallery of Art, Washington, and has kindly allowed the results to be published here. Jo Kirby has contributed HPLC results and useful discussions about documentary sources. For discussions about blanching, I would like to thank Carol Christensen, Rosanna Eadie, Mette Bjarnhof, and Sophie Plender, who also very kindly contributed her photograph of a detail of *View on a Plain.*

For information on Cuyp's early paintings, see Alan Chong, "New Dated Works from Aelbert Cuyp's Early Career," *Burlington Magazine* 133 (September 1991), 606–612.

2. Small paint samples were mounted as cross sections and the pigments examined by light microscopy and EDX analysis in the scanning electron microscope. Detailed descriptions of the mixtures found in the green paint in each of the paintings examined can be found in the table in the appendix.

3. David Saunders and Jo Kirby, "Light Induced Color Changes in Red and Yellow Lake Pigments," *National Gallery Technical Bulletin* 15 (1994), 79–97.

4. Erma Hermens and Arie Wallert, "The Pekstok Papers, Lake Pigments, Prisons and Paint Mills," in *Looking through Paintings,* Leids Kunsthistorisch Jaarboek 11, eds. Erma Hermens, Annamiek Ouwerkerk, Nicola Costaras (London and Baarn, 1998), 269–295.

5. Hermens and Wallert 1998, 284. EDX analysis on samples of green paint revealed that the yellow lake pigment contains a large amount of chalk and almost undetectable amounts of alumina.

6. Saunders and Kirby 1994.

7. I would like to thank Jo Kirby (Scientific Department, National Gallery, London) for analysis of the dyestuff by HPLC. The paintings in which weld was identified in the yellow lake pigment are *Landscape with Two Windmills* (Statens Museum for Kunst, Copenhagen), *View on a Plain* (Dulwich Picture Gallery, London), *River Landscape with Horseman and Peasants* (cat. 45), and *Landscape with Horse Trainers* (cat. 39). The analysis also serves to confirm that the paint contains a yellow lake pigment, and that the chalk detected by EDX analysis is not a colorless extender added to the paint.

8. Johannes A. van de Graaf, *Het De Mayerne manuscript als bron voor de schildertechniek van de barok* (Utrecht, 1958), 142. See also Jo Kirby and David Saunders, "Sixteenth- to Eighteenth-Century Green Colors in Landscape and Flower Paintings: Composition and Deterioration," in *Painting Techniques: History, Materials and Studio Practice,* Preprints of the IIC Dublin Congress (7–11 September 1998), ed. Ashok Roy and Perry Smith (London, 1998), 155–159.

9. Margriet van Eikema Hommes, "Painters' Methods to Prevent Color Changes Described in Sixteenth to Early Eighteenth Century Sources on Oil Painting Techniques," in Hermens and Wallert 1998, 102.

10. Samuel van Hoogstraten, *Inleyding tot de Hooge Schoole der Schilderkonst* (Rotterdam, 1678) (facsimile ed. Holland, 1969), 221.

11. Ernst L. Richter, "Seltene Pigmente im Mittelaltar," *Zeitschrift für Kunsttechnologie und Konservierung* 2 (1988), 1: 171–176. Helen Howard, "Techniques of the Romanesque and Gothic Wall Paintings in the Holy Sepulchre Chapel, Winchester Cathedral," in *Historical Painting Techniques, Materials and Studio Practice,* Preprints of a Symposium, University of Leiden, eds. Arie Wallert, Erma Hermens, Marja Peek (Getty Conservation Institute) (Los Angeles, 1995), 91–104.

12. The presence of vivianite is difficult to determine by optical microscopy, particularly in green mixtures in which tiny grayish particles are embedded in a matrix of yellow lake and yellow earth; vivianite only really becomes apparent when analyzed by SEM-EDX.

13. Koos Levy-Van Halm, "Where Did Vermeer Buy His Painting Materials? Theory and Practice," in *Vermeer Studies,* National Gallery of Art, Studies in the History of Art, eds. Ivan Gaskell and Michiel Jonker, vol. 55 (Washington, 1998), 137–141.

14. Cornelis van Bolenbeek was recorded as selling painting materials, as well as other supplies in Dordrecht in about the middle of the seventeenth century. Xenia Henny, "Hoe kwamen de Rotterdamse schilders aan hun verf?" in *Rotterdamse Meesters uit de Gouden Eeuw,* ed. Nora Schadee [exh. cat., Historisch Museum Rotterdam] (Zwolle, 1994), 48. Cuyp would not necessarily have bought his supplies in Dordrecht, since documentary sources record instances of artists traveling to other towns to buy materials. See Levy-Van Halm in Gaskell and Jonker 1998.

15. Richard V. Gaines, M. Catherine W. Skinner, Eugene E. Foord, Brian Mason, Abraham Rosenzweig, *Dana's New Mineralogy,* 8th ed. (New York, 1997), 791.

16. Jan van de Vries, "The Dutch Rural Economy and the Landscape," in Christopher Brown, *Dutch Landscape: The Early Years, Haarlem and Amsterdam 1590–1650* [exh. cat., National Gallery] (London, 1986), 83. Deposits of vivianite have been found in the Netherlands. See P. A. Riezebos and M. Rappol, "Gravel- to Sand-Sized Vivianite Components in a Saalian Till Layer Near Borne (The Netherlands)," *Geologie en Mijnbouw* 66 (1987), 21–34.

17. The name vivianite was not applied to the mineral until the nineteenth century, when it was named for the mineralogist J. G. Vivian.

18. Mary Beal, *A Study of Richard Symonds: His Italian Notebooks and Their Relevance to Seventeenth-Century Painting Techniques* (London, 1984), 225. Van Leemput stated that this "blew clay earth" was "much usd in faces by all ye face makers in London." Rosamund Harley has already suggested that this blue earth might be vivianite, or another blue earthy mineral, ilsemannite. See Rosamund D. Harley, *Artists' Pigments c. 1600–1835, A Study in English Documentary Sources,* 2d ed. (London, 1982), 59.

19. M. Kirby Talley, *Portrait Painting in England: Studies in the Technical Literature before 1700* (London, 1981), 194. Talley proposed a link between Haarlem ultramarine and the Haarlem blue mentioned in Houbraken's life of Jan van Goyen. Houbraken 1718–1721 (1893 ed.), 135, cited the deterioration of Haarlem blue as the cause of the monochrome coloring of Van Goyen's landscapes, but Melanie Gifford has shown that his use of somber colors was deliberate and that the grayish skies contain a pale grade of smalt. This suggests that the name Haarlem blue was used rather inconsistently. See E. Melanie Gifford, "Jan van Goyen en de techniek van het naturalistiche landschap," in *Jan van Goyen* [exh. cat., Stedelijk Museum De Lakenhal] (Leiden, 1996), 70–81.

20. For *"The Small Dort,"* see Reiss in London 1973, 116, no. 79; for *"The Large Dort,"* see Reiss in London 1973, 120, no. 83.

21. Leiden 1996.

22. Brad Epley, "Jan Both's *Italian Landscape,"* *The Hamilton Kerr Institute Bulletin,* no. 3 (2000), 121–128. David Bomford, Christopher Brown, Ashok Roy, with contributions from Jo Kirby and Raymond White, *Art in the Making. Rembrandt* [exh. cat., National Gallery] (London, 1988), 31. A similar double ground has been found on *A Landscape with the Judgement of Paris,* attributed to Jan Both and Cornelis van Poelenburch (National Gallery, London).

23. Karin Groen and Ella Hendriks, "Frans Hals: A Technical Examination," in Seymour Slive ed., *Frans Hals* [exh. cat., National Gallery of Art] (Washington, 1989), 114–116.

24. Epley 2000. Epley stated that complex mixtures of ultramarine, smalt, green earth, copper blue, yellow and red earths, lead-tin yellow, yellow lake, chalk, lead white, and black were used for the foliage.

25. Cases of blanching in seventeenth-century paintings and possible causes are discussed in Martin Wyld, John Mills, Joyce Plesters, "Some Observations on Blanching with Special Reference to the Paintings of Claude," *National Gallery Technical Bulletin* 4 (1980), 49–63. Blanching is common on paintings by Claude and Gaspard Dughet. See also Epley 2000. For blanching in paintings by Cuyp see Richard Beresford and Giles Waterfield, eds., *Conserving Old Masters.*

Paintings Recently Restored at Dulwich Picture Gallery [exh. cat., Dulwich Picture Gallery] (London, 1995).

26. For an illustration of this painting, see Reiss in London 1973, 75, no. 42.

27. Vivianite is of only medium stability, but blanching has also occurred in those paintings in which it is not a component of the green mixtures; therefore, it is unlikely to be the cause. The blue jacket of one of the horsemen in *Horsemen and Herdsmen with Cattle* (cat. 38), which is painted with vivianite, does show some sign of deterioration, however. See Helen Howard, "Romanesque and Gothic Wall Paintings in Winchester Cathedral: An Unusual Use and Alteration of Vivianite," *Journal of the Russell Society* 6, no. 2 (1996), 93–96. Green earth has been implicated in previous studies of blanching, but it is only a minor component of the paint in deteriorated areas in paintings by Cuyp. See Karin Groen, "Scanning Electron Microscopy as an Aid in the Study of Blanching," *The Hamilton Kerr Institute Bulletin,* ed. Ian McClure, no. 1 (1988), 48–65.

28. Saunders and Kirby 1994.

29. Epley 2000 also made the point that the hygroscopic nature of chalk may have contributed to the blanching in a painting by Jan Both.

30. Van de Graaf 1958, 145.

Summary of the preparation of the support and the composition of areas of green paint

Date	Title and Support	Preparation of the support	Composition of areas of green paint
1640–1641	*Landscape with Two Windmills*, Statens Museum for Kunst, Copenhagen, panel	Thin off-white priming (lead white and a little yellow earth)	Greenish yellow foliage in the foreground: mainly yellow lake, a little red lake, vivianite, and cassel earth
1644	*View on a Plain*, Dulwich Picture Gallery, London, panel	Thin pale beige priming (lead white, yellow earth, black, and umber) over chalk bound in glue	Grayish green foliage in the foreground: mainly yellow lake, some vivianite, silicon-rich yellow earth, a little cassel earth, and lead-tin yellow
c. 1645	*Herdsmen with Cattle* (cat. 14), canvas	Beige ground (lead white, yellow earth, black, and umber)	Gray-green foreground near the bottom edge: yellow lake, vivianite, cassel earth, yellow earth, a little vermilion Yellow-green hill on the right: mainly yellow lake, some silicon-rich yellow earth, a little vivianite, lead white, and red earth Dark brown foreground paint: yellow lake, yellow earth, bone black, umber, vermilion Gray-green grass in the middle distance: yellow lake, yellow earth, green earth, vermilion, brown, black, a little lead white
1650	*"The Large Dort,"* The National Gallery, London, canvas	Beige ground (lead white, yellow earth, black, and brown)	Grayish green of the grass in front of the cow near the left edge: yellow lake, vivianite, silicon-rich yellow earth, a little green earth, lead white, lead-tin yellow, and cassel earth
1650–1652	*"The Small Dort,"* The National Gallery, London, panel	Pale beige priming (lead white, yellow earth, black and brown) over chalk bound in glue	Yellow green of the grass in the foreground: yellow lake, vivianite, silicon-rich yellow earth, a little lead-tin yellow, and bone black Light green leaf on the bushes in the foreground: lead white, lead-tin yellow, a little green earth, and yellow lake
1655–1660	*A Hilly River Landscape with a Horseman Talking to a Shepherdess*, The National Gallery, London, canvas	Beige layer (lead white, charcoal black, yellow earth, red earth) over a brownish yellow layer (chalk, yellow, and red earth)	Dark green of the leaves on the branch hanging over the horseman: green earth, lead-tin yellow, yellow earth, a little black Yellow brown of the leaves on the bush, lower left: lead-tin yellow, yellow earth, yellow lake, a little black, green earth, and cassel earth Dull khaki green of the leaves on the trees beside the tower: silicon-rich yellow earth, lead white, a little black, green earth, red earth, cassel earth
late 1650s	*Horsemen and Herdsmen with Cattle* (cat. 38), canvas	Pale gray layer (lead white, charcoal black, aluminosilicate clays) over a light red layer (red earth, chalk, lead white)	Dark vegetation in the foreground: lead-tin yellow, charcoal black, yellow lake, lead white, a little red earth
late 1650s	*Landscape with Horse Trainers* (cat. 39), canvas	NA	Gray green of the foreground landscape: yellow lake, lead-tin yellow, green earth, silicon-rich yellow earth, manganese black, bone black Light gray-green leaves on the tree: yellow lake, yellow earth, brown, charcoal black, green earth

Date	Title and Support	Preparation of the support	Composition of areas of green paint
begun c. 1655 completed 1660 / 1665	*Lady and Gentleman on Horseback* (cat. 40), canvas	Light gray layer (lead white, charcoal black, chalk) over an orange-red layer (red earth, chalk, umber, lead white)	Dark green of the burdock leaf: yellow lake, vivianite, lead white, charcoal black, yellow earth, lead-tin yellow Green of the uppermost burdock leaf in the lower left corner: yellow lake, vivianite, lead-tin yellow, orpiment
late 1650s	*Evening Landscape* (cat. 44), canvas	Warm pale gray layer (lead white, charcoal black, umber, chalk) over a red layer (red earth, chalk, red lead)	Foliage at the right edge of painting: yellow lake, vivianite, yellow earth, cassel earth, a little lead white
c. 1660	*River Landscape with Horseman and Peasants* (cat. 45), canvas	Beige ground (lead white, black, umber, yellow earth, some chalk)	Gray green of the burdock leaf in the foreground: yellow lake, vivianite, yellow earth, some lead-tin yellow, bone black, and umber

The Beauty of Holland: Aelbert Cuyp as Landscape Draftsman *Egbert Haverkamp-Begemann*

Cuyp's major artistic interest was landscape.[1] About five out of six of his drawings are landscapes, and most of the others are studies of plants, animals, and shepherds.[2] He favored simple rural motifs observed from close proximity, views of forests, distant panoramas, and views of towns, particularly Dordrecht, Nijmegen, and Cleves. Cuyp usually sketched the first three subjects with chalk and brush in gray, often with the addition of color; the fourth, with black chalk only and rarely touched with color. His choice of subjects and their interpretation, his interest in light, and his very personal application of color set him apart from his contemporaries.

The functions of verisimilitude and fantasy differ in painting and drawing. Cuyp sketched nature for its intrinsic qualities. In each of his drawings (with the exception of foregrounds and, possibly, a few imaginary views), he strived for topographical correctness.[3] By contrast, he painted most of his landscapes from imagination, at times incorporating motifs he had observed in nature or combining some he had seen and drawn separately. Topographic accuracy in Cuyp's drawings does not surprise in views of towns like Dordrecht or Nijmegen in which recording the town and its buildings was the main purpose. It is astonishing, however, to realize that drawings of simple rural motifs without man-made structures, or drawings in which a shed, a barn, or a church tower is almost entirely hidden by shrubs, trees, or an elevation in the terrain were largely true to nature as well. Certainly the repetitive, somewhat stereotypical foregrounds composed of reeds on watery banks or hilly terrain, which effectively provided a pictorial *repoussoir,* were pure constructs.

The great majority of Cuyp's drawings is characterized by the absence of man and an understatement of his intrusion in the landscape in any form. Even the idea of the pastoral, prominent in his later paintings, is rarely evoked. When he did include figures, he did so to indicate scale rather than to convey the role of man or to enliven the scenery. By contrast, in the landscape drawings of his close contemporaries, Jan van Goyen and Pieter Molyn, human activities are included to emphasize man's link to nature. In Cuyp's drawings, man's work, his mills, his farm buildings, and his churches have become part of nature, with light and air used as unifying elements. The dominance of landscape over man is also emphasized in Cuyp's drawings of panoramas in which the towns are submerged as part of the landscape rather than as its dominant feature.[4]

Aelbert's father, Jacob Cuyp, initiated Aelbert's fundamental artistic direction by exerting the greatest formative influence on him as a landscape artist. This assertion may seem surprising, since Jacob is known principally as a portraitist. However, Aelbert's interpretation of the rural surroundings of Dordrecht, known from a large group of drawings, clearly reflects his father's influence. According to Houbraken, Jacob had been a pupil of Abraham Bloemaert, whose art was certainly familiar to him; Jacob's wife came from Utrecht, a very active art center not far from Dordrecht; and Jacob may well have sent Aelbert there to broaden his horizons. His drawings, in the use and application of color, are reminiscent of those by Roelandt Savery, Abraham Bloemaert, and Cornelis Saftleven; these artists all lived and worked in Utrecht, where Aelbert also became acquainted with some of the remarkable medieval monuments that he chose for his drawings. This orientation toward Utrecht distinguishes Aelbert from other Dordrecht artists who went to Amsterdam to be trained by Rembrandt and who subsequently returned to the city on the Merwede.[5]

Cuyp's Drawings in Context

Landscape and Autonomous Drawing

To understand Cuyp's significance as a draftsman, it is necessary to review some aspects of his work that touch on broader issues, such as landscape as a specialty and drawing as an autonomous art form. After a flourishing beginning in Flanders, the subject of landscape acquired an unparalleled significance in Holland in the first decades of the seventeenth century.[6] During Cuyp's lifetime the number of artists specializing in landscape in Holland was far greater than anywhere else, and these artists were able to make a living (although sometimes only by producing enormous quantities of paintings). Cuyp's specialization was far from unusual and his chosen field was respectable, in spite of the low ranking it traditionally received in art-theoretical writing.

Particularly in Holland, autonomous drawing had a place among the other arts at the time. Besides drawings made as preliminary sketches or complete designs for other works of art, such as paintings or prints, many drawings were made as self-contained or autonomous works of art. Their status was similar to paintings or prints. Most of these self-contained drawings were finished, rather detailed, complete subjects. But sketchy drawings were also considered complete in themselves. Many of the drawings of biblical subjects by Rembrandt and his pupils were autonomous rather than preliminary studies. Elsewhere in Europe — in Italy, France, Spain — a drawing more frequently served a preliminary function in the artistic process and less often played an independent, autonomous role.

Cuyp's drawings were self-contained, autonomous works of art. In some cases, like the large and elaborate panoramas, the independence of the drawings is evident, but in others (which are in the majority), the seemingly casual selection of the motif, the appearance of effortless execu-

tion, and an overall informality seem to belie the status of autonomy. They were not quick sketches or recordings of motifs wanted for future incorporation in paintings (as are Van Goyen's quick sketches of 1650 / 1651).[7] The drawings are complete, the compositions are thoughtfully constructed, the space is convincingly suggested, the interplay of light and shadow fully rendered, and the color applied with great sophistication. These elements indicate a certain degree of finish; they do not imply that he made such works as preparatory designs for paintings — though he from time to time used drawings for motifs in paintings and, in a few instances, used an entire drawing as a *modello* for a painting (cats. 4, 64). He molded unassuming but picturesque rural sites into autonomous works of art, preserving both topographical truth and a sketchy, informal appearance.[8]

As an art form the autonomous landscape drawing was practiced not only "for the market" by such artists as Jan van Goyen and Pieter Molyn, but also frequently by independent, well-educated, and intellectually sophisticated amateur artists. One thinks of Cuyp's younger contemporaries Jan de Bisschop (1628–1671) and Constantijn Huygens the Younger (1628–1697),[9] accomplished draftsmen who made large numbers of landscape drawings, most of them topographically faithful, when they were not busy as prominent lawyers. Huygens' drawings remained together until 1823, when they were sold at auction.[10] Cuyp, too, did not dispose of his drawings, and although he was not one of the amateurs, he may have shared their attitude toward the self-contained landscape drawing as a special type of work of art.

Technique (Black Chalk, Brush, Watercolor, Gum Arabic)

Cuyp combined traditional and recently developed media in a personal way. He used black chalk for the main structure of his drawings, usually applying it very lightly at first, then with more pressure, and finally moistening it for black accents (with water or, presumably if need be, with his tongue).[11] He introduced other accents, from various shades of gray to black, with a brush and suggested shadows and clouds with washes from light to dark gray (in this sequence, but he reverted to materials used earlier whenever necessary), finally covering the darkest parts of the drawing with gum arabic. In his later drawings he combined black chalk with graphite, for the lighter tone and sharper detail it could produce.

One of the main features that sets Cuyp's drawings apart from those of his contemporaries is the subtle yet decisive use of color. Others in Holland in the seventeenth century applied color to their landscape drawings. One of them, Hendrick Avercamp (1585–1634), did so in ways that demonstrate the very different effects that could be obtained. Early in the century, circa 1613, he enlivened some of his black-chalk landscapes with lightly applied, pastellike, transparent watercolors; later he used strong colors, often with bodycolor, as the main element of a design and actually made little paintings on paper.[12] In the earlier works, black chalk defined the design; in the later ones, the colors. Aelbert Cuyp also defined his subjects in black chalk, fusing it with lines and dashes drawn with the brush in color, sometimes including touches of white bodycolor. In contrast to the later Avercamp, Cuyp preferred not to color or "wash" entire sections with the brush only (except for clouds), but to sketch with the brush in conjunction with black chalk; neither did he make drawings in color only, without any black chalk.[13]

Cuyp's use of color was also sophisticated because of his habit of constantly creating new colors and shades of tints, such as yellowish green or greenish brown, or grayish pink and the like. Max Friedländer rightly wrote in 1901 about "the great colorist's characteristic blond olive-green tonality in its manifold variations."[14] Of all Cuyp's predecessors, Roelandt Savery presents the closest parallel, for he also sketched with colors, usually together with black chalk, mixing them (although less frequently than Cuyp) to create new tones. After a sojourn in Prague at the court of Rudolf II and in Bohemia — where Pieter Stevens and Paulus van Vianen also applied colors to their landscapes — and after a short residence in Amsterdam, Savery came to Utrecht in 1619. Cuyp must have seen Savery's drawings, especially *A Mill Tower on the Moldau near Prague* (fig. 1),[15] for not only are the colors related but its composition, adopted in reverse, also appears in Cuyp's *Utrecht with the Vecht River and the Pellekussenpoort* (cat. 49).

Cuyp frequently covered parts of his drawings with a transparent, colorless, varnishlike substance consisting of gum arabic (presumably diluted with water).[16] He applied it carefully, with a rather broad brush, only going over the darkest areas of his drawings, such as foregrounds and adjoining sections, for instance, trees and hills that were in shade. He applied it after finishing the design, although he sometimes added a few lines over the substance as an afterthought. His purpose undoubtedly was to prevent the black chalk from rubbing off, and to intensify and preserve the contrasts between light and dark. Cuyp was not the first one to use gum arabic as a fixative or a varnish; Pieter Molyn had preceded him in one drawing and apparently never used it again.[17] Very few did.

The Series as Format
Cuyp liked to produce drawings in series. This practice is reflected in his frequent use of sketchbooks or drawing books (or, in at least one instance, a number of unbound sheets of the same paper). The drawings of each series represent similar subject matter, are the same size, and are executed with the same materials used in a similar way. Most series can be reconstructed at least in part.[18] They vary in length from a few sheets to no less than twenty. Cuyp also made drawings in pairs, but rarely single drawings by themselves. For some series he used one sketchbook, for others, more than one, but that does not imply that sketchbooks were completed in a narrow time span; he may have expanded a series in one sketchbook with intermissions. Although the format of the sketchbook must have facilitated making drawings in series, producing series of like drawings must have answered a more fundamental need. The series was more than a matter of convenience. Each series and each pair represented a type of landscape. The drawings were not meant to

be in a specific order, and Cuyp did not number them, but he must have seen them as variations on a theme: not as imaginary modifications of a central idea, but rather as a collection of existing sites that resembled each other and that he represented in a similar way.

The series had a specific function with a long tradition. In the fifteenth century, the print series became a tool to improve the transmission of ideas and was later used for many subjects, religious as well as secular. The "instructive series" not only organized data, it intensified the cumulative message of its components.[19] In the Netherlands, earlier than elsewhere, the series became the vehicle for landscape scenery, in prints as well as in drawings. Pieter Bruegel the Elder's series of large mountain landscapes was made into print by the Van Doetecom brothers and published by Hieronymus Cock about 1555, marking a most impressive beginning of the series as a format for publishing landscapes. Only a few years later, in 1559 and 1561, the same Hieronymus Cock published views of the rural surroundings of Antwerp in two series of fourteen and at least twenty-seven prints respectively.[20]

These series of rural landscapes had a great impact in the Northern Netherlands in the early seventeenth century. Not only did Claes Jansz Visscher copy a number of prints from Hieronymus Cock's series, publishing them in 1612 as a series entitled *Regiunculae…(Little Landscapes)*, he also portrayed similar rural scenes in the environs of Haarlem in his drawings and prints of 1607 and shortly thereafter (fig. 2). Esaias van de Velde similarly adopted the series as a format for ten landscape etchings, most of which also show rural sites near Haarlem. The most prolific producer of landscape series was Jan van de Velde. About 1616 Visscher published three of Jan van de Velde's series (totaling sixty etchings), and Robert de Baudous published two more (comprising thirty-six etchings).[21]

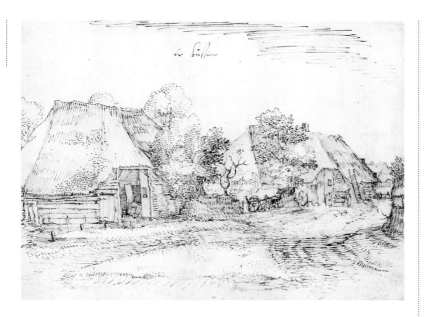

Aelbert Cuyp was much impressed by Claes Jansz Visscher's village views. He used the idea for his own drawings of the environs of Dordrecht, and the concept of the series for many of his drawings. By the time he became active as an artist, the format of the series had already been adopted for landscapes by draftsmen of the previous generation, among them Esaias van de Velde, Willem Buytewech, Jan van de Velde, and Jan van Goyen. And the format would remain valid later in the century: Allart van Everdingen, Roelant Roghman, Lambert Doomer, and Willem Schellinks used it. Outside the Netherlands, Claude Lorrain in particular arranged his landscape drawings in series or groups.

The Landscapes

A brief discussion of the characteristics that differentiate Cuyp's series provides insight into his contribution to the art of landscape. A chronology of his drawings can be established only in its broad outlines. One reason for this difficulty is that Cuyp did not date any of his drawings. Approximate dates, therefore, are based largely on the occasional use he made of drawings for dated paintings or on stylistic similarities to those paintings. Moreover, the series demonstrate that Cuyp changed his style frequently, varying it over time as well as according to the type of landscape (for example, a close-up village view, a panorama, or the interior of woods). The different styles, it is important to note, are not necessarily sequential. Despite these difficulties of dating, Cuyp's drawings seem to be concentrated in three distinct periods of his career. His most active period as a draftsman was between 1639 / 1640, when he was about nineteen or twenty years old, and 1642. During the mid-1640s Cuyp made a group of panoramic drawings of Dutch towns and another group of forest scenes. In the early 1650s he made a remarkable series of at least twenty black-chalk sketches of Nijmegen, Cleves, and other sites near these towns. No drawings can be securely dated later than the early 1650s.

Cuyp, in the short, very intense, early period of circa 1639 / 1642, executed the majority of his drawings, usually in series. The very first drawings were two detailed renderings of Dordrecht's main watergate, the Groothoofdspoort, in black chalk only (Gemeentearchief, Dordrecht; Hamburg Kunsthalle). They are in a generalized black-chalk style that has no specific precedent. At about the same time Cuyp made large, autonomous drawings of historic monuments and town views, here referred to as the Utrecht Group. For these he used complex techniques, including watercolor, heightening in white, and gum arabic, over a basic structure of black chalk. *Utrecht with the Vecht River and the Pellekussenpoort* (cat. 49) and views of the Mariakerk (cats. 46, 47) and the Buurkerk (cat. 48) are among them. He used the Frankfurt drawing for a painting that can be dated to the early 1640s (see cat. 5), which provides a clue for the dating of the entire Utrecht Group. These drawings reflect the artist's familiarity with drawings by Roelandt Savery, specifically his views of sites in Bohemia and his use of watercolor and gouache.

During this early period Cuyp also sketched distant views of towns like Rhenen, Utrecht, and Amersfoort, placing them in the middle distance beyond hilly foregrounds; these drawings are here referred to as Small Panoramas (Teylers Museum, Haarlem; F. Koenigs, formerly Haarlem; Kupferstichkabinett, Berlin; and cat. 71). The *View of Rhenen*

in Haarlem (fig. 3) was used for the background of a family portrait set in a landscape that he painted with his father in 1641 (see cat. 3, fig. 1). This group of Small Panoramas, therefore, also dates from circa 1641. The precedents for Cuyp's distant Small Panoramas, such as the drawing in Haarlem, are the prints in Georg Braun and Franz Hogenberg's *Civitates orbis terrarum* (1572–1618), many of them designed by Joris Hoefnagel or under his guidance. Cuyp must have known them, but modified the concept by bringing the foreground closer and introducing color. Cuyp made at least four more drawings of a similar concept, showing a valley or flat lands beyond a dark foreground, but sketching them more loosely and only in black chalk and gray wash with a touch of white bodycolor in some (for instance, cat. 58).

Country Road with a Cottage alongside a River (cat. 64) is totally different from the Haarlem *View of Rhenen*, in motif, perspective, and detail. Cuyp used it for a painting that can be dated to 1640/1641 (cat. 4). The gray and colored washes and the distribution of light and dark were applied very skillfully — the road and the barn lie in direct sunlight while the foreground is in shade. Cuyp used the same composition in his drawing *View of 's-Gravendeel* (cat. 64, fig. 1) in Saint Petersburg.[22] In both drawings the light comes from the side and from behind, a device Cuyp used frequently to model contrasts between light and shade that define subject and space. These two drawings of rural motifs, forming a pair or part of a group (here called River Borders), differ greatly from the Small Panoramas and the Utrecht Group, but nevertheless were done about the same time, on paper of the same size (approximately 19 × 30 cm).

The largest single group of Cuyp's drawings from this early period, and one of his major achievements, represents subjects near his hometown. To judge by those that are identifiable, Cuyp sketched no less than

twenty-five views of rural subjects in the environs of Dordrecht, two of them in the town itself (cat. 61). Originally part of various sketchbooks, the drawings are all approximately the same size (about 14 × 19 cm) and were done in black chalk and gray wash; the majority was colored with watercolor in a variety of tints, and a number were heightened with white bodycolor. At present they cannot be dated more precisely than circa 1640 / 1642. They exude an air of simplicity and spontaneous enjoyment of nature. They also seem to follow, chronologically, the drawings of the Utrecht Group and the Small Panoramas, but may have been done concurrently. One of the drawings of the Environs of Dordrecht Group is *Fields, a Tree to the Left, and Farm Buildings in the Distance* (Museum Boijmans Van Beuningen, Rotterdam), which in composition and light-dark contrasts is similar to *A Farm with Cottages and Animals* (cat. 10).

The Environs of Dordrecht Group demonstrates Jacob's formative influence on Aelbert. Jacob did not limit himself to portraiture, and as early as 1627 he painted a *Fish Market* (fig. 4)[23] with a background of farm buildings and trees that in motifs and composition is very similar to some of Aelbert's drawings in the Environs of Dordrecht Group. Other landscapes painted by Jacob in 1627 and 1628 for two versions of a shepherdess with a little boy[24] (possibly portraying his wife and son; see Wheelock essay, fig. 3) anticipate later drawings and paintings by Aelbert. The farm settings in his designs for a series of prints of animals by Reinier Persyn (1641) also resemble the scenery in some of the Environs of Dordrecht drawings, and the execution of Jacob's extant drawing for one of Persyn's prints is very close to Aelbert's way of handling such subjects (see cat. 2, fig. 1).[25] Father and son sometimes worked together, Jacob portraying families seated or standing in the open air with a view of fields or a town behind them painted by Aelbert. Two such comparatively large joint works date from 1641 (cat. 3, and fig. 1 in that entry).[26]

At least fifteen broad panoramas of Dutch towns and distant views, here referred to as Large Panoramas, rank among Cuyp's most impressive landscapes. They are difficult to date precisely, but they seem to have followed the small rural scenes and distant views of towns just mentioned, and probably date from the years 1642–1646. These large panoramic views (they measure about 18 × 45 / 50 cm) are characterized by hilly foregrounds that serve not merely as *repoussoir* or elevated vantage points, but that tend to absorb the main motif or constitute the main emphasis of the drawing.

Most Large Panoramas are broadly sketched and are colored, usually yellowish green. Cuyp sketched the broad outlines first in thin and light black chalk, making the details gradually heavier and adding accents by moistening the chalk and by using a brush and gray ink; he then applied gray and colored washes, fusing the colored washes with the chalk, and

frequently reverting to black chalk and brush in dark gray to make the dark accents stand out. Frequently he added gum arabic to the darkest areas, both to fix the chalk and to produce a deeper black.

Among the towns represented in this group are Arnhem, The Hague, Rhenen, Harderwijk, and Calcar, all places near hills or dunes that gave him the opportunity to make nature the dominant feature. Prints by Jan van de Velde, who frequently used the oblong format for landscapes seen from a distance, provided the starting point for Cuyp's Large Panoramas. One of Van de Velde's series, comprising eighteen oblong prints dating from 1615, includes a view across fields beyond an elevated foreground (fig. 5)[27] that anticipates Cuyp's panoramas. Cuyp created his own view of such motifs, and in contrast to Jan van de Velde, he emphasized the foreground terrain to enhance the impression of depth.

About the same time, 1642–1646, Cuyp made about eight sketches of roads through or along the edges of forests, consisting largely of old oaks (cats. 51–53). They are rooted in the wooded scenes by Gillis van Coninxloo and more closely related to views of woods etched by Willem

Buytewech circa 1616 (see Wheelock essay, fig. 14).[28] Cuyp, however, totally changed their ideas by making the woods look old and inhospitable rather than contrived and mannerist. He sketched these views, here called Forest Edges, broadly with black chalk and brush lines and washes in gray, suggesting the wildness of nature. His wooded scenery resembles Jacob van Ruisdael's painted forests of the 1650s, leading one to conclude that Cuyp must have seen such motifs east of Utrecht and in Guelderland, where Ruisdael found them.

In 1645 or somewhat earlier, Cuyp made four large oblong drawings of Dordrecht seen from across the river (cats. 80, 82–84). Two of them are in black chalk and gray watercolor only; the other two have touches of color. The emphasis on the linear structure of the houses, the church, and other buildings aligned along the river sets these drawings apart from his other works. Cuyp's goal was to render the town as it stretched out along the river, absorbed by light and confined between an endless sky and a wide body of water, and to provide topographic accuracy at the same time.

Cuyp adopted the precision applied to these profile views of Dordrecht to a group of at least sixteen large views of the towns of Nijmegen, Cleves, and their surroundings, which he made about 1651/1652 using smaller sheets of paper (about 14/19 × 24/27 cm). Cuyp also used black chalk, as he had for the profiles of Dordrecht, but for the Nijmegen and Cleves views he sometimes combined it with graphite in order to obtain greater precision in small details and more tonal gradation. The project was well defined, although whether he carried it out for himself or as a commission is not clear. His goal was to make topographically correct views of towns and their settings.

The towns (Nijmegen, Cleves) and the hills in between — situated in a small region along the Rhine on both sides of the present border between Holland and Germany — were tourist attractions and were frequently chosen for representation in paintings and drawings by Jan van Goyen, Herman Saftleven, Lambert Doomer, and others. These views of hills bordering meadows, of towns in their hilly settings combining distant precision with nearby boldness of detail, of towns seen across a body of water, and of buildings selected for scrutiny incorporate all the interests he had expressed in his earlier drawings. He found the subjects that satisfied these preferences in this one area around Nijmegen. He sketched them in black chalk and pencil, without color, with great care for rendering space, light, and detail. They demonstrate great accomplishment. But then he quit drawing.

Cuyp rarely disposed of his drawings. They had little influence on other artists,[29] and they rarely appear in auction catalogues until 1767, when more than eighty were sold in a Dordrecht sale; they may well have been part of Cuyp's estate.[30] The commercial aspect of his drawings apparently did not interest him very much.

Aelbert Cuyp the Draftsman

Like all artists, Cuyp reacted to his surroundings and his background, which provided stimuli that are largely imponderable. One may conjecture, however, that his thorough familiarity with the insular setting of Dordrecht and its neighboring villages opened his eyes for the particular beauty of the Hoekse Waard and Alblasserwaard and other reclaimed lands. Whatever one may think about evaluating an artist's personality, Cuyp certainly seems to have loved nature as he knew it in his immediate sur-

roundings and, later, to have been taken by the vistas that the hilly terrain in the eastern part of Holland provided. They presented different challenges, and he changed his "style" accordingly.

As far as one can establish an artistic personality on the basis of the artist's work, Cuyp was clearly not a revolutionary who was out for change. The general conservative nature of his hometown and more specifically of the circles in which he and his father were moving facilitated the adaptation of existing artistic achievements. Cuyp was active as a draftsman at a time and in a culture that witnessed the representation of nature as a more sophisticated and popular activity than ever before in Europe. He came late on the scene in the sense that those aspects of depicting nature that interested him had all been developed: perspective and space had been mastered, the panoramic view had been worked out, the simple rural subject matter had been established as an acceptable, even attractive subject.

Cuyp took advantage of all these achievements and used them to shape his own vision of the Dutch countryside. He used the village views of his older contemporaries as a point of departure for his own: he noted the colors in the works of Savery and Bloemaert and changed them into a personal, integrated, and fundamental part of many of his landscapes. Cuyp's artistic and technical mastery — in the true sense of the word — turned the achievements of the past into a base to start from rather than a level to attain. In his drawings Cuyp conveyed the beauty of nature for its own sake, rather than as a setting for man or for the pleasure and relaxation it provided. The allusion to arcadia is absent from the drawings; it was added to the paintings in which a more public purpose required the depiction of grander expectations.

1. I am much indebted to the partial manuscript catalogue raisonné of Aelbert Cuyp's drawings prepared by J. G. van Gelder and Ingrid van Gelder-Jost circa 1964–1975. I am presently editing and completing the catalogue for publication, together with a study of Aelbert Cuyp as a draftsman.

2. His drawings include no biblical scenes or history subjects, and only three portraits (of superior quality, witness cats. 108, 109).

3. Verisimilitude is difficult to substantiate in individual instances. J. G. van Gelder and I. van Gelder-Jost addressed this issue in Poughkeepsie 1976, 61–69, and Washington, Denver, and Fort Worth 1977, 59, 60, no. 57; Broos 1993, 71, also took up the issue. As the Van Gelders concluded, whenever a subject or site can be checked, Cuyp observed topographical truth (except in foregrounds). By inference this holds true for similar views. Martin Royalton-Kisch wrote an illuminating study on the role and history of drawing from nature, emphasizing the beginning of the seventeenth century and selecting impressive drawings to illustrate his points, in Antwerp and London 1999.

4. Both Van Goyen and Molyn assigned a significant role to man in their autonomous drawings, frequently stereotyping their activities.

5. Chong 1994a.

6. The synthetic studies of landscape in art, particularly Dutch art, from Deperthes 1822 to Grosse 1925, Stechow 1966, and Sutton 1987–1988 are still worth reading. Recently Gibson 2000 and Sluijter 2000 each have contributed an excellent analysis of the effect of Flanders on the revival of landscape in art in Haarlem and other artistic centers in the Northern Netherlands.

7. Beck catalogued Van Goyen's sketchbooks, whether existing or reconstructible, in a separate section (see Beck 1972, 1: 254–315); the many sheets of the 1650–1651 sketchbook are listed and partly illustrated under no. 847.

8. In spite of the different subject matter and "style" of works by Cuyp and Claude Lorrain, the relationship between the self-contained aspect of a drawing and its role as a source for a painting in Cuyp's case is similar to Claude Lorrain's approach, as described by Roethlisberger 1968, 1: 8, 9.

9. Studies on both artists appeared recently, both in the form of exhibition catalogues: Amsterdam 1992 and Amsterdam 1982.

10. Heijbroek 1996, 42.

11. Although moistening black chalk with water (or more likely with the tongue) is described by Meder 1919, 110, the procedure is usually omitted from descriptions of drawings. Only catalogues recently published by the Courtauld pay attention to this basic feature of many drawings in black and also in red chalk (most consistently in New York and London 1986; Van Oosterzee 1998, 29, also mentions it). Moistened black chalk is often misinterpreted as brush and black watercolor or pen and black ink or, sometimes, as oiled black chalk.

12. To the first category belongs the drawing *Country Road Bordering a River*, which is dated 1613, in the Fondation Custodia (Institut Néerlandais, Collection Frits Lugt) in Paris (Brussels, Rotterdam, Paris, and Bern 1968–1969, no. 2). Among Avercamp's fully colored, "finished" drawings should be mentioned *A Winter Landscape* in the Fogg Art Museum, Harvard University Art Museums (Collection Maida and George Abrams) because having been mounted on a panel until recently and framed, it demonstrates the custom to make such drawings as little paintings to be hung on the wall. This drawing and one of the earlier category are discussed by William W. Robinson in Amsterdam, Berlin, and London 1991–1992, nos. 24, 25, with a fruitful discussion of the complexities in establishing a chronology of Avercamp's drawings; the drawing is illustrated in a contemporary frame in Amsterdam 2000b, 121.

13. The resemblance between Avercamp's *Flat Landscape with a Windmill, a Village, a Church and a Farm Building* in Berlin and drawings by Cuyp (as rightly suggested by Royalton-Kisch in Antwerp and London 1999, no. 29) concerns the subject, space, and composition rather than the use of the brush or the color, since Avercamp sketched his remarkable panorama with the brush only, in blue with touches of other colors and some bodycolor. Pieter Saenredam's *View of Bleaching Houses near Haarlem* (dated 1617 but probably drawn later after a work of that year) and *Studies of Two Trees* on the same page (Kupferstichkabinett, Berlin) are also drawn entirely (or almost entirely) with the brush (ill. in Amsterdam 2000b, 31).

14. Friedländer 1901, 214.

15. The colors, partly mixed, are mainly yellow, green, blue, gray, and pink (for the roofs). Paris and Hamburg 1985–1986, no. 118, ill. on xxxiv, 229; Amsterdam 1993c, 219, no. 193; Antwerp and London 1999, 44–46, fig. 40.

16. Although the contrasting and preserving effect of gum arabic in Cuyp's drawings is an integral aspect of the appearance of the drawing, whether under glass or not, the actual presence can be seen only in reflecting light, therefore without the interference of glass or Plexiglass. Cuyp's practice was adopted by an artist who imitated him (Johan van Almeloveen) and another one who copied him (Hendrik Dubbels). It was described as a personal feature of Cuyp's work by Christian Josi in Ploos van Amstel 1821, 2: 107, 108, and it was recognized by J. G. van Gelder and I. van Gelder-Jost (Poughkeepsie 1976, nos. 46, 47, 48, 50, 63, 66, 68). Samuel van Hoogstraten 1678, 32, wrote about gum arabic for fixing black chalk and similar materials (but only as used by submerging a drawing in a watery solution of the gum). Meder 1919, 104, 136, 191, discussed the medium broadly, and recently Royalton-Kisch reviewed other early references to gum arabic (in Antwerp and London 1999, 132, under no. 34). Cuyp's use of gum arabic remained an exception.

17. See Pieter Molyn's, *Distant View over Flat Land with a Road and a Waterway in the Foreground* (Rijksprentenkabinet, Amsterdam, inv. RP-T-1948-405), illustrated in color in Amsterdam 1987, no. 27, and in Antwerp and London 1999, no. 34. The date on this most remarkable drawing, signed and dated by Pieter Molyn but so unusual for him, seems to be written as 1630, but according to Beck 1998, no. 47, more likely should be read as 1636. The drawing resembles work by Hendrick Avercamp and Pieter Saenredam (who never applied gum arabic over their drawings).

18. Some of Cuyp's sketchbooks can be reconstructed partially on the basis of the paper used, watermarks, size of the sheets, drying folds, and by the smudging that appears in the same place on each sheet caused by viewers leafing through the sketchbooks. Sketchbooks or drawing books were frequently vehicles for like drawings, as were the sketchbooks by Jan van Goyen that are preserved or can be reconstructed (see note 7). A study of the history and function of the sketchbook and the album would be a rewarding enterprise. (The discussion of Claude Lorrain's sketchbooks, drawing books, and albums by Marcel Roethlisberger [1968] would be an obvious starting point.) The sketchbook with thirty-nine leaves representing mainly subjects from the environs of The Hague in the Rijksprentenkabinet, Amsterdam (Amsterdam 1987, 36), is one of the few Dutch seventeenth-century sketchbooks that has not been dismantled.

19. The function of the series as a format in the arts has not been studied. Such a study might lead to a better understanding of tapestries, prints, and paintings — any works of art that in series have a significance beyond the sum of the individual items. The exhibition *Leerrijke Reeksen* and its catalogue by B. L. D. Ihle (Museum Boijmans Van Beuningen, Rotterdam, 1966), and many of her exhibitions demonstrated various functions of the series.

20. The most recent and best assessment of the seminal significance of the two series is found in Gibson 2000, 1 – 31, 47, 173, 174, with bibliography.

21. Gibson 2000, 43.

22. The village of 's-Gravendeel is situated on the Dortse Kil and had a ferry link to nearby Dordrecht. Here the topography is correct. The drawing was illustrated in New York 1998, no. 54.

23. Dordrechts Museum, no. DM / 937 / 95; Dordrecht 1977, 28 – 29, no. 3; Dordrecht 1992, no. 26.

24. Amsterdam, Rijksmuseum (no. A 1793; Dordrecht 1977, 26 – 27, no. 2; Chong 1992, no. JC 76). The year before, he had painted the same subject (formerly in the Van Nesselrode Collection; Reiss 1975, 199 ill.; Chong 1992, no. JC 75) with a different background. The interpretation of the figures as portraits was suggested by Reiss.

25. The prints of the series entitled *Diversa animalia quadrupedia*…are listed by Hollstein, under Persijn, nos. 11 – 23. The drawing in the Albertina, Vienna, was recognized by Jaap Bolten and illustrated by Van Gelder and Jost 1969, 101, note 14, fig. 1.

26. As late as 1649 the father used a drawing by Aelbert (London, British Museum; Hind 1915 – 1932, 2: no. Cuyp 4) for the background behind the portrait of Michiel Pompe van Slingeland as a six year old in the guise of a hunter (see Gordenker essay, fig. 5; Dordrecht 1977, 38 – 39, no. 8; Dordrecht 1992, no. 30).

27. Jan van de Velde's *Landscape with a Man at a Draw-Well* (119 × 316 mm) is one of a series of eighteen Landscapes and Ruins (Hollstein 1949 – , 33: nos. 173 – 195; this particular print is in 34: 100, no. 192).

28. For instance, the drawing by Gillis van Coninxloo, *View in the Woods* in the Van Regteren Altena Collection, Amsterdam, ill. in J. G. van Gelder, *Jan van de Velde (1593 – 1641): Teekenaar Schilder* (The Hague, 1933), pl. 1.

29. Two drawings made by Anthonie Waterloo early in his career, formerly in the Oskar Huldschinsky Collection in Berlin (sale Berlin, Paul Graupe, 3 Nov. 1931, nos. 99 and 100, illustrated; no. 98 may have been similar), were clearly influenced by Aelbert Cuyp's Environs of Dordrecht Group. Their sizes (c. 29 × 35, 19 × 29, 19 × 29 cm) were also similar to Cuyp's. No. 100 was later in the Klaver collection, Amsterdam (Amsterdam 1993a, no. 52, ill. in color; present location not known).

30. As mentioned by J. G. van Gelder in Dordrecht 1977, 112. More than eighty lots of drawings, some with more than one item, were among the drawings and books of Matthijs Balen and Jacob van Meurs, both deceased, held in Dordrecht, 23 – 25 July 1767 (Lugt 1938, no. 1629). Matthijs Balen probably was the historian of that name (1611 – 1691) whose *Beschryvinge der Stad Dordrecht* in two volumes was published in 1677. The only copy of the auction catalogue was recorded by Frits Lugt in the printroom in Dresden from where it apparently was removed to Moscow with parts of the library at the end of World War II. Recent efforts to find it there were in vain.

• In his *Metamorphoses* (book 10, lines 86 – 105), Ovid narrated the tale of Orpheus, who not only charmed wild animals and birds with his playing and singing, but also attracted trees that sheltered him from the sun. Cuyp's graceful branches and lacy foliage gently shade Orpheus, cloaked in red and playing his viol. A wide assortment of wild and domesticated animals gathers to listen. Nearest him are several dogs, a cat, and a monkey, often considered the mirror of man. To the right are a large dromedary and a macaw resting in the tree above.

Silhouetted on a distant ridge are an ostrich, elk, and elephant. Domesticated animals such as cattle and sheep graze at the left, while two fine jaguars dominate the immediate foreground. The brilliant patch of light in the middle ground, which creates rich shadows in the surrounding areas, anticipates Cuyp's later specialized light effects.

The *Metamorphoses* was widely known in the sixteenth and seventeenth centuries through translations and illustrated editions,[1] and the subject of Orpheus was occasionally taken up by artists,

particularly by specialists in painting animals, such as Cuyp's contemporary Paulus Potter (*Orpheus*, dated 1650, Rijksmuseum, Amsterdam). The most important influence on Aelbert Cuyp was Roelandt Savery, who painted at least twenty-three depictions of Orpheus Charming the Animals, as well as numerous paintings of such related subjects as the Garden of Eden and Noah's ark.[2] Like Savery, Aelbert Cuyp arranged his beasts in luxuriant and naturalistic landscapes: here he profiled an elephant against a distant panorama and shaded other animals under a grove of trees — a composition very close to Savery's in his *Orpheus* in Frankfurt (see Wheelock essay, fig. 18).[3] In addition, Cuyp may have modeled the two jaguars after a Savery drawing of jaguars that was reproduced in Crispijn van de Passe's drawing handbook of 1643, which also illustrates other exotic animals similar to those seen in Cuyp's painting.[4] It is possible that Cuyp saw Savery's drawings before they were reproduced or encountered individual prints before they were compiled into a volume in 1643. The jaguars reappear in several other works by Aelbert Cuyp as well as in a painting by his father dated 1639.[5]

Aelbert Cuyp may have based his depictions of some of the rare animals on stuffed specimens. The pangolin, the spiny Asian mammal seen at right, was just the kind of exotic creature that was preserved and displayed in a Cabinet of Wonders, a collection type that had long been favored in European aristocratic circles and was finding growing popularity in the Netherlands in the early sev-

1 Aelbert Cuyp, **Orpheus Charming the Animals**, Anhaltische Gemäldegalerie Dessau

Orpheus Charming the Animals

enteenth century. Rare animals had been an almost constant theme in European art since antiquity,[6] and occasionally curious beasts were brought back to Holland by Dutch trading ships.[7]

Cuyp painted three versions of Orpheus, beginning in the first recorded year of his career, 1639. The imposing scale, complexity, and detailed finish of the exhibited picture mark it as his first significant artistic statement. At about the same time, Cuyp painted a much smaller treatment of the subject on wood (fig. 1). Many of the same animals and details reappear, and the distant panorama is almost identical. The smaller painting should not be considered a preparatory work in the conventional sense because the composition remains distinct, but its scale and simpler composition indicate that it was an initial attempt at mastering a subject that Cuyp then developed in a more challenging picture. Also very close in style and subject matter is the recently discovered *Adam Naming the Animals* (fig. 2). This work is signed and dated 1639, providing firm evidence for dating the large Orpheus. About 1645, Cuyp returned to the subject of Orpheus yet again (marquess of Bute,

Mount Stuart). This exceptionally large canvas retains certain features from the earlier works, including Orpheus' pose and details such as the kneeling greyhound and the cat. In all three versions, Cuyp set Orpheus in a vast landscape and surrounded the figure with a variety of wild and

domesticated animals. Orpheus is always shown playing a violin, or *lira da braccio*, as was typical of Netherlandish representations of the subject.

In his commentary on Ovid appended to *Het Schilder-boeck* of 1604, Karel van Mander associated Orpheus with artistic inspiration.[8] Orpheus' musical and poetic eloquence, along with his ability to tame animals, also made him a symbol of wise and peaceful government. Citing Horace, Van Mander connected Orpheus with the power "to build city and law, in order to live justly."[9] In addition, political pamphlets sometimes used Orpheus to represent harmonious government.[10] Aelbert Cuyp's diminutive Orpheus now in Dessau may have acted as an allegory of good government in an official setting,[11] for it may once have belonged to the stadtholder Frederik Hendrik and Amalia van Solms. Nonetheless, one of Cuyp's principal motivations for painting the subject of Orpheus must have been the opportunity to depict a wide range of unusual animals that emphasize the general theme of a bounteous and harmonious nature.[12] **AC**

2 Aelbert Cuyp, **Adam Naming the Animals,** dated 1639, private collection

2 Open Countryside with Shepherds and Animals

c. 1640, oil on panel, 40 × 59 (15 ¾ × 23 ¼). The Trustees of Dulwich Picture Gallery, London

1 Jacob Cuyp, Plate 12 from the series **Diversa animalia,** 1641, Rijksmuseum, Amsterdam

• This peaceful panoramic landscape is one of Cuyp's earliest depictions of the native Dutch landscape. Seen from a low vantage point, a sandy path leads the viewer from the bottom edge of the picture past a group of goats and a herd of cows toward a sunny elevation populated by a flock of sheep and a group of shepherds silhouetted against the bright sky. The vast expanse of a "marshy distance" can be glimpsed beyond.[1] The figure pointing to the distance suggests that the scenery extends far beyond the borders of the picture, a motif also occasionally employed by the painter Herman Saftleven from Rotterdam (see Wheelock essay, fig. 15).[2] The deep recession of the space is underscored by both the shaded left foreground with the two goats, which functions as a *repoussoir,* and by the diagonal formation of the clouds. At the same time, the goat that is placed parallel to the picture plane functions as a barrier and prevents the viewer's eye from plunging into the depth of the seemingly infinite space.

Although lighter in tone and not as monochromatic as Jan van Goyen's works of that period (Cuyp's paintings were to become more monochromatic a short while later), this sandy landscape betrays, in composition, the influence of the Leiden artist[3] and resembles, in general, Van Goyen's dune landscapes painted between 1629 and circa 1631. Nonetheless, while similarities exist in the brushwork of the two artists,[4] Cuyp's handling of the paint is denser and more vigorous than Van Goyen's.

Close in date to the present picture is a lost painting, formerly in the Kaiser-Friedrich-Museum in Berlin.[5] The panoramic views into the distance are comparable in the two pictures, as is the manner in which the cattle are depicted.[6] The striking resemblance between these goats and cows and the animals in the prints of Reinier van Persyn after drawings by Jacob Cuyp, published with the title *Diversa animalia* in 1641 (fig. 1), suggests that Cuyp followed his father's models for his early portrayals of animals and livestock.[7] **AR**

Open Countryside with Shepherds and Animals

3 Portrait of a Family in a Landscape

Jacob and Aelbert Cuyp, 1641, oil on canvas, 155 × 245 (61 × 96 7/16). Collection the Israel Museum, Jerusalem, Gift of Mr. and Mrs. Joseph R. Nash, Paris

1 Jacob and Aelbert Cuyp, **Portrait of a Couple and Their Child**, 1641, present location unknown, last recorded in the collection of Comtesse Souboff, Geneva

• In sweeping countryside broken in the distance by some cattle and windmills, a family gathers to welcome their eldest son, who returns from a successful hunt accompanied by his servant and dog. He offers a game bird to his youngest sister, who rushes out to greet him. Sheltered by a tree, the rather stiff and evenly spaced figures turn toward the viewer. The portrait's awkwardness is partly relieved by the strongly modeled landscape marked with strong light and long shadows.

The painting is a collaborative effort between Jacob Cuyp, who was responsible for the figures and the foliage in the immediate foreground, and Aelbert Cuyp, who rendered the landscape background and the trees in a thick, yellowish brushwork typical of his early paintings. Jacob Cuyp was Dordrecht's principal portraitist and, almost certainly, the director of this commission. In the same year, Jacob and Aelbert Cuyp collaborated on another group portrait (fig. 1), which shows a couple seated in a landscape with their child. Both works are signed solely by Jacob Cuyp. The two artists worked together on at least two other occasions: a painting of about 1640 showing shepherds in a landscape (Musée Ingres, Montauban), and a portrait of two children dated 1645 (private collection).[1]

The theme of the returning hunter often had amorous or marital references in Dutch painting (see cats. 26, 27, 40), but here the figures seem to be members of the same family. In this context, hunting suggests an abundant household, a theme reinforced by the grapes held by the girl at the right, which can be associated with nature's fertility.[2] Game and fruit commonly denoted a bounteous farm or estate. The servants who appear at the far left and right edges (they do not have their ages inscribed below) support the well-being of the family: The manservant has assisted in the hunt, while the maid holds chickens and bellows, indicating that she will soon be preparing a meal. The painting as a whole indicates that a prosperous and harmonious family depends on agricultural gifts such as fruit, game, and even the dairy products represented by the milking of cows in the distance.

Emile Michel was the first writer to notice the painting in 1892, when it was in the Rothschilds' opulent mansion Ferrières outside Paris. Noting that it was attributed to Jacob Cuyp, Michel found that "la composition est un peu gauche." By 1952, when the work was auctioned in Paris, the attribution had been changed to Aelbert Cuyp. The compiler of that sales catalogue had already grasped the nature of Jacob and Aelbert Cuyp's collaboration. The painting was found to be "already very typical in the distant landscape and animals. For the figures Aelbert has still used the manner of and perhaps with the collaboration of his father, Jacob Gerritsz Cuyp."[3] Several group portraits by Jacob or Aelbert Cuyp appear in Dordrecht inventories in the seventeenth century. One example is from the estate of the wine dealer Abraham Sam, who died in 1692: "A painting in which is depicted the whole family of their parents, by Aelbert Cuyp."[4] **AC**

Portrait of a Family in a Landscape

• The broad rivers passing near Dordrecht provided Cuyp with numerous opportunities to portray life along the water's edge. Here, from a low viewpoint near the bank of one such river, Cuyp indicated the wide expanse of this countryside, whose flatness is relieved only by a few windswept trees and a lonely hut with a large chimney. As clouds swirl overhead, daily life unfolds in predictable rhythms: cattle rest on the bank, sailboats glide quietly across the smooth waters, and two workmen busy themselves with boats filled with peat. One of the workmen has pulled his boat (a *plemp*) to shore, probably to unload the peat in the wheelbarrow that lies upside down behind him.

Peat not only had domestic uses, such as cooking and heating, but was also essential for a number of industries, such as brick and pottery making, beer brewing, and cloth bleaching.[1] And, as Marika Spring notes, vivianite, one of Cuyp's favorite pigments, was made from peat. Still, the production and transportation of peat hardly seem like subjects that would have inspired Dutch artists and poets. Nevertheless, a surprising number of poems and pictorial images celebrate these seemingly mundane activities. For example, Claes Jansz Visscher (1586 / 1587 – 1652) executed a number of prints depicting the making of peat. Often included in the decora-

1 Claes Jansz Visscher, Detail from **Comitatus Hollandia,** Pieter van den Keere, ed. (1610), Palacio Royal, Madrid

tive borders of maps — borders whose texts and images helped express the ideals and character of the land and the people (fig. 1)[2] — such depictions of daily activities emphasized the industry of the Dutch in making their land more productive. The making of peat was also featured in 1618 in *Deliciae Batavicae (Batavian Delights)*, a series of prints of topographical scenes and images of daily life published by Jacobus Marco in Leiden. In this instance, however, the text accompanying the illustration of peat diggers accords peat an importance beyond being a significant industry. Peat is celebrated as a Dutch miracle: "Come from afar you physicians, see the miracles of the Batavian lands; the water and marsh yield their own fire."[3] Adriaen van de

Venne (1589 – 1662) also included images of peat diggers in his 1626 watercolor album *'tLants Sterckte (The Land's Strength)*, some of which he derived from Marco's publication.[4]

Cuyp probably chose to depict this theme because the transport of peat was commonly seen when traveling through the countryside. Nevertheless, his river view projects a positive image of the peat industry and of the workmen who were responsible for its distribution. The boats are well maintained, and the peat is neatly stacked in each vessel as the workmen undertake their deliveries. Thus, Cuyp's approach to the subject of peat is similar to that found in *Deliciae Batavicae*, *'tLants Sterckte*, and the decorative borders of maps, which celebrate the productivity of the land and the industriousness of its people as integral components of the Dutch Republic.

Despite its convincing atmospheric character, Cuyp did not paint this scene from life. As in so many other instances, he executed this work on the basis of a drawing made at the site (cat. 64). **AKW**

Cattle and Cottage near a River

5 Cattle and Herders, with Mariakerk, Utrecht

early 1640s, oil on panel, 49 × 74 (19 5/16 × 29 1/8). Residenzgalerie Salzburg, Salzburg

• That Aelbert Cuyp traveled around the Nether-lands on a number of occasions throughout his career is evident from his drawings and paintings. And Utrecht must undoubtedly have been a fre-quent destination, not in the least because of the strong connections Cuyp's family had with the town.[1] As a result Cuyp included buildings and monuments from Utrecht and the town's environs in several of his early drawings and paintings (see cats. 47, 48).[2]

Remarkably, in this picture Cuyp depicted the Mariakerk, a large church located in the center of Utrecht, nestled between the trees beyond a gently rolling imaginary landscape.[3] Behind the church a sunny flat landscape extends into the dis-tance. In a manner similar to that in *Open Country-side with Shepherds and Animals* (cat. 2), the viewer is taken into the painting along a sandy path that leads past a herd of cattle on the left and two shep-herds enjoying a rest in the sun on the right. The general atmosphere of this sun-drenched landscape populated by shepherds and cattle is a peaceful one evoking an afternoon in a countryside where man and nature coexist in perfect harmony.

Cattle and Herders, with Mariakerk, Utrecht demon-strates the stylistic refinements characteristic of Cuyp's paintings from the early 1640s. The trees

have become more elegant, the recession of the landscape reveals greater subtlety, and the impasto in the sky effectively evokes rays of light. Only the cattle in the left foreground are still reminiscent of those in his earlier works, such as the paintings in Dulwich and Rotterdam (see cats. 2, 4).[4]

J.G. van Gelder and Ingrid Jost first noted in 1969 the relationship between this painting and two drawings by Cuyp.[5] One drawing, formerly in a collection in Iowa (fig. 1), shows a landscape with two large groups of trees, while the other, now in Frankfurt, represents the Mariakerk in Utrecht (cat. 47). For this composition Cuyp inserted the view of the Mariakerk into an expanded landscape flanked by the two groups of trees from the drawing formerly in Iowa.[6] AR

1 Aelbert Cuyp, **Landscape with Two Groups of Trees,** formerly in the Brower Collec-tion, Central College, Pella, Iowa

Cattle and Herders, with Mariakerk, Utrecht

early 1640s, oil on panel, 40.3 × 54.9 (15 ⅞ × 21 ⅝). Graphische Sammlung im Städelsches Kunstinstitut, Frankfurt am Main

• Cuyp's painting is a quiet reflection on the care, nurturing, and proper husbandry of the land. The artist has situated the viewer along the near bank of a small inlet crossed by a simple wooden bridge, a vantage point that reveals a landscape in which man has created a flourishing agricultural environment. The contented appearance of the cattle resting in the fields, the well-maintained fences and boats, and the harmonious way in which the farm buildings lie nestled amidst a copse bespeak of man's easy rapport with nature.

This rapport is also evident in the relaxed demeanor of the group in the foreground that has gathered to discuss the day's affairs. The standing burgher wearing a black hat may well be the owner of the property who has come to speak with the two seated herdsmen and the standing laborer holding a pike. The pike, or more aptly boat hook, indicates that this man works by the water's edge, probably to retrieve logs, some of which can be seen floating in the water.[1] Other logs, already attended to, have been carefully piled near the thatch-covered haystack. Cuyp, however, stressed neither the identity of the individuals nor the actual workings of this specific farm.[2] Rather, his concern seems more general, a reflection on the idea that careful oversight and proper husbandry of nature's resources make not only for a harmonious existence, but also for economic viability.

The clarity of Cuyp's composition, which he executed with vigorous yet delicate brushwork, has no evident prototype in Dutch painting traditions. Not only is the landscape's horizontal structure striking, but so also is the linearity of his touch, particularly in the pronounced accents that articulate and enliven forms. Cuyp, like Esaias van de Velde and other early seventeenth-century landscape painters, may well have thought first as a draftsman and then only subsequently as a painter. Indeed, in this work, as in so many of his other paintings, he used drawings to establish the fundamental framework for the composition. He developed the general compositional character of the image in a pen and wash drawing now in the British Museum (cat. 66). The specific disposition of the boats near the bridge and the farm on the right is found in a drawing in the Kunsthalle, Hamburg (see cat. 7, fig. 1).

The importance of the graphic tradition for Cuyp's paintings appears to extend beyond the impact of his own drawings. Similar views of farms situated in copses near wooden bridges are found in early seventeenth-century landscape prints by Haarlem artists, among them Jan van de Velde and Esaias van de Velde. The elegant rhythms of the trees in Cuyp's images, however, are more specifically related to those in the landscape drawings and prints of a Rotterdam artist active in

Haarlem, Willem Buytewech (see Wheelock essay, fig. 14). In fact, Buytewech's landscape print series, first published in 1616, not only provided stylistic inspiration for Cuyp, but also presented conceptual ideas that foreshadow those found in paintings such as *River Landscape with Bridge*.

Buytewech was an artist who had been extremely conscious of the political and social benefits to be gained by peace with Spain — the resulting prosperity, he felt, would be manifest in the nurturing of the land through the diligent labor of all its people. This ideal, explicit in a political print of 1615, is implicit in his landscape series of 1616.[3] Buytewech's prints, which include scenes of laborers reinvigorating the land by clearing and tending the forests and cultivating the soil, are infused with the ideals of Virgil's *Georgics*.[4] Such images, and the ideas underlying them, had an enormous impact on Cuyp during his formative years. They help explain the extraordinary impact of seemingly straightforward paintings such as *River Landscape with Bridge*. **AKW**

River Landscape with Bridge

1 Aelbert Cuyp, **A Boat**, Hamburg Kunsthalle

⸱ Together with *Cattle and Cottage near a River* from Rotterdam and *River Landscape with Bridge* from Frankfurt (cats. 4, 6), this picture clearly reveals Cuyp's early distinctive approach to landscape painting. A vast river — seen from a low vantage point that seats the viewer in a boat — stretches from the immediate foreground. On the banks in the far distance, silhouetted against the sky, are a number of majestic windmills as well as the bell tower of a village church.[1] The deeply receding view toward the brightly lit horizon contrasts with the shaded patch of land and the boat with two men in the foreground. It and an almost identical boat just beyond the bridge in *River Landscape with Bridge* (cat. 6) are based on a drawing by the artist, now in the Kunsthalle in Hamburg (fig. 1).[2]

The most intriguing aspect of the picture is the simplicity of its composition.[3] Cuyp relied almost exclusively on the use of light and color rather than on any compositional elements, such as diagonally placed paths or clouds, in order to evoke a sense of pictorial depth. Moreover, while both the Rotterdam and Frankfurt pictures include several small figures and herds of cattle in the foreground, in this painting Cuyp eschewed anecdotal details almost entirely. Only traces of human activity are indicated by the farm building nestled beneath the large tree on the right, the windmills and village in the distance, and the boat with two fishermen quietly going about their business.[4] Nothing, it seems, could disturb the general atmosphere of harmony and peacefulness.

Although the picture shows several parallels with works by Jan van Goyen and Salomon van Ruysdael from the late 1630s and the first half of the 1640s, the linearity of the composition, as well as the vigorous handling of the brush, is rather different from the works of these two masters. The tonality of this picture, which ranges from light yellow to greenish brown, remains on the whole lighter and somewhat cooler than Van Goyen's and Van Ruysdael's colors. Cuyp also employed a more dramatic mode of lighting, using slightly nervous yellow highlights that play across the different surfaces in the picture.

Cuyp regularly made sketches in the countryside that he later used as models for his compositions.[5] Besides the sketch of the boat in Hamburg, Cuyp used a drawing in the Kröller-Müller Museum in Otterlo as the model for the landscape and a drawing preserved on a sketchbook page (cat. 61) for the distant view of windmills.[6] **A R**

A River Scene with Distant Windmills

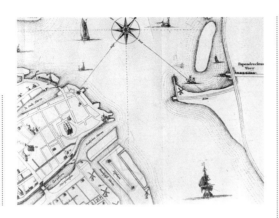

1 Romeyn de Hooghe, Detail of **Map of Dordrecht**, from Matthijs Balen, **Beschryvinge der stad Dordrecht** (Dordrecht, 1677)

2 Simon de Vlieger, **View of the Oostpoort**, c. 1640, Hamburg Kunsthalle

· Cuyp is not known as a marine painter, largely because he never ventured too far from land. Nevertheless, his numerous views of river life are extremely varied and demonstrate a remarkable sensitivity to the changing light and water conditions encountered on inland waterways. He could comfortably set boats in the water, even as he visually contrasted water's translucent and changing surface with the physical presence of heavy wooden hulls and weighty canvas sails. Cuyp's pictorial sensitivities were also directed toward human and animal activities revolving around the water, ones that added visual and thematic interest to the inherent beauty of the river scenes.

This luminous painting, executed in the early 1640s, depicts Dordrecht from the northeast as seen from Papendrecht veer (Papendrecht ferry), situated near the small village of Papendrecht on the far side of the river Merwede (fig. 1). To the right of Dordrecht's city walls rises the thin spire of the Groothoofdspoort, while before this major gateway are docked a number of sailing ships. Ferry transportation was provided by sailboats or rowboats that constantly traveled back and forth across the Merwede. In Cuyp's painting a small rowboat carrying two burghers, distinguishable by their dress, approaches a roughhewn pier where a group of travelers awaits the return voyage to Dordrecht. Whether or not the travelers on the pier are rural folk or city dwellers dressed for a day in the country (the man holding a rifle presumably went for the hunt), Cuyp has effectively shown the different character of the lands on either side of the Merwede through the figures' costumes.

Cuyp was particularly intrigued with life along the piers during the early years of his career, perhaps because of the variety of scenarios that could be portrayed in this setting.[1] The inspiration for this interest may have been the Rotterdam painter Simon de Vlieger, who also starkly contrasted the architectural forms of the pier and adjacent buildings with vigorous skies and sun-filled distant river views (fig. 2).[2] De Vlieger, however, differs from Cuyp in that he did not focus on the human aspect of the scene as much as the Dordrecht artist did.

The forceful, even monumental character of Cuyp's painting comes largely from the juxtaposition of the boldly modeled foreground forms with the light-filled riverscape beyond them. This monumentality is reinforced by the strong emphasis on the horizontal, not only of the pier and the distant horizon, but also of the ripples in the water. With this solid framework firmly established, the sailboats seem to glide effortlessly back and forth, catching the light winds that fill the air. This controlled yet vigorously executed manner of painting is one of Cuyp's most distinctive characteristics; it is also unlike that of any of his contemporaries. Given the freshness of his touch, it is always surprising to discover that Cuyp often repeated compositional elements in different paintings. For example, the rowboat and oarsman in this work appear, in reverse, in *Cattle and Cottage near a River* (cat. 4). **AKW**

A Pier in Dordrecht Harbor

105

1 Jan van Vliet after Rembrandt, **Baptism of the Eunuch**, 1631

· According to the Acts of the Apostles (8.26 – 40), Christ's disciple Philip met an Ethiopian eunuch on the road from Jerusalem to Gaza. Treasurer to Candace, queen of Ethiopia, the eunuch had been to Jerusalem to worship. Philip rode with the eunuch in his chariot and explained that a passage in Isaiah prophesied Christ's crucifixion. Having arrived at some water, the eunuch asked why he should not be baptized. Philip replied that if he believed with all his heart, he could be baptized. Cuyp depicted the eunuch dressed in sumptuous golden robes, kneeling near a shallow stream as the aged Philip scoops up some water for the baptism. The eunuch's carriage and servants wait on the ridge above while a page hovers nearby with a large book — the text of Isaiah. With visible skepticism, one of the retinue casually leans on the richly bedecked carriage. A tower and shallow-domed building crown a distant hill, surely a reference to Jerusalem.

Cuyp's arrangement of figures is dependant on a widely copied painting by Rembrandt of about 1630. Now lost, the composition is recorded in Jan van Vliet's etching of 1631 (fig. 1) as well as in several painted copies.[1] The characterizations of Philip and the eunuch are similar to Rembrandt's, as is the disposition of figures and a chariot around a small hillock. Cuyp even repeated details such as the large leafy plants that anchor the foreground. Since Aelbert's uncle Benjamin Cuyp was strongly influenced by Rembrandt, he probably provided the conduit to Rembrandt's work.[2]

On the other hand, the impact of Aelbert Cuyp's picture differs considerably from Rembrandt's. Where Rembrandt dramatically arranged his figures in a steep vertical pattern, Cuyp dispersed the group slightly within a rich and expansive landscape setting. The eunuch's pious humility, in contrast to his servant's arrogance, remains. Cuyp also subtly varied Philip's pose, so that it is not the traditional gesture of baptism, but actually a subtle variation on a familiar formula. The motif of a page carrying a large Bible is missing in Rembrandt's composition of 1630, but it does appear in his painting of the subject dated 1626 (Museum Catharijneconvent, Utrecht) and in Pieter Lastman's picture of 1623 (Staatliche Kunsthalle, Karlsruhe).

As a setting for the biblical narrative, Cuyp carved an almost circular space out of soft vegetation and rocky outcroppings. Feathery foliage frames the scene, while the nearly monochromatic palette further sets off the figures. Aelbert Cuyp seems to have been influenced not just by Jacob and Benjamin Cuyp, both experienced figural painters, but also by Herman Saftleven, who perfected the blending of narrative scenes in rich natural settings. Cuyp's soft organic forms and whitish tonality are also similar to the work of Gijsbert de Hondecoeter, namely his *Landscape with Animals* of 1641 (private collection, Boston).

In seventeenth-century Holland, the subject was known almost exclusively as the Baptism of the

The Baptism of the Eunuch

Moor.[3] The Acts of the Apostles had been extensively analyzed by Protestant theologians, most crucially by John Calvin (1509–1564), whose commentaries were published in 1552 and translated into Dutch as early as 1582.[4] Calvin noted that since Near Eastern monarchs often made eunuchs their most trusted ministers, the term eunuch was often employed simply to describe important court officials. Therefore, most seventeenth-century Dutch viewers probably did not realize that the Greek text of the Acts calls the figure a eunuch. Calvin also stressed that the eunuch had studied the scripture but remained modest about his understanding, and was thus ready to be baptized. Quite naturally, the episode was used by Protestant writers as a model of adult baptism. Dutch Remonstrant preachers such as Simon Episcopius (1583–1643) cited the Baptism of the Eunuch as an example of free will because the eunuch's purposeful study of scripture brought about his salvation.

The freedom of brushwork and a feathery treatment of foliage found in this painting and in related works (cats. 10, 11) suggest an evolution away from Cuyp's paintings produced in 1641 and immediately afterward under Jan van Goyen's influence. These later, occasionally awkward canvases are larger, more broadly handled, and more ambitious in scale. This period of Cuyp's career, dating about 1643, has long confused scholars precisely because their experimental nature seems less advanced than the graceful control of Cuyp's diminutive river landscapes painted on panel (cats. 4–7).[5] Like Cuyp's paintings of Orpheus (cat. 1) and *Adam Naming the Animals* (cat. 1, fig. 2), this representation of the Baptism of the Eunuch demonstrates the artist's ambition to become a history painter as well as a landscapist—an inspiration that would remain largely unrealized. AC

· This ravishingly beautiful — unlined — farmyard scene is one of the most accomplished of Cuyp's early depictions of the Dutch countryside. The artist has placed the viewer in a sun-drenched pasture populated by herds of cattle and sheep, beyond which extends a vast landscape. In contrast to some of the artist's other early landscapes where shepherds and peasants rest and converse (cats. 2 – 5), the two peasants (on the right) in this picture busy themselves with their daily farm chores. The pervasive mood is one of quiet peacefulness, celebrating the wealth and prosperity of the Dutch countryside — and by extension of the Dutch Republic — which is afforded by the harmonious relationship between nature and man.

Among Cuyp's early pictures are several that combine an idyllic setting of a pasture with humans and animals with a vast panoramic landscape. Here Cuyp placed a stronger emphasis on the gradual recession of the space than he did in other paintings through the use of a diagonal extending from the farmhouses to the small trees in the distance. This rather large picture — which must have been commissioned rather than painted for the open market, as some of Cuyp's smaller early works may have been — reveals the artist's distinctive, more mature approach to composition, lighting, and the use of atmospheric effects.

The debate around the dating of this picture sheds some light on the changing appreciation of Cuyp's early oeuvre. Hofstede de Groot considered it a "very large early work" in the style of Cuyp's earliest known landscape, dated 1639, now in Besançon.[1] Reiss as well as the authors of the Dordrecht exhibition catalogue of 1977 generally shared this view, largely because the work bears no resemblance with Cuyp's slightly later, so-called Van Goyenesque works.[2] However, by 1987 Chong had noted that the picture's brushwork was neither close to the painting from Besançon nor as "monochromatic and calligraphic" as his works of about 1641, but was instead closer to his later paintings, especially in the foliage. He therefore concluded that the picture should be dated to about 1642, at which time Cuyp must have been "capable of working simultaneously in two styles."[3] But why Cuyp would have felt it necessary to work in two considerably different styles at the same time is not clear from this argument. In his dissertation, Chong noted the more accomplished handling of the spatial recession, the palette that is markedly different from his early pictures, and the "more flowing foliage."[4] Based on these considerations, he revised his earlier opinion and dated the picture to 1642 / 1643, which immediately precedes the period when Cuyp began to change his approach and turn his attention to the works of Dutch artists returning from Italy, in particular, to the works of Jan Both. **AR**

A Farm with Cottages and Animals

• This work, a strikingly large and bold depiction of the edge of a forest, is Cuyp's only known woodland scene. It is also one of the rare instances in which he depicted an artist, with sketchbook in lap, recording the scene before him.[1] Perhaps the artist's interest, and that of his companion, lay in the dramatically craggy trees with broken trunks that guard the forest's inner realm or, perhaps, in the two picturesque younger trees near the path emerging from the woods. This path seems to have been frequented by travelers of all types, for one sees not only riders on horseback, but also a farmer returning home after haying and three elegantly dressed city burghers. The presence of these burghers, who have paused to converse while on their country outing, indicates that this woodland site was near an urban center, presumably Dordrecht.[2] Their presence also suggests that the site was deemed worthy of an excursion, comparable to the "pleasant places" near Haarlem that Jan van de Velde, Esaias van de Velde, and Willem Buytewech depicted in their landscape print series from the 1610s.

The painting would seem to indicate the way Cuyp, with sketchbook in hand, traveled into the countryside to draw after nature. As with many artists, he clearly followed the advice so clearly articulated by P.C. Ketel in Karel van Mander's 1604 treatise on painting: "take charcoal and chalk, pen, ink, paper / and draw what you see, whatever pleases your eye."[3] As Ketel recommended, Cuyp would then return home to paint, bringing the drawings "to life in colors / which you have ground yourself." One can imagine Cuyp sitting before such a forest bordered by rugged, weatherworn trees, for he often focused on precisely such elements in his chalk drawings of the early-to-mid 1640s (cats. 51, 52, 55). Nevertheless, no known drawing served as a model for any of the trees in this painting.

Cuyp's brushwork in this large painting on canvas is distinctly broader than that of his small-scale panel paintings executed during the first years of the 1640s.[4] For example, the tree branches are heavier and the leaves are less precisely defined than in *River Landscape with Bridge* in Frankfurt (see cat. 6). The differences almost certainly relate to changes in scale and support, but also suggest a different period of execution. An indication of date comes from the costumes worn by the city burghers and the artist and his companion, which relate in style to those found in Dutch paintings from the early-to-mid 1640s.[5]

Although Cuyp generally preferred to depict scenes that included distant landscapes, the only suggestion of such a view is provided by the small figure of a man seated to the left of the forest who appears to gaze across a wooded valley. The source of inspiration for this focus upon the forceful character of the forest edge is unknown. Although this compositional type is unusual for Cuyp, it is one associated with Herman Saftleven or Simon de Vlieger, artists whose work seems to have influenced Cuyp on other occasions during the 1640s (see cats. 8, 19).[6] However, Saftleven and De Vlieger apparently only began depicting forest scenes in their etchings and large-scale paintings during the mid-1640s, slightly after Cuyp executed this work. Nevertheless, as few of these woodland landscapes are dated, the relationship of this subject in the work of these three artists cannot be firmly established. AKW

* Gift of Dr. and Mrs. Charles C. Beach, Charles B. Curtis, Mr. and Mrs. Eugene L. Garbaty, Dr. Francis Goodwin, Walter K. Gutman, Mrs. Walter Keney, Lyman Mills, in memory of Mr. and Mrs. Clement Scott by their children, Mrs. H. K. Welch and Horace B. Clark, Mrs. Charles B. Wood, Hans Wreidt, Bequest of Warren H. Lowenhaupt, The Ella Gallup Sumner and Mary Catlin Sumner Collection Fund by exchange; The Ella Gallup Sumner and Mary Catlin Sumner Collection Fund, the Douglas Tracy Smith and Dorothy Potter Smith Fund, and the Evelyn Bonar Storrs Trust Fund

Wooded Landscape with an Artist

• The first critic to describe Cuyp's work was Arnold Houbraken, whose treatise provides the biographical framework for the study of Dutch seventeenth-century artists.[1] As a native of Dordrecht, this artist-theorist had ample opportunities to view Cuyp's work, thus his well-informed comments are important for assessing the artistic qualities of Cuyp paintings and drawings that were most admired by early eighteenth-century connoisseurs. Houbraken's description of Cuyp's work is particularly germane to *Dordrecht Harbor by Moonlight*,

for he listed among Cuyp's specialties depictions of "still water with ships." More important, Houbraken admiringly noted how Cuyp "paid much attention to the time of day in which he portrayed his subjects, so that one can distinguish in his paintings the misty early morning from the bright afternoon and that again from the saffron-colored evening time." He continued, "I have also seen various moonlight scenes by him which were very realistic and arranged in such a way that the moon was beautifully reflected in the water."[2]

Cuyp's ability to convey the character of different times of the day and varied weather situations is an aspect of his art that has continued to elicit the admiration of collectors and connoisseurs. This atmospheric painting of sailboats at a dock across the harbor from Dordrecht's Rietdijkspoort (see Wheelock essay, fig. 1) is one of the few, surviving moonlight scenes by Cuyp.[3] It is a supremely quiet painting, the only sounds imaginable being the gentle lapping of water against the wooden hulls of the moored ships. Under darkly billowing clouds, the moon casts a cool light on the boats' sails, the windmill, and the ripples of the water. A few figures stand on the pier, perhaps travelers awaiting the early morning ferry to destinations along the Merwede or one of the other waterways passing by Dordrecht.

The earliest reference to this painting is probably that found in the 1729 inventory of Elisabeth Francken, widow of Mattheus vanden Broucke, which describes "a moonlight" as a pendant to "a lightning," almost certainly Cuyp's dramatic *Dordrecht from the South, in a Storm* (fig. 1).[4] The paintings, which have identical dimensions, remained together until 1802. The artist most likely intended them as pendants: they both feature unusual light and atmospheric phenomena, ones that Cuyp rarely explored in his work.

In the mid-1640s, Dutch painters were fascinated with depicting unusual light and weather conditions. The origins of this interest are not entirely clear, although the depiction of ephemeral

1 Aelbert Cuyp, **Dordrecht from the South, in a Storm**, Foundation E.G. Bührle Collection, Zurich

Dordrecht Harbor by Moonlight

light and weather conditions had long been recognized as one of the most difficult challenges a landscape artist could face.[5] Apelles, the celebrated Greek painter of the late fourth century B.C., was often cited as an artist worthy of emulation, partly because he, reputedly, could depict thunder and lightning.[6] Van Mander noted Apelles' achievements in his theoretical poem *Den grondt der edel vry schilder-const* (1604) when urging landscape artists to capture a variety of natural effects, including the color of reflections created in moonlight.[7] Depictions of weather also entered into seventeenth-century disputes about the *paragone*, which contrasted the relative merits of painting, poetry, and sculpture. Philips Angel, who published a defense of the art of painting in Leiden in 1642, wrote that, unlike sculpture, painting can "depict a rainbow, rain, thunder, lightning, clouds, vapor, light, reflections…the rising of the sun, early morning, the decline of the sun, evening, the moon illuminating the night, with her attendant companions, the stars, reflections in the water."[8]

The visual tradition for night scenes in Dutch art stems from prints made by Hendrick Goudt (1580 / 1585 – 1648) after paintings by Adam Elsheimer (1578 – 1610) (see cat. 41, fig. 1). Goudt's impact was particularly important for the Haarlem printmaker Jan van de Velde, who exploited the graphic medium to depict the times of the day, the seasons of the year, and windy and rainy weather. However, with the exception of early seventeenth-century marine specialists who depicted stormy seas, painters of Dutch landscapes rarely represented extreme weather conditions or moonlight until the late 1630s and early 1640s. The artist who first developed an interest in such scenes was Jan van Goyen.[9] Other artists soon followed suit, among them Aert van der Neer (1603 / 1604 – 1677), Simon de Vlieger, and, of course, Aelbert Cuyp.[10] His *Dordrecht Harbor by Moonlight* is one of the largest and most hauntingly beautiful of these night scenes, capturing the sense of quiet and serenity evoked by moonlight flooding across this inland waterway. **AKW**

Landscape with Shepherds and Shepherdesses

c. 1643 – 1645, oil on panel, 77.5 × 107.5 (30 ½ × 42 ⁵/₁₆). Private collection, Belgium *(Amsterdam only)*

· In his *Eerlycke tytkorting* of 1634, the poet and playwright Jan Hermansz Krul published a number of love songs that focus on the romantic yearnings of shepherds and shepherdesses. The pictorial settings described by the poet, as well as the engraved images accompanying these songs, are remarkably similar to a number of Cuyp's pastoral scenes, including this one. For example, one of Krul's songs introduces the shepherdess Galathee in the following manner: "Not long ago, before the sun sent its golden rays from Heaven's top over the misty earthly valleys, I saw my beloved Galathee driving her flock from the cold dry beach, coming barefoot through wet sand to the heath, in order to graze her sheep on the grassy land."[1] The engraving accompanying this love song (see Wheelock essay, fig. 5) depicts a young man gesturing toward the comely Galathee, much as the shepherd in Cuyp's painting points toward a shepherdess as she passes through the landscape tending her herd.

Cuyp's lyrical scene does not depict a specific text, but it does share the spirit of Dutch pastoral literature, whether the songs of Krul, the poems of the *Nederduytschen helicon,* or the writings of J. van Heemskerk (see Wheelock essay). Much as these Dutch poets used evocative words to create a setting for their human encounters, so Cuyp created the pastoral mood of his scenes with carefully chosen pictorial motifs and atmospheric effects. In this instance, he situated the shepherd group on a hill before a copse of windswept trees, while he bathed the misty river valley beyond in golden light. Distant hills, one of which is covered by buildings that have the character of ruins, enhance the painting's arcadian character.

Cuyp seems to have imaginatively created his setting from views he saw on a trip along the Rhine in the early 1640s. The distant hill surmounted by buildings is reminiscent of Elten, which was situated near the confluence of the Rhine and the Maas.[2] The irregularly shaped stone table in the left foreground apparently depicts a stone marker on a hill overlooking the Rhine near Rhenen.[3] Anthonie van Borssum (1629 / 1630 – 1677) made a drawing of a six-sided stone table on a hill overlooking the Rhine that almost certainly represents the same structure.[4]

Cuyp was probably working from this location when he made a drawing of the landscape surrounding Rhenen (see Haverkamp-Begemann essay, fig. 3), a study that served as the basis for the background of a 1641 family portrait (see cat. 3, fig. 1) and for his *View on a Plain* (c. 1644, Dulwich Picture Gallery, London).[5] Both the Dulwich painting and *Landscape with Shepherds and Shepherdesses* include a standing shepherd that is based on a chalk drawing now in a private collection in Vorden.[6] Cuyp derived many of the sheep in *Landscape with Shepherds and Shepherdesses* from studies that appear on another of his chalk drawings.[7] **AKW**

Landscape with Shepherds and Shepherdesses

119

• Since the nineteenth century *Herdsmen with Cattle* has vied with several other works by Cuyp for the accolade of being the master's most accomplished work.[1] When the English critic and essayist William Hazlitt saw the painting he extolled it as "the finest Cuyp perhaps in the world," praising the light and atmospheric coloring as having been "woven of ethereal hues" and describing "the tender green of the valleys beyond the gleaming lake, the purple light of the hills" as having "an effect like that of the down of an unripe nectarine."[2] With the exception of the painter John Ruskin, who parodied Hazlitt's praise (and prose) by describing the coloring of Cuyp's sky as "very like an unripe nectarine," the painting has been much admired by critics and the public alike.[3]

The picture belongs to a group of works from the mid-1640s in which Cuyp began to explore the use of Italianate and *contre-jour* lighting. In the foreground two herders rest and converse on a sunny pasture, a recurring motif in Cuyp's paintings.[4] At the foot of the hills are the rest of the herd and more herders, while beyond the stagelike plateau of the foreground, a flat and watery landscape extends toward the far hills. The deep orange-yellow tints of the sunlight and the long shadows clearly indicate that this is a late sunny afternoon scene.[5] The impressive luminosity of the painting and the accomplished handling of the atmospheric effect are remarkable for a work that must date in the mid-1640s.[6] The reflections of the light on the edges of the foliage in the foreground already point to Cuyp's later pictures in which this becomes one of the most characteristic features.

This painting represents one of Cuyp's earliest endeavors in combining native rural scenes — ordinary Dutch peasants and herders tending to their livestock — with a setting and lighting effects inspired by Dutch Italianate painters such as Herman van Swanevelt, Claes Berchem, Herman Saftleven, and, perhaps most significantly, Jan Both.[7] The majestic hills in the distance and the warm golden sunlight infuse the scene with a sense of classical grandeur that contrasts sharply with the flat landscape and Dutch climate. The paintings from this period add a new dimension to Cuyp's idealized visions of life in the countryside, a vision of a Dutch arcadia in which man coexists in perfect harmony with animals and nature.[8] **AR**

Herdsmen with Cattle

• The imagery of Cuyp's stable interior closely echoes the title plates to series of prints of farm animals.[1] For example, Boëtius Bolswert's print dated 1614 after a design by Abraham Bloemaert (fig. 1) similarly depicts a farm woman with brass vessels, baskets laden with produce, cattle, and even the farm cat—familiar elements in any barn.[2] The print is a contrived allegory meant to introduce a series of twenty etchings depicting farmhouses; inscribed on the title plate is a Latin poem that celebrates farm life:

Oh most happy is he, and truly blessed,
who may spend his years free from civic duties,
living safely under the roof of his shed!
His mind is not disturbed by various complications,
He does not struggle with whims,
But is happy with the work of his ancestors, and
    contentedly
Harvests yellow grain or the ripe apples from the trees,
or herds productive cattle to his pastures.
When a diligent wife takes part of the work,
Oh most happy is he, and most highly blessed![3]

These lines by G. Ryckius reiterate the sentiments and even the language of Horace's famed celebration of the simplicity of rural life, the second epode "Beatus ille."[4] The general thrust of the text is also directly relevant to Cuyp's painting. A title plate very similar to Bloemaert's was designed by Jacob Cuyp for his series of prints depicting various animals, etched by Reinier van Persyn. These prints suggest that the stable was the center of farm life, a role emphasized by both ancient and seventeenth-century agricultural poetry, especially that inspired by Virgil's *Georgics*. Cuyp too made this clear by allowing a glimpse of the sunlit landscape through the open stable door at the left. While the stable housed cattle, a variety of farm equipment, and produce grown on the farm, it was also a preparatory area for food and acted as an adjunct to the kitchen.

In Cuyp's depiction, a woman scours a brass kettle with some straw, while vegetables and game are piled on a nearby bench.

Bloemaert's image and Ryckius' poem, like Cuyp's painting, clearly show that these farms were simple but not poverty stricken. Dutch prints from the early years of the century often depict farmhouses as ramshackle ruins, a tradition also evident in the paintings of barn interiors by Roelandt Savery (for example a circular painting dated 1615 in the Rijksmuseum, Amsterdam). In addition, Netherlandish artists had long favored depicting the Nativity of Christ in ruined stables to indicate the humility and virtuous poverty of the holy family.[5] In nearby Rotterdam, several painters specialized in simple stable interiors.[6]

However, Cuyp's stable is evidently more prosperous than any of these examples. The interior is clean and well lit, the woman neatly dressed. An analogy can be found in Peter Paul Rubens' grand depictions of flourishing barns. Like Cuyp's painting, Rubens' *Prodigal Son* (Koninklijk Museum voor Schone Kunsten, Antwerp) and *Winter Landscape* (Royal Collection, London) suggest the bounteous productivity of a farm. Cuyp's depiction of a stable interior contains many of the same associations with prosperity and the happiness of rural life found in the artist's more celebrated paintings of cattle. **AC**

1 Boëtius Bolswert, after Abraham Bloemaert, **Stable Interior**, 1614

Woman in a Stable

16 Conversion of Saul

c. 1645 – 1648, oil on panel, 71 × 91 (27 15/16 × 35 13/16). Private collection

· After witnessing the stoning of Saint Stephen, the first Christian martyr, Saul had proceeded to Damascus to capture more Christians. But on the way, he was engulfed by heavenly light. A voice from above asked him, "Saul, Saul, why do you persecute me?" Saul, who became known as the apostle Paul after the conversion, was left blind for three days. Like most painters before him, Cuyp depicted the scene in a violent flash of light. Horses bolt in all directions as Saul lies on the ground, his turban tossed aside. One of Saul's soldiers struggles to control his rearing horse as other men are thrown to the ground. At the right, a group trembles in awe at the heavenly voice.

This painting shows the influence of the artist's uncle Benjamin Cuyp. Benjamin favored dramatic bursts of light and complex arrangements of figures. Benjamin painted at least five versions of the Conversion of Saul, as well as numerous battle scenes that share such similar motifs as fallen horsemen and fleeing soldiers.[1] Aelbert's arrangement of figures, which comes to an apex with the man on horseback silhouetted against a brilliant light, is closely derived from Benjamin's versions (see Wheelock essay, fig. 11). But other aspects of the painting are Aelbert's own: the light has a golden tonality, and careful attention is paid to the depiction of the costumes and horses. Lying on the ground dazed, Saul gestures as though he were listening intently to the words of Christ. The figure thus possesses a sense of calm amidst the surrounding tumult. This motif is not found in other Netherlandish depictions of the subject and may be Aelbert's own invention, although it partially resembles Saul's pose in a print by the German artist Johann Ladenspelder.[2]

Cuyp painted two versions each of the Baptism of the Eunuch (cats. 9, 30) and the Conversion of Saul (fig. 1). The two subjects provided rich and varied opportunities to paint horses and exotic costumes — motifs Cuyp favored. Moreover, theologians drew instructive comparisons between the two narratives. Saul and the eunuch underwent two very different types of conversion. The eunuch

discovered Christ through careful study of scriptural text and was therefore baptized, whereas Saul was converted by Christ's sudden, miraculous appearance. Erasmus, for example, contrasted the humbleness of the eunuch with the arrogance and persecutory zeal of Saul. Some commentators noted that both the eunuch and Saul were Jewish, but became Christian missionaries.[3] In his widely read commentaries on the Bible, Calvin specifically compared Saul before his conversion to a violent animal, a "beast that was unbridled."[4] The violent confusion of the horses in Cuyp's picture may recall this reading. Saul's conversion also led Calvin to draw broad conclusions about intolerance.[5]

The Conversion of Saul had long been a popular theme throughout Europe, and although it was employed prominently in Counter-Reformation symbolism, especially in Jesuit iconography, the subject continued to be painted by Dutch Calvinist artists.[6] Aelbert Cuyp's other depiction of the subject (fig. 1) belonged to the Pompe van Meerdervoort family, important patrons of the artist (see cat. 29).[7] This larger, probably later version is less a landscape and more a figural composition. The painting gives greater prominence to Saul (and his horse), who remains essentially the same except that he turns his hand away from his face in a gesture of comprehension. AC

1 Aelbert Cuyp, **Conversion of Saul**, Musée de Picardie, Amiens

Conversion of Saul

• The rolling countryside that Aelbert Cuyp discovered on his trip along the Rhine in the early 1640s provided him with a visual vocabulary that transformed the character of his art. Although the specifics of Cuyp's trip are not known, one can envision the artist's excitement when he first reached the summit of Grebbeberg, an overlook situated between Rhenen and Wageningen, and gazed in wonder at the full extent of the landscape unfolding

1 Aelbert Cuyp, **View of Rhenen with Travelers,** c. 1645, private collection

before him. This panoramic view of the Rhine valley was unlike any he had experienced in the flat river landscape surrounding Dordrecht. Surmounting this height was an imposing stone marker, named Koningstafel (kings table), that also lent its name to the overlook. Koningstafel was named in honor of the Elector Palatine Frederick v, who reportedly enjoyed viewing the Rhine valley and surrounding countryside from this spot, much as do the two travelers in this luminous painting.[1]

Koningstafel was a popular destination for travelers to the region. An eighteenth-century traveler's pocket atlas specifically recommended visiting this "high mountain" near Rhenen, "which is frequently climbed to gaze at one of the finest views over the Rhine, as well as onto the Neder-Betuwe, and over the Rheensche Veenen."[2] Following the lead of other Dutch artists who had visited this area, among them Hercules Seghers (c. 1589 / 1590 – c. 1638) in the late 1620s and Jan van Goyen in 1640, Cuyp pulled out his sketchbook and made drawings of Rhenen and its surroundings (see cat. 73).[3] Quite possibly, Cuyp, like the figure in this painting, may have laid his papers on the flat surface of the Koningstafel before beginning to draw.

One of the views of Rhenen Cuyp made from this site (Haverkamp-Begemann essay, fig. 3) served as the model for the landscape in three of his paintings, among them *View of Rhenen with Travelers* (fig. 1), c. 1645, a work that includes a figural group resting at the Koningstafel that is comparable to the one in *Two Horsemen on a Ridge*. A now-lost drawing probably was the basis for the panoramic landscape stretching out in this small panel painting.[4] The view, which is toward the south, depicts the peacefully flowing Rhine with its low-lying surrounding floodplain. Beyond the river's bank can be seen the church steeple from the small village of Ter Lee.[5]

Because this small painted panel exhibits the forceful, vigorous brushwork found in Cuyp's works from the mid-to-late 1640s, he appears to have executed it somewhat after he executed his *View of Rhenen with Travelers*. The energetic handling of the sky particularly resembles that in *River Landscape with Cows* (cat. 19). This later dating is also supported by subtle differences in the men's costumes — the shapes of their hats, jackets, and boots all reflect the fashion of the mid-to-late 1640s. **AKW**

Two Horsemen on a Ridge

18 The Maas at Dordrecht in a Storm

c. 1648–1650, oil on panel, 49.8 × 74.4 (19 ⅝ × 29 ⁵⁄₁₆). The National Gallery, London

1 Aelbert Cuyp, **Shipping on the Maas, Dordrecht,** The Wallace Collection, London

2 Jan van Goyen, **View of Dordrecht from the Dortse Kil,** 1644, National Gallery of Art, Washington, Ailsa Mellon Bruce Fund

• In contrast to Cuyp's numerous shipping scenes in which he presented majestic ships in the calm waters of the rivers surrounding Dordrecht, here the artist confronts the viewer with a dramatic scene of a sailing vessel caught in a storm on the river Merwede. Against the backdrop of Dordrecht as seen from the southwest — the view has been taken from the Meerdervoort dike — a *smalschip* is sailing close-hauled across the choppy river.[1] The sky is filled with thick dark clouds, and in the distance a jagged line of lightning momentarily casts light on the city's roofs. The light coming from the left, where the sky appears to be clearing, illuminates the taut sail of the boat, its backwash, and the whitecaps on the water.

Cuyp's shipping pictures often portray life on and around Dordrecht's rivers, ranging from mundane subjects such as people working on the riverbanks (cat. 4), fishing (cat. 7), or transporting goods and passengers to more majestic views of the river (cats. 35, 36) and grand celebrations of the gathering of the Dutch fleet (cat. 28). With its vigorous and sketchy brushwork, the present picture conveys a sense of precariousness and drama that is quite unusual within Cuyp's oeuvre. The threat of being struck by lightning literally hangs over the ship's mast. The same boat sailing in a stiff breeze, though in a less dramatic storm and more closely seen, appears in a work by Cuyp in the Wallace Collection, London (fig. 1).[2]

Aside from Cuyp's direct observation of the world around Dordrecht, this painting may well have been inspired by works by Jan van Goyen. In the 1630s and 1640s the latter painted a number of views of Dordrecht whose compositions, in both quiet and stormy waters, are similar to the present picture (fig. 2).[3] Aside from Van Goyen, the subject of a relatively small vessel sailing in a strong breeze with a close-hauled sail, at times brightly lit and set off against the dark unruly water, appealed to many painters. Jan Porcellis (1584–1632), Abraham van Beyeren (1620/1621–1690), and later Jacob van Ruisdael (1628/1629–1682) and Willem van de Velde the Younger (1633–1707) also show boats in similar predicaments.[4] Indeed, Van Goyen's depictions of storms of the 1640s bear striking similarities to Cuyp's interpretation of the subject.[5]

The depiction of thunderstorms, an ephemeral and essentially "unpaintable" phenomena, occupied an important place in the art theoretical discussions of the sixteenth and seventeenth centuries. Among the publications in which this issue is raised are Karel van Mander's *Den grondt der edel vry schilderconst* (1604), which challenges young painters to emulate Apelles in his reputed skill in painting thunder and lightning, and Philips Angel's *Lof der schilder-konst* (1642), which emphasizes the illusionistic capacities of painting. Many of the ephemeral atmospheric qualities ("rain, thunder, lightning, clouds, vapour, light, reflections") stressed by these authors are convincingly portrayed in this small view of Dordrecht.[6] **AR**

The Maas at Dordrecht in a Storm

19 River Landscape with Cows

1648–1650, oil on panel, 68 × 90.2 (26 ¾ × 35 ½). National Gallery of Art, Washington, Gift of Family Petschek (Aussig)

• Cuyp was not the first Dutch artist to focus on a herd of cows for his subject matter, but in his hands the theme took on a grandeur and dignity lacking in the work of his predecessors. Whether in the hilly, dense forest landscapes of Roelandt Savery (see Wheelock essay, fig. 18) or the flatter fields of scenes by Cornelis Saftleven, cows were portrayed as inelegant, graceless animals that mill together in rather haphazard formations. Cuyp, however, seems to have perceived a certain nobility in the beast, one he emphasized by placing the viewer at a low vantage point and by silhouetting the cattle against a light-filled background. He simplified and purified their forms to give their heads sharp, angular shapes. He emphasized these ennobled profiles by orienting his herd on a horizontal axis along which their overlapping forms become visually connected. Finally, he projected their heads forward, even those lying in the grass, in a way that suggests a degree of alertness and even intelligence not normally associated with this species.

This painting is one of a number of similar images that Cuyp painted in the late 1640s and early 1650s, when he was beginning to incorporate stylistic elements from Simon de Vlieger and the Dutch Italianate artists. While the painting's dramatic cloud formations, broken by shafts of light, reflect the impact of De Vlieger's paintings of the mid-1640s (see Wheelock essay, fig. 4), the impact of the Italianate artists is evident in Cuyp's placement of large foreground forms (cattle) within a more generalized, arcadian landscape. The mood is idyllic. As the herd of eight cows quietly enjoys the gentle winds of a late afternoon summer day, a few sailboats glide along the inland waterway, their reflections shimmering in the peaceful water. On the crest of the gentle rise to the right, two herdsmen converse with a rider mounted on a large brown horse. Shafts of light breaking through the billowing clouds not only accentuate their diminutive forms, but also seem to provide a spiritual blessing upon their presence. The overriding sense is that this is a blessed land, fertile, prosperous, and at peace.

As with some of his other paintings, Cuyp may well have used drawings made from life when composing this work. His drawing of a horse in the Abrams collection (cat. 99) was probably the source for the image of the horse seen from behind on the crest of the hill. Although a number of Cuyp's studies of cows resemble cows in this painting, no known drawing served as a direct prototype for any of them. **AKW**

River Landscape with Cows

• *A Herdsman with Five Cows by a River* represents one of the most characteristic types of pictures painted by Aelbert Cuyp. A herd of cows stands in the shallow water of the banks of a river (possibly in the vicinity of Dordrecht), grazing, drinking, and enjoying the warm, golden afternoon sun that floods the scene. Their shepherd crouches by the water on the far right, and on the left two fishermen go about their business in their small rowboat. The animals are placed close to the foreground, partly silhouetted against the bright sky and partly against the rising land on the right. The vast expanse of the river, dotted with a few sailing boats, extends from the immediate foreground toward a thin strip of landscape along the horizon. The contrast between the closely seen cattle in the foreground and the distant view is underscored by Cuyp's use of color. The boat with the fishermen, the cattle, and the land range in tone from a light, warm brown to dark browns, greens, and black, while the view across the river is suffused with the pale, hazy light streaming in from the left. The swirling clouds are painted in thick, vigorous brushstrokes in shades of blue, gray, and light yellow.

The painting belongs to a group of cattle pictures with very similar compositions. They are the first "pure cattle paintings" by Cuyp.[1] The other works are two pendant paintings in a private collection in London (cats. 22, 23), another pair of pendants from another private collection (cats. 22, 23, figs. 1, 2), *Cattle in a River*, now in Budapest (cat. 21), and a painting in the collection of Lord Samuel, England.[2] There seems to be little disagreement on the dating of these paintings. While MacLaren had suggested a date of the mid-1650s for the National Gallery painting, more recent authors seem to agree on a date of circa 1650.[3]

The present painting may well represent the first work in the series, since Cuyp included a number of details (such as the boat with the fishermen and the land) that somewhat detract from the impact of the group of cattle.[4] By contrast, the painting from Budapest (cat. 21) dispenses with these additional details and focuses on the group of cattle instead. In that work the animals are closer to the foreground than in *A Herdsman with Five Cows by a River*, which enhances their majestic appearance. Nonetheless, the present picture must have served as a model for the subsequent interpretations of the theme, for Cuyp repeated the arrangements of cows (for instance, in cat. 22).

Indeed, the depiction of the cattle in these paintings lends them a new degree of idealized grace and nobility not found in any of the cattle pictures of Cuyp's predecessors and contemporaries, such as Abraham Bloemaert, Roelandt Savery, and, later, Jan Asselijn and Karel Dujardin.[5] Equally, Paulus Potter's works of the same period depict cattle in a far less idealized manner, as common, rough, and imperfect farm animals — a far cry from Cuyp's beautiful and monumental bulls and cows.[6]

Whether these portrayals of cattle carry any symbolic overtones is a matter of debate. The traditional role of cows as part of representations of *Terra* does not seem applicable in the case of animals wading in shallow water, especially in the later versions of this series.[7] However, cows have also traditionally been associated with earth, fecundity, prosperity, and spring. In the Netherlands of the seventeenth century, where dairy farming played an important role in the country's economy, the cow was seen as a symbol of national pride that connects general concepts of spring and fertility with the economic success and productivity of the Dutch nation.[8] Cuyp's idealized depictions of cattle clearly resonate with these overtones without ever being specifically symbolic or overtly moralizing. **AR**

A Herdsman with Five Cows by a River

133

• Water, sky, and cattle: these are the simple elements that constitute a remarkable group of paintings Aelbert Cuyp painted around 1650. The sight of cattle wading in shallow water was very common in spring when the wide banks of Dutch streams would flood. Cuyp must have found the composition especially rich and satisfying because he completed so many different versions with such subtle variations. The extremely low horizon and mirrored surface of the water eliminate distracting details. The herd of cattle forms a unified shape terminated by the sharp angle of one animal drinking from the water. The shimmering reflections of the legs seem to give the cattle even greater substance. This almost abstract foundation leaves most of the picture's surface for the sky — a dramatic swirl of energetically brushed gray clouds. The wood support of these pictures allowed the artist to display the rich textures of his brushwork. Pentimenti above the herd not only show that Cuyp worked to refine the composition, but also indicate that it is earlier than the other version (cat. 22), which is neater and more geometric. This simplicity may also be explained by its role as a pendant to another painting of cattle (cat. 23), while the painting in Budapest appears to have been conceived as a stand-alone work. This exhibition affords the first opportunity to compare this beautifully preserved painting with its near mirror image.

Cattle had long been associated with a set of meanings and associations tied to prosperity and well-being. Traditionally a symbol of agricultural bounty, the cow became specifically associated in about 1600 with the peaceful affluence of the Dutch nation.[1] The town of Dordrecht was especially proud of its cattle farming because, after the catastrophic flooding of the region in 1421, numerous polders had been reclaimed for agricultural use. Many of Cuyp's patrons helped finance drainage projects and owned land in the new agricultural polders,[2] and Dordrecht collectors may possibly have associated cattle pictures with the renewed agricultural industry of the region — a meaning also connected with the cow's symbolic identification as *Terra*.[3] Indeed, Cuyp's depictions of cattle always seem to be set along the waterways near Dordrecht. In the so-called *"Large Dort"* (The National Gallery, London) cattle and a milkmaid are set before an idealized representation of the city itself, strengthening the connection between Dordrecht and the theme of agricultural bounty. Printed views often contain similar combinations of cattle with a panorama of Dordrecht.

Nearly perfect blocks of color, the cattle depicted by Cuyp here (and in cats. 22, 23) are idealized animals. They are certainly very different from the spotty, shaggy beasts that the artist depicted in his early paintings (cats. 2, 4, 5, 10), but are closer to the beautiful specimens painted by Italianate artists such as Claes Berchem and Karel Dujardin. The little information we have about dairy farming in the Dordrecht region during the seventeenth century indicates that most cattle were reddish, some 30 percent were black, while only 4 percent were spotted.[4] Obviously, Cuyp could easily manipulate the color of his cattle to achieve picturesque effect.

Cuyp's attention to the uniformity and coloristic beauty of cattle accords well with Karel van Mander's instructions to the artist interested in depicting cattle:

Then go to try to practice
You must also further study the colors
Of oxen and cows, red, gray, and pale
How wonderfully spotted they are, all
Having ears always like all the others
One not having a hair that's differently spotted
     from another.[5]

Van Mander could almost be describing Cuyp's painting when he stresses the regularity of cattle, their variety in color, and how they look in groups. AC

Cows in a River

22 Cows in a River

c. 1650, oil on panel, 59 × 72.5 (23 ¼ × 28 ⁹⁄₁₆). Private collection *(London, Amsterdam only)*

23 Bulls on a Riverbank

c. 1650, oil on panel, 59 × 72 (23 ¼ × 28 ⅜). Private collection *(London, Amsterdam only)*

1 Aelbert Cuyp, **Cattle in a River**, private collection

2 Aelbert Cuyp, **Cattle and a Horse with a Shepherd Boy,** private collection

• While cattle, sheep, and other farm animals appear even in Cuyp's earliest pictures, the artist only began to concentrate on cattle in about 1650, when he made a number of cattle paintings with different landscape settings. In these two paintings, Cuyp depicted the animals as nearly uniform blocks of color — forms to be arranged and lit as though components of a still life. Cuyp applied layers of paint quickly and forcefully. Much of the picture — the distant bank, the boats, and the edges of the clouds — was brushed wet in wet.

Cuyp's initial attempt to depict cattle wading in water appears to be a painting at Petworth, where the motif can be glimpsed in the distance.[1] A work in the National Gallery, London (cat. 20), established the basic motif, but the view is wider than in the exhibited painting, while the rowboat and the man squatting at the right distract from the principal subject. Cuyp probably next painted the work in Budapest (cat. 21), and then, in another picture, reversed the herd of cattle, turning the drinking cow to face the viewer (fig. 1). This painting has a pendant depicting cattle with a horse and a shepherd boy (fig. 2). The exhibited pair of pictures seems to be the culmination of this process. While the composition of the cows in the water remains essentially the same as in *Cattle in a River* (fig. 1), a new pendant has been devised showing bulls on a riverbank. Pendant paintings of cattle are rare in seventeenth-

century Holland, and prominent cattle specialists such as Paulus Potter and Karel Dujardin do not seem to have conceived their depictions of animals in pairs. However, in 1616, Roelandt Savery had painted pendants showing cows and bulls, purposefully contrasting docile cows with belligerent bulls fending off a fox.[2] Cuyp had turned periodically to Savery for inspiration (see cat. 1), and was very likely once again influenced by the older artist. In Cuyp's pendants, the traditional significance of bulls as protectors is missing, since Cuyp's bulls do not seem especially defensive or aggressive.[3]

The paintings have been in the same collection since 1829 and in the nineteenth century were widely praised as prime examples of Cuyp's art. In 1877 a reviewer for the *Athenaeum* wrote, "in no instance is the art of Cuyp more enjoyable than in the pair of small works ... extremely fine and simple compositions — an atmosphere of apparently illimitable loftiness, pregnant with the pure, warm, and silvery vapours of a fine evening." The writer thought the painting of cattle on the bank was rendered in the contrasting light of early morning. Only Gibson in 1928 found the paintings "unusually rough and thick for Cuyp, and for once his sense of form has relatively failed him." **AC**

Cows in a River

Bulls on a Riverbank

Travelers in a Hilly Countryside

c. 1650–1652, oil on panel, 48.1 × 74.8 (18 ¹⁵⁄₁₆ × 29 ⁷⁄₁₆). The Cleveland Museum of Art, Bequest of John L. Severance

• Muleteers make their way onto a ridge in a hilly landscape. Led by a young man in improbably pristine clothing, a donkey carries a woman as another mule laden with bundles and a shiny brass jug follows. Behind them, another man encourages a recalcitrant animal up the hill. The scene is disarmingly simple. Little disturbs the sweeping lines of the countryside, an effect enhanced by the long evening shadows. Shaded from the sun, the cool green and brown foreground sets off brilliantly lit hills in back. The intense sunlight refracts the farmhouses and the buildings on the hill, turning them into crystalline forms. The edges of the clouds above are delicately tinged with color. So convincing is this evocation of the atmosphere and light of Italy that it is difficult to believe that Aelbert Cuyp never saw the country for himself.[1] Did he simply master the artistic tricks he saw in the pictures of Jan Both, Claes Berchem, and Cornelis van Poelenburch? In particular, Van Poelenburch's renderings of distant ridges and hill towns seem to have been the model for this landscape. Cuyp probably made this painting, his most believable depiction of Italian scenery, just before his 1652 journey along the Rhine, for after that date he almost always included motifs derived from his travel sketches.

Aelbert Cuyp is perhaps the most prominent Dutch Italianate landscapist not to have gone to Italy, although no conclusive evidence yet proves that Claes Berchem or Adam Pynacker actually traveled there either. While modern art historians have coined the terms "Italianate" and "Italianizing" to categorize Dutch views of Italy, how did seventeenth-century viewers appreciate such pictures? Only a handful of landscapes were described as Italian in inventories from the end of the seventeenth century and beginning of the eighteenth: these include works by Jan Asselijn, Claes Berchem, Adam Pynacker, Abraham Storck, Jan Baptist Weenix, and Thomas Wijk.[2] In 1718, Arnold Houbraken characterized the landscapes of Jan Asselijn and Karel Dujardin as painted in a "zuivere en heldere wyze" (pure and bright manner).[3] More important are a few references that characterize landscapes as made in an Italian manner, as opposed to simply Italian in subject. A 1672 inventory drawn up in Dordrecht describes two works as a "lantschap, op zijn Italiaens" (landscape, in an Italian manner).[4] In 1689, a London auction catalogue employed an analogous term in listing a painting as "An Original Landscape the Italian way."[5] These are sure indications that the Italianate landscape style practiced by Dutch painters was becoming recognized by a wider public.

The group of riders in this painting inevitably recalls the holy family, perhaps journeying to Bethlehem or fleeing into Egypt. Painters such as Jan Both, Claes Berchem, and Karel Dujardin frequently included such figures in their works, which, while they lack specific attributes or symbols, are strong reminiscences of a biblical story. Apparently, the Italianate style permitted a deliberately ambiguous treatment of figure types that allowed viewers to construct their own narratives. **AC**

Travelers in a Hilly Countryside

25 Landscape with Herdsmen

c. 1650 – 1652, oil on panel, 48 × 82.5 (18 ⅞ × 32 ½). The Corcoran Gallery of Art, Washington, William A. Clark Collection

Dordrecht was situated near the confluence of a number of major waterways — the Maas, the Merwede, the Waal, and the Rhine — rivers that allowed easy access by boat to the eastern regions of the Netherlands. Cities lying on these waterways — Arnhem, Nijmegen, Rhenen, and Wageningen — were some of the oldest and historically most important of the region, and Aelbert Cuyp, following Van Goyen's lead, recorded their appearance in landscape drawings executed during his journeys to that region (see cats. 73 – 76), where he discovered panoramic views of broad river valleys dotted with towns, churches, and windmills, views whose impressions he captured with expressive chalk drawings in horizontally shaped sketchbooks (see Haverkamp-Begemann essay). Partial views of these areas must have found a ready market, for Cuyp translated his drawings of the early-to-mid 1640s into impressive panoramic paintings that stressed the hilly terrain and dramatic sites of cities near the eastern frontier of the Dutch Republic. Once he returned to Dordrecht, the visual vocabulary provided by these landscape studies allowed him to develop his ideals of the Dutch arcadia in paintings he executed throughout the rest of his career.

This beautifully preserved, luminous work from the Corcoran Gallery of Art is one of the earliest instances in which Cuyp incorporated references to this distant landscape. The background of this work depicts a view of the Rhine river valley virtually identical to that found in a panoramic drawing he made near Cleves, just over the Dutch border (cat. 76). The most prominent feature of this landscape is Monterberg, the distant hill barely visible through the gentle haze of the river valley.[1] In his later paintings (see cat. 38), Cuyp took more liberties with the topographic character of the landscape than he did here, not only exaggerating the height of Monterberg but also expanding the breadth of the river valley.

The cattle resting on the foreground, some of which are derived from existing drawings (see cat. 103), enframe the landscape with quiet dignity, a sense Cuyp reinforced through the weight and repetition of their forms. In these respects, as well as in their general disposition, they resemble the cattle Cuyp depicted in *River Landscape with Cows* (cat. 19). Cuyp may even have adapted some of the same preliminary drawings for cows for both works, as

he did with *Two Studies of a Horse* (cat. 99), in which one of the studies coincides with a horse in *River Landscape with Cows* and one with a horse in *Landscape with Herdsmen*. Indeed, the two paintings also share the theme of horsemen stopping to ask local herdsmen for directions.

Such repetitions of motifs may account for the reservations some scholars have quietly expressed about the painting's attribution.[2] Nevertheless, Cuyp generally worked in this manner, readapting drawn studies to create a surprising range of compositions with a rather limited range of subject matter. Although his *River Landscape with Cows* and *Landscape with Herdsmen* both portray a realm where man, animal, and nature coexist in peaceful harmony, the impact of the two works is strikingly different. The emphasis of the earlier work is on the drama of the sky, where shafts of light break through billowing clouds. In the latter work, Cuyp emphasized the quiet stillness of the air, which has been warmed by the sun — an effect he reinforced by silhouetting the cattle prominently against the golden sky and the muted tones of the distant river valley. **AKW**

Landscape with Herdsmen

26 Portrait of a Woman Aged Twenty-One, as a Hunter

1651, oil on panel, 80.5 × 68.5 (31 ⅝ × 27 ¹⁵/₁₆). Private collection

27 Portrait of a Man with a Rifle

c. 1651, oil on panel, 80 × 68.5 (31 ⅜ × 26 ⅞). Rijksmuseum, Amsterdam

• Portraiture occupies a curious position in Aelbert Cuyp's oeuvre. Although Aelbert began his career in a workshop that was known for portraiture (see Wheelock essay, figs. 9, 10), his father was the portrait specialist. Aelbert painted landscapes in Jacob's pastoral portraits until at least 1645, long after he had begun working as an independent landscape artist, but he does not appear to have assisted with the portraits themselves.[1] No portraits by the artist are known until 1646, the year in which he executed the pendant portrait drawings now in Berlin (cats. 108, 109). During the late 1640s and early 1650s, he painted relatively few half-length portraits, probably because he gravitated more easily to landscape images. In these works Cuyp focused, as did his father, upon the sitter's physical rather than emotional character.[2] Indeed, it is fair to say that most of the painted portraits Aelbert created during the early part of his career are relatively uninspired, for his figures lack animated gestures or expressions that would compensate for the absence of psychological penetration.

Given this background, the expressive, forceful character of these half-length oval portraits of 1651 comes as a surprise, and one wonders if new stylistic influences expanded the range of Cuyp's portraits at this time. In 1651 Jacob was at the end of his life, and the traditional style of portraiture coming from the workshop may have been seen as decidedly outmoded. The paintings have a dramatic flair vaguely reminiscent of works painted by Rembrandt and his school, particularly ones executed by Paulus Lesire and Ferdinand Bol. Both of these artists were from Dordrecht and had studied with Jacob Gerritsz Cuyp before adapting Rembrandt's manner of painting. Although Bol had moved to Amsterdam in the mid-1630s and Lesire had moved to The Hague in the 1640s, Cuyp must have known their portraits, including their pastoral portraits, in which sitters are similarly modeled in strong light and dressed in exotic costumes.[3]

Cuyp's sitters are richly garbed in fanciful costumes with attributes associated with the hunt. The young woman, who wears two white feathers in her hair and a gold-trimmed, split-sleeve dress, rests a spear against her shoulder and holds the fruits of her hunt: small birds suspended from a split willow branch. Her male counterpart, who wears a split-sleeve doublet and a hat festooned with two white ostrich feathers, proudly holds the barrel of a rifle in his left hand. The similarities in costume and attribute, as well as the identical size and shape of the panels, confirm that Cuyp intended these portraits to be pendants.[4]

The pastoral poems of Pieter Cornelisz Hooft (1581–1647), Giovanni Battista Guarini (1538–1612), and Jan Hermansz Krul (1602–1646) recount the joys and laments of arcadian lovers with names such as Granida and Daifilo, Silvia and Dorinda or Coridon, or Laura and Tyter. Widespread interest in these romantic stories, which stress the purity and innocence of country life, helped spawn the blossoming of pastoral portraiture in the Netherlands during the second quarter of the seventeenth century, primarily in Utrecht, but also in The Hague, Amsterdam, and Dordrecht.[5] While Cuyp's portraits belong to this broad tradition, his sitters have not posed as arcadian shepherds or shepherdesses, but as hunters. The distinction may relate to class consciousness, for hunting was a privilege reserved only for aristocrats.

Seventeenth-century emblematic literature and pastoral poems also often associated the hunt with love. This thematic association would be particularly appropriate should the portraits have been commissioned to commemorate an engagement or marriage, a distinct probability given the ages of the sitters. For example, Otto van Veen referred to the hunt as a prelude to love ("The chasing goeth before the taking") in *Amorum emblemata*.[6] Crispijn van de Passe similarly noted how the pleasures of love often replace the joy of the hunt: "Sometimes I was a Shepherdesse / within the Tuscane plaine / But when unto dame Venus I did render up my name, / I lost my shepheards crooke, and then / betooke me to this game."[7] **AKW**

Portrait of a Man with a Rifle

Portrait of a Woman Aged Twenty-One, as a Hunter

early 1650s, oil on canvas, 114.9 × 170.2 (45 ¼ × 67). National Gallery of Art, Washington, Andrew W. Mellon Collection

In the mid-1830s, Gustav Waagen, director of the Royal Gallery at Berlin, made an extensive tour of British private collections and, in 1838, published an account of the works of art he had seen.[1] When he expanded upon his account in his *Treasures of Great Britain* (published in four volumes from 1854 to 1857), he wrote enthusiastically of Aelbert Cuyp's *The Maas at Dordrecht* in the collection of Sir Abraham Hume:

The chief picture, however, of the whole collection is a view of the Maas, with the town of Dort, and numerous ships, by this master, in a moderately warm but extremely clear evening light. The delicacy of aërial gradation in a series of vessels seen one behind the other is not to be described, and, at the same time, all is executed with the greatest ease and freedom. This picture, 3 ft. 10 in. high, by 5 ft. 6 ½ in. wide, is a proof not only of the extraordinary talent of this master, but also of the astonishing height which the art of painting in general had attained in Holland in the seventeenth century.[2]

Waagen's enthusiastic response to *The Maas at Dordrecht* has been widely shared, and the painting has been featured in a number of exhibitions of Dutch painting since it was first brought to England in 1804.[3] The appeal, as Waagen suggested, owes much to the extraordinary light effects that Cuyp achieved, for rays of the early morning sun stream across the landscape, striking at full force the tower of the great church of Dordrecht and the sails of the ships.[4] Much of the painting's appeal is also owed to the massive scale of the work, which gives the scene a dominating presence, one enhanced by the sweep of the clouds and the powerfully conceived composition.

Cuyp portrayed Dordrecht and the river Maas as it is seen from the north, across the river Merwede. From this vantage stretches an impressive panorama of the city, a view accented by the distinctive port building, the Groothoofdspoort, and the Grote Kerk, with its massive yet unfinished tower. As with his depictions of Dordrecht at Ascott (cat. 35) and Kenwood (cat. 36), Cuyp based this view on a drawing of the site from the mid-1640s (cat. 84). Not only are the three paintings topographically similar, but they all include two sailboats to the right of the Groothoofdspoort that appear in the drawing.[5]

The Washington painting differs from those in Ascott and Kenwood in the drama and activity of a great number of ships assembled near Dordrecht, each crowded to capacity with passengers. In the midst of these transport boats are a few yachts, including one firing a salute. Cuyp has apparently portrayed an uncommon event taking place on the river Maas, for which a number of distinguished officials are being ferried to a large sailing ship (right foreground). As an officer wearing an orange sash and feathered hat awaits them and a drummer beats on his instrument, the boat carrying two gentlemen reaches its destination. A bugler in the second rowboat announces the imminent arrival of the other dignitaries.

When the painting was in the Van Slingeland collection in the eighteenth century, the subject was identified as a rendezvous of Prince Maurits (1567–1625) with several other princes of the city of Dordrecht.[6] However, neither the style of the costume nor the physiognomy of the officer standing in the sailing ship (*pleyt*) resembles Maurits.[7] Another fanciful interpretation, first proposed in 1929, was that the scene "represented Charles II in the Dordrecht roads, May 26th, 1660, during his journey from Breda … to The Hague and thence to England."[8] Several objections weigh against this theory: not only are English flags or other signs of English royalty absent[9] but stylistic considerations also make it probable that Cuyp executed this scene in the early 1650s. In the 1660s Cuyp painted with less emphasis on the weight, density, and textures of materials than is evident here in the hull and sail of the *pleyt*, whose effects he achieved through the application of thick impastos. Finally, the style of the figures' costumes is comparable to clothes worn in the late 1640s and early 1650s.[10]

As Margarita Russell has persuasively proposed, the probable subject matter of Cuyp's painting is the great assembling of the Dutch fleet at Dordrecht in July 1646.[11] Matthijs Balen, who extensively described this event in his chronicle of the city's history, wrote that for two weeks an enormous transport fleet, consisting of more ships than had ever before come together at Dordrecht and over 30,000 foot soldiers, had gathered at Dordrecht.[12] The city magistrates ordered that free board and

The Maas at Dordrecht

lodging should be provided for the men. Everything the soldiers needed for the festive occasion was provided: beer as well as bacon, bread as well as cakes. Onlookers from Haarlem, Delft, Amsterdam, Rotterdam, The Hague, and elsewhere crowded into the city.

Balen precisely described the ships and their locations as they anchored in the tidal current of the Merwede. As is clear from his account, the "fleet" was a disparate group of ships, consisting of not only warships but also utilitarian and transport boats. Among them were the kitchen boats, which were also used as sleeping accommodations for the personnel of the princely household; sailing vessels called *uytlegers*, which were used for guard and pilot duties when approaching internal waterways; and *pleyten*, single-masted, wide-bodied ships used as ferry boats. On 12 July, the fleet set sail as a last show of force against the Southern Netherlands at the onset of negotiations for the truce (which would ultimately be signed at Münster in 1648).[13] However, nothing ever came of the expedition, thus this event of such significance in the history of Dordrecht was of no consequence in the broader course of Dutch political history.

Balen's description of the locations of the ships carrying the various regiments can be applied to the situation depicted in Cuyp's painting. In the foreground left a warship flying the Dutch tricolored flag seems under sail in midstream. The large massing of ships beyond it may be those containing the Frisian and English troops that Balen described as

being anchored near the Groothoofdspoort. Beyond these ships, to the right of the Grote Kerk, a large yacht fires a gun salute. This ship, which displays the Orange coat of arms, must be that of the lifeguards (*Lijf-Scut-Bende*) of Prince Frederik Hendrik that Balen indicated was anchored near the Blaupoort.

The focal point of Cuyp's composition is not an elaborate warship but the relatively simple *pleyt* in the right foreground. The ship is at anchor, with her bow in an easterly direction, not to the wind, but with the tidal current to the bow. The large, wide jib is lowered and the spritsail is in a half-lowered position.[14] In all likelihood the officials who are approaching the *pleyt* are coming to bid farewell just before the fleet's departure. With the exception of the *pleyt*, all the ships have their sails fully raised. They would have waited for the ebb tide to help carry them along the inland waterways to Bergen op Zoom and Sas van Ghent.

The identity of the portly officer standing on the *pleyt* is unknown.[15] However, the officials in the rowboats are probably representatives of Dordrecht, since the young, standing officer wears a sash of red

and white, the city's colors. Indeed, this dignitary, who is given such prominence through his central placement, may have commissioned this large, complex painting. It is possible that he was Matthijs Pompe van Slingeland, who in 1646 at the age of twenty-five already held the public office of *schepen* (judge, alderman). Not only was Matthijs Pompe married to one of the daughters of Dordrecht's burgomaster, Cornelis de Beveren, he was also the brother of Michiel Pompe van Meerdervoort, one of Cuyp's important patrons (see cat. 29).[16] Given his official position and family connections, Matthijs Pompe could have been granted the honor of presenting the burgomaster and other high-ranking city officials to an officer of the fleet at the moment it was about to set sail. Whether he was an ancestor of Johan van der Linden van Slingeland, the eighteenth-century Dordrecht collector who is the first documented owner of this work, is not known.

When the Washington painting belonged to the Van Slingeland collection, it had a pendant, a painting that now hangs in Waddesdon Manor (fig. 1). The two works, which are virtually identical in size, together depict a continuous panoramic sweep of this impressive assemblage of ships anchored off of Dordrecht in 1646.[17] In the pendant, a comparable scene unfolds, with distinguished individuals being transported to an awaiting sailing ship. Reiss proposed that the rowboat contains Prince Frederik Hendrik inspecting the Dutch fleet, an uncertain but plausible identification.[18] Frederik Hendrik was present at the Groote Vergaderinge in Dordrecht

since Balen mentioned that his lifeguard was there. It seems, however, that the prince accompanied the troops by land rather than by water, at least as far as Breda.[19]

Cuyp's masterful depictions of the Groote Vergaderinge of 1646 in Dordrecht stem from his long-abiding interest in depicting scenes along the Maas and Merwede. For example, in *A View of the Maas at Dordrecht*, c. 1644 (see Wheelock essay, fig. 2), he similarly depicted a panoramic, light-filled river view that focuses on a sailing boat with its jib lowered.[20]

Nevertheless, Cuyp's *Maas at Dordrecht* is directly related to the marine "parade" pictures created in the late 1640s by Simon de Vlieger, specifically his imposing yet atmospheric image of this very event, which he executed in 1649 (fig. 2). Although De Vlieger provided Cuyp with the visual vocabulary necessary to create such a compositionally complex and yet balanced image, Cuyp gave his scene an immediacy and physical tangibility matched only by the later marine paintings of Willem van de Velde the Younger (1633–1707). **AKW**

29 Michiel and Cornelis Pompe van Meerdervoort with Their Tutor

c. 1652 – 1653, oil on canvas, 109.8 × 156.2 (43 ¼ × 61 ½). The Metropolitan Museum of Art, New York, The Friedsam Collection, Bequest of Michael Friedsam

· In an expansive landscape, a party prepares to hunt. Two boys, Michiel Pompe van Meerdervoort (1638 – 1653) and his younger brother Cornelis (1639 – 1680), sit astride diminutive horses. Just behind them is their tutor, identified in an inventory of 1680 as a man named Caulier, who gives instructions to Willem, their coachman (see Chong's essay). He holds two greyhounds, animals capable of running down game; in the center of the picture are two mastiffs, more powerful animals used for the kill. In the background, similar hounds pursue a small animal. The boys, costumed in lush velvet jackets of exotic provenance, are being taught equestrian skills by taking part in a hunt, a pursuit traditionally reserved for the aristocracy. A tower and some partly ruined fortifications just behind the riders suggest that this castle belongs to the Pompe van Meerdervoort family and that the landscape we survey is part of their estate. However, since the same structure recurs in *Lady and Gentleman on Horseback* (cat. 40), much of this image is fictional.

This painting is well documented: Inventories identify the principal figures with certainty. The death of the older boy in 1653 establishes a date for the work; this is confirmed by the view of Elten in the distance, which Cuyp sketched in 1652.[1] Cuyp traveled up the Rhine as far as Nijmegen and Cleves, and filled sketchbooks with topographic drawings in black chalk — a rich source of motifs that directly or indirectly affected all of his late landscapes.[2] The artist employed the same view in a more personal landscape showing two horsemen stopped near the vast panorama (fig. 1). One of the men sits to draw the view, clearly a depiction of Cuyp himself on his sketching expedition.

The portrait of the Pompe van Meerdervoort boys brings together several factors that had preoccupied Cuyp. It is the first in a line of apparently popular equestrian portraits crafted for members of a social class that would provide much of his future patronage. The painting also blends the artist's first-hand experience of the expansive scenery around Elten with his study of the golden light and Italian motifs found in the landscapes of Jan Both. This combination became the essence of Cuyp's landscape production for the rest of his career.

Netherlandish hunting portraits often have an informality and anecdotal atmosphere that distinguishes them from state equestrian portraits. Paulus van Somer, Daniel Mijtens, and Anthony van Dyck crafted hunting portraits for the English court that may have provided inspiration for Cuyp. His depiction of two young seigneurs being taught the arts of riding and hunting by a tutor specifically recalls prints by Crispijn van de Passe showing Antoine de Pluvinel giving riding lessons to Louis XIII (see cat. 39, fig. 1).[3] Cuyp could easily have encountered Pluvinel's popular illustrated treatise, since it was reprinted in Utrecht in 1625. An illustration by Abraham van Diepenbeeck for a similar equestrian manual of 1658 also shows two young princes being taught to ride.[4] These images by Netherlandish artists leave little doubt that horsemanship and the equestrian hunt were essential components of noble life.

Although the educational allusions of the portrait are quite clear, they differ from the moralizing elements frequently discerned in seventeenth-century Dutch portraits of children.[5] These young aristocrats are being readied for a sophisticated and cultured life in the manner recommended by Baldassare Castiglione in *Il libro del cortegiano* of 1528, which specifically required princes and courtiers to be taught the equestrian arts. Nicolas Faret's paraphrase of Castiglione was revised by the Dordrecht artist and writer Samuel van Hoogstraten in 1657, and a Dutch translation of the *Courtier* was published in Dordrecht in 1662.[6] Aelbert Cuyp's equestrian portrait belonged equally to this social milieu in Dordrecht that aspired to proper aristocratic behavior. AC

1 Aelbert Cuyp, **Landscape with a Sketcher**, c. 1652, Marquess of Tavistock and the Trustees of the Bedford Estate, Woburn Abbey, Bedfordshire

Michiel and Cornelis Pompe van Meerdervoort with Their Tutor

151

The Baptism of the Eunuch

c. 1653, oil on canvas, 117 × 171 (46 ⅟₁₆ × 67 ⁵⁄₁₆). Anglesey Abbey, The Fairhaven Collection (The National Trust) *(Washington, London only)*

· In a lush landscape, a sumptuous open carriage draped with velvet and golden fabrics, and sheltered by a blue silk umbrella, has stopped near a small pool. The Ethiopian eunuch, treasurer to Queen Candace, has alighted and kneels at the edge of the water, where the apostle Philip baptizes him.

The manner of painting in the foliage and the form of the signature suggest that this painting dates shortly after the equestrian portrait in the Metropolitan Museum of Art, made about 1653 (cat. 29). As Cuyp developed a new Italianate landscape style that found favor with patrons in Dor-

1 Jan Both, **Landscape with the Baptism of the Eunuch**, Royal Collection, London

drecht, he returned to the historical subjects that had interested him at the very beginning of his career. In the decade between his first treatment of the subject (cat. 9) and this painting, Cuyp discovered the Italianate landscape style of Claes Berchem and Jan Both. Cuyp retained several elements from his earlier essay, particularly the general point of view, which brings the eunuch and Philip to the immediate foreground and isolates the carriage and the eunuch's retinue on the road above — a scheme first developed by Rembrandt in 1630. In Cuyp's second version, the eunuch's retinue has grown considerably in size and opulence. Two beautifully attired outriders now accompany the official, and two impressive white steeds draw the elaborate chariot. The entire party is sheltered by cool trees, in marked contrast to the hot sun of the open countryside in the distance. The effect is strengthened by streaks of impasto above the umbrella that depict intense rays of sunlight penetrating the leafy shade. The trees also shade the calm pool, which reflects the figures and draws them close to the viewer. Above, a leafy branch frames the figural group. As in so many of his mature landscapes, these equestrians journey through an exotic land — whether Italy, the Near East, or some unspecified, idealized locale. Then too, Cuyp had acquired a new technique and palette that allowed him to render more convincingly the luxurious textures of fabric and the brilliance of light.

The Baptism of the Eunuch was only occasionally painted by Dutch artists in the seventeenth century. Rembrandt and his teacher Pieter Lastman favored the subject,[1] as did the Dutch Italianate painters Herman van Swanevelt and Jan Both.[2] Both's approach to the narrative was very different from Cuyp's (fig. 1): Jan separated the baptismal group from the carriage, which waits around a bend in the road, while Cuyp brought his figures forward on a tiered stage. In addition, Jan Both frequently arranged trees in the foreground in order to delineate space. Cuyp, in the exhibited *Baptism of the Eunuch*, used a grove of trees as a backdrop for the figures. Jan Both's painting remains a beautiful landscape with staffage — appropriate to almost any historical narrative — while Cuyp molded his landscape setting around the biblical subject.

In 1683, Roeloff Francken, who was from Dordrecht but lived near The Hague, owned a painting by Aelbert Cuyp of the *Baptism of the Eunuch*.[3] A large *Baptism of the Eunuch* painted by Aelbert Cuyp was also recorded in the collection of the Dordrecht merchant and art dealer Aert Teggers in 1688, when it was valued at twenty guilders.[4] Several other depictions of the *Baptism of the Eunuch* are recorded in Dordrecht inventories, which suggests that the subject may have been more popular there than in other cities.[5] **AC**

The Baptism of the Eunuch

• Unlike some of the other historic monuments and ruins Cuyp depicted in his paintings — for example, the Valkhof in Nijmegen (cats. 33, 34) or Huis te Merwede (cat. 32), whose remains survive to the present day — Ubbergen castle does not exist anymore. The identification of the castle is based on a drawing by Cuyp in Vienna, which bears an inscription identifying the building (cat. 88).

The castle was probably built during the second half of the fourteenth century for Johan van Ubbergen, Count of Nijmegen, at the foot of the Ubberger Berg (Ubbergen mountain) on the banks of the Ubberger Meer, a lake that has since disappeared.[1] At that time it was meant to replace a nearby castle, which was torn down after the new building had been erected. The new castle had a square ground plan with four corner towers, similar in type to the castles of Moyland, Ammersoyen, Brederode, and Muiden. The earliest depiction of Ubbergen castle can be found on a map drawn by the surveyor Thomas Witteroos in 1570.[2]

The true significance of the castle for the history of the area and of the country as a whole, however, derives from its role in the Dutch revolt against Spain in the sixteenth century. On the evening of 23 August 1582, the castle was incinerated by the citizens of Ubbergen, probably to prevent it from being used as a base by Spanish troops.[3] The present picture shows the ruins that were left after the fire (although parts of the building had been refurbished during the first half of

the seventeenth century to make it habitable).[4] Like Ubbergen castle, two other Dutch buildings, the Huis ter Kleef in Haarlem and Brederode castle near Leiden, were destroyed during the conflict with the Spanish, who had besieged the two cities. Because of their association with the war, these two buildings became important national symbols representing the struggle of the Dutch for independence from the despised Spanish oppression; this historic role turned them into popular subjects for numerous paintings and prints.[5] For the same reasons, Ubbergen castle also became a national symbol, and Cuyp's depiction of its ruins must have evoked similar patriotic feelings with seventeenth-century viewers.[6] Eventually the castle was demolished in 1742 and Baron Johan van Weldern built a new country house in its place, which was torn down in 1868 to make room for yet another building.

Cuyp would have seen the castle when he visited Nijmegen and its environs on his journey up the Rhine in 1651 – 1652. The drawing of the ruins in Vienna (cat. 88) sheds some light on Cuyp's working method.[7] When he saw the castle, he probably made the drawing of the building on the site; back home in his studio, however, he added the hills in the background and the tree at the left.[8]

The painting, which follows the drawing quite faithfully, including the added background scenery, is generally considered one of Cuyp's small masterpieces.[9] It shows the ruins of the castle surrounded by the still water of the lake. The view is bathed in a hazy golden light, which subtly fuses the different elements of the composition and lends the scene a unified warm tonality ranging from light beige to dark brown and green. Here the drawing differs from the painting in that in the drawing the pronounced plasticity of the castle contrasts considerably with the much flatter background of the mountains. Also, Cuyp evidently decided not to use the prominent tree from the drawing as a *repoussoir* in the painting. Instead, the painting's composition is anchored by the figures of the horseman and shepherd on the near bank of the lake, silhouetted against the silvery water and the landscape in the distance. Faint outlines of these figures are also visible in the drawing. Once again, as in a number of other pictures, Cuyp juxtaposed a shepherd with a man on horseback (see, for example, cat. 45). Different interpretations account for this pairing of figures. The man on horseback could be a traveler who, having come to see the castle, is discussing the famous landmark with a local herder. Or, equally possible, the contrast between the two figures may serve to emphasize the elevated social position of the horseman, who might own an estate with a country house and land for hunting or agricultural production. The figure would thus represent the seigneurial privileges and responsibilities that Cuyp's patrons from the "striving classes" enjoyed and undoubtedly recognized in many of his paintings.[10] **AR**

Ubbergen Castle

155

32 Ice Scene before the Huis te Merwede near Dordrecht

mid-1650s, oil on panel, 64 × 89 (25 3/16 × 35 1/16). Private collection

1 Aelbert Cuyp, **Ruins of the Huis te Merwede**, The British Museum, London

2 Aelbert Cuyp, **Fishing under the Ice near Dordrecht**, Marquess of Tavistock and the Trustees of the Bedford Estate, Woburn Abbey, Bedfordshire

· With this picture Cuyp takes us to the ruins of the Huis te Merwede on a sunny, late-winter afternoon. The river next to the towering remains of the fortress is frozen, and people have gathered on the ice around a *koekenzopie* (a tent where refreshments are offered) to chat, eat, drink, and generally enjoy each other's company. Toward the right and in the distance other people can be seen walking and skating across the ice. The white swan decorating the barrel on the horse-drawn sleigh in the foreground indicates that the beer has been provided by Dordrecht's main brewery.[1]

The Huis te Merwede just outside of Dordrecht was built at the beginning of the fourteenth century as a residence for Daniel IV van der Merwede on land leased from the Count of Holland. Two events have been connected to its eventual destruction. After the siege of Dordrecht in 1418, when Jan van Beieren, duke of Brabant, had turned the fortress into his residence, the city's inhabitants, in a fit of revenge, attempted to destroy the building.[2] The enormous Saint Elizabeth's Flood of 1421 further damaged the structure and completely submerged the land around it. The ruins have been surrounded by water ever since. The flood was one of the most momentous and dramatic events in the history of Dordrecht. Not only did it harm the Huis te Merwede, but it also destroyed large parts of the environs of Dordrecht — much of this land was not reclaimed until well into the seventeenth century.[3] The Huis te Merwede thus gained its historic significance through the two most disastrous events of Dordrecht's past. Although not a patriotic symbol, such as Ubbergen castle (cats. 31, 88), the

remains of the building became a popular monument that reminded the people of Dordrecht of the trials their city had overcome in order to become the prosperous economic center it was in Cuyp's own day. Numerous artists, among them Abraham van Beyeren, Jan Porcellis, and, perhaps most frequently, Jan van Goyen, painted the Huis te Merwede,[4] while Cuyp included the structure in several of his other works, as did some of his followers.[5] The depiction of the ruins in the present painting is based on one of several sketches by Cuyp, now in the British Museum (fig. 1).

This picture is unusual within Cuyp's oeuvre in that it is one of only three known winter scenes by his hand.[6] Although the painting of winter landscapes had a long tradition in the Northern Netherlands, no other artist before Cuyp had combined the subject of a typical northern winter scene with this type of brilliant Italian lighting (see also fig. 2).[7] Cuyp's interpretation of the warm and atmospheric light — and its subtle reflections off the ice — infuses the picture with a bright mood and an almost cozy atmosphere, which stands in marked contrast to the much cooler, pale light of many of his colleagues' winter landscapes. The handling of the structure of the ruin and the light appear close to Cuyp's depiction of Ubbergen castle (cat. 31) as well as to his *Landscape with Horse Trainers* (cat. 39).

Indeed, Cuyp's sensitive rendering of the shimmering light, comparable to that in his views of Nijmegen and Dordrecht (cats. 33–36), makes this painting one of his greatest accomplishments, a picture that "has not its equal of that Master in Europe," as one nineteenth-century observer noted.[8] **AR**

Ice Scene before the Huis te Merwede near Dordrecht

33 **The Valkhof at Nijmegen from the Northwest**

mid-1650s, oil on panel, 48.9 × 73.7 (19 ¼ × 29). Indianapolis Museum of Art, Gift in commemoration of the 60th anniversary of the Art Association of Indianapolis in memory of Daniel W. and Elizabeth C. Marmon (*Washington only*)

34 **The Valkhof at Nijmegen from the East**

mid-1650s, oil on panel, 48.3 × 74 (19 × 29 ⅛). Private collection (*Washington only*)

· The medieval citadel called the Valkhof (falcon court), nestled within the town walls of Nijmegen, became a popular subject for Dutch artists in the early seventeenth century. Aelbert Cuyp was especially fascinated with the site, which he visited in 1652. He made numerous sketches and at least six paintings of Nijmegen, including the only known repetition of a composition in his oeuvre. Jan van

Goyen had popularized the subject of Nijmegen in more than thirty paintings dating between 1635 and 1654.[1] His favorite vantage point seems to have been from a boat in midstream, amid ferries and fishing boats, with the Valkhof looming steeply upward. In two of Cuyp's paintings of Nijmegen (cat. 33; and cat. 43, fig. 1), the point of view is similar to Van Goyen's, but very different in atmo-

sphere. The Valkhof is seen from a greater distance from across the river while Van Goyen's sharp diagonals are entirely eliminated. Cuyp's depictions, filtered through hazy yellow sunlight, take on a classical symmetry and repose. Cuyp's paintings are closely based on a drawing he made on the spot (fig. 1).[2] While he straightened out some of the buildings to create a tidier composition, the paintings are faithful to the original sketch and even retain the borders of the composition determined by the edge of the sheet. This *mise-en-page*, encountered in other works by Cuyp, demonstrates the central role that Cuyp's on-the-spot sketches played in the development of his paintings.

The Indianapolis painting is paired with a depiction of the Valkhof from the east, a view that had also been painted by Jan van Goyen. Cuyp again followed his sketch closely in creating his painting.[3] The city fortifications follow the downward descent of the hill to the river — a composition that nearly mirrors the painting in Indianapolis. Both paintings are adorned with idealized shepherds tending their flocks. While the architecture in the Indianapolis picture glistens brilliantly in the morning sun, the pendant landscape is deeply shadowed by the setting sun, accompanied by a darker tone in the clouds. The paintings therefore represent contrasting times of day — such pairings of landscapes are

1 Aelbert Cuyp, **The Valkhof at Nijmegen from the Northwest**, private collection

encountered in other works by Cuyp and were commonly recorded in seventeenth-century collections.[4]

Nijmegen was popularly known as the capital city of the ancient Batavians, the supposed precursors of the Dutch. Tacitus, in his *Historiae*, described the Batavians (a Germanic tribe that provided auxiliary troops for Roman legions) as having settled in the estuaries of the Maas and the Rhine. Their leader, the facially disfigured Gaius Julius Civilis (known as Claudius Civilis in the seventeenth century), had been brought before Nero on charges of rebellion, but had been acquitted. Civilis remained firmly opposed to Roman rule and organized a revolt to expel them.[5] He set fire to his capital (the "Oppidum batavorum") in order to prevent its use by the Romans.

During the sixteenth century, Netherlandish scholars became especially interested in the Batavian revolt because it was such a compelling ancient precedent for the Dutch struggle for independence from Spain.[6] This nationalistic myth grew in importance during the early years of the Dutch Republic. Justus Lipsius, for example, revised his edition of Tacitus in 1588 to include a call to arms: Claudius Civilis showed what the Dutch could do when their liberty was threatened by a distant, oppressive empire.[7] The most influential writer on this subject was probably Hugo Grotius, who in 1610 freely interpreted the story of Claudius Civilis in contemporary terms in order to establish ancient precedents for the government of the new Dutch Republic.[8] Grotius also popularized the notion that ancient Batavia covered all of the Seven United Provinces.[9] Nijmegen's identification as the Batavian capital became especially important because it lay on the very border of the seventeenth-century Dutch Republic. Nijmegen's role in the Batavian revolt became fixed in the popular imagination, as the tale was recounted in nearly all civic and national histories.[10] Artists such as Otto van Veen, Govaert Flinck, and most famously Rembrandt (his *Oath of the Batavians* is in the Nationalmuseum, Stockholm) depicted episodes from Claudius Civilis' revolt.

Cuyp's paintings of Nijmegen were produced for collectors in Dordrecht, not for residents of Nijmegen itself. The images were not exercises in city pride, but signifiers of a national mythology, a role shared by contemporary literature on the subject. Through his gilded light and timeless peasants, Cuyp emphasized the role of the Valkhof as the capital of ancient Batavia. The herders contemplate the citadel from afar, just as figures in Batavian times must have gazed upon Nijmegen. Cuyp's depictions of Nijmegen are classical landscapes in the most general sense: they are ennobled and glorified reminiscences of a distant antiquity. **AC**

The Valkhof at Nijmegen from the East

The Valkhof at Nijmegen from the Northwest

35 Dordrecht from the North

mid-1650s, oil on canvas, 68.5 × 190 (26 15/16 × 74 13/16). Ascott, The Anthony de Rothschild Collection (The National Trust) *(Washington, London only)*

• The view of Dordrecht was one of the most prominent subjects within Aelbert Cuyp's oeuvre, with depictions of the city and its environs appearing in more than twenty-five paintings and ten drawings (see also cats. 8, 18, 28, 36, 72, 80–84). What distinguishes this picture from the other representations of the city is the spectacular golden light of the afternoon sun, which floods the scene from the right (an unusual choice for Cuyp). Once again, much like in his view of *Ubbergen Castle* and the *Ice Scene before the Huis te Merwede near Dordrecht* (cats. 31, 32), Cuyp combined an identifiable northern setting with the warm, slightly hazy light he had adopted from his Italianate colleagues. Particularly noteworthy is the deft handling of the reflections of the light on the water's surface and off the buildings in the distance. On the whole, the spectacular lighting transforms a depiction of everyday life on a river into a scene of unprecedented serenity and grandeur.

The painting shows Dordrecht from the northeast at the junction of several of the city's most important and busiest waterways. At this point the river Beneden Merwede becomes the Oude Maas, and the Noord and the Dortse Kil split off toward Rotterdam and Antwerp respectively.[1] The view of the city was based on a drawing now in Amsterdam (cat. 84), while the depiction of the boats and rafts was taken from a drawing in the British Museum (cat. 85). The painting depicts the harbor of Dordrecht after its rebuilding in 1647, when the old walls and turrets had been removed.[2] To the left one can see the Groothoofdspoort, whose spire

preceded the dome put on in the 1690s, and the Korenbeurs (corn exchange). To the right of the Groothoofdspoort are the Joppentoren (Joppen tower), the Damiatenbrug, and the Damiatenbolwerk (Damiaten bridge and bastion, respectively). In the back one can make out the Grote Kerk and further to the right the windmill, also known as the Standaardmolen, at the junction of the river and the Dortse Kil.[3] The view of Dordrecht from the north was the most common prospect of the city.[4] An important model must have been Adam Willaerts' view of the city (see Wheelock essay, fig. 8), which in the seventeenth century hung in the council chamber of the town hall.[5]

The view of the river is dotted with different types of ships, ranging from a grand three-masted merchant ship to small cargo vessels and ferries. Adam Willaerts' picture similarly focuses on the activities that take place on the river before the city, highlighting the importance of river trade and traffic for Dordrecht. An unusual feature of the present picture is the inclusion of the wooden rafts visible in the middle distance.[6] Cuyp and Willaerts seem to be the only seventeenth-century Dutch artists who ever depicted them in their paintings. These floats consist of timber felled in Westphalia and Bavaria, and floated down the Rhine to supply hardwood for Dordrecht's shipbuilding industry and timber trade. Although Rotterdam, Zaandam, and Hoorn had overtaken Dordrecht's shipbuilding industry in the seventeenth century and cheaper timber was increasingly imported from Scandinavia

and the Baltic region, the wood industry remained important and large floats of timber continued to arrive in Dordrecht.[7] In the eighteenth century, Claes Bruin still described the floats in exuberant terms:

What do we see here floating on the water
what great monster rushes towards us?
It has drifted down stream,
and is full of life and motion.
It is an oak float,
chopped from German forests;
and, through commerce, is turned into gold.[8]

The view of Dordrecht combined with its emphasis on the river as one of the main resources of Dordrecht's economy must have resonated strongly with Cuyp's fellow townsmen and wealthy patrons, and probably would have filled its viewers with civic pride.[9]

The pronounced oblong format of the painting seems unusual, yet scholars have been divided as to whether it may have been cut along the top.[10] The picture had actually been cut into two halves before 1774. Smith evidently had no idea that the two fragments once belonged together and described them, respectively, as a scene of early morning and as a scene "represented under the agreeable illusion of sunset."[11] The two pieces were only rejoined by a restorer in 1842.[12] Although a nineteenth-century commentator who had seen the two halves side by side did not find them particularly noteworthy, today the painting certainly represents one of the most spectacular accomplishments within Cuyp's idiosyncratic oeuvre. **AR**

Dordrecht from the North

163

• Cuyp's *Dordrecht from the North* at Kenwood House is very similar to the larger version at Ascott (cat. 35) — both show Dordrecht from the northeast and probably date from the same period. The buildings in the background can be clearly identified. On the extreme left one can just make out the entrance to the Voorstraatshaven (Voorstraats harbor) with the Boombrug (Boom bridge), followed by the Groothoofdspoort and the Korenbeurs, and further to the right the Joppentoren, the Damiatenbrug, and finally the Damiatenbolwerk.[1] In the back one can see the Grote Kerk dominating the cityscape and further to the right, at the junction of the river and the Dortse Kil, the windmill that was known as the Standaardmolen. The clock on the spire of the Groothoofdspoort shows five minutes past five, which means that the golden light flooding the scene from the right (the west) is that of the setting sun. As Arnold Houbraken wrote, Cuyp "paid attention to the time of day in which he portrayed his subjects, so that one can distinguish in his paintings the misty early morning from the bright afternoon and that again from the saffron-colored

evening time."[2] As in the Ascott version, Cuyp's great mastery is revealed in the handling of the warm light, which plays across the silvery water, the wooden ships, the plain sails, and the silhouette of the city in the distance and which infuses this scene of everyday life with a sense of majestic grandeur.

The painting shows Dordrecht's newly rebuilt harbor (which had just been completed in 1647). On the water, various types of ships and boats pursue their daily business. The focal point of the composition is the large three-masted seagoing merchant ship lying at anchor. Behind it are several smaller sailing ships that were used as cargo vessels on inland waterways. The rowing boat at the left may be one of the ferries that regularly ran between Dordrecht and its neighboring towns. Floating by in front of an anchoring inland watercraft (on the right) is a raft — a common sight on the rivers around Dordrecht, though an uncommon feature in seventeenth-century Dutch art.[3] Like Adam Willaerts' 1629 "portrait of the city," with its focus on Dordrecht's busy waterways (see Wheelock essay, fig. 8), Cuyp's views of the river would have made an equally strong impression

on his patrons, the aspiring patricians and merchants of Dordrecht, who must have seen them as celebrations of the city's beauty and economic success. Thus, Willaerts' view may well have served as a source of inspiration for both the present painting and the picture from Ascott.

The relationship between the two pictures is difficult to determine. While the motif is almost identical in both paintings, the proportions of the Kenwood version are different — less oblong, with the raft and boats on the right moved closer to the city. The view thus appears somewhat compressed, which has led to discussions on whether it was cut along the right edge. Van Gelder and Jost suggested that the float must have once been complete, but no evidence exists to support such an alteration of the picture.[4] Finally, whether this painting was executed before or after the Ascott version seems impossible to ascertain. Neither the presence of pentimenti, which occur in both pictures, nor the preparatory drawings in Amsterdam and London (cats. 84, 85) allow for any conclusions as to which picture may have been painted first.[5] **AR**

Dordrecht from the North

•   Before an expansive countryside, two horsemen have paused to rest under some trees. Having dismounted from his dappled gray horse, one sits to adjust his boot. Both riders wear exotic velvet jackets, which were probably part of Cuyp's stock of studio costumes because they recur in other images.[1] The two men have apparently been hunting, since they are accompanied by two dogs. The scene distills and simplifies the imagery that Aelbert Cuyp first perfected in his portrait of Michiel and Cornelis Pompe van Meerdervoort (cat. 29) and employed in several other equestrian portraits.

Not only is the setting comparable to the painting in the Metropolitan Museum of Art, but the costumes and accompanying dogs are also almost identical. However, such details as supporting servants and the depiction of an active hunt are missing. Instead, Cuyp imbues his picture with idyllic calm, undisturbed by any activity beyond the peaceful herder who tends a few cattle. Long shadows fall across the foreground and a ruddy light filters through the picture, setting this scene in the late afternoon, with hunters nearing the end of a long, exhausting day.

The wide river and distant mountain generally recall the scenery along the Rhine valley without being a topographically specific depiction of a site that Cuyp actually saw. The painting resembles the Wylerberg and the Wylermeer that Cuyp sketched in 1652 (a sheet formerly in the Duits collection) and employed in a painting (cat. 42).[2] In his equestrian pictures, Cuyp often included a figure adjusting his boot, as for example in a painting of riders stopping for refreshment at an inn (private collection)[3] and in a depiction of riders with an African page (see Gordenker essay, fig. 7). **AC**

Horsemen Resting in a Landscape

late 1650s, oil on canvas, 120 × 171.5 (47 ⅜ × 67 ½). National Gallery of Art, Washington, Widener Collection

This broad, panoramic view of a river valley has long been considered one of Cuyp's most masterful works.[1] The golden light of the late afternoon sun and the moist air in the broad valley soften the landscape, casting a quiet, peaceful spell over the scene. In the foreground two elegant horsemen, whose exotic costumes indicate that they have come from a distant land, pause to discuss their route. Behind them, in the shadow of a group of large trees, two shepherds rest amidst their animals. Another herdsman and his cows appear at the left, while a lone rider gallops along in the middle distance.

The pastoral quality of the scene reflects the influence of Dutch artists who had traveled to Italy and brought back images of the Roman *campagna*. Particularly important was the work of Jan Both, who similarly set off views of distant river valleys with elegant trees grouped to one side (see Wheelock essay, fig. 19). Jan Both also favored the *contrejour* effects of the late afternoon light and frequently painted long diagonal shadows cast by the setting sun, atmospheric elements particularly apparent in this work. However, the connections between Cuyp's pastoral scenes and Both's Italianate views can be overstated. Peasants with their donkeys pass through Both's mountainous landscapes, whereas in this work, elegant foreigners ride finely bred steeds through a broad, open landscape. The distinctive character of Cuyp's travelers indicates that his approach is fundamentally different from Jan Both's, whose peasants fit comfortably into his landscapes as integral components of the artist's idealized vision of the Roman *campagna*. Cuyp's travelers, on the other hand, do not belong to the land nor do they fit within it. The exotic horsemen provide striking visual accents for the composition, but they also engage the viewer, raising questions about the riders' identities, their travels, and their destination.

Despite the evocative quality of Cuyp's pastoral scene, the landscape is based on a real site: the Rhine valley near the towns of Cleves and Calcar, not far from the Dutch border. The identifying features are two background hills: Monterberg, the steep-sided hill on the left with twin towers at its summit, and Eltenberg, surmounted by the partially ruined monastery of Hochelten. These hills, also depicted in other paintings (see cat. 29), are recognizable from drawings of these sites that Cuyp made on his trip to this area of the Rhine in about 1651–1652 (see cats. 91, 92).[2]

Nevertheless a comparison with these drawings indicates that Cuyp freely interpreted topographic elements in this painting. He represented Monterberg as a much higher hill than it actually was, and the two towers are only seen to such advantage from the opposite viewpoint.[3] Finally, Monterberg and Eltenberg do not lie in such close proximity and cannot be seen together in the way Cuyp represented them.[4] Given the freedom with which the artist combined these landscape elements, the towns vaguely discernible in the river valley are probably Cuyp's own creations, intended to suggest the character of this beautiful stretch along the Rhine.[5]

Aside from reusing landscape motifs, Cuyp also repeated figures and animal motifs in his paintings. For example, the gray horse is identical to that in *Lady and Gentleman on Horseback* (cat. 40), and the galloping horse and rider reappear in *Michiel and Cornelis Pompe van Meerdervoort with Their Tutor* (cat. 29). The ease with which Cuyp reused motifs in his paintings and the fact that he rarely dated his landscapes make it difficult to establish an exact chronology for his work. Nevertheless, the expansiveness of the panorama; the soft, atmospheric qualities of the river valley, which derive from Cuyp's broad, planar technique of applying paint; and the elegance of the riders are elements associated with paintings Cuyp started in the mid-to-late 1650s. Other distinctive characteristics of Cuyp's mature style are an increasing artificiality of light effects and the introduction in the foreground of twisted saplings and large decorative leaves. This artificiality is particularly striking in this painting, in which diagonal shadows fall across rocks and foliage without any indication of the three-dimensionality of the landscape elements. A painting in the Toledo Museum of Art contains similar characteristics: *Landscape with Horse Trainers* (cat. 39) hung as pendant to the Washington picture, which is exactly the same size, when the two paintings were together in the Van Slingeland collection in the eighteenth century.[6] AKW

Horsemen and Herdsmen with Cattle

late 1650s, oil on canvas, 118.7 × 170.2 (46 ¾ × 67). The Toledo Museum of Art, Purchased with funds from the Libbey Endowment, Gift of Edward Drummond Libbey

• Horsemen played a surprisingly important role in Aelbert Cuyp's pictorial world. Many of his paintings focus upon riders journeying through a landscape (cat. 38), some capture a moment of interaction between horsemen and shepherds (cat. 25), while still others include hunters at full gallop in pursuit of game (cat. 29). He also painted portraits of wealthy aristocrats astride horses, generally but not always preparing for the hunt (cats. 29, 40). Among the most fascinating and unusual of Cuyp's equestrian paintings is this remarkable work, which depicts an elegantly dressed equestrian directing two grooms training a horse in the art of dressage. This work may well be the painting Arnold Houbraken considered one of Cuyp's finest.[1]

They are teaching the horse to perform a levade, a movement (requiring great skill from both horse and rider) in which the horse rises on its hind legs while keeping its forelegs tucked in.[2] The codification of such specific formal movements in equitation developed in European courts in the latter half of the sixteenth century. One of the most successful riding masters of this period was Antoine de Pluvinel, who founded a riding academy in Paris in 1594.[3] He eventually became riding instructor for the French dauphin, later Louis XIII. Pluvinel's fame was extended throughout Europe by his treatise *L'Instruction du Roy en l'exercice de monter à cheval* (Paris, 1625), which was lavishly illustrated by the Dutch engraver Crispijn van de Passe (c. 1597 – c. 1670) (fig. 1).[4] In the Netherlands, the publication served as a model not only for young aristocrats intent upon learning the equitation fashions then current in the French court, but also for the artists they commissioned to portray their equestrian achievements.[5] When Cuyp came to paint this work, he similarly turned to Van de Passe's engravings in De Pluvinel's manual to find a model for representing the levade. Interestingly, Cuyp may have actually known Van de Passe, who lived in Utrecht from 1630 to 1639, the very period in which Cuyp probably visited that city to enhance his artistic training.[6]

The Toledo landscape's idyllic setting is far more Mediterranean in character than Dutch. Warmed by the golden light of the setting sun, the scene is situated on a field before an imposing Romanesque

church, whose softly diffused form is silhouetted against the late afternoon sky. Nearby, two classicizing figural sculptures on large pedestals reinforce the aristocratic tenor of the subject, while fragments of classical columns in the foreground left and ruins flanking the scene reinforce the sense of nostalgia for faraway times and lands.[7] Nevertheless, as in *Horsemen and Herdsmen with Cattle* (cat. 38), Cuyp derived elements of his scene from Dutch sources. He based the church on the imposing Mariakerk in Utrecht, while the distant hills reflect the landscape he recorded on his Rhine trip of 1651 – 1652.[8]

In both the subject matter and style, this scene seems to reflect the aristocratic aspirations of Cuyp's wealthy patrons during the mid-1650s.[9] The painting's large scale, similar to that of other works by Cuyp from this period, indicates that it was probably destined for a country house located near Dordrecht.[10] Such properties were then being built near most Dutch urban centers, as both country retreats and symbols of a patrician status.[11]

Although the patron who commissioned this work is unknown, it formed part of Johan van der Linden van Slingeland's extensive collection of Cuyp paintings.[12] Since Van Slingeland hung this work as a pendant to *Horsemen and Herdsmen with Cattle* (cat. 38), he probably acquired the two identically sized, related paintings from the same collection. Thematic and compositional relationships, however, are not sufficiently strong to argue that Cuyp originally conceived the two works as pendants. **AKW**

1 Crispijn van de Passe, **King Louis XIII Performing a Levade**, from Antoine de Pluvinel, **L'Instruction du Roy en l'exercice de monter à cheval** (Paris, 1625)

Landscape with Horse Trainers

40 Lady and Gentleman on Horseback

begun c. 1655, completed 1660 / 1665, oil on canvas, 123 × 172 (48 ½ × 67 ¾). National Gallery of Art, Washington, Widener Collection

· Although the hunt became a popular pastime for Dutch patricians in the second half of the seventeenth century and numerous representations of the sport exist, Cuyp was the only Dutch artist to create large-scale formal portraits of aristocrats engaged in this activity (see also cat. 29). *Lady and Gentleman on Horseback*, which is the largest and most imposing of these works, is unique in that it represents an elegant equestrian couple, probably a husband and wife, setting out for the hunt. With an expansive light-filled arcadian landscape stretching behind them, they

embark with two types of hounds: tufters to track the deer and follow the scent and greyhounds (under the control of an attendant) to run after the deer and bring them to bay.[1]

The names of the sitters are not known with certainty.[2] Nevertheless, a promising clue to their identity is a bust-length portrait, based on the male rider in this painting, which has been traditionally identified as Adriaen Stevensz Snouck (c. 1634 – 1671).[3] Alan Chong, who discovered the resemblance between the two heads, has noted that

Snouck, originally from Rotterdam, lived in The Hague until his marriage to Erkenraad Berk Matthisdr (1638 – 1712) in 1654. This marriage would have brought Snouck into contact with Cuyp since Erkenraad was the daughter of Matthijs Berk, Raad-Pennsionaris of Dordrecht and an important patron of the artist. This theory may well account for the prominence given the female sitter, who, resplendent in her gorgeous blue dress, is mounted on a white horse with a brilliant red and gold saddlecloth.[4]

Chong's identification of the sitters accords well with technical examinations of the painting. As is evident in the x-radiographs (fig. 1), Cuyp overpainted and changed major portions of *Lady and Gentleman on Horseback*. The man originally wore a hat, had shorter hair, and his collar lay flat on his shoulders. He also wore a military-style tunic-and-cape combination, adorned with braids and buttons (presumably gold). This costume, whose overall color was apparently a brilliant red rather than the current brown, was in many respects not unlike that worn by Jan Six in Rembrandt's famous portrait of 1654 in the Six Collection, Amsterdam.

The woman's costume was also substantially changed: her hat was a different shape and its feathers sat farther back on her head. Her dress fit more loosely and seems to have fallen over the right flank of her horse. In place of the fairly low, elegantly gathered neckline of the final version, Cuyp originally painted a plain flat collar that covered her

1 X-radiograph of Aelbert Cuyp, **Lady and Gentleman on Horseback**

172

Lady and Gentleman on Horseback

shoulders. The costume was comparable to that
seen in Bartholomeus van der Helst's 1654 portrait
of *Abraham del Court and Maria de Keerssegieter* (fig. 2).
From the stylistic characteristics of their outfits, one
can conclude that Cuyp painted the original version
in about 1654 – 1655. As this probable period of
execution coincides with the 1654 date of the marriage of Adriaen Snouck and Erkenraad Berk, Cuyp
may possibly have received the initial commission
to commemorate that event.

Aside from changes in the figures' costumes,
Cuyp also substantially modified the mood of
the painting through changes in the woman's pose
and in the arrangement of figures in the landscape.
The woman originally assumed a less demure position, with her right arm extended, presumably to
hold the reins tightly. This gesture would have given
her a more active appearance than is evident in
the final version. The background was also more
dynamic. Instead of the two greyhounds and the
young attendant walking behind the riders, Cuyp
originally included five running greyhounds and
a somewhat larger young man in red socks running
with them.[5] The juxtaposition of the portraits and
the background figures would thus have been similar to that seen in the painting of the Pompe van
Meerdervoort family in the Metropolitan Museum
of Art (cat. 29).[6] Finally, the landscape also sloped
in from the left, and Cuyp may have made changes
to the fanciful castlelike building at the far left.

Although no specific symbolism relating to
marriage exists in the painting, the hunt as a theme
was metaphorically linked with the game of love.[7]
Also, the large burdock leaves in the foreground were
frequently associated with love.[8] Cuyp had a special
fondness for this plant and included it in the foreground of a number of his paintings (see cat. 39). In
most of these works the symbolic associations of the
burdock leaf seem irrelevant to the meaning of the
painting, but in this instance, with the dog calling
attention to its presence, Cuyp may have intended to
convey its symbolic associations.

The remarkable revisions in the painting suggest
that the patrons were dissatisfied with the original
composition. One may speculate that the activity
of the hunt distracted from the formal character of
the double portrait. The substantial modifications
in costume, however, also suggest that the sitters
wanted to update their image. For example,
the male rider's dignified brown jacket crossed by
a sash and his long, wavy hair worn falling over
the shoulders only came into vogue about 1660.
Cuyp's patrons may also have desired a more refined
style of portraiture than the artist had provided
in his initial version. Indeed, these portraits are
remarkably elegant for Cuyp, who is not noted for
his nuanced modeling of the human form. Their
style reflects that of Nicolaes Maes (1634 – 1693),
who, after returning to Dordrecht in the mid-
1650s, initiated a new vogue of portraiture in
Dordrecht patterned on the model of Anthony van
Dyck (1599 – 1641). Maes' Dordrecht portraits
captured the elegant, aristocratic aspirations of a
society that had begun to fashion itself after French
styles of dress and decorum, and Cuyp clearly
learned from his example. **AKW**

late 1650s, oil on panel, 68 × 90.8 (26 ¾ × 35 ¾). Los Angeles County Museum of Art, Partial gift of Hannah L. Carter (*Washington only*)

· On the night after the three wise men had found the newborn Jesus in Bethlehem, Joseph had a dream in which the Lord commanded him to "Arise, and take the young child and his mother, and flee into Egypt, and be thou there until I bring thee word: for Herod will seek the young child to destroy him." So, Joseph arose and "took the young child and his mother by night, and departed into Egypt" (Matthew 2:13 – 14).

This short narrative describing the Christ child's escape from certain death at the hands of Herod the tyrant is among the most compelling episodes from Christ's childhood. Of the legends and depictions of this event that have since sought to capture the essence of the story, Cuyp's is one of the more benign and genteel ever created. Instead of portraying the holy family apprehensively wending its way across unknown lands under a moonlit sky, as did Adam Elsheimer (fig. 1), Cuyp depicted the journey as one without urgency or danger: it takes place in the fullness of daylight with gentle clouds wafting overhead. As Joseph leads the donkey carrying Mary and the Christ child to their distant destination, the late afternoon sun casts a warm and embracing light, illuminating the landscape of steep cliffs and placid water through which they pass. The well-worn path they travel offers no resistance to their progress, and their presence elicits little notice from two nearby cowherds.

This sun-filled scene has long been admired, among others by Gustav Waagen, who commented in 1854 that "the composition itself has something more noble and poetical than is usual with [Cuyp]; to this is added a rare power and energy of foreground with the most delicate gradation of the clear tones to the warm evening sky, so that the picture is one of the most beautiful that ever came from the hand of this master."[1] Despite his enthusiastic comments, Waagen apparently did not realize that the foreground group is the holy family, probably because comparable motifs of peasants traveling through the countryside are commonly found in Cuyp's work (see cat. 24).[2] In this instance, Cuyp clearly identified the family by placing Joseph's saw in the donkey's pack.

Flight into Egypt generally reflects the influence of Jan Both's Italianate views of the late 1640s and early 1650s, in which peasants and their donkeys similarly travel along winding paths (see Wheelock essay, fig. 19).[3] Nevertheless, Cuyp's work, which is one of the purest expressions of his late painting style, has a clarity of light quite different from that found in landscapes by the Utrecht artist. Cuyp grounded his scene with more defined compositional elements, including the horizontal flow of the river, the vertical thrust of the cliffs, and the weighty mass of the foreground trees.

The cliffs along this river valley are reminiscent of the landscape that Cuyp witnessed during his trip along the Rhine in the early 1650s (see cats. 33, 42), particularly between Nijmegen and Elten. However, the painting must date some years later, probably in the mid-to-late 1650s, when Cuyp began to feature the elegant tracery of foreground bushes and generalized, atmospheric, distant river valleys.[4] Similar landscape features in Cuyp's paintings from the mid-1650s remain truer to the actual topography of the area than those in this work. **AKW**

1 Adam Elsheimer, **The Flight into Egypt**, 1609, Bayerische Staatsgemäldesammlungen, Alte Pinakothek, Munich

Flight into Egypt

1 Aelbert Cuyp, **Wylermeer between Nijmegen and Cleves,** formerly Duits and Co., London

• One of the most curious aspects of Aelbert Cuyp's works is their scarcity in Dutch collections.[1] After the (late) discovery of the artist by English collectors in the eighteenth century, "the flight of his paintings from Holland was immediate and total"[2] — particularly with the sale in 1785 of the collection of Johan van der Linden van Slingeland, who had owned forty-one paintings by the master. By the turn of the century, hardly any paintings of significance by Cuyp remained in the country — a notable exception is the *Equestrian Portrait of Pieter de Roovere*, which was sold by a descendant of its original owner directly to the Mauritshuis in The Hague in 1820.[3] *River Landscape with Two Horsemen* is one of the few paintings by Cuyp (and probably the most important) that has found its way back to the Netherlands. With its acquisition in 1957, the Rijksmuseum was able to fill an all too noticeable gap in its otherwise comprehensive and distinguished collection of Dutch paintings.

Typically for Cuyp's late works, the painting shows a sun-drenched landscape that extends along the banks of a river. In the middle distance the setting is framed on the right by a row of hills with some farm buildings nestled at their base. In the hazy light of the distance, a town is silhouetted against some distant hills. In contrast to most of Cuyp's late landscapes (see cats. 38, 44, 45) here he avoided the inclusion of any large trees that separate the foreground from the deeply receding landscape. The entire scene is bathed in Cuyp's characteristic golden sunlight, with long shadows cast across the

scene. Particularly noteworthy is Cuyp's adept handling of the shimmering light on different surfaces. The focal point of the composition is the foreground group of two men on horseback, who have evidently interrupted their journey in order to water their mounts. Judging by the light armor (breastplate and backplate) and the orange sash, the man on the left must be a Dutch soldier, while his traveling companion appears to be an elegantly dressed civilian.[4] Cuyp juxtaposed the horsemen with a shepherd who, momentarily distracted from his herd, watches them from a distance. This contrast between members of different groups of society is a frequent ingredient in Cuyp's "landscapes of power," most likely because it would have resonated with his patrons, the economically and socially ambitious patricians and merchants of Dordrecht who often aspired to the lifestyle of feudal landlords.[5]

The picture rather accurately portrays a view of the landscape between Nijmegen and Cleves, the Wylermeer and Wylerberg. Cuyp must have seen this area on his travels along the Rhine in the

early 1650s,[6] for his painted view very closely follows a drawing he seems to have made on the spot (fig. 1).[7] The peaceful scenery with its hills and still water, the beautiful resting cows, the picturesque farm, and, above all, the golden afternoon light lend the picture a sense of artifice and grandeur, which suggests a world far removed from the prosaic, flat, wet, and cold scenery of the Northern Netherlands. One is meant to behold and quietly enjoy this idealized world of pastoral beauty and serene tranquility. Typically for Cuyp, this elevated, vaguely arcadian mood is evoked by the setting itself rather than through the inclusion of classically inspired staffage acting out scenes taken from literary sources. By contrast, arcadian and pastoral paintings by Claude Lorrain and Nicolas Poussin as well as by earlier Dutch painters such as Abraham Bloemaert, Cornelis van Poelenburch, and Bartholomeus Breenbergh rely on the inclusion of scenes from classical mythology and pastoral plays.[8] Based on Cuyp's spectacular handling of the light and atmospheric effects in this picture, Smith had already recognized it in 1842 as one of the artist's finest accomplishments: "It is impossible to commend too highly this beautiful work of art … the wonderful and lovely gradation of tints and atmospheric truth, justly entitle it to the first rank among his best productions."[9] **AR**

River Landscape with Two Horsemen

43 Landscape with a View of the Valkhof, Nijmegen

late 1650s, oil on canvas, 113 × 165 (44 ½ × 64 ¹⁵⁄₁₆). National Gallery of Scotland, Edinburgh

1 Aelbert Cuyp, **The Valkhof at Nijmegen from the Northwest**, Marquess of Tavistock and the Trustees of the Bedford Estate, Woburn Abbey, Bedfordshire

2 Aelbert Cuyp, **Water Festivities at Nijmegen**, Duke of Sutherland Collection

· Several years after painting a pair of views of Nijmegen (cats. 33, 34), Aelbert Cuyp created a second set of pendants on a much larger scale. Cuyp repeated the view of the Valkhof from the northwest (fig. 1), but constructed a different companion piece — a view of the Valkhof's southwest gate. Like the artist's other paintings of Nijmegen, this was based on a sketch that the artist had made on his visit to Nijmegen in 1652 (The Pierpont Morgan Library, New York). The long shadows framing delicately striated clouds and the direction of the sunlight indicate that this is a summer afternoon.[1] As with *The Valkhof at Nijmegen from the East* (cat. 34), the rich browns of the picture contrast with the brighter tones of its pendant.

The figures encountered in the two sets of pendants create different effects and moods. While the earlier set of pendants is peopled by contented shepherds, Cuyp depicted elegant horsemen in the later pair. Here, a rider on horseback, his cape artfully arranged, is the most prominent of the travelers who pass through the city gate. Whereas peasants occupy centerstage in the earlier northwest view (cat. 33), in the later view (fig. 1) they have been moved to the edge of the bank, where they watch two elegant horsemen ride past. The imagery that Cuyp perfected in his equestrian portraits — wealthy horsemen set against deferential peasants — is deployed here against an imposing historic site.

Although the identification of Nijmegen as the ancient Batavian capital appears to have been the predominant association in the seventeenth century,

more recent events connected with the site were also well known. The town had been a seat of Charlemagne and had played a major role in the Dutch Revolt.[2] Nijmegen had fallen to the Spanish in 1585, and the Dutch general Marten Schenk had drowned attempting to recapture it. In 1591, Prince Maurits had liberated the town and declared the Valkhof a palace of the stadtholder. Louise Henriette, daughter of stadtholder Frederik Hendrik, and her new husband Friedrich Wilhelm, Kurfürst of Brandenburg, had paid a state visit to Nijmegen in 1647. Brandenburg had long been a close ally of the Dutch Republic and controlled the neighboring territories of Cleves and Emmerich. In addition, a cousin of the stadtholder, Jan Maurits of Nassau-Siegen (the Brazilian adventurer and builder of the Mauritshuis), had just been appointed stadtholder of Cleves, which strengthened ties between Brandenburg and the house of Orange. The elaborate ceremonies welcoming the guests are the subject of Cuyp's depiction of waterborne festivities at Nijmegen (fig. 2).[3]

Images of Nijmegen were widely circulated and immediately recognizable to seventeenth-century viewers. The distinctive outline of the Valkhof graced numerous maps and atlases. Joan Blaeu's popular atlas of Dutch towns included a map and view of Nijmegen, along with an extended commentary describing the city's history. Seventeenth-century inventories also attest that collectors recognized paintings, including works by Cuyp, as depictions of Nijmegen.[4] **AC**

Landscape with a View of the Valkhof, Nijmegen

late 1650s, oil on canvas, 101.5 × 153.6 (39 15/16 × 60 ½). Her Majesty Queen Elizabeth II
(*Washington, London only*)

•   This spectacular painting of a hilly landscape suffused with the golden, hazy light of the setting afternoon sun belongs to a group of pictures that stands at the end of Cuyp's career as a painter.[1] One of the common denominators shared by Cuyp's late landscapes is the setting. As John Smith had already observed, both the *River Landscape with Two Horsemen* from Amsterdam (cat. 42) and the present work depict the landscape of the environs of the Rhine between Nijmegen and Cleves. Cuyp had traveled to this region in 1651–1652 and produced numerous sketches of the local scenery with its steep and sloping hills, views of the river and its tributaries, and silhouettes of distant towns (see cat. 92). While the painting in Amsterdam is topographically accurate, here Cuyp freely varied different aspects of the landscape he had encountered, without forfeiting its general recognizable character.

However, while a number of parallels exist between these late paintings, the composition of the present picture varies in a significant way. In contrast to the works in which the viewer enters the picture on a sandy path that extends from the immediate foreground (cats. 42, 45), here access is almost blocked by the "barrier" of plants and the pool of water in the immediate foreground. On the path beyond are two men on horseback, who, in characteristic Cuyp fashion, have interrupted their journey to ask a shepherd for directions.[2] The group appears almost sheltered by the screen of tall trees to their left. The path continues farther toward the left, turning into a ridge that is sharply outlined against the softly lit landscape beyond — a contrast that is underscored by the silhouette of the man riding on a donkey.[3] Although this composition relates thematically to earlier works by Cuyp, the use of a ridge and a screen of tall trees to structure the composition suggests a renewed interest in the work of Jan Both (see Wheelock essay, fig. 19).[4]

What connects this picture most closely to Cuyp's *River Landscape with Horseman and Peasants* (cat. 45), formerly in the collection of Lord Bute and now kept at the National Gallery, London, is the artist's accomplished — and somewhat contrived — handling of light and atmospheric effects. While the town in the distance is engulfed by the bright haze of the moist atmosphere, in the foreground the warm afternoon sunlight coming in from the left casts long shadows across the scene and creates subtle *contre-jour* lighting effects. The pronounced highlights — "gilded edges" — on the different elements of the composition add what Gustav Waagen had already referred to as a "brightness of tone, approaching a silvery quality," that was to become even more pronounced in the painting from the Bute collection.[5] Smith, although not exactly exuberant in his praise, had already found that "the beauty of a fine summer's evening gives value to the scene."[6] As with all of Cuyp's late landscapes, the Italian lighting infuses the native northern setting with a sense of splendor and elegance, which evokes an idealized world of quiet peace and pastoral tranquility that would have appealed to the imagination of Cuyp's wealthy urban clientele, who often owned sizeable country estates. **AR**

Evening Landscape

45 **River Landscape with Horseman and Peasants**   c. 1660, oil on canvas, 123 × 241 (48 7/16 × 94 7/8). The National Gallery, London

· Besides being perhaps Cuyp's most accomplished picture, this work also represents one of the high points of Dutch landscape painting of the seventeenth century.[1] The scene — a path winding along a river at the foot of a range of hills, with a town visible in the distance — was inspired by the area along the Rhine between Nijmegen and Cleves, where Cuyp had traveled in the early 1650s. On the sandy path that extends from the immediate foreground, past a herd of resting cows, an elegantly dressed rider has stopped to speak to the cowherd. From the latter's gesture, one may surmise that the horseman has asked for directions. Ahead of the rider walks a man, and just beyond, a shepherdess tends to a flock of sheep. The warm light of the late afternoon sun suffuses the entire picture, shrouding the distant scenery in Cuyp's characteristic golden haze, which depicts the effect of moisture in the air. The foreground figures, animals, and trees cast long shadows across the path. The light, coming diagonally from behind, creates a *contre-jour* effect, which emphasizes the contours of the figures, animals, and plants with bright silvery highlights. Nothing, it seems, could disturb the sense of peace and tranquility that pervades the scene — until the gun of the barely noticeable duck hunter crouching in the left foreground goes off!

It has been suggested that the confrontation between an elegant figure on horseback, most likely of elevated social position, and a simple herdsman (a recurring motif in Cuyp's paintings) was meant to underscore the former's superiority. He would

have been the figure in the painting with whom the artist's wealthy patrons would have easily identified.[2] However, this interpretation relies on a view of herders and shepherds as lowly and inferior. Contemporary pastoral literature, on the other hand, often celebrated the "wise herder" and his simple and virtuous life by contrasting it with the potentially corrupt life of the ambitious courtier.[3]

Although this scene was inspired by views Cuyp had encountered and recorded during his trip along the Rhine, nothing indicates that it was meant to be topographically accurate. Indeed the tall mountains seem entirely imaginary.[4] This type of artistic license is not unusual; Cuyp occasionally embellished actual views he had recorded in his sketchbook (see cat. 38). The lighting and the composition, particularly the screen of trees, are similar to those in *Evening Landscape* in the British Royal Collection (cat. 44) and appear to have been inspired by Cuyp's renewed interest in the work of Jan Both.

The common impression that this picture was the first painting by Cuyp to enter the United Kingdom when it was bought by William Baillie, who thereby set off a craze for Cuyp's pictures among English collectors, is based on a discussion between Benjamin West and Joseph Farington during their visit to the British Institution exhibition of 1818.[5] However, if one is to believe Noel Desenfans, the dealer who bought several paintings by Cuyp for the collection of the king of Poland, works by the master had already been

imported into England in 1740 by a Swiss merchant.[6]

Very early on, the picture was held in high regard in England, where John Boydell published a laudatory description of it in 1769. This passage, which accompanies *A View on the Maese near Maastricht*, a print of 1764 by William Elliott (see Chong essay, fig. 7), refers to Cuyp as the "Dutch Claude," a label that was to stay with Cuyp until well into the nineteenth century.[7]

The print by Elliott, which not only shows the sky extending farther at the top but also gives the dimensions of the pictures as 60 by 65 inches, has raised the question of whether the painting was cut along the top in the late eighteenth or early nineteenth century. However, careful examination in the conservation studio of the National Gallery, London, has shown that the picture's original unpainted edges are intact on all four sides. Possible explanations for the discrepancy between the painting and Elliott's print are that either the painting at one stage had an addition at the top or that the engraver simply applied artistic license when he copied the work.[8] Unfortunately no preparatory drawings, which might provide further clues, have been identified for the print.[9] However, even without the extension, the picture is the largest painting Cuyp ever executed. Although nothing is known about its original whereabouts, it most likely was destined for the grand home of one of Cuyp's wealthy patrons from Dordrecht's regent class — a world the artist himself had joined by this time. **AR**

River Landscape with Horseman and Peasants

I

Orpheus Charming the Animals

c. 1640, oil on canvas, 113 × 167 (44 ½ × 65 ¾).
Private collection, Boston

Inscription

Signed, lower right: *A. cuyp*

Provenance

Probably Johan van Nispen; (probably sale, The Hague,
12 September 1768, lot 5). Probably Hendrik Verschuuring;
(probably sale, The Hague, 17 September 1770, lot 38,
to Lemmens). Harper family, London. Private collection,
Madrid; (sale, Sotheby's, London, 6 July 1994, lot 8, to
Johnny van Haeften, Konrad Bernheimer, Artemis Ltd.,
and Otto Naumann); private collection

Exhibitions

Amsterdam 2000a

Literature

Chong 1994b, 30 – 31, repro.

Endnotes

1. See Sluijter 1986, 295 – 339.

2. Müllenmeister 1988, 129 – 132, nos. 203 – 225. Arnold
Houbraken specifically praised Savery's paintings of
Orpheus; Houbraken 1718 – 1721 (1753 ed.), 1: 58 – 59.

3. Müllenmeister 1988, 129 – 132, no. 203. Müllenmeister
believed this was Savery's earliest depiction of Orpheus.

4. Van de Passe 1973. The jaguars appear in plate 20,
an etching by Robert de Vorst after Savery.

5. Jacob Cuyp's painting, which is signed and dated 1639
(Sotheby's, New York, January 2001), indicates how closely
father and son were working at this period. Although Jacob
was the senior artist, there is no reason to believe that he
took up the subject first. In 1994, I believed that the 1639

painting of jaguars by Jacob Cuyp suggested that the jaguars
in the exhibited work were also by Jacob (Chong 1994b, 31),
but when the paintings were brought together at the Dordrechts Museum in 1995, it was evident that the jaguars in
the large Orpheus were entirely by Aelbert.

6. See Lloyd 1971, 16, 32, 61, 88.

7. For example, Rembrandt had the opportunity to see and
sketch an elephant, a lion, and a camel. See Benesch 1973,
nos. 453, 454, 457 – 459; 1211 – 1216; Schatborn in Amsterdam, Berlin, and London 1991 – 1992, no. 13.

8. "Wtlegghinghe op den Metamorphoseon Pub. Ovidij
Naso…" in Van Mander 1604; fols. 83 – 86 are devoted
to Orpheus.

9. Van Mander 1604: "Wtlegghinghe," fol. 84r.

10. For example, a pamphlet discussing the 1609 truce:
*Afbeedlinge vanden Oude ende Nieuwentijt waer met Orpheus
wandelt, spreekt, singt ende speelt* (c. 1615); catalogued in
Muller 1863, no. 1302C.

11. Cuyp's painting is recorded in the 1696 inventory of
Albertina Agnes van Nassau (daughter of Amalia van Solms
and Frederik Hendrik), who inherited nearly all of her
paintings from her mother. See Drossaers and Lunsingh
Scheurleer 1974 – 1976, 2: 223.

12. Willem Goeree in 1670 exhorted artists, "In particular,
one must take the chance to observe the exotic, such as
lions, tigers, bears, elephants, camels, and similar animals,
which one rarely sets eyes on, and which must be had for
one's inventions." Goeree 1670, 121. A depiction of Orpheus
could form the introductory vignette to a series of prints
showing various animals, as found in Roger Danell's
Animalium quadrupedum, avium of 1628.

2

Open Countryside with Shepherds and Animals

c. 1640, oil on panel, 40 × 59 (15 ¾ × 23 ¼).
The Trustees of Dulwich Picture Gallery, London (348)

Inscription

Signed, lower right: *A cůÿp*

Provenance

Noel Desenfans (collected for the king of Poland);
(sale, London, 18 March 1802, no. 158); Francis Bourgeois;
bequeathed to the Dulwich Picture Gallery 1811

Exhibitions

London 1947, no. 8; London 1952, no. 358; London 1973,
no. 1

Literature

Smith 1829 – 1842, 5 (1834): 306, no. 77; Dulwich Picture
Gallery 1858, no. 192 (as after Cuyp); Richter and Sparkes
1880, no. 192; HdG 1907 – 1927, 2 (1909): nos. 239 and 697;
Reiss 1975, 43, no. 15; Murray 1980, 48 – 49; Chong 1992,
273 – 274, no. 12; Beresford 1998, 82 – 83, no. 34

Endnotes

1. HdG 1907 – 1927, 2 (1909): 208.

2. Paulus Potter used a similar device: his cows turn away
from the viewer and, standing on a ridge, stare into a landscape that remains largely hidden. See for example his *Bull*,
signed and dated 1649 (Gemäldegalerie, Staatliche Museen
zu Berlin, inv. no. 872B; The Hague 1994, 31, fig. 22).

3. J. P. Richter in the catalogue of the Dulwich Picture
Gallery was the first to identify the painting as an early work
by Cuyp in the style of Jan van Goyen (Richter and Sparkes
1880, no. 192). The earlier catalogues of 1859 and 1876 had
dismissed it as a copy. See also Chong 1991, 606, note 2.

4. Commonly, the *Dune Landscape* of 1631 (Herzog Anton Ulrich-Museum, Braunschweig, inv. no. 340; Beck 1973, no. 1110) is cited as a related example. Chong 1992, 255, has observed similarities in the "brushing in of blue patches among the swirling clouds." Other examples include a *Dune Landscape*, signed and dated 1629 (Städelsches Kunstinstitut, Frankfurt, inv. no. 1271; Beck 1973, no. 1077) and a *Dune Landscape* from a private collection, signed and dated 1630 (Beck 1973, no. 1081; Leiden 1996, no. 12).

5. *Road through Dunes*, signed, destroyed (formerly Kaiser-Friedrich-Museum, Berlin, inv. no. 861G; Chong 1992, no. 11).

6. The cattle also relate to a slightly earlier picture in a private collection (*Milking near a River with an Alley of Trees*, Reiss 1975, 27, no. 2; Chong 1992, 268, no. 3), to a drawing in the British Museum (*Pasture with Cattle*, Hind 1915–1932, 33, inv. no. Gg 2-294; see also Chong 1991, 606–608, figs. 41 and 44), and to a much earlier painting in another British private collection (*Farm Scene with a Panorama*, Chong 1992, no. 7; see also sale, Amsterdam, Sotheby's, 14 November 1990, no. 89). It has also been suggested, albeit less convincingly, that the somewhat awkward anatomy of Cuyp's "spiny and curvaceous" cows may have originated from the paintings of Cornelis van Poelenburch (1594–1667) (Chong 1992, 254).

7. Reiss 1975, 43 and Beresford 1998, 83. Comparable goats also occur in the *River Valley with Panorama*, signed and dated 1639 (private collection, The Netherlands; Chong 1991, 607, fig. 40; Chong 1992, 269, no. 6).

3
Portrait of a Family in a Landscape

Jacob and Aelbert Cuyp, 1641, oil on canvas, 155 × 245 (61 × 96 ⁷⁄₁₆). Collection the Israel Museum, Jerusalem, Gift of Mr. and Mrs. Joseph R. Nash, Paris (166.4.65)

Inscription
Signed by Jacob Cuyp, lower center: *JG. cuijp Fecit / Aᵒ. 1641* (*JG* ligated, partially effaced); the age of each figure is inscribed below it, except for the two figures at the far left and far right: *AE 22* (or *23*), *AE 11*, *AE 20*, *AE 58*, *AEtatis 49*, *AE 15*, *AE 13*

Provenance
Alphonse de Rothschild, Ferrières, by 1892; by descent to Edouard de Rothschild, Paris (seized by German forces in 1941, returned in 1946); (sale, Charpentier, Paris, 2 December 1952, no. 66). Mr. and Mrs. Joseph Nash, Paris; The Israel Museum, Jerusalem (Gift of Madeleine and Joseph R. Nash, Paris), 1965

Exhibitions
Dordrecht 1977, no. 17, repro.

Literature
Michel 1892, 14–15, 18; Von Wurzbach 1906–1911, 1 (1906): 369; Heyligers 1924, 219, no. 64; Reiss 1953, 45, note 2; Burnett 1969, 372; Van Gelder and Jost 1969, 100–102, fig. 7; Van Gelder and Jost 1972, note 10; Reiss 1975, no. 16; Sullivan 1984, 44, fig. 75; Amsterdam 1987, 291, fig. 2; Chong 1992, no. 17; Lewitt 1995, 164

Endnotes
1. Chong 1991, 606–612.

2. The painting lacks the moralizing element often discerned in Dutch portraits. On the interpretation of grapes as symbols of virginity and chastity, see De Jongh 1974; on fertility, see Bedaux 1990, 71–108. For an erotic interpretation of birds, see De Jongh 1968–1969.

3. Burnett 1969 as well as Van Gelder and Jost 1972 later concluded that the figures in the painting were by Jacob Cuyp and the landscape by Aelbert. Reiss 1953 had already implied as much. The signature is Jacob Cuyp's, although the initial monogram had later been effaced and changed into an *A*, an addition removed in 1966.

4. Gemeente Archief, Dordrecht: ONA 262, f. 37–38, 69r; ONA 172, f. 213v. A painting that is probably a group portrait by Jacob Cuyp dated 1641 appeared in the sale of Jacob Hendrik Voet, The Hague, 25 September 1780, no. 62, "De Aankomst van Vader Jacob met zyne Zoonen, beneevens Vrouwen en Kinderen by Joseph, door J. Kuyp, Ao. 1641," 13.5 guilders to Fouquet, which suggests that the painting was sent to France, where this work was first recorded.

4
Cattle and Cottage near a River

early 1640s, oil on panel, 43.5 × 74 (17 ⅛ × 29 ⅛). Museum Boijmans Van Beuningen, Rotterdam (no. 2490)

Inscription
Center on plank: *A. cuyp*

Provenance
(Asscher and Welker, London, 1925); D.G. van Beuningen, Vierhouten; Museum Boijmans Van Beuningen, Rotterdam, 1958

Exhibitions
Rotterdam 1949, no. 43, repro.; Paris 1952, no. 87; Rotterdam 1955, no. 55, repro.

Literature
Stechow 1960a, 87; Boymans-van Beuningen 1972, 208, repro.; Reiss 1975, 38, no. 10, repro.; Chong 1992, 280–281, no. 21

Endnotes

1. For a discussion of the importance of peat for the Dutch economy, see De Vries 1986, 83–84. De Vries also noted that in the area north of Rotterdam, peat was generally found under water level, thus its production altered the character of the land by creating new lakes.

2. See, in particular, Levesque 1994, 38–39. Levesque cited, and illustrated, another important early seventeenth-century map that includes Visscher's images of peat: Herman Allertsz' *Land Caerte ende Water Caerte van Noordt Hollandt ende West Vrieslandt met de aenliggende Lande* (1608).

3. Royalton-Kisch 1988, 102 and 254.

4. This extraordinary album is in the British Museum. For Van de Venne's three images related to the peat industry, see Royalton-Kisch 1988, 252–256. In 1634, the artist/poet also wrote a humorous poem, *Sinne-Vonck op den Hollandtschen turf*…(1634, The Hague), about a farmer smoking tobacco on a peat boat and the comic fears that fire was threatening the cargo.

5
Cattle and Herders, with Mariakerk, Utrecht

early 1640s, oil on panel, 49 × 74 (19 5/16 × 29 1/8). Residenzgalerie Salzburg, Salzburg (534)

Inscription
Signed, lower right: *A cuyp. Fec*

Provenance
Graf (Count) Rudolf Dzernin, Vienna, 1844; by descent; Residenzgalerie, Salzburg, 1980

Literature
HdG 1907–1927, 2 (1909): no. 712; Stechow 1960a, 86 (as very early Van Goyen); Van Gelder and Jost 1969, 100,

101, fig. 8; Reiss 1975, 39, no. 11; Washington, Denver, and Fort Worth 1977, 66; Salzburg 1980, 52, pl. 17; Chong 1992, 283, no. 25

Endnotes

1. Chong 1992, 86–87.

2. See for example the *View of Utrecht with the Pellekussenpoort* (Musée des Beaux-Arts, Strasbourg, inv. no. 539; Chong 1992, no. 15); and a depiction of the *Duitsche Huis and Maria-kerk* (private collection; Chong 1992, no. 57). For a more detailed discussion of Cuyp's depictions of Utrecht see Van Gelder and Jost 1969, 100–103.

3. Hofstede de Groot already identified the church as the Mariakerk "set in a fanciful landscape" (HdG 1907–1927, 2 [1909]: 211).

4. Chong 1992, 283. See also the much earlier *Milking near a River with an Alley* (private collection; Reiss 1975, 27, no. 2; Chong 1992, 268, no. 3).

5. Van Gelder and Jost 1969, 101.

6. See also Chong 1992, 283. He observed that Cuyp remained "faithful to many small details of the [landscape] sketch."

6
River Landscape with Bridge

early 1640s, oil on panel, 40.3 × 54.9 (15 7/8 × 21 5/8). Graphische Sammlung im Städelsches Kunstinstitut, Frankfurt am Main (1242)

Inscription
Lower right: *A.. cúÿp.*

Provenance
Moritz Gontard, Frankfurt, by 1869; Städelsches Kunst-institut (Moritz Gontard bequest), Frankfurt, 1892

Exhibitions
Munich 1869, no. 185

Literature
Burnett 1969, 372, repro.; Reiss 1975, no. 18, 46, repro.; Chong 1992, no. 23, 282; Sander and Brinkmann 1995, 27

Endnotes

1. For the importance of the wood trade for Dordrecht's economy, see Chong 1992, 168–171. Dordrecht achieved much of its wealth as a trading center for wood, which was floated there as rafts from Germany. For a comparable boat hook in an image by Adriaen van de Venne (1589–1662), see Royalton-Kisch 1988, 338–339.

2. Cuyp did not reveal the purpose for the logs (whether, for example, they were to be used for building materials or for burning to make charcoal); the answers to these questions, however, would probably have been self-evident to his contemporaries.

3. This print on the deceitfulness of Spain and the liberty and prosperity of Holland illustrated the title page of an anonymous pamphlet, *Merckt de Wysheyt vermaert vant Hollantsche huyshouwen en siet des luypaerts aert die net is te vertrouwen* (published 1615). For an excellent discussion of the print, see Levesque 1994, 75–80.

4. Virgil's ideas were well known in the Netherlands through the writings of a number of early seventeenth-century Dutch poets. See, in particular, the *Nederduytschen helicon* (Helicon 1610).

7
A River Scene with Distant Windmills

early 1640s, oil on panel, 35.6 × 52.4 (14 × 20 5/8). The National Gallery, London (2545)

188

Inscription

Signed, bottom right corner: *A cuÿp*.

Provenance

Charles Bredel; Miss Bredel; (sale, Christie's, London, 1 May 1875, no. 111, to Rutley). Jean Louis Miéville; (sale, Christie's, London, 29 April 1899, no. 60, bought by Thomas Agnew & Sons); George Salting, London; The National Gallery, London (Salting Bequest), 1910

Exhibitions

London 1841, no. 59 (according to Chong 1992); London 1903, no. 82; Stoke-on-Trent 1928; London 1973, no. 3; London 1976, no. 24

Literature

Waagen 1854, 2: 292 (as style of Van Goyen); HdG 1907 – 1927, 2 (1909): nos. 638, 667, 677; MacLaren 1960, 90 – 91, no. 2545; London 1973, no. 3; Reiss 1975, 47, no. 19; Brown 1979, 32, 34, pl. 32; Brown 1990, 87, 89; MacLaren and Brown 1991, 1: 94 – 95, 2: pl. 81; Chong 1992, 281 – 282, no. 22

Endnotes

1. On the mount of a photo of the picture at the Rijksbureau voor Kunsthistorische Documentatie (RKD) in The Hague, the village has been identified as Beverwijck, a town Cuyp had depicted in his *View of Beverwijck* (Harold Samuel Collection, London; Reiss 1975, 37, no. 9; Chong 1992, no. 19). Indeed the church towers in both pictures bear a certain resemblance with that town's church, but it is not clear whether Cuyp had intended to depict a recognizable location in the present painting. Without giving any specific reasons, MacLaren and Brown 1991, 94, have argued that "it seems unlikely that Cuyp intended to show a precise topographical location." Also, it is unclear whether the cluster of windmills on the horizon has been taken from an existing example. Their relative remoteness in the scene makes it unlikely that they were intended to carry any symbolic connotations. Recognizable as a characteristic feature of the Dutch landscape, they were probably simply used as a compositional device to enliven the horizon.

2. Hamburg, Kunsthalle, inv. no. 21.822.

3. See Reiss in London 1973, no. 3. Reiss 1975, 47, even notes: "Cuyp never came closer to the plein-air technique of the Impressionists, nor painted a picture more daring in its simplicity."

4. Evidently river fishing represented an important source of income for Dordrecht's economy, for the fish caught were exported to England. See Dordrecht 1992, 35.

5. See also Chong 1992, 257 – 258.

6. Chong 1992, 281; *Landscape*, Kröller-Müller Museum, Otterlo.

8
A Pier in Dordrecht Harbor

early 1640s, oil on panel, 44.5 × 75.5 (17 ½ × 29 ¾).
Mr. and Mrs. George M. Kaufman

Inscription

Signed, lower right (on pier): *A. Cuyp*

Provenance

(Sale, Jeronimo de Vries, Amsterdam, 10 May 1853, no. 16). Herman de Kat, Dordrecht (sale, Lamme, Petit, Paris, 2 May 1866, no. 17). Louis Viardot, Paris (sale, Féral, Paris, 30 April 1884, no. 2); Alfred Thieme, Leipzig, by 1889. (Galerie Sedelmeyer, Paris). Private collection, Basel (sale, Christie's, London, 20 November 1973, no. 124); (Brod Gallery, London, 1974); (Julie Kraus, Paris, 1976). (Sale, Christie's, London, 18 April 1985, no. 2); Mr. and Mrs. George M. Kaufman, Norfolk, Virginia

Exhibitions

Leipzig 1889, no. 44

Literature

HdG 1907 – 1927, 2 (1909): 635, 662.; Reiss 1975, 49; Chong 1992, 284 – 285, no. 28

Endnotes

1. For an illustration of Cuyp's earliest depiction of a pier, *The Melkpoortje on the Dordrecht Harbor*, 1639, see Wheelock essay, fig. 12. For further information about this painting, see Chong 1992, 268, no. 4.

2. Reiss 1975, 56, was the first author to suggest De Vlieger's influence on Cuyp for the depiction of such scenes.

9
The Baptism of the Eunuch

c. 1642 – 1643, oil on canvas, 108 × 151.1 (42 ½ × 59 ½).
The Menil Collection, Houston (CA 6140)

Inscription

Signed, lower left of center (on log): *A cuÿp*

Provenance

Probably widow of C. S. Roos; (sale, R. W. P. de Vries, Roos, Amsterdam, 26 November 1827, no. 71, to Gruyter). Alexander Cuninghame, Craigends, Renfrewshire (mid-1800s); by descent to Mrs. A. Cuninghame (sale, Christie's, London, 11 July 1930, no. 89, unsold); by descent to John Charles Cuninghame, Craigends; by descent to his widow's sister, Helen Laura Pearson; (sale, Christie's, London, 24 November 1961, no. 12); (Hanover Gallery, London); Dominique de Ménil, Houston and New York

Exhibitions

Houston 1971 – 1972, 19 (as "unattributed 17th century"); Jerusalem 2000, no. 35

Literature

HdG 1907 – 1927, 2 (1909): no. 11a; Reiss 1975, no. 6; *The Menil Collection* 1987, 106 – 110; Musée des Beaux-Arts de Bordeaux 1990, 252 – 253 (as Cornelis Saftleven); Chong 1992, no. 35

Endnotes

1. Bartsch 1803 – 1821, 2: no. 12. See Bruyn in *Corpus* 1982 –, 1 (1983): 35 – 51; a painted copy formerly in Oldenburg is reproduced in fig. 4.

2. No painting of the Baptism of the Eunuch by Benjamin Cuyp is known, but his depictions of the Adoration of the Magi in the Konstmuseum, Göteborg (Ember 1979, no. 18), and in the Dordrechts Museum (inv. 985 / 606) are influenced by Rembrandt's composition.

3. The Getty Provenance Index database records twenty-eight references in Holland between 1627 and 1710, all of which identify the subject as the "Moorman" or "Moor." Literary sources only rarely call the figure "kamerling" (chamberlain), the preferred modern Dutch rendering.

4. John Calvin, *Harmonia* (Leiden, 1582). This is a translation of *Commentarii integri in acta apostolorum* (Geneva, 1552 – 1554). Also see Calvin 1965.

5. Stephen Reiss dated the exhibited painting and cat. 10 to 1639 – 1640 and rejected several large canvases from the period 1642 – 1645 (Reiss 1975, 32 – 33, 83 – 105).

10
A Farm with Cottages and Animals

c. 1642 – 1643, oil on canvas, 105 × 155 (41 5/16 × 61). Private collection

Inscription

Signed, lower center: *A cuÿp*

Provenance

Probably Hendrick Verschuring; (probably sale, Rietmulder, The Hague, 17 September 1770, no. 39, to Lemmens). John Blackwood (sale, Christie's, London, 20 February 1778, no. 2: 77); 2d earl of Ilchester, Redlynch House, then Melbury Park, Dorset; by descent to Lady Teresa Agnew, daughter of the 7th earl. Private collection

Exhibitions

London 1973, no. 5; Dordrecht 1977, no. 18; Amsterdam 1987, no. 20

Literature

HdG 1907 – 1927, 2 (1909): nos. 228b, 699; Reiss 1975, 33, no. 7; Plomp 1986, 146 – 147, note 7; Chong 1992, 292, no. 36

Endnotes

1. HdG 1907 – 1927, 2 (1909): 209, no. 699. The picture at the Musée des Beaux-Arts et d'Archéologie in Besançon is *A Farm*, signed and dated 1639, inv. no. 840.8.1 (Reiss 1975, 26, no. 1; Chong 1992, 267 – 268, no. 2).

2. Reiss in London 1973, no. 5, and Reiss 1975, 33, no. 7; Dordrecht 1977, 64 – 65, no. 18.

3. Amsterdam, Boston, and Philadelphia 1987, 291.

4. Chong 1992, 292.

11
Wooded Landscape with an Artist

c. 1643, oil on canvas, 98.5 × 136 (38 ¾ × 53 9/16). Wadsworth Atheneum, Hartford, Gift of Dr. and Mrs. Charles C. Beach, Charles B. Curtis, Mr. and Mrs. Eugene L. Garbaty, Dr. Francis Goodwin, Walter K. Gutman, Mrs. Walter Keney, Lyman Mills, in memory of Mr. and Mrs. Clement Scott by their children, Mrs. H. K. Welch and Horace B. Clark, Mrs. Charles B. Wood, Hans Wreidt, Bequest of Warren H. Lowenhaupt, The Ella Gallup Sumner and Mary Catlin Sumner Collection Fund by exchange; The Ella Gallup Sumner and Mary Catlin Sumner Collection Fund, the Douglas Tracy Smith and Dorothy Potter Smith Fund, and the Evelyn Bonar Storrs Trust Fund (1996.26.1)

Inscription

Signed, lower right: *A. cuyp f.*

Provenance

Miss P. M. Young, Faringdon, 1942. (Thomas Agnew & Sons, London). Prof. Singer, London. (P. de Boer, Amsterdam, by 1954). Mrs. Morris Dalinon; (sale, Sotheby's, 27 March 1968, no. 49). (Sale, Sotheby's, 13 July 1977, no. 15). (Noortman Gallery, Maastricht, by 1996); Wadsworth Atheneum, Hartford

Literature

Burlington Magazine 1942, 81: 259, fig. A

Endnotes

1. Chong 1992, 432, B6, has noted that the sketching figure is close to that in *The Huis te Merwede, with an Artist in a Boat*, Musée des Beaux-Arts, Château des Rohan, Strasbourg (Chong 1992, 430 – 431, B4; ill. in Reiss 1975, 105, no. 70).

2. Reiss 1975, 104, believed that the painting was a collaboration between Cuyp and a staffage painter who executed the burghers. He associated their style with Dordrecht genre painters Jan Olis (c. 1610 – 1676) and J. F. van der Merck (c. 1610 – 1664).

3. For the original Dutch of this poem by P. C. Ketel, which introduces Van Mander 1604, see essay by Wheelock, note 18. The English translation is taken from Buijsen in Leiden 1993, 47.

4. Before seeing the painting, Chong doubted its attribution because he considered the execution "too rough and clumsy for Cuyp." See Chong 1992, 432, B6.

5. The shapes of the men's hats, collars, cloaks, and boots are consistent with costumes worn during the first half of the 1640s. For example, the turned-up front brim of the hat worn by the burgher on the left is comparable to that worn by an unknown man portrayed by Frans Hals in 1644 (Amsterdam, Six Collection). See Slive 1970–1974, 2: pl. 242.

6. See Stechow 1966, 69–70, figs. 129, 131, 132, 133.

12
Dordrecht Harbor by Moonlight

c. 1643–1645, oil on panel, 76.5 × 106.5 (30 ⅛ × 41 ¹⁵⁄₁₆). Wallraf-Richartz-Museum, Cologne

Inscription
Signed, lower left: *A. cuyp*

Provenance
Probably Mattheus vanden Broucke; by descent to his widow Elisabeth Francken, by 1729; by descent to Margarita vander Burch; by descent to Johan vanden Broucke, by 1731; earl of Halifax (sale, Christie's, London, 19 April 1782, no. 68); William Nisbet (sale, Coxe, London, 25 February 1802, no. 70). William Prideaux, by 1823. Wynn Ellis, London, by 1862 (sale, Christie's, London, 27 February 1876, no. 14); Adolph von Carstanjen, Cologne, to Wilhelm Adolph von Carstanjen, Berlin, bequest to Wallraf-Richartz-Museum, Cologne, 1936

Exhibitions
London 1862, no. 122; Cologne 1876, no. 58; Berlin 1890, no. 36; Essen 1938, no. 6, repro.; Cologne 1946–1947, no. 24, repro.; Cologne 1954, no. 6

Literature
Bode 1890, 235; Michel 1892, 228; Von Wurzbach 1906–1911, 54; Walpole 1927, 68; Bode 1956, 266, 284, repro.; Stechow 1966, 181, repro.; Vey 1968; Farington 1978–1984, 5, 781; Repp-Eckert 1989, 50–52, 67, repro.; Chong 1991, 610, repro.; Chong 1992, 306–308, no. 60

Endnotes
1. Houbraken 1718–1721, 1: 248–249.

2. Houbraken 1718–1721, 1: 248. "Ossen, Koeijen, Schapen, Paerden, Fruit, Landschap, stil water met Scheepen; 't scheen hem alles onverschillig te wezen, en daar men zig over verwonderen moet, is, dat hy alles even fraai en natuurlyk schilderde. Daarenboven heeft hy inzondeheid wel in agt genomen de tydstonden waar in hy de voorwerpen verbeelde, zoo dat men den benevelden morgenstond van den klaren middag, en dezen weer van den saffraan-werwigen avondstond in zyn tafereelen kost onderscheiden. Ook heb ik verscheide maanligten van hem gezien die heel natuurlyk verbeeld waren, en zoo geschikt dat dezelve een aangename spiegeling in't water maakten." The English translation is taken from Reiss 1975, 198.

3. Reiss 1975, 65, identified two night scenes that are currently lost (his catalogue numbers 75 and 77). See also Chong 1992, 306, no. 59; 310–311, no. 62, 63.

4. This document, first published by Chong 1992, 307–308, records "een blixim van Kuyp / een Maneschijn van deselve."

5. In Montias 1987 and Montias 1990, the argument is made that economic factors influenced an artist's decision to introduce new subject matter and develop new stylistic modes of painting. This theory was expanded in Sluijter 1996, 52–54, in reference to the innovations of Jan van Goyen. These theories were modified in Falkenburg 1997, who questioned whether seventeenth-century viewers were aware of different categories of landscape painting. See also Montias 1987, 455–466; Montias 1990, 49–57.

6. See Buijsen in Leiden 1993, 170–171. Buijsen noted that Van Goyen painted eight scenes of thunderstorms between 1641 and 1647. His first moonlit scene dates to 1643 (Strasbourg, Musée des Beaux-Arts).

7. See Melion 1991, 73–75.

8. This point is made by Falkenburg 1997, 144. The English translation of Angel's text is taken from Angel 1996, 137.

9. See Falkenburg 1996–1997, 60–69.

10. Falkenburg 1997, 135, note 67, also mentioned that a series ("een reeks") of moonlight scenes by Maerten van der Hulst (active 1630–1645) and Pieter Molyn (1595–1661) are recorded in Haarlem archival documents from the late 1640s.

13
Landscape with Shepherds and Shepherdesses

c. 1643–1645, oil on panel, 77.5 × 107.5 (30 ½ × 42 ⁵⁄₁₆). Private collection, Belgium

Inscription
Signed, lower left: *A: cuijp*

Provenance
Mrs. Cosmo Bevan (sale, Robinson, Fisher & Harding, London, 10 November 1938, no. 178). Rita Bellesi, New York, by 1950; (Frederick Mount, New York, 1951). (Newhouse Galleries, New York, by 1978); S. T. Fee, Oklahoma City (sale, Christie's, New York, 9 May 1985, lot 9, bought in); (sale, Sotheby's, New York, 4 June 1987, lot 69); (Johnny van Haeften, London); private collection; (Noortman, Maastricht); private collection

Exhibitions
Fort Worth 1982, no. 4

Literature

Buchanan 1824, 1: 282, no. 26; Reiss 1975, 71, no. 38; Dordrecht 1977, 132, note 1

Endnotes

1. Krul 1634b, 142 – 143. "Onlanghs geleden, eer dat de Zon / Van's Hemels-top zijn gulde stralen / Liet over 't vochtigh Aerdrijck dalen: / Sagh ick mijn beminde Galathee / Komen drijven met haer Vee / Van de Kouwe dorre strand, / Barrevoets door 't natte zand, / Na de heyden, om te weyden / Hare Schaepjes, na 't begraesde Land."

2. For a comparable view of this hill, see the painting of the *Battle of Schenkenschanz* (1629, Gemeentemuseum Arnhem), by Pauwels van Hillegaert (1595 – 1640), ill. in Dattenberg 1967, 234 – 235.

3. Reiss 1975, 71, no. 38, describes this structure as a well. Deys 1981, 59, fig. 167, identifies the site as the Tafelberg near Rhenen. It would seem unlikely, however, that this structure is the Koningstafel (see cat. 17), since that stone marker had a square top. Deys 1981, 59, fig. 166, illustrates an anonymous drawing of a square stone table that includes the following handwritten inscription: "a stadt Reene b des Conincks v. bohemens taeffel op den Rondebergh c den Rijn fluv d dorp."

4. Sumowski 1979, 2, 686, no. 321, ill.

5. Reiss 1975, 75, no. 42.

6. Dordrecht 1977, 150 – 151, no. 59, repro.

7. Dordrecht 1977, 158 – 159, no. 63, repro.

14
Herdsmen with Cattle

c. 1645, oil on canvas, 99 × 144 (39 × 56 11/16).
The Trustees of Dulwich Picture Gallery, London (128)

Provenance

Probably Michael Bryan; (probably sale, Coxe, Burrell & Foster, London, 17 May 1798, no. 3:39). Francis Bourgeois, London; bequeathed to the Dulwich Picture Gallery 1811

Exhibitions

London 1824, no. 72; London 1903, no. 97; London 1952, no. 185; The Hague and London 1970 – 1971, no. 57

Literature

Smith 1829 – 1842, 5 (1834): 302, no. 65 and 306, no. 80; Dulwich Picture Gallery 1858, no. 169; Richter and Sparkes 1880, no. 169; HdG 1907 – 1927, 2 (1909): no. 237e and no. 330; Reiss 1975, 77, no. 44; Murray 1980, 48, no. 128, repro.; Chong 1992, 257, 323 – 325, no. 80; Beresford 1998, 83, 128

Endnotes

1. See, for example, *Ubbergen Castle* (cat. 31), *Ice Scene before the Huis te Merwede near Dordrecht* (cat. 32), *Dordrecht from the North* (cats. 35, 36), *River Landscape with two Horsemen* (cat. 42), and *River Landscape with Horseman and Peasants* (cat. 45).

2. Hazlitt 1824, 30. See also Hazlitt 1942, 669. Peter George Patmore (1824, 171) used remarkably similar terms in his description of the painting in the same year: "It seems all — cattle, men, ground, hills, clouds, and all — made of woven air and sunshine. There are no marks of the pencil about it. You cannot tell how it got there — unless, as I before said, it has been *breathed* there."

3. Ruskin wrote, "Now I dare say that the sky of this first-rate Cuyp is very like an unripe nectarine: all that I have to say about it is that it is exceedingly unlike a sky. The blue remains unchanged and ungraduated over three-fourths of it, down to the horizon, while the sun, in the left-hand corner, is surrounded with a halo, first of yellow and then of crude pink, both being separated from each other, and the last from the blue, as sharply as the belts of a rainbow…There is no such thing — there never was, and never will be such a thing, while God's heaven remains as it is made — as a serene sunset sky with its purple and rose *belts* around the sun." Ruskin also included a more personal attack on the artist: "Now it is difficult to conceive how any man calling himself a painter could impose such a thing on the public, and still more how the public can receive it." See Ruskin 1843, 1: part 2, section 3, chapter 1, paragraph 11; Ruskin 1903 – 1912, 3 (1903): 350; and Ruskin 1987, 91 – 92. See also Beresford 1998, 83, and Waterfield 1988, 22, 48.

4. See for example *Landscape with a View of Beverwijck*, (Harold Samuel Collection, Mansion House, London; Reiss 1975, 37, no. 9; Chong 1992, 279 – 280, no. 19); *Cattle and Herders, with Mariakerk, Utrecht* (cat. 5); *River Landscape with Bridge* (cat. 6); *Herdsmen and Cattle near Rhenen* (Dulwich Picture Gallery, London, inv. no. 4; Reiss 1975, 75, no. 42; Chong 1992, 315 – 316, no. 68). While Reiss (1975, 77) had suggested that the picture "can be connected with Cuyp's etchings" Chong has argued that the standing cow may be similar but not identical to the one in the print illustrated by Reiss (Hollstein 4; Chong 1992, 324). Also, the herder seen from the back appears in a painting attributed to Cuyp of *Shepherds Overlooking Amersfoort* of before 1651 (Von der Heydt-Museum, Wuppertal, inv. no. G 198; Reiss 1975, 52, no. 24; Chong 1992, 431 – 432, no. B5, who doubts the attribution).

5. Even though Houbraken celebrated Cuyp's ability to depict convincingly specific times of day, some earlier descriptions of the painting have confused the hour shown as early morning. Smith identified the scene as "representing the morning of a fine summer's day" (Smith 1829 – 1842, 5 [1834]: 302, no. 65). Hofstede de Groot mentioned the picture twice, referring to it as "a fine summer morning" and as "a blue sky, with red evening tints to the left" respectively (HdG 1907 – 1927, 2 [1909]: 78, no. 237e and 101, no. 330).

6. See also Chong 1992, 324.

7. Chong 1992, 256 – 257.

8. Peter George Patmore, writing in the same year as William Hazlitt, had already noted this aspect when he referred to the painting as "a more apt idea of the Golden Age of classical poets than all the classical work expressly intended to typify it — even those of Claude and Poussin, and this notwithstanding the perfect truth of the details introduced in them, and above all, the rude and altogether modern character of the figures, and the dresses they wear" (Patmore 1824, 171). For more on this subject, see also the essay by Arthur Wheelock in this catalogue.

15
Woman in a Stable

1645 – 1648, oil on panel, 65 × 92 (25 ⁹/₁₆ × 36 ¼).
Dordrechts Museum (DM / 983 / 580)

Inscription
Signed, lower right[7]: *A. cuyp*

Provenance
Perhaps Woollett; (sale, Christie's, London, 8 May 1813, no. 48, to Philip Hill). Comte de Morny, Paris; (sale, Phillips, London, 20 June 1848, no. 86, to Baron Chippendale). (Sale, Febrve and Delbergue-Cormont, Paris, 9 May 1856, to Durant). (Sale, Galliera, Paris, 3 December 1966, no. 16). George Heine, Paris; (sale, Galliera, Paris, 23 March 1971, no. 10). (Bruno Meissner, Zurich, 1975); (Galerie Nicoline Pon, Zurich, 1977); (sale, Sotheby's, London, 12 December 1979, no. 280, unsold). (Edward Speelman, London, 1982); sold to the Dordrechts Museum, 1983

Exhibitions
Dordrecht and Leeuwarden 1988, no. 23; Dordrecht 1992, no. 17

Literature
Blanc 1857 – 1858, 2: 516; HdG 1907 – 1927, 2 (1909): no. 54; De Groot 1983, no. 6, pl. 1; Chong 1992, no. 103; Gemar-Koeltzsch 1995, 2: 274, no. 87 / 1, repro.

Endnotes
1. Cuyp painted two other stable interiors: private collection and the Nationalmuseum, Stockholm. Dordrecht and Leeuwarden 1988, no. 20, repro., 75, fig. 73; Chong 1992, nos. 49, 55.

2. Hollstein 1949 –, 3: 67, no. 338. See Chong 1988, 75.

3. "O nimium felix, et vera sorte beatus, / Cui licet immunes curis civilibus annos / Degere, dum tugurI tutus sub arundine vivat! / Non illi varijs anfractibus intricatur / Pectus, non dubio luctatur corde voluntas: / Composita sed mente, opibus contentus avitis, / Aut flavam segetem, matura aut arbore poma / Colligit, aut laetum pecus in sua pascua ducit. / Quod si uxor subeat partem officiosa laboris, / O nimium felix, et summa sorte beatus!" The lines are signed "G. Ryckius," probably the Latinist Josse de Rijcke (1586 – 1627).

4. There is no suggestion that the dilapidated farmhouses that Bloemaert depicted in the series were meant to represent sloth or vice, as suggested by J. Bruyn in Amsterdam, Boston, and Philadelphia 1987, 85 – 86.

5. For example, Robert Campin's Nativity (Dijon). See Baldwin 1985, 122 – 135. A seventeenth-century example of this is Abraham Bloemaert's *Holy Family* (1632, Rijksmuseum, Amsterdam).

6. Rotterdam 1994, 132 – 141, 222, 228. In particular, the work of Herman Saftleven may have influenced Cuyp (see Schulz 1982, nos. 1 – 4).

7. A piece of wood about 4 cm wide has been added to the top of the painting at some point after the work was first completed; this appears to have been done by Cuyp himself.

16
Conversion of Saul

c. 1645 – 1648, oil on panel, 71 × 91 (27 ¹⁵/₁₆ × 35 ¹³/₁₆).
Private collection

Inscription
Signed, lower right: *A. cuyp*

Provenance
Johan van der Linden van Slingeland, Dordrecht (sale, Yver, Delfos, Dordrecht, 22 August 1785, no. 101, to Kielmans). Probably Philip Hill; (sale, Christie's, London, 20 June 1807, no. 76, unsold). J.R. West, Alscot Park, 1831; by descent to Capt. James Alston-Roberts-West, Alscot Park; (sale, Christie's, London, 26 June 1964, no. 122); Dr. H. Wetzlar, Amsterdam; (sale, Mak van Waay, Amsterdam, 9 June 1977, no. 66); J.H. van Litsenburg, Amsterdam; (Charles Roelofsz, Amsterdam, 1984); Gerald Gutterman, New York; (sale, Sotheby's, New York, 14 January 1988, no. 8, unsold). Private collection

Exhibitions
Birmingham 1831, no. 24; Laren 1966, no. 18; Dordrecht 1977, no. 27; Washington, Detroit, and Amsterdam 1980, no. 80

Literature
Smith 1829 – 1834, (1834): 296, under no. 35; HdG 1907 – 1927, 2 (1909): no. 10; Reiss 1975, 212 (as doubtful); Halewood 1982, 108, note 4; Chong 1992, no. 101

Endnotes
1. Ember 1979, nos. 99 – 103.

2. Hollstein 1949 –, no. 13, repro.

3. Grotius 1646, 2, 8: 46. Lightfoot 1645 (1822 ed., 7: 129 – 130).

4. Calvin 1965, 257.

5. "A general warning is also given to us all, so that not one of us may attack Christ by injuring his brother unjustly, but especially so that not one of us resist the truth rashly and in a blind fury under the pretence of zealousness" (Calvin 1965, 257).

6. See Drexelius 1627; Philip Sadeler produced a print of the Conversion of Saul for the book. See Martone 1977.

Thirty-six depictions of the Conversion of Saul are recorded in Dutch inventories between 1628 and 1710 (Provenance Index database). There is no real indication that the Conversion of Saul was preferred by Catholic collectors in Holland, although one of Cuyp's Catholic patrons owned an anonymous depiction of the subject (ONA 160). See Montias in Freedberg and De Vries 1991, 356, 358.

7. Johan Diederik Pompe van Meerdervoort and Jan van Huysum sale, Amsterdam, 14 October 1749 (no. 15): "Een stuk verbeeldende de Bekeering van Paulus," 32 × 45, 13 guilders to Claes Mol. Although the properties of Pompe van Meerdervoort and the flower painter Jan van Huysum were not divided, the Cuyp painting almost certainly belonged to the former.

17
Two Horsemen on a Ridge

c. 1646 – 1648, oil on panel, 33 × 42.5 (13 × 16 ¾).
Private collection, New York

Inscription
Signed, lower left: *A. cùÿp*

Provenance
Walter Fawkes, Farnley Hall, Yorkshire, 1822; Ayscough Fawkes, Farnley Hall, Yorkshire; (sale, Christie's, 28 June 1890, lot 79); (Thomas Agnew & Sons, London); Edward C. Guinness; by descent to Lady Bridget Ness; private collection

Exhibitions
London 1922, no. 32

Literature
Neale 1818, no. 13; Stephens 1873, 407

Endnotes
1. Frederick v and his consort Elizabeth Stuart (also known as the Winter King and Winter Queen) had settled in the Netherlands in 1621 after he was deposed as king of Bohemia. Although they lived primarily in The Hague, they also resided in Rhenen after constructing a palace there in 1631. As noted by Huys Janssen and Sutton in The Hague 1991, 62, it is not known when the large stone table on top of Grebbeberg was erected or when it became known as Koningstafel.

2. Sepp 1773, 85: "Aan de Westzyde [traveling from Wageningen to Rhenen] heeft men een zeer hoogen Berg, welke veeltyds beklommen word, om van daar een der fraaiste Gezichten over den Rhyn, als mede op de Neder-Betuwe, en over de Rheensche Veenen te aanschouwen."

3. For depictions of Rhenen by Seghers and Van Goyen, as well as a list of Dutch artists who visited this region, see Deys 1981 and Sutton in Amsterdam, Boston, and Philadelphia 1987, 329 – 330.

4. Cuyp used this now-lost drawing when depicting a comparable river view in three other works: *Shepherds with Their Flocks*, private collection (Reiss 1975, 88, no. 53); *Landscape with Two Horses*, Mittelrheinisches Landesmuseum, Mainz (Reiss 1975, 89, no. 54); and *A Horseman with a Cowherd*, The National Gallery, London (inv. no. 822).

5. The situation is visible on map 24 of Sepp 1773 (see note 2).

18
The Maas at Dordrecht in a Storm

c. 1648 – 1650, oil on panel, 49.8 × 74.4 (19 ⅝ × 29 ⁵⁄₁₆).
The National Gallery, London (6405)

Inscription
Signed, lower right: *A. cùÿp*

Provenance
(Sale, Hobbs, London, 23 February 1764, no. 57). Possibly earl of Halifax; (possibly sale, Christie's, London, 20 April 1782, no. 67, to Nisbet). Michael Bryan (sale, Coxe, Burrell & Foster, London, 17 – 18 May 1798, no. 1798). Probably Sir Francis and Sir Thomas Baring, Bt.; The Prince Regent, Carlton House, 1814; (anonymous sale [The Prince of Wales], Christie's, London, 29 June 1814, no. 56, to Norton). Francis Jordan; Thomas Barber, Cheltenham, by 1844; (sale, Thomas Barber, Christie's, London, 5 May 1862, no. 54, to Peacock); (P. and D. Colnaghi); Willam C. Alexander, Aubrey House, London, 1886; by descent to Misses Rachel F. and Jean I. Alexander; presented by deed of gift to The National Gallery; entered The National Gallery's collection in 1972

Exhibitions
London 1887, no. 50; London 1929, no. 291; London 1952, no. 365; Norwich 1954, no. 5; London 1972, no. 6405; London 1976, no. 25; Dordrecht 1977, no. 28; Rotterdam and Berlin 1996, no. 50

Literature
HdG 1907 – 1927, 2 (1909): nos. 167a, 167c, 636; Reiss 1975, 140, no. 101, repro.; Brown 1979, 14, pl. 14; Minneapolis, Toledo, and Los Angeles 1990, 25, fig. 20; MacLaren and Brown 1991, 1: 95 – 06, 2: pl. 82; Chong 1992, 359 – 361, no. 119

Endnotes

1. In the literature the identification of the vessel is somewhat confusing. Chong 1992, 160, refers to the ship in the present picture (as well as in the painting in the Wallace Collection) as a *wijdschip*, an identification that is, surprisingly, taken up in the catalogue entry on the picture in the 1996 exhibition on Dutch marine painting (Rotterdam and Berlin 1996, 244). Rather, the vessel depicted is a *smalschip*, a freighter that was designed for inland waterways (Rotterdam and Berlin 1996, 30, where the ship from the present painting is illustrated as an example). See also the glossary of ships in Robinson 1990, 2: 1134.

2. Inv. no. P49 (Chong 1992, 370, no. 130). Another comparable scene that also includes storm and lightning as well as several of the boats from the present composition, painted by a follower of Cuyp, is *Ships in Stormy Weather* (Musée du Louvre, Paris, inv. no. 1195; Chong 1992, 476 – 477, no. C84).

The comparison of this work and the picture from the Wallace Collection has in the past been used in order to determine a date for the present picture. Reiss argued for a date of the early 1650s for the Wallace Collection picture and, based on the hypothesis that the work from the National Gallery is a sketch for it, suggested a similar date for the present picture (Reiss 1975, 140). However, Chong has convincingly shown that the National Gallery painting could not have been a sketch for the painting in the Wallace Collection (Chong 1992, 360, 370).

MacLaren and Brown 1991, 1: 95, notes the considerable discrepancy in the handling of the brush and placed the present picture among Cuyp's "early, Van Goyenesque" works from the mid-1640s, partly based on a comparison with *Dordrecht from the South, in a Storm* (see cat. 12, fig. 1), which has been dated to the same period (for this picture, see Reiss 1975, 55, no. 27; Chong 1992, 309 – 310, no. 61). Chong, on the other hand, identified the "strong brushstrokes of the gray sky" as "typical of Cuyp's work around 1650" (Chong 1992, 360).

3. See, for example, Beck 1973, nos. 294, 295, 299, 304, 305.

4. For an example by Jan Porcellis see *Sailboats in a Breeze* (signed and dated 1629, Stedelijk Museum De Lakenhal, Leiden, inv. no. 877; Minneapolis, Toledo, and Los Angeles 1990, 135 – 137, no. 24); for Van Goyen see Beck 1973, no. 798; for Abraham van Beyeren see *Ships Sailing in a Strong Breeze* (c. 1640 – 1650; private collection, Bahamas; Rotterdam and Berlin 1996, 248 – 249, no. 51); for Jacob von Ruisdael see *Rough Sea* (c. 1670, Museum of Fine Arts, Boston, inv. no. 57.4; Minneapolis, Toledo, and Los Angeles 1990, 138 – 140, no. 25); for Willem van de Velde the Younger, see the *Kaag Close-Hauled in a Fresh Breeze* (c. 1672, The Toledo Museum of Art, Ohio, inv. no. 77.62; Minneapolis, Toledo, and Los Angeles 1990, 169 – 171, no. 38).

5. Beck 1973, nos. 803, 804, 807, 811 and 833. For a much broader discussion of the subject of thunderstorms as a pictorial theme in Dutch art of the first half of the seventeenth century, and in particular as a subject within the oeuvre of Jan van Goyen, see Falkenburg 1997.

6. Van Mander and Miedema 1973, 1: chap. 8, fol. 35, 12 – 13. Also quoted by Falkenburg 1997, 143 – 144, in the context of his discussion of the *paragone* debate as well as questions regarding the *aemulatio* of older artists. See also Angel 1642, 25 – 26, and Sluijter 1993, 21. For a full discussion of this topic, see Wheelock's entry for *Dordrecht Harbor by Moonlight* (cat. 12).

19
River Landscape with Cows

1648 – 1650, oil on panel, 68 × 90.2 (26 ¾ × 35 ½).
National Gallery of Art, Washington, Gift of Family Petschek (Aussig) (1986.70.1)

Inscription
Signed, lower right: *A: cuÿp*

Provenance
Caroline Anne, marchioness of Ely, Eversley Park, Winchmore Hill, London; (sale, Christie's, London, 3 August 1917, no. 43); (C. Huggins, London); (Thomas Agnew & Sons, London, 1917 to 1919); Guston Neuman, Brussels. (Sale, Frederik Muller & Co., Amsterdam, 30 November 1920, no. 1024, bought-in). (Perhaps Steinmeyer, Lucerne, by 1923); (Paul Cassirer & Co., Berlin, by 1924). Ignaz Petschek, Aussig, Czechoslovakia, by 1927; by descent to his son Frank C. Petschek, New York City; by descent to his daughters Elisabeth de Picciotto, New York City, and Maria Petschek Smith, Falls Church, Virginia; gift of Family Petschek (Aussig) to the National Gallery of Art, Washington, 1986

Exhibitions
Madrid 1921, no. 51; Copenhagen 1922, no. 30; Dordrecht 1924, no. 10

Literature
HdG 1907 – 1927, 2 (1909): no. 243; Reiss 1975, 206; Sutton 1987, 294; Chong 1988, 82, repro.; Chong 1992, 362, no. 121; Wheelock 1995, 33 – 36

20
A Herdsman with Five Cows by a River

c. 1650, oil on panel, 45.4 × 74 (17 ⅞ × 29 ⅛).
The National Gallery, London (823)

Inscription
Signed, lower right: *A: cuyp:*

Provenance
Probably De Nogaret; (probably sale, Lebrun, Paris, 2 June 1780, no. 12, to Vicomte Choiseul). Probably duc de Choiseul-Praslin; (probably sale, Paillet, Paris, 18 February 1793, no. 97, to Struber). John Smith; Joseph Barchard, 1822. (Charles J. Nieuwenhuys, Brussels); Sir Robert Peel, Bt., by 1834; purchased by The National Gallery, London, 1871

Exhibitions

London 1822, no. 128; Norwich 1925, no. 6; Newcastle-upon-Tyne 1927

Literature

Smith 1829–1842, 5 (1834): 287, no. 7, 299, no. 43, 331, no. 164; HdG 1907–1927, 2 (1909): nos. 325, 391; MacLaren 1960, 85–86, no. 823; Müllenmeister 1973, 2: no. 103; Reiss 1975, 125, no. 88; MacLaren and Brown 1991, 1: 89–90, no. 823; Chong 1992, 363–364, no. 122

Endnotes

1. Chong 1992, 179.

2. Reiss 1975, 124, no. 87, identified the painting as being in The Hermitage, Saint Petersburg. However, in Amsterdam, Boston, and Philadelphia 1987, 295, note 2, the owner is identified as Lord Samuel, England.

3. MacLaren 1960, 85; MacLaren and Brown 1991, 89; Reiss 1975, 125. Chong cited by way of comparison the brushwork in *Equestrian Portrait of Pieter de Roovere* (see Chong essay, fig. 3), which can be dated to before 1652 (Amsterdam, Boston, and Philadelphia 1987, 294; see also Chong 1992, 259 and 372–373, no. 132).

4. Chong 1992, 363: "It appears to be the earliest because it is slightly warmer in coloring, and includes more traditional elements such as the rowboat with fishermen and shows more of the river bank."

5. Examples by Bloemaert might be his *Expulsion of Hagar* (signed and dated 1635, private collection), an engraving by Jan Saenredam after Bloemaert showing a *Farmyard with the Prodigal Son,* and his two animal series engraved by Adam Bolswert and Frederick Bloemaert (Roethlisberger and Bok 1993, nos. 511, 71, 135–148, 149–162). For Roelandt Savery see his *Cows in a Meadow* (1616, whereabouts unknown; see Spicer 1983, fig. 5); *Stable Interior* (Rijksmuseum, Amsterdam,

inv. no. A2211); and Jan Asselijn's *River Landscape* (Gemäldegalerie der Akademie der Bildenden Künste, Vienna, inv. no. 810); *River Landscape* (Statens Museum for Kunst, Copenhagen); *Shepherd and Cows with Ruins* (Staatliche Kunstsammlungen, Gemäldegalerie Alte Meister, Dresden, inv. no. 1583; see Steland Stief 1971, nos. 101, 152, 153).

6. See for example Potter's *Landscape with Cattle and Milkmaid* (signed and dated 1646, private collection, England); *Farmyard near The Hague* (signed and dated 1647, collection of the duke of Westminster, Chester); and certainly *The Farmyard,* which was known in the seventeenth century as *"The Pissing Cow"* (signed and dated 1649, The Hermitage, Saint Petersburg, inv. no. 820; see also The Hague 1994, nos. 5, 9, 15).

7. See also Chong 1992, 180.

8. For a more detailed discussion of the symbolism associated with cattle, see Spicer 1983, 251–256; Chong 1988, 56–86; and Chong 1992, 173–184.

21
Cows in a River

c. 1650, oil on panel, 59 × 74 (23 ¼ × 29 ⅛).
Szépmüvészeti Múzeum, Budapest (408)

Inscription

Signed, lower left: *A. cùÿp*

Provenance

John Barnard, by 1784, London; by descent to his nephew Thomas Hankey; (sale, Christie's, London, 7 June 1799, no. 35, to Bryan). Sir Simon Clarke, Bt., and George Hibbert (sale, Christie's, London, 14 May 1802, lot 63, to Charles Birch). Prince Miklós Esterházy zu Galántha, by 1810, Laxenburg and Vienna; collection bought by the Hungarian government in 1871

Exhibitions

Lugano 1985, no. 28, repro.; Amsterdam, Boston, and Philadelphia 1987, no. 21, repro.

Literature

Fischer 1812, 148; Smith 1829–1842, 5 (1834): no. 170; Viardot 1844, 269; Cundall 1891, 159; Frimmel 1892, 1: 196; Michel 1892, 236; HdG 1907–1927, 2 (1909): no. 390, repro.; Rosenberg, Slive, and Ter Kuile 1966, 159, pl. 141B; Budapest Szépmüvészeti Múzeum 1968, 174–175, pl. 278; Reiss 1975, no. 85; Chong 1992, no. 123

Endnotes

1. Chong 1988; Chong 1992, 173–184; Walsh 1985; Spicer 1983.

2. Van Beveren archive, Gemeente Archief, Dordrecht, inv. 123; Van Slingeland archive, Hoge Raad van Adel, The Hague, inv. 1954–1959. Baars 1973, 2: app. 1, 3, 9, 10, 17, 19.

3. Spicer 1983; for example, Van Mander 1604, fol. 125r.

4. Inventory description compiled by Baars 1973, 171, table 26. Between 1701–1750, the proportions reverse (59 percent black, 22 percent red, 15 percent gray).

5. Van Mander 1604, fol. 41r (*Grondt* 9:34); Van Mander and Miedema 1973, 1: 230–231:

dan gaen soeck te practiseren
Noch moet ghy oock letten in't coloreren
Op Ossen en Koeyen, roo, grys' en vale,
Hoe wonderlijck ghevleckt dats'altemale,
Hebben d'ooren altyt ghelijck malcander,
D'een niet een hayr ghevleckt onghelijck d'ander.

22
Cows in a River

c. 1650, oil on panel, 59 × 72.5 (23 ¼ × 28 ⁹/₁₆).
Private collection

Inscription

Signed, lower right (false?): *A. cuyp*

Provenance

Abraham Widley Robarts, M.P., London, by 1829.
Private collection

Exhibitions

London 1829, no. 81; London 1877a, no. 76; London 1891,
no. 87; London 1903, no. 83; London 1924, no. 22; London
1929, no. 279, pl. 14; London 1945, no. 4; London 1973,
no. 11

Literature

Smith 1829 – 1842, 5 (1834): no. 222; Waagen 1854, 4, 163
(both paintings); *Athenaeum* 1877, 86 (both paintings); HdG
1907 – 1927, 2 (1909): no. 393; Gibson 1928, 114 – 115, repro.;
Reiss 1975, no. 86; Chong 1987, 293 – 294 (both paintings);
Chong 1988, 79, figs. 76, 77 (both paintings); Chong 1992,
nos. 126, 127 (both paintings)

23
Bulls on a Riverbank

c. 1650, oil on panel, 59 × 72 (23 ¼ × 28 ⅜). Private collection

Inscription

Signed, lower left (false?): *A. cuyp*

Provenance

(See cat. 22)

Exhibitions

London 1877a, no. 78; London 1891, no. 81

Literature

Smith 1829 – 1842, 5 (1834): no. 223; HdG 1907 – 1927,
2 (1909): no. 205; also see cat. 22

Endnotes

1. Reiss 1975, pl. 63; Chong 1992, no. 50.

2. Spicer 1983, 254 – 255, figs. 5, 6. The painting of cows
was sold at Christie's, London, 8 December 1967; the painting of bulls is in the Musée d'Art et d'Histoire, Geneva.
Spicer stressed the importance of Savery for the early development of Dutch cattle painting.

3. For these various traditional meanings, see Chong 1988.

24
Travelers in a Hilly Countryside

c. 1650 – 1652, oil on panel, 48.1 × 74.8 (18 ¹⁵/₁₆ × 29 ⁷/₁₆).
The Cleveland Museum of Art, Bequest of John L. Severance
(1942.637)

Inscription

Signed, lower right: *A. cuyp*

Provenance

Johan van der Linden van Slingeland, Dordrecht (sale,
Dordrecht, 22 August 1785, no. 87, to Beekmans).
(Galerie Charles Brunner, Paris, 1912); (P. W. French and
Co., New York, from 1917 – 1921, owned with M. Knoedler,
New York); John L. Severance, Cleveland; bequeathed
to the Cleveland Museum of Art, 1936, transferred 1942

Exhibitions

Cleveland 1936, no. 214; Ann Arbor 1964, no. 29

Literature

Smith 1829 – 1842, 5 (1834): no. 27 (in part); Cleveland
Museum of Art 1942, no. 3; Coe 1955, 230 – 231; Gimpel

1963, 236; Gerson 1964, 347 – 348; Stechow 1966,
161 – 162; Reiss 1975, no. 46; Duparc 1980, 25; Cleveland
Museum of Art 1982, no. 97; Chong 1992, no. 11

Endnotes

1. Strangely, Gerson 1964, 347 – 348, used this of all paintings to remark that Cuyp's "objects and his scenery are never
really Italian."

2. A landscape by Pynacker is called "Italiaansche" in
the 1672 inventory of Franciscus de la Boë Silvius, Leiden;
in 1674 a landscape by Berchem is similarly termed (Pieter
Davidts, Leiden). See also Provenance Index database.
Unattributed landscapes are termed "Italian" by 1657.

3. Houbraken 1718 – 1721 (1753 ed.), 3: 64, 108. Dujardin's
style is contrasted by the "bruine wyze" (brown manner) of
Jacob van der Does.

4. Estate of Matthys Helwigh van Alsem (Gemeente Archief,
Dordrecht, ONA 154); also "Alnogh een cleijn lantschap,
op zijn Italiaens, met een breede leyst." I am grateful to John
Loughman for this reference; see also Loughman 1993,
154. The term is used again in the 1707 inventory of Roeland
Teerlink (Gemeente Archief, Dordrecht, ONA 574).

5. Sale, London, 6 November 1689 (lot 270), as by
John Peters.

25
Landscape with Herdsmen

c. 1650 – 1652, oil on panel, 48 × 82.5 (18 ⅞ × 32 ½).
The Corcoran Gallery of Art, Washington, William A.
Clark Collection

Inscription

Lower right: *A. Cuyp*.

Provenance

(Sale, Jolles de Winter, Amsterdam 23 May 1764, no. 41). C. Price, London. 5th earl of Carlisle, London, by 1771, Castle Howard in 1865, thence by descent; (P. and D. Colnaghi, half-share with M. Knoedler, London and New York, 1907); Senator William Andrews Clark, New York, 1909 – 1926; Corcoran Gallery of Art, W. A. Clark Collection

Exhibitions

London 1815, no. 57; London 1822, no. 136 or 138; London 1828, no. 83; London 1853, no. 7; New York 1959, 14, repro.

Literature

Smith 1829 – 1842, 5 (1834): 309, no. 93; HdG 1907 – 1927, 2 (1909): no. 424; Breckenridge 1955, 11, repro.; Dattenberg 1967, no. 82; Reiss 1975, 218, no. 89, repro.; Chong 1992, 373 – 374, no. 133

Endnotes

1. Dattenberg 1967, no. 82, identifies the view as depicting Calcar, near Cleves, and Monterberg.

2. Reiss 1975, 218, addendum, expresses "lurking doubts" about the painting. Chong 1992, 374 – 375, accepts the attribution of the painting to Cuyp, but describes it as "Somewhat harder than other Cuyp works, the arrangement of the riders is also unusual." He also notes that J. G. van Gelder and I. Jost state in their manuscript notes of 1977 that the painting was a replica.

26

Portrait of a Woman Aged Twenty-One, as a Hunter

1651, oil on panel, 80.5 × 68.5 (31 ⅝ × 27 ¹⁵⁄₁₆).
Private collection

Inscription

Signed and dated, left: *Aetatis. 21 / A.cúÿp. fecit . / 1651*

Provenance

M. J. Alexander, London, by 1935; (sale, Sotheby's, London, 18 December 1935, no. 118, to A. Asscher). L. van Santen, by 1936; (Galerie Sanct Lucas, Vienna); private collection, France, by 1938; by descent to current owner

Exhibitions

Boston 1992, 142

Literature

Rijksmuseum 1960, 79; Virch 1970, 6; Chong 1991, 617, fig. 55; Chong 1992, 336, no. 94

27

Portrait of a Man with a Rifle

c. 1651, oil on panel, 80 × 68.5 (31 ⅜ × 26 ⅞).
Rijksmuseum, Amsterdam (c 120)

Provenance

(Sale, Albertus Brondgeest, Amsterdam, November 1839, no. 191); Adriaan van der Hoop; bequest to the city of Amsterdam, Museum van der Hoop, 1845; on loan to the Rijksmuseum from the city of Amsterdam since 1885

Exhibitions

Bolsward 1950, no. 4 (no catalogue)

Literature

Museum van der Hope 1855, no. 30 (ed. 1872, no. 26); Thoré 1858 – 1860, 2: 144; Michel 1892, 114; Rijksmuseum 1976, 184, repro.; Chong 1991, 612, repro.; Chong 1992, 336, no. 93

Endnotes

1. Chong 1991, 611, fig. 54.

2. Indeed, some of Cuyp's portraits from these years are copies of Jacob's works. See Chong 1991, 612.

3. For Bol, see Blankert 1982, particularly 99 – 100, nos. 22 and 23. For Lesire, see Amsterdam and Groningen 1983, 188 – 191, nos. 48 – 49.

4. Nevertheless, since their known provenances are entirely different, this exhibition will be the first opportunity to compare the two works side by side to confirm this hypothesis.

5. For a comprehensive discussion of this tradition, see Kettering 1983.

6. Van Veen 1608, 130 – 131.

7. Quoted in Kettering 1983, 44.

28

The Maas at Dordrecht

early 1650s, oil on canvas, 114.9 × 170.2 (45 ¼ × 67).
National Gallery of Art, Washington, Andrew W. Mellon Collection (1940.2.1)

Inscription

Right foreground (on sideboard of ship): *A. cúÿp*

Provenance

Johan van der Linden van Slingeland, Dordrecht, by 1752; (sale, Yver, Delfos, Dordrecht, 22 August 1785, no. 70). (Alexis Delahante, London, c. 1804 to 1814); Abraham Hume, Bt. Wormley, Hertfordshire; by inheritance to his grandson, John Hume Cust, Viscount Alford, M.P., Ashridge Park, Hertfordshire; by inheritance to his son, John William Spencer, 2d earl Brownlow, Ashridge Park; by inheritance to his brother, Adelbert Wellington, 3d earl Brownlow, P.C., G.C.V.O., Ashridge Park and London; (sale, Christie's, London, 4 May 1923, no. 75); (Duveen Brothers, Inc., New York and London); The A. W. Mellon Educational and Charitable Trust, Pittsburgh, 1940; National Gallery of Art (Andrew Mellon Collection), Washington, 1940

Exhibitions

London 1815, no. 67; London 1838, no. 37; London 1867, no. 21; Nottingham Castle 1878, no. 78; London 1892, no. 85; Detroit 1925, no. 3; Toronto 1926, no. 143; London 1928a, no. 1424; London 1929, no. 267; Brussels 1935, no. 714; Amsterdam 1936, no. 37; Detroit 1939, no. 7; Liège 1939, no. 54; The Hague and San Francisco 1990–1991, no. 17

Literature

Hoet 1752, 2: 490; Descamps 1753–1765, 2 (1754): 80; Buchanan 1824, 2: 192, no. 10; Smith 1829–1842, 5 (1834): 311, no. 98; Waagen 1838, 2: 206; Waagen 1854, 2: 316; HdG 1907–1927, 2 (1909): no. 28; Berenson and Valentiner 1941, no. 209, repro.; Mellon 1949, 97, repro.; Stechow 1966, 119, fig. 237; Reiss 1975, 143, no. 104, repro., 204, 212; Walker 1976, 296–297, repro.; Wheelock 1984, 22–23, repro.; Russell 1990, 31–82, repro.; Chong 1992, 409–411, no. 161; Wheelock 1995, 36–43, color repro.

Endnotes

1. This entry is based on Wheelock 1995, 36–43.

2. Waagen 1854, 2: 316.

3. In addition to its popularity in exhibitions, a number of copies of the work were executed. They include a signed copy (oil on panel, 59 × 74 cm) by Jacob van Strij (1756–1815), with Rob Kattenburg, Aerdenhout in 1983; a copy formerly in the collection of Matthew Anderson, exhibited in Leeds in 1868 (no. 898); and a copy (oil on canvas, 43 × 65 in.), formerly owned by Guy Sebright, exhibited at the Royal Academy in 1907 (no. 57).

4. Waagen wrongly believed that the scene was illuminated by a setting sun.

5. This drawing was made after 1647, when modifications were made to buildings along the water's edge. (Another drawing of the same site is in the Stichting P. and N. de Boer, Amsterdam. See cat. 83)

6. Hoet 1752, 2: 490. Van Slingeland's inventory describes two paintings as "Two pictures showing the view of Dordrecht as far as the *Huys Merwede* with many yachts and ships, showing a rendezvous of Prince Maurits of Orange in a boat with several other princes being taken from the town to the yacht, opposite which boat is another with *Oldenbarnevelt* standing up and looking at Prince Maurits. Painted from life, by *Aelbert Cuyp*. Each picture high 43 *duim*, wide 64 ½ *duim*." The first half of this description seems to refer to Cuyp's painting at Waddesdon Manor (fig. 1), while the second half of the description refers to *The Maas at Dordrecht*. As Oldenbarnevelt was executed in 1619 and as Prince Maurits had died in 1625, however, these identifications were clearly fanciful.

7. They are also unrelated to other princes of Orange — Frederik Hendrik (1584–1647) or Willem II (1626–1650) — with whom the scene might be associated. Only two references record visits made to Dordrecht by Frederik Hendrik and his family. The first was in 1638 when they accompanied Marie de Medicis on 20 September during her exile from France. The second was in 1643 when the prince of Orange and Amalia van Solms, accompanied by their son Willem II and his fourteen-year-old wife Mary, anchored for the night at Zwijndrecht, on the opposite side of the river Merwede from the city of Dordrecht.

8. London 1929, 29.

9. Moreover, the elaborate account of Charles II's trip published in 1660 makes it clear that the royal fleet sailed past Dordrecht and only anchored beyond the city. Upon anchoring, the king first heard the dramatic news that he had been restored to the crown, news that quickly changed his plans to spend the night before proceeding to the city of Delft. As the message also indicated that an English fleet was off the coast of Holland ready to bring the royal couple back to London, they embarked immediately.

10. See, for example, Govaert Flinck's *The Amsterdam Civic Guard Celebrating the Signing of the Peace of Münster*, 1648 (Rijksmuseum, Amsterdam, inv. no. C.1).

11. Russell 1990, 31–82. Russell's article is the outgrowth of research she undertook at the National Gallery of Art (NGA) in 1981–1982. Her article also incorporated a number of observations provided by Commodore C. J. W. van Waning, who undertook an in-depth study of the painting in the fall of 1982. The text of his research, as well as navigational charts he provided, are in NGA curatorial files.

12. Balen 1677, 880–881.

13. According to Professor Paul Hofsÿzer (letter, 6 August 1986, in NGA curatorial files), the intent of the expedition was to lay siege to Antwerp. Antwerp, however, was heavily defended and by autumn the campaign had become bogged down.

14. As is characteristic of these ships, the wooded hull is broader along the waterline than at the deck level. This profile kept the ship high in the water and allowed it to sail along the shallow inland waterways. One of the sideboards used to stabilize the craft when it was under sail is seen drawn up midway along its side.

15. The distinctive flags on the ship — that hanging from the stern with blue-white-blue bars, the smaller orange flag atop the mast, and the small red flag atop the mast — may well provide a clue to the officer's identity. Unfortunately, despite the kind assistance of both T. N. Schelhaas, M.A., director of the Centraal Bureau voor Genealogie, The Hague (letter, 5 March 1982, in NGA curatorial files), and H. C. 't Jong, archivist at the Gemeentelijke Archiefdienst, Dordrecht (letter, 10 March 1982, in NGA curatorial files), all efforts to identify these flags have been unsuccessful. One possibility is that the flags are related to Colonel Varik, the only officer mentioned by Balen. Although the exact identity of Colonel Varik is not known, one form of the Varik family

crest was a diagonal cross (color unknown) that in shape is not unrelated to the flag at the stern of the *pleyt*. See Anspach 1892, 68–69, 149. Commodore Van Waning (see note 11) believed that the small orange flag represented a "banner or regimental colour with its finely carved top and wooden bar along the topside of the flag." He believed that the flag may well represent the regimental colors of Colonel Varik. Schelhaas, however, believes that the flag depicts a fleur-de-lis and thus may relate to the coat of arms of the De Beveren family. Finally, H.C. 't Jong suggested that the flag depicts a tower or castle on a red field, which would associate the ship with Middelburg.

16. De Beveren was also the head of a family that was one of Cuyp's important patrons. He is certainly not the relatively youthful officer standing in the small rowboat, since in 1646 he was fifty-six years old. Serving with De Beveren on the city council were three treasurers, Jacob de Witt, Johann Dionijsz, and Cornelius van Someren.

17. For the text of Van Slingeland's inventory, see note 6. For an assessment of the relationship between these two paintings, see Russell 1990, 34–35.

18. Reiss 1975, no. 106.

19. Ter Raa 1918, 4: 151.

20. Reiss 1975, no. 32.

29
Michiel and Cornelis Pompe van Meerdervoort with Their Tutor

c. 1652–1653, oil on canvas, 109.8 × 156.2 (43¼ × 61½).
The Metropolitan Museum of Art, New York, The Friedsam Collection, Bequest of Michael Friedsam (32.100.20)

Inscription
Signed, lower left: *A. cuyp. fecit.*

Provenance
Cornelis Pompe van Meerdervoort, Zwijndrecht, 1680; by descent to Johan Diederik Pompe van Meerdervoort, Zwijndrecht, 1749. L. L[apeyrière], Paris; (sale, Henry, Paris, 19 April 1825, no. 103); Thomas Emmerson, London; (sale, Phillips, London, 2 May 1829, no. 165). Richard Sanderson, London, 1834; (sale, Christie's, London, 17 June 1848, no. 25, to Norton). Mrs. Lyne Stephens, Lynford Hall, Norfolk; (sale, Christie's, London, 11 May 1895, no. 332); (Charles Wertheimer, London, and Galerie Sedelmeyer, Paris); Maurice Kann, Paris, 1895; (sale, Petit, Paris, 9 June 1911, no. 12); Eugène Fischof; (sale, Petit, Paris, 14 June 1913, no. 50); (Kleinberger, Paris). Séquestre Magin; (sale, Petit, Paris, 23 June 1922, no. 12); (Kleinberger, Paris). Michael Friedsam, New York; The Metropolitan Museum of Art (The Friedsam Collection bequest), 1931

Exhibitions
Santa Barbara 1954, no. 5; Dordrecht 1991, 14, fig. 31

Literature
Smith 1829–1854, 5 (1834): no. 150; Waagen 1838, 2: 400; Jervis 1854, 326; Waagen 1854, 2: 289; HdG 1907–1927, 2 (1909): nos. 85, 617; Bode 1911, 23; Holmes 1930, 168, no. 38; The Hague 1933, no. 938; Reiss 1953, 45, fig. 15; Staring 1953; Dattenberg 1967, 72, no. 78; Brussels, Rotterdam, Paris, and Bern 1968–1969, 35; Reiss 1975, no. 121; Dordrecht 1977, 174; De Marly 1978, 750; Leeuwarden, Den Bosch, and Assen 1979; Chong 1987, 111; Herbert 1988, 163, fig. 165; Franits 1989, 219, fig. 4; Liedtke 1989, 83, fig. 68, pl. 28, no. 184; Chong 1992, no. 143, 385–387; New York 1995, 326, repro.; Chong 1996, 295, fig. 2; Dordrecht and Enschede 2000, 105, fig. 145

Endnotes
1. The drawing (cat. 93) in the Collection Frits Lugt, Institut Néerlandais, Paris, depicts a view of Elten from the Sternberg. See Dordrecht 1977, no. 71, repro.

2. Topographical details from his sketches of Cleves show that Cuyp must have seen the town between late 1651 and November 1652, when a tower was removed. See Gorissen 1964, 94, nos. 13, 14, 141; also Van Gelder and Jost 1973.

3. De Pluvinel 1623. Revised editions were published in Paris and Utrecht in 1625 under the title: *L'Instruction du Roy en l'exercise de monter à cheval.*

4. Cavendish 1657–1658.

5. Bedaux 1990. Franits 1989, 219, in an article devoted to the pedagogical associations of portraits of children with horses, specifically dismissed the educational allusions of this portrait. While the painting may not support an emblematic reading, the boys are depicted being tutored in riding and hunting.

6. *Den Eerlyken Jongeling, Of de Edele Kunst, Van zich by Groote en Kleyne te doen Eeren en Beminnen* (Dordrecht, 1657). Castiglione's book was translated into Dutch by the Dordrecht writer Lambert van den Bos: *De volmaeckte hovelinck, Van de graef Baldazar de Castiglione* (Dordrecht and Amsterdam, 1662).

30
The Baptism of the Eunuch

c. 1653, oil on canvas, 117 × 171 (46 1/16 × 67 5/16).
Anglesey Abbey, The Fairhaven Collection (The National Trust)

Inscription
Signed, lower right: *A. cuyp.fe.t.*

Provenance
(Sale, Paillet, Paris [probably the property of John Bertels], 27 March 1786, no. 3); (Lebrun, Paris). Widow Lebas-Courmant le jeune (sale, Paillet, Paris, 26 May 1795, no. 10). 1st duke of Buckingham and Chandos, Stowe, Buckinghamshire, 1834; to the 2d duke (sale, at house, Christie's, 15

August 1848, no. 437); (Thomas B. Brown, London). Sir Hugh Hume Campbell, Bt., Marchmont House, Scotland, 1857. Baron Gustave de Rothschild, Paris, 1908; by descent to his grandson Sir Philip Sassoon, Bt., London; (Asscher, Koetser and Welker, London, 1926). (Sale, Sotheby's, London, 27 June 1928, no. 65); (G. Matthiesen, Berlin; Reinhardt Gallery, New York; Arthur Ruck, London). Sir Duncan Watson (sale, Christie's, London, 12 December 1947, no. 53); (Hugh Leggatt, London); (Arthur Tooth & Sons, London). 1st Baron Fairhaven, Anglesbey Abbey, Cambridgeshire; collection bequest to National Trust, 1966

Exhibitions

London 1866, no. 63; London 1929, no. 276; London 1952, no. 567; London 1976, no. 29; Dordrecht 1992, no. 19

Literature

Smith 1829–1842, 5 (1834): no. 36; Buckingham 1838, 72, no. 301; Waagen 1854, 4: 441; HdG 1907–1927, 2 (1909): nos. 11, 12; Holmes 1930, 167, 185, no. 28; Reiss 1953, 46; Anson 1973, 595, fig. 38; Reiss 1975, no. 118; Edwards 1982, 227, 462; Loughman 1991a, 535, fig. 55; Chong 1992, no. 147, 389–390

Endnotes

1. Rembrandt: paintings of 1626 (Utrecht) and c. 1630 (lost). Lastman: paintings of 1608 (Berlin), c. 1615 (Lugt Collection, Paris), 1620 (Munich), and 1623 (Karlsruhe).

2. Herman van Swanevelt: paintings in Bordeaux and the Rijksmuseum, Amsterdam. Jan Both: Prado, Madrid; Royal Collection, London (fig. 1); Christie's, 1928.

3. Gemeente Archief, Dordrecht, inv. ONA 189: "Een groote schilderije vanden Moorman door Aelbrecht Cuyp" (A large painting of the Moor by Aelbrecht Cuyp) — written first as "Benjamin," then crossed out and changed. The painting hung in the large upper room ("Groote boven camer"). This painting may have been inherited from Roeloff Francken's sister Elisabeth, who owned an unattributed

painting of the same subject; inventory of 1671 (ONA 153): "een lantschap metten doop vande Moorman" (A landscape with the baptism of the Moor). Their father, Sebastian Francken, owned seven paintings by Cuyp in The Hague, 1656 (ONA 101), but they are not specifically described.

4. Gemeente Archief, Dordrecht, inv. ONA 561: "De dooping vande moorman door A. Kuyp" (The baptism of the moor by A. Kuyp). The painting hung in the rear salon ("achter op de sael"). See Loughman 1991a, 535.

5. Pieternella Palm (1674 Inventory: "Een van de Moorman"), who also owned four landscapes by Cuyp (ONA 365), and in estates of Gijsbrecht van Beaumont (1648), Jan Diemers (1650; he owned a portrait by Jacob Cuyp), Aeltgen Dircxdrs (1652), and Claertgen Tack (1661). When it was inventoried in Amsterdam in 1710 (Provenance Index, inv. N-431), the estate of Jan Six and Margaretha Tulp, who were originally from Dordrecht, also contained an anonymous Baptism of the Eunuch.

31
Ubbergen Castle

mid-1650s, oil on panel, 32.1 × 54.5 (12 ⅝ × 21 ⁷⁄₁₆).
The National Gallery, London (824)

Provenance

Said to have been bought in Hoorn from an old clothes man for about 15 pence; D[e] P[reuil]; (sale, Lebrun, Paris, 25 November 1811, no. 69, to Lebrun). L[apeyrière]; (sale, Paris, 14 April 1817, no. 25, to Perignon). Varroc; (sale, Paris, 28 May 1821, no. 24, unsold); (sale, Phillip's, London, 22 March 1822, no. 87); Sir Robert Peel, London; by descent to his son; The National Gallery, London, 1871

Exhibitions

London 1822, no. 38; Dordrecht 1992, no. 21

Literature

Smith 1829–1842, 5 (1834): 317, no. 118; Peel 1845, no. 5; HdG 1907–1927, 2 (1909): no. 176; MacLaren 1960, 86, no. 824; Roberts 1973, 135; Reiss 1975, 175, no. 132; Brown 1979, 34, pl. 33; Brown 1990, 90; MacLaren and Brown 1991, 90–91, no. 824; Chong 1992, 399, no. 154

Endnotes

1. This and most of what follows on the history of the castle has been taken from Gorissen 1959, which appears to be the only publication to discuss the history of the building in any detail. For this as well as several other references I am enormously grateful to Ms. G. G. J. A. Bosman of the Gemeente Archief Nijmegen.

2. The map is kept in the Rijksarchief Gelderland, Arnhem, Rekenkamer, inv. no. 112. A detail showing the castle is illustrated in Gorissen 1959, pl. XXXII. See also Van Schevichaven 1898–1904, (1901): 23.

3. Gorissen 1959, 159, quotes a document stating that on 23 August 1582 "heft die burgerie het huis Ubbergen den avot in brant gesteken" (in the evening the citizens set fire to the Huis Ubbergen). Chong 1992, 205–206, based on Arkstée 1738, 202, suggests that the castle "was burnt by Spanish troops to forestall its use by troops of the United Provinces."

4. By 1660 Klaes Vijghe (d. 1663) had added a baroque park to the property, a plan of which survives in the library of Leiden University (collection Bodel Nyenhuis; see Gorissen 1959, 159, note 8, and Schulte 1973). Another illustration of the ruins of the castle seen from the same direction but from a more elevated vantage point can be found in Arkstée 1738, following page 202 ("In den jare 1582 vertoonde zich het Huys of Slot te Ubbergen op dusdanige wyze, als het hier gezien word").

5. One of the earliest depictions of Brederode castle may be the drawing by Hendrik Goltzius of c. 1600 in Amsterdam (Rijksprentenkabinet, inv. no. 1879-A67; see Reznicek 1961,

1 [text]: 423, no. 391). See also Meindert Hobbema's *Ruins of Brederode Castle*, signed and dated 1671 (National Gallery, London, inv. no. 831). For a discussion of this subject in the context of Cuyp's paintings, see Chong 1992, 195–199, 205–206.

6. A seventeenth-century poem by Johan van Someren, entitled "Wandelingh van Nijmegen op Ubbergen," published in his book *Uyt-spanning der vernugten, bestaende in geestelijcke ene wereltlijcke poësy* (1660), describes the fate of the castle and celebrates its importance by comparing it to the stadtholder's castles of Rijswijck and Honselaersdijk (partially quoted in Chong 1992, 206).

7. New York 1995, 112–113, no. 52.

8. Chong 1992, 399. See also Kloek and Niemeijer 1990, 50 and note 11.

9. According to John Smith "this little picture, although simple in its composition, possesses every charm for which the master is so justly admired" (Smith 1829–1842, 5 (1834): 317, no. 118; quoted by HdG 1907–1927, 2 [1909]: no. 176). Roberts 1973, 135, found the painting lacking: "The little panel of *Ubbergen Castle*…is among the best of his small pictures; but it is only necessary to compare the passage of the rising ground on the left with the strictly comparable area of Claude's *Cephalus and Procris* [signed and dated 1645, National Gallery, London, inv. no. 2] to see that Cuyp misses a whole dimension of atmospheric feeling. And he loses it because his actual observation of light is often inaccurate; Cuyp's tone is invariably too yellow."

10. See the essay by Alan Chong in this catalogue as well as Chong 1992, chapter 4 and 145–147.

32
Ice Scene before the Huis te Merwede near Dordrecht

mid-1650s, oil on panel, 64 × 89 (25 ³/₁₆ × 35 ¹/₁₆).
Private collection

Inscription
Signed, lower right: *A cuijp*

Provenance
Johan van der Linden van Slingeland, Dordrecht, 1752; (sale, Yver, Delfos, Dordrecht, 22 August 1785, no. 78, to Fouquet). Probably duke of Bridgewater; (probably sale, Coxe, London, 12 May 1802, no. 63, to Squibb); probably Michael Bryan (probably sale, Coxe, Burrell & Foster, London, 10 May 1804, no. 65, to Bettesworth). William Dermer; Sir Richard Worsley, Bt., Appuldurcombe House, Isle of Wight, 1805; by descent to his niece Henrietta Simpson (wife of 2d baron, later created earl of Yarborough); by descent to earls of Yarborough, London, and Brocklesby Park, Lincolnshire; private collection

Exhibitions
London 1832, no. 47; London 1847, no. 55; London 1849, no. 18; Manchester 1857, no. 1035; London 1875, no. 145; London 1890, no. 96; London 1894, no. 54; London 1949a, no. 5; London 1952, no. 340; London 1976, no. 26; Kingston-upon-Hull 1981, no. 27; Amsterdam, Boston, and Philadelphia 1987, no. 23, pl. 58

Literature
Hoet 1752, 2: 496; Smith 1829–1842, 5 (1834): 292, no. 19; London 1851, no. 20; HdG 1907–1927, 2 (1909): no. 737; Reiss 1975, 150, no. 111; Chong 1992, 400–401, no. 155

Endnotes
1. Amsterdam, Boston, and Philadelphia 1987, 300. The catalogues of the Van Slingeland collection from the eighteenth century have identified the town on the distant bank as Papendrecht, yet none of the buildings give

any reliable indication to that effect (Hoet 1752, 2: 496; catalogue of sale Johan van der Linden van Slingeland, Dordrecht, 22 August 1785, no. 78; Chong 1992, 401).

2. Buvelot 1998, 39. For more literature on the Huis te Merwede, see also Amsterdam 1981, 184, and note 7; Dordrecht 1976; and Chong 1992, 197, 171–172 and note 58.

3. Chong 1992, 197–198, quotes the notes of the Englishman Thomas Coryat, taken during his visit to Dordrecht in 1608, in which he mentions the effects of the flood on the Huis te Merwede. William Lord Fitzwilliam noted in his diary on 29 June 1663: "Anno 1421 was this town by an inundation separated from firm ground. There was at that time drowned seventy-two villages [sic], many gentleman's houses and above a hundred thousand men and women" (quoted in Van Strien 1998, 129).

4. Amsterdam, Boston, and Philadelphia 1987, 300, notes 6 and 7. In Jan van Goyen's *Scene on Ice*, the Huis te Merwede dominates the skyline in the far distance (The National Gallery London, inv. no. 1327; Beck 1973, no. 63).

5. Amsterdam, Boston, and Philadelphia 1987, 300, note 5. In the painting at the Musée Fabre in Montpellier (inv. no. 836-4-7)—whose attribution has been accepted by Chong with qualifications (Chong 1992, 329–330, no. 87) but which in the most recent catalogue of the museum has been attributed to a "follower of Cuyp"—the ruins are seen from a slightly different angle and overgrown with greenery (see Buvelot 1998, 39–42, no. 11). Chong 1992, 401, lists eight other versions of the present picture, albeit "with significant differences in composition."

6. The two other paintings are *Fishing under the Ice near Dordrecht* (fig. 2; Reiss 1975, 151, no. 112; Chong 1992, 402–403, no. 156) and *Landscape with Hunters and Dead Birds*, Gemäldegalerie, Staatliche Museen zu Berlin, inv. no. 861K; see Bock 1996, fig. 1231).

7. Most closely related to the present picture is probably Jan van Goyen's *Winter Scene next to the Hius te Merwede with Dordrecht in the Background* (signed and dated 1649, Musée du Louvre, Paris, PF3726; Beck 1973, no. 80), which shows a similar scene (including a refreshments stall) in front of the Huis te Merwede, albeit seen from the opposite direction. On this subject, see also Amsterdam, Boston, and Philadelphia 1987, 299; Chong 1992, 260, referred to these winter scenes as "Cuyp's most innovative pictures."

8. See a letter from the dealer William Dermer to Sir Richard Worsley on 25 April 1805, just before the latter acquired the picture (quoted in Chong 1992, 401). John Smith called it "a superlative production" (Smith 1829–1842, 5 (1834): 292).

33
The Valkhof at Nijmegen from the Northwest

mid-1650s, oil on panel, 48.9 × 73.7 (19 ¼ × 29). Indianapolis Museum of Art, Gift in commemoration of the 60th anniversary of the Art Association of Indianapolis in memory of Daniel W. and Elizabeth C. Marmon (43.107)

Inscription
Remains of a signature lower right

Provenance
Dukes of Sachsen-Coburg-Gotha, Schloss Friedenstein, Gotha, by 1826; Herzogliche Gemäldegalerie, Gotha; sold around 1937. (Galerie Sanct Lucas, Vienna, 1937); (Cassirer Gallery, Amsterdam); (Rudolph Heinemann, New York); (Arnold Seligmann, Rey and Co., New York, 1939); John Herron Art Institute, Indianapolis, 1943 (Gift of Mrs. James Fesler in commemoration of the 60th anniversary of the Art Association of Indianapolis in memory of Daniel W. and Elizabeth C. Marmon)

Exhibitions
San Francisco 1939–1940, no. 54; Toronto 1940, no. 17; Amsterdam, Boston, and Philadelphia 1987, no. 22

Literature
Rathgeber 1839, 144; Herzoglichen Gemäldegalerie zu Gotha 1858, 50; Parthey 1863, 723, no. 62; Schneider 1883, 6, no. 55; HdG 1907–1927, 2 (1909): no. 196; Stillson 1944, 7–9; Stechow 1960b; Stechow 1966, 56, 59, 61–62, 119; Miller 1970, 92–94; Reiss 1975, no. 130; Fuchs 1978, 140, fig. 121; Janson and Fraser 1980, 106; Chong 1992, no. 152; Janson and Janson 1995, 582, fig. 797

34
The Valkhof at Nijmegen from the East

mid-1650s, oil on panel, 48.3 × 74 (19 × 29 ⅛). Private collection

Provenance
Rev. J. Image, 1855; (John Smith, London); Richard Foster, Clewer Manor (sale, Christie's, London, 3 June 1876, no. 3); baron Alphonse de Rothschild, Paris; to Edouard de Rothschild, Ferrières; by descent; private collection

Exhibitions
Paris 1946, no. 82

Literature
Waagen 1854, 4: 288; HdG 1907–1927, 2 (1909): nos. 274, 667a; Reiss 1975, no. 29; Amsterdam 1987, 297, fig. 4; Chong 1992, no. 153

Endnotes
1. Beck 1973, 2: nos. 144, 342–373.

2. The drawing is continued to left on the verso of a sheet in Besançon (inv. D513). The boats are based generally on a drawing in Nijmegen (Dordrecht 1977, no. 72, repro.).

Burnett 1969, 379, stated that Cuyp was less concerned with topographical accuracy than Jan van Goyen or Salomon van Ruysdael, when in fact he was far more exacting.

3. Drawing in the British Museum, London.

4. Cuyp's night scene in Cologne (cat. 12) is paired with a stormy landscape in the Bührle Collection, Zurich (see cat. 12, fig. 1); see also the 1674 inventory of Pieternella Palm: "Een morgen stont door Cuyp / Een avont stont door Cuyp" (A sunrise by Cuyp / A sunset by Cuyp); ONA 365. See also Moiso-Diekamp 1987, 545–548.

5. Tacitus, *The Histories*, book 5.19. On the rebellion of A.D. 69, see Sprey 1953.

6. See Kampinga 1917; Schöffer 1975.

7. See Schöffer 1975, 78–101; Ruysschaert 1949; Saunders 1955, 14, 17.

8. Grotius 1610. The book appeared simultaneously in Latin and was reprinted twelve times in the seventeenth century. See the 1988 edition with an introduction by G.C. Molewijk. For example, Grotius wrote that the Batavians rejected not only the Roman Empire, but also the centralized power of a monarch in favor of collective responsibility — a system not unlike the sharing of power between the Dutch provinces, cities, and stadtholder.

9. Grotius 1610, chapter 2. Similar ideas had been put forward by Hadrianus Junius, Kornelis van Haemrode, and Jan van Reygersbergh. See Kampinga 1917, 66; Chong 1992, 202–205.

10. Petrus Scriverius compiled an anthology of sources and interpretations of the Batavian story entitled, *Batavia illustrata* (Leiden, 1609), later revised as *Beschrijvinghe van out Batavien* (Arnhem, 1612).

35
Dordrecht from the North

mid-1650s, oil on canvas, 68.5 × 190 (26 ¹⁵/₁₆ × 74 ¹³/₁₆).
Ascott, The Anthony de Rothschild Collection
(The National Trust)

Provenance
(Sale, Sir George Colebroke, Bt., Christie's, London,
22 April 1774, nos. 2: 22, 23, to C. Bathall); Lady Stuart
(c. 1757–1841), Scotland Yard, London; (sale, Christie's,
London, 15 May 1841, nos. 74, 75 to Thomas B. Brown;
Brown rejoined the canvases); Robert Holford (18-8-1892),
Dorchester House, London; by descent to Sir George L.
Holford; (sale Christie's, 17 May 1928, no. 10, to Thomas
Agnew & Sons, London) for Anthony de Rothschild,
Ascott; National Trust bequest, 1949

Exhibitions
London 1815, nos. 133, 134; London 1843, no. 115; London
1852, no. 68; London 1862, no. 4; London 1887, no. 75;
London 1900, no. 31; Paris 1921, no. 5; London 1929, no. 265;
London 1936, no. 68; London 1967, no. 9; London 1973,
no. 13; London 1976, no. 27; Dordrecht 1992, no. 22; London
1995b, no. 29

Literature
Smith 1829–1842, 5 (1834): 337–338, nos. 187, 188; supplement (1842): no. 52; HdG 1907–1927, 2 (1909): no. 164;
MacLaren 1960, 72; Van Gelder and Jost 1972, 223, note 15;
Reiss 1975, 137, no. 98; Dordrecht 1977, 88; MacLaren and
Brown 1991, 1: 71; Chong 1992, 415–417, no. 163

Endnotes
1. London 1995b, 84.

2. Chong 1992, 416.

3. London 1995b, 84.

4. See also Abraham van Calraet, *Scene on Ice outside Dordrecht* (The National Gallery, London, inv. no. 3024), which
shows a similar view of Dordrecht, albeit during the winter
and with slight variations (MacLaren and Brown 1991, 71).

5. Adam Willaerts, *View of Dordrecht* (Dordrechts Museum).
See also the essay by Arthur Wheelock in this catalogue.

6. See also the large raft on the left of Adam Willaerts'
View of Dordrecht.

7. See also the lumber yard depicted in Cuyp's *View of
Dordrecht from the South* (collection Eugène Heimgartner,
Geneva; Reiss 1975, 28, no. 3; Chong 1992, 269, no. 5).

8. Bruin 1716, 129; quoted by Chong 1992, 170: "Wat zien
wy hier op 't water zweeven, / Wat groot gevaart bestormt
ons hier? / Het komt van boeven afgedreeven, / en 't is vol
leeven en gezwier. / 't zyn eike vlotten, / Daar men 't Duitse
Woud / Om af moest knotten; / Dus verkeert het hout /
Door koopmanschap, in goud." For a more detailed discussion of this subject see Chong 1992, 168–171 and notes
48–49. See also Dordrecht 1992, 132.

9. Chong 1992, 170.

10. Because of the picture's format and the fact that it does
not bear a signature nor is anything known about a possible
commission or an original owner, it has been suggested that
Cuyp may have painted it "for his own pleasure and use"
(London 1995b, 85). Although it seems certainly true that
Cuyp was no longer dependent on the sale of his pictures
after his marriage in 1658, it does not seem very likely that
he would have painted such an ambitious work without
having a particular patron in mind. Chong, based on a comparison with the loftier sky in the picture from Kenwood
House (cat. 36), suggested that the picture may well have lost
about a fourth of its original height, but there does not seem
to be any technical evidence to support this hypothesis
(Chong 1992, 416).

11. Smith 1829–1842, 5 (1834): 337, 338, nos. 187 and 188.

12. The picture had been cut in half by the time it appeared
as two pendants in the sale of Sir George Colbrooke in 1774.
Hofstede de Groot mentioned that "the portions were reunited
by the London dealer Brown, 1841" (HdG 1907–1927, 2
[1909]: no. 164). More specifically, the work must have been
done between the sale of the two pictures in the auction of
Lady Stuart (Christie's, London, 15 May 1841, nos. 74, 75)
and the publication of Smith's supplement of his *Catalogue
raisonné...*in 1842 (no. 52; see Van Gelder and Jost 1972, 236,
note 5). Evidently, the severing and rejoining were handled
in such a manner that "virtually nothing has been lost from
the centre of it" (London 1995b, 85). However, another
author found the "excessively bright and hard-edged sky"
"unlike anything Cuyp ever painted"—although parallels
have been perceived in the sky of *The Baptism of the Eunuch*
from Anglesey Abbey (cat. 30) (Chong 1992, 416). Reiss
(1975, 137) compared this with the two fragments of a *View
of Dordrecht*, now kept in Los Angeles (left half, Los Angeles
County Museum of Art, inv. no. 50.43) and Leipzig (right
half, Museum der Bildenden Künste, inv. no. 1001) (Chong
1992, 286–287, nos. 30, 31).

36
Dordrecht from the North

mid-1650s, oil on canvas, 97.8 × 137.8 (38 ½ × 54 ¼).
English Heritage (The Iveagh Bequest, Kenwood) (46)

Inscription
Signed, lower right (on oar): *A. cuyp*

Provenance
(Probably sale, Jan Danser Nijman, Amsterdam, 16 August
1797, no. 48, to J. Spaan). Private collection, Brussels;
(C. J. Nieuwhuys, 1829); Edward Gray, Harringay House,

London, by 1834; (James Morrison, William Buchanan, 1838); 3d marquess of Lansdowne, London, and Bowood, 1838; (Thomas Agnew & Sons, 1888); Sir Edward C. Guiness, Bt., later baron, viscount, and earl of Iveagh, Elveden Hall, Suffolk and Kenwood House; bequest 1927

Exhibitions

London 1839, no. 12; London 1867, no. 128; London 1903, no. 94; London 1928b, no. 191; Manchester 1928, no. 12; London 1952, no. 163; New York, Toledo, and Toronto 1954, no. 19; London 1963, no. 2; The Hague and London 1970–1971, no. 55; Dordrecht 1977, no. 30; Birmingham 1989, no. 101

Literature

Smith 1829–1842, 5 (1834): 339, no. 193; supplement (1842): 658, no. 29; HdG 1907–1927, 2 (1909): nos. 165, 631; London 1928b, no. 46, pl. 31; Van Gelder and Jost 1972, note 5; Reiss 1975, 136, no. 97; Bryant 1990, 29, 72; Chong 1992, 417–418, no. 164

Endnotes

1. For the identification of the individual buildings see Dordrecht 1977, 88.

2. Houbraken 1718–1721, 248: "Daarenboven heeft hy inzonderheit wel in acht genomen de tyd stonden waar in hy de voorwerpen verbeelde, zoo dat men den benevelden morgenstont van den klaren middag, en dezen weer van den saffraanverwigen avonstont in zyn tafereelen kost onderscheiden."

3. See also the entry on the painting from Ascott (cat. 35); Dordrecht 1992, 34–35, fig. 1; and Chong 1992, 171.

4. Van Gelder and Jost 1972, 236, note 5; Chong 1992, 418.

5. The drawing from Amsterdam also served as a model for Cuyp's *Maas at Dordrecht* in Washington (cat. 28). Both Reiss and Chong — evidently considering the present picture somewhat inferior to the Ascott version — suggested that the present work must have been painted slightly later (Reiss 1975, 136; Chong 1992, 416).

37
Horsemen Resting in a Landscape

late 1650s, oil on canvas, 116 × 168 (45 11/16 × 66 1/8). Dordrechts Museum (DM / 978 / 526)

Inscription

Signed, lower right: *A. cuyp*

Provenance

John Cator, Beckenham Place, Kent, by 1834; by descent to Albemarle Cator, Kent, 1890, and to John Cator, Woodbastick Hall, Norwich; (sale, Sotheby's, London, 24 June 1970, no. 17); (H. Baer); (David Koetser, Zurich); acquired by the Dordrechts Museum, Dordrecht, with the support of the Vereniging Rembrandt, 1978

Exhibitions

London 1890, no. 86; London 1964, no. 5; Norwich 1964, no. 18; Dordrecht 1977, no. 29; Dordrecht 1991, fig. 24; Dordrecht 1992, no. 20; Nagasaki 1993, no. 15

Literature

Smith 1829–1842, 5 (1834): no. 191; HdG 1907–1927, 2 (1909): no. 509; Dumas in Leeuwarden, Den Bosch, and Assen 1979, 105, no. 70, repro.; Chong 1992, no. 146

Endnotes

1. These include Cuyp's first equestrian portrait, depicting Pieter de Roovere (Chong essay, fig. 3) and the painting in the Barber Institute of Fine Arts, Birmingham (Gordenker essay, fig. 7).

2. De Bruyn Kops 1965; Dattenberg 1967, 64–66. The scene is also similar to the large landscape in Waddesdon Manor (Reiss 1975, pl. 137).

3. Reiss 1975, pl. 115.

38
Horsemen and Herdsmen with Cattle

late 1650s, oil on canvas, 120 × 171.5 (47 3/8 × 67 1/2). National Gallery of Art, Washington, Widener Collection (1942.9.16)

Inscription

Bottom right corner: *A.cuijp*.

Provenance

Johan van der Linden van Slingeland, Dordrecht, by 1752; (sale, Yver, Delfos, Dordrecht, 22 August 1785, no. 71, to Fouquet). M. Albert Dubois, Paris; (sale, Lebrun, Paris, 20 December 1785, no. 16, bought in). William Smith, Norwich; Edward Gray, until 1830. Alexander Baring, later 1st Baron Ashburton, London, and The Grange, Hampshire, by 1834; by descent to the 5th Lord Ashburton, until 1907; (Thomas Agnew & Sons, London). (Arthur J. Sulley, London); Peter A.B. Widener, Lynnewood Hall, Elkins Park, Pennsylvania, 1909–1915; Joseph E. Widener, Lynnewood Hall, Elkins Park, Pennsylvania, 1915–1942; National Gallery of Art (Widener bequest), 1942

Exhibitions

Montreal 1990, 109–110, no. 28

Literature

Hoet 1752, 2: 495; Smith 1829–1842, 5 (1834): 288, no. 10; Waagen 1838, 2: 282–283; HdG 1907–1927, 2 (1909): no. 430; Widener 1913, no. 12, repro.; Holmes 1930, 165–185;

Hutton 1961, 79 – 85, repro.; Dattenberg 1967, 72 – 73, repro. 79a; Reiss 1975, 179, no. 136 repro.; Walker 1976, 298 – 299, color repro.; Chong 1992, 405 – 406, no. 158; Wheelock 1995, 46 – 50, color repro.

Endnotes

1. The auction catalogue of the sale held in Dordrecht in 1785 described the painting as having "an unusually beautiful execution" and as being "one of the best of this master" ("dit Konstuk is van een ongemeene schoone uitwerking, en een der beste van deezen Meester").

2. Cuyp based another painting upon the view from the opposite direction. Several versions of this composition exist, the best of which seems to be that in the Castle Howard Collection, Yorkshire (HdG 1907 – 1927, 2 (1909): no. 71).

3. Cuyp originally painted Monterberg as a somewhat lower hill. He seems to have enlarged it for compositional reasons.

4. Compare with the more topographically accurate depictions of the area produced by Joris van der Haagen (drawing, Kupferstichkabinett, Berlin, inv. no. 11821) or Romeyn de Hooghe (engraving, reproduced in Gorissen 1964, no. 106).

5. J. K. van der Haagen, former chief, museum and monuments division, UNESCO, Paris (letter, 29 November 1964, in NGA curatorial files), tentatively identified the towns as Griethausen (to the left) and Emmerich (immediately to the left of the pale horse, partly behind the twigs of the foreground sapling).

6. Smith 1829 – 1842, 5 (1834): 288, and HdG 1907 – 1927, 2 (1909): no. 430, both stated that the two pictures were hung as pendants in the Van Slingeland collection, information that they would have gained from Hoet 1752, 2: 495, who listed *Horsemen and Herdsmen with Cattle* as one of a "pair of landscapes," the other of which was probably *Landscape with Horse Trainers*. The Toledo picture, moreover, came

directly after the Washington picture in the 1785 Van Slingeland sale catalogue (see note 2) and was described as "een Meesterstuk van konst en een weerga van de vorige" (a masterpiece of art and a pendant of the previous [work]; see cat. 39).

39
Landscape with Horse Trainers

late 1650s, oil on canvas, 118.7 × 170.2 (46 ¾ × 67).
The Toledo Museum of Art, Purchased with funds from the Libbey Endowment, Gift of Edward Drummond Libbey (1960.2)

Inscription
Signed, lower right: *A. cuyp*

Provenance
Johan van der Linden van Slingeland, Dordrecht, by 1752; (sale, Yver, Delfos, Dordrecht, 22 August 1785, no. 72, to Fouquet). M. Albert Dubois, Paris; (sale, Lebrun, Paris, 20 December 1785, no. 17). 5th earl of Hopetoun, by 1826; by descent probably until 1908. Edouard de Rothschild, Ferrières, by 1912 and by descent. (André Seligmann, Paris). (Rosenberg and Stiebel, New York, 1960); The Toledo Museum of Art, 1960

Exhibitions
Edinburgh 1826, no. 60; Edinburgh 1883, no. 276; London 1883, no. 238; Edinburgh 1992

Literature
Hoet 1752, 2: 495; Waagen 1854, 3: 309; HdG 1907 – 1927, 2 (1909): no. 448; Hutton 1961, repro.; Stechow 1966, 162; Toledo Museum of Art 1976, 46 – 47, pl. 121, col. pl. VII; Chong 1992, 404 – 405, no. 157; Hutton 1995, 97, repro.; Wheelock 1995, 48, repro.

Endnotes

1. Houbraken listed some of Cuyp's favorite subjects, including the riding school: "de Pikeurbaan, daar hy dan de schilderagtigste Paerden die daar gewoonlyk kwamen, in te pas bragt, zoo dat men dezelve kost onderkennen" (the riding school, in which he depicted the most picturesque horses that usually came there, so that one could recognize them); see Houbraken 1718 – 1721 (1753 ed.), 1: 248 – 249.

2. The horse in Cuyp's painting has not accurately performed the levade: its front legs are too extended.

3. See Liedtke 1989, 89 – 90.

4. An earlier edition of the treatise is De Pluvinel 1623.

5. See Liedtke 1989, 296 – 298, figs. 177 – 180.

6. In 1640 Van de Passe moved to Amsterdam.

7. This point is made by William Hutton in Hutton 1995, 97.

8. See Hutton 1961, 84, who notes that the church's tower, cupola, and façade resemble those of the Mariakerk. Hutton, however, also adds that "Cuyp has flattened the roof, suppressed later Gothic elements and raised the arcading. He then added a half-round apse like the one still in the Valkhof at Nijmegen." See Boymans-van Beuningen 1972, 51, repro., for a painting by Pieter Saenredam (1597 – 1665) of the Mariakerk, signed and dated 1663.

9. See the essay by Gordenker for a discussion of the date and style of the outfits worn by the horsemen in riding coats.

10. Inventories of country houses near Utrecht indicate that many collectors preferred paintings by artists working in an Italianate mode, among them Herman Saftleven, Cornelis van Poelenburch, and Jan Both. Poelenburch's influence is stressed by Chong 1992, 148. For inventories of Utrecht collections, see Olde Meierink and Bakker 1997, 72 – 85.

11. See De Jongh 1990, 29.

12. The Toledo picture and its pendant were listed in the 1652 inventory of the Van Slingeland collection. This work followed directly after the Washington picture in the 1785 Slingeland sale, where it was described as "een Meesterstuk van konst en een weerga van de vorige" (a masterpiece of art and a pendant of the previous [work]).

40
Lady and Gentleman on Horseback

begun c. 1655, completed 1660 / 1665, oil on canvas, 123 × 172 (48 ½ × 67 ¾). National Gallery of Art, Washington, Widener Collection (1942.9.15)

Inscription

Lower left: *A.Cuijp.*

Provenance

Thomas Emmerson, London, before 1834. Edmund Higginson, Saltmarshe Castle, Herefordshire, before 1842; (sale, Christie's, London, 16 June 1860, no. 34 to Charles J. Nieuwenhuys, Brussels). Probably Lord Henry Francis Hope Pelham-Clinton-Hope; (sale, Christie's, London, 30 June 1894, no. 22); Charles Wertheimer, London. (Galerie Sedelmeyer, Paris, by 1894); Peter A.B. Widener, Lynnewood Hall, Elkins Park, Pennsylvania, 1894–1915; Joseph E. Widener, Lynnewood Hall, Elkins Park, Pennsylvania, 1915–1942; National Gallery of Art (Widener bequest), Washington, 1942

Literature

Smith 1829–1842, 5 (1834): 334, no. 177; 9 (1842): 664, no. 48; Widener 1885–1900, 2 (1900): 142; HdG 1907–1927, 2 (1909): no. 618; Widener 1913, unpaginated, no. 11; Holmes 1930, 168, 185, no. 35; Reiss 1953, 45, pl. 14, no. 599;

Reiss 1975, 165, no. 124, repro.; Walker 1976, 298–299, color repro.; Leeuwarden, Den Bosch, and Assen 1979, 104–105, no. 69, repro.; Chong 1992, 391–392, no. 148; Wheelock 1995, 50–56, color repro.

Endnotes

1. I would like to thank Ann P. Wagner, a graduate student at the University of Maryland, for informing me about the character of these hounds. For further information, see Anthony Dent, *Horses in Shakespeare's England* (London, 1987), 128.

2. Reiss 1975, 165, proposed that the gentleman was "a member of the Pompe [van Meerdervoort] family, perhaps Cornelis Pompe (1639–1680), the younger of the two boys seen in the New York picture" (cat. 29), but this conclusion rests on the assumption that the star-shaped horse-brass in the Washington picture, which resembles that in the New York picture, relates to the family crest. On the other hand, in a letter dated 25 February 1984 (NGA curatorial files), Alan Chong noted that the horse-brass in the National Gallery's picture is similar to the stylized five-pointed oak-leaf that appears in the Berk family crest. In fact, according to the archivist of the Municipal Archives in Dordrecht, these horse-brasses were standard decorative elements of Turkish origin and cannot be connected with family crests. Indeed, exactly the same motifs occur on the horse-brass on Paulus Potter's 1653 life-size equestrian portrait of Dirck Tulp, in the Six Collection, Amsterdam. The suggestion has also been made in a number of the Widener catalogues that the woman, because of her younger appearance, may be the man's daughter.

3. The painting is in the Zeeuws Genootschap van Kunst en Wetenschap, Middelburg. Alan Chong kindly provided this information in a letter, 5 February 1990 (NGA curatorial files).

4. However, this identification does not explain the two letters, *JH*, embroidered on the woman's saddlecloth. These initials have not yet been connected with any name.

5. The red socks can be seen through the somewhat translucent surface paint.

6. Another connection is the architecture of the building; though not identical, it is similar in character to that in the Washington painting. This structure is probably a fanciful evocation of an ancient fortified chateau such as Cuyp may have seen on his trip along the Rhine.

7. De Jongh 1968–1969, 34, wrote: "The hunt is synonymous with the game of love and it…was a current and naturally obvious metaphor."

8. Although the symbol of the burdock leaf can be either that of virtue and fidelity or vice and lust, the context of the scene clearly points toward the first alternative. See Parsons and Ramsay 1983.

41
Flight into Egypt

late 1650s, oil on panel, 68 × 90.8 (26 ¾ × 35 ¾). Los Angeles County Museum of Art, Partial gift of Hannah L. Carter

Inscription

Signed, lower left: *A. cuyp*

Provenance

Servad, Amsterdam (sale, Yver, Amsterdam, 25 June 1778, no. 48); Prince Charles-Maurice de Talleyrand, Paris (sale, Henry, Paris, 7 July 1817, no. 10); (James Buchanan, London); John Webb, London; Alexander Baring, later 1st Baron Ashburton, London, and The Grange, Hampshire, by descent to the 5th Lord Ashburton, until 1907; (Thomas

Agnew & Sons, London); Alfred de Rothschild, Halton Manor, by descent to Rothschild heirs; (Arthur Ruck and M. Knoedler, New York, by 1924); Charles T. Fisher, Detroit, by 1925; Thomas K. Fisher (sale, Christie's, 28 June 1974, no. 79); (Richard L. Feigen, New York, 1977); Mr. and Mrs. Edward Carter, Los Angeles

Exhibitions
London 1819, no. 105; Detroit 1926, no. 24, repro.; Detroit 1927, no. 31; Detroit 1929, no. 16, repro.; Detroit 1939, no. 10; New York 1939, no. 66, pl. 77; Detroit 1949, no. 6, pl. 7; Los Angeles, Boston, and New York 1981, 40 – 45, no. 10, repro.

Literature
Buchanan 1824, 2, 312, 321 – 322; Waagen 1838, 2, 283; Waagen 1854, 2, 110; Valentiner 1929, 3, repro.; Holmes 1930, 167, no. 27, repro.; Montreal 1990, 87, repro.; Chong 1992, 422 – 423, no. 168

Endnotes
1. Waagen 1854, 2: 110, no. 2.

2. This point was made by Walsh and Schneider in Los Angeles, Boston, and New York 1981, 43. These authors noted that the painting's biblical subject was not identified until the 1929 Detroit exhibition catalogue.

3. This comparison was made in Montreal 1990, 87.

4. Walsh and Schneider in Los Angeles, Boston, and New York 1981, 45, dated the painting in the "early to middle 1650s."

42
River Landscape with Two Horsemen

late 1650s, oil on canvas, 128 × 227.5 (50 ⅜ × 89 ⁹⁄₁₆). Rijksmuseum, Amsterdam (A 4118)

Inscription
Signed, lower center: *A. cuyp.*

Provenance
Jacob Odon; (sale, Van de Sley, Yver, Amsterdam, 6 September 1784, no. 51, to Coclair); (Noel Desenfans); John Joseph Martin, Ham Court, about 1796; G. E. Martin; Alfred de Rothschild, Halton; Lionel de Rothschild, Exbury, Hampshire, 1920; by descent to Edmund de Rothschild; (Thomas Agnew & Sons, London, and Rudolf Heinemann by 1957); acquired by the Rijksmuseum, Amsterdam, with the aid of the Vereniging Rembrandt, the Prins Bernhard Fonds, and the Commissie voor Fotoverkoop, 1965

Exhibitions
London 1850, no. 20; London 1862, no. 34; London 1880, no. 114; London 1938, no. 127; London 1952, no. 170; London 1957, no. 19; Dordrecht 1977, no. 34; Amsterdam 2000a, no. 151

Literature
Smith 1829 – 1842, supplement (1842), 659 – 660, no. 35; Burnett 1969, 377 – 379, fig. 16; Reiss 1975, 182, no. 139; Chong 1992, 423 – 424, no. 169

Endnotes
1. See Chong's essay in this catalogue and Chong 1992, 53 – 56.

2. Quoted from Chong's conclusion in his essay in this catalogue.

3. A few more works left the country over the course of the nineteenth century, for instance, *Ships on a River* and *A Landing Party on the Maas at Dordrecht*, both now at Waddesdon Manor (see cat. 28, fig. 1; Chong 1992, nos. 159, 160).

4. De Bruyn Kops 1965, 162 – 176. Uniforms had not been introduced yet and soldiers recognized friend and foe by the colors of their sashes and feathers. The light armor suggests that the soldier is a harquebusier.

5. Chong 1992, 145 – 147 and 224.

6. For the identification of the landscape see Dattenberg 1967, 66 – 67.

7. Chong 1992, 424, and De Bruyn Kops 1965, 165, have argued that the topographical fidelity of the drawing suggests that it was actually made from nature and not sometime after the journey in the studio, as Burnett implied. (Burnett 1969, 378). However, Cuyp may have added the range of hills in the back sometime later. Presumably without knowing the drawing, John Smith in his *Catalogue raisonné* had already identified the location as "on the banks of the Rhine, and apparently in the vicinity of Nijmegen." Smith 1829 – 1842, supplement (1842): 659. Another drawing of the same scene, although with different staffage, identified by Chong as a copy, is kept in the Städelsches Kunstinstitut in Frankfurt (inv. no. 3721).

8. This is discussed in more detail in Maisak 1981, 188 – 192. Already in 1769 the description accompanying William Elliott's print after Cuyp's *River Landscape with Horseman and Peasants* (then in the earl of Bute's collection), remarks, if somewhat critically, on this aspect (see Chong essay, fig. 7 and note 7 in cat. 45).

9. Smith 1829 – 1842, supplement (1842): 660.

43
Landscape with a View of the Valkhof, Nijmegen

late 1650s, oil on canvas, 113 × 165 (44 ½ × 64 ¹⁵⁄₁₆).
National Gallery of Scotland, Edinburgh (2314)

Inscription
Signed, lower right: *A. cuyp*

Provenance
Perhaps Sir James Colebrooke, Bt., Gatton, Surrey. (sale, Prestage, London, 3 February 1762, no. 67), to Sir George Colebrooke, Bt., the brother of Sir James Colebrooke, Bt.); (sale, Christie's, London, 22 April 1774, no. 47); (Dr. Chauncey). 2d earl of Ashburnham, London, and Ashburnham Place, Sussex, by 1784; (sale, Christie's, London, 20 July 1850, no. 89); sold by Lady Ashburnham in 1895 to Alfred de Rothschild, Halton; by descent to Lionel de Rothschild, Exbury, Hampshire, 1920; to Edmund de Rothschild; (Thomas Agnew & Sons, London, 1966); L.R. Bradbury; (Thomas Agnew & Sons, London); National Gallery of Scotland, 1972 (acquired in recognition of the services of the earl of Crawford and Balcarres to the National Arts-Collection Fund and the National Galleries of Scotland)

Exhibitions
London 1815, no. 100; London 1903, no. 98; London 1957, no. 16

Literature
London 1815, 50; Neale 1818, series 2, vol. 4 (1828); Smith 1829–1842, 5 (1834): no. 260; Waagen 1854, 3, 28; Cundall 1891, 160; HdG 1907–1927, 2 (1909): nos. 173, 174; Burnett 1969, 379, fig. 21; Reiss 1975, no. 128; Poughkeepsie 1976, 67; Nijmegen 1980, 89, fig. 3; Chong 1992, no. 165

Endnotes
1. Noted by J.G. van Gelder and I. Jost in Poughkeepsie 1976, 67. The same view was drawn several times by Lambert Doomer; see Schulz 1974, nos. 188–190. The version in the Staatliche Kunstsammlungen, Weimar (4894), even includes, in reverse, almost the same rider as seen in the Edinburgh picture.

2. See Hogenberg 1983. A print of the 1591 siege of Nijmegen can also be found in Orlers 1610, 84.

3. Boudewijnse 1959, 177–184.

4. The 1673 inventory of Anthonetta van Bouthem, Dordrecht: "een groote schilderije wtbeeldende een leger ofte Rendevou van schepen leggende voor Nummegen, gemaeckt door Aelbert Cuyp" (a large painting depicting an army or meeting of ships before Nijmegen, made by Aelbert Cuyp); ONA 157. The 1723 inventory of Pompejus de Roovere: "Het hoff van Nijmegen door kuyp" (The court of Nijmegen by Cuyp); Hoge Raad van Adel, The Hague, Van Slingeland archive. An anonymous view of Nijmegen is recorded in 1669 in the collection of Cornelis Bloesem, Dordrecht. See also Getty Provenance Index.

44
Evening Landscape

late 1650s, oil on canvas, 101.5 × 153.6 (39 ¹⁵⁄₁₆ × 60 ½).
Her Majesty Queen Elizabeth II (314)

Inscription
Signed, lower right: *A cuÿp.*

Provenance
Johan van der Linden van Slingeland, Dordrecht; (sale, Yver, Delfos, Dordrecht, 22 August 1785, no. 82, to Fouquet). Jan Gildemeester, Amsterdam; (sale, Amsterdam, 11 June 1800, no. 30, to Telting). Sir Francis Baring, Bt., London; by descent to Sir Thomas Baring, Bt.; The Prince Regent, later George IV, Carlton House, London, 1814; by descent to H.M. the Queen Elizabeth II, Buckingham Palace, London

Exhibitions
London 1826, no. 28; London 1827, no. 28; London 1837, no. 24; London 1885, no. 101; London 1946, no. 391; The Hague and London 1970–1971, no. 17; Amsterdam, Boston, and Philadelphia, 1987, no. 24; London 1991, no. 44

Literature
Smith 1829–1842, 5 (1834): 293, no. 22; HdG 1907–1927, 2 (1909): no. 432; Millar 1968, 278; Reiss 1975: 176, no. 133; White 1982, 32–33, no. 35; Chong 1992, 425–426, no. 171

Endnotes
1. In this context it is interesting to note, as Chong has pointed out, that Cuyp is actually never referred to as a "painter" in contemporary documents (see Chong 1992, 225). Cuyp's 1658 marriage to Cornelia Boschman, the widow of the wealthy Dordrecht regent Johan van den Corput, left him financially secure and admitted him to the city's regent class. He may have reduced his activities as a painter in order to pursue the responsibilities and lifestyle (alluded to so often in his grand landscapes) that his new social position demanded. However, it seems unlikely that he gave up painting altogether, for evidence suggests that he reworked one of his earlier pictures (cat. 40) in the early-to-mid 1660s, and Houbraken reported that Barent van Calraet became apprenticed to Cuyp about 1665 (Houbraken 1718–1721 (1753 ed.): 230).

2. This is a recurring motif in Cuyp's paintings. For more on the subject see also cat. 45.

3. A variant of this composition, painted by a follower of Cuyp, is now kept at Petworth House (National Trust) (Reiss 1975, 190, no. 145; Chong 1992, 451, no. C16).

4. See, for example, his etching of *Travelers in a Landscape* (Amsterdam, Boston, and Philadelphia 1987, 398, fig. 2). A comparable composition can also be found in Cuyp's *Three Horsemen, Herdsmen, and Shepherdess* (British private collection; Reiss 1975, 177, no. 134). Less convincingly Reiss 1975, 176, suggested that the painting also reflects the influence of Adam Pynacker's compositions, for example his *Bridge in an Italian Landscape* (Dulwich Picture Gallery [inv. no. 183]).

5. Waagen 1838, 2: 371.

6. Smith 1829 – 1842, 5 (1834): 293.

45
River Landscape with Horseman and Peasants

c. 1660, oil on canvas, 123 × 241 (48 7/16 × 94 7/8).
The National Gallery, London (6522)

Inscription
Signed, lower right: *A: cuÿp.*

Provenance
Acquired in Holland by Capt. William Baillie; 3d earl of Bute, Luton Hoo; by descent to marquess of Bute, Luton Hoo, by 1799; in London in 1865, later at Mount Stuart; acquired by The National Gallery, London, 1989, with contributions from the National Heritage Memorial Fund and from the National Art Collections Fund

Exhibitions
London 1818, no. 85; London 1819, no. 37; London 1847, no. 92; London 1870, no. 102; London 1883, no. 202; Glasgow 1884, no. 38; Manchester 1885, no. 56; Edinburgh 1949, no. 7; London 1973, no. 14; London 1976, no. 31; London 1984, no. 45; Amsterdam, Boston, and Philadelphia, 1987, no. 25

Literature
Smith 1829 – 1842, 5 (1834): 361, no. 264; HdG 1907 – 1927, 2 (1909): no. 433; Burnett 1969, 380; Roberts 1973, 135; Reiss 1975, no. 140; Kingston-upon-Hull 1981, 7; MacLaren and Brown 1991, 1: 555; Chong 1992, 426 – 428, no. 172

Endnotes
1. Although Cuyp may have reduced his activities as a painter because of his new position and responsibilities in the wake of his marriage of 1658, Reiss suggested that the present picture "is so perfectly wrought that it is almost understandable he should have felt inhibited from proceeding further" (Reiss 1975, 183).

2. Chong 1992, 147.

3. For more on this subject see the essay by Mieke B. Smits-Veldt and Hans Luijten, "Nederlandse poëzie in de 17de eeuw: verliefde en wijze herders" in Utrecht, Frankfurt, Luxemburg 1993 – 1994, 58 – 75 and also Gibson 2000, 133 – 140.

In this context it may be worth noting that the motif of asking for directions occurs in a poem, entitled "Van den Wegh" (About the Way), published in Haarlem in 1610 as part of the *Nederduytschen helicon*. The subject of the poem is man's journey through life — contrasting a world full of dangers and corruption as symbolized by the woods with fertile lands that promise a joyful and virtuous life. But in order to stay on the proper path — and thus is the reader reminded twice at the end of the poem — it is necessary

to "ask for the way" (*Vraeght naer de wegh*) (see *Helicon* 1610, "Van den Wegh," 230 – 233, fols. P3v – P5r). However intentional this parallel may have been, it is not inconceivable that some of Cuyp's more educated and well-read patrons would have noticed it. I would like to thank Anna Tummers, who drew my attention to this source.

4. Chong 1992, 261.

5. See Farington's diary (1978 – 1984, 15 [1984], 5203): "While looking at Lord Bute's picture by Cuyp, He [Benjamin West] sd. that picture was brought to England by the late Captn. Baillie, and was the first picture by that Master known in England. Having been seen, pictures by Cuyp were eagerly sought for & many were introduced & sold to advantage!"

6. Desenfans 1802, 2: 142 – 145. The first paintings to appear at auction in London were in the Glover sale, 16 – 17 March 1741, nos. 58 and 115.

7. The passage reads as follows: "Cuyp may, with great propriety, be styled the *Dutch Claude*. It must be confessed, that this scenery is not of so fine a goût as that great master's, nor had he any idea of embellishing his pictures by the introduction of poetical subjects; but the chief design of both was to represent the beautiful effects of the sun upon terrestrial objects in different parts of the day ... nor is the colouring of Cuyp any way inferior to that of Claude in producing those effects. In some respects, he was certainly superior to him, particularly in designing and painting cattle, and the representation of the effect of moon-light, which, perhaps, Claude never attempted." (Boydell 1769, 12). In 1837 Gustav Waagen in his account of the paintings by Cuyp he had seen in the National Gallery also used the comparison with Claude: "In greatness of design, knowledge of aërial perspective, combined with the greatest glow and warmth of the misty or serene atmosphere, Cuyp stands unrivalled, and takes the same place for Dutch scenery as Claude Lorrain for the Italian, so that he might justly be called the Dutch Claude." (Waagen 1838, 1, 227 – 228). For a more detailed discussion of this aspect see Chong 1992, 32 – 34. John Ruskin, on the other hand, held a generally dismissive attitude toward the artist's paintings: "A brewer by trade, he [Cuyp] feels the quiet of a summer afternoon, and his work will make you marvellously drowsy. It is good for nothing else I know of; strong, but unhelpful and unthoughtful. Nothing happens except some indifferent person's asking the way of somebody else, who, by the cast of countenance, seems not likely to know it." (Ruskin 1843, 5: part 9, chapter 6, paragraph 12; Ruskin 1903 – 1912, 7, [1903]: 333 – 334; Ruskin 1987, 562; partially also cited by Gibson 2000, 133.)

8. MacLaren and Brown 1991, 1: 555.

9. In 1770 Boydell exhibited the drawings for the prints he had published a year earlier. They were sold at Christie's on 22 April 1771, yet the drawing for the present painting is missing (Chong 1992, 427).

Drawings

black chalk, gray wash, watercolored in brown, yellow, green, and pink, 22 × 31 (8 11/16 × 12 3/16).[1]
The British Museum, London

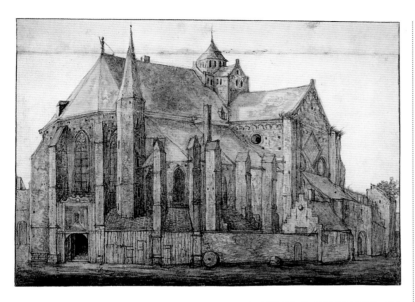

1 Pieter Saenredam, **View of the Choir and the Transept of the Mariakerk in Utrecht,** Het Utrechts Archief

· Aelbert Cuyp, as a draftsman, primarily a landscapist, turned his hand at the beginning of his career to the portrayal of the Utrecht Mariakerk, evidently in order to discover his abilities as a topographical artist. However, one may hardly speak of Cuyp's view of the Mariakerk without taking into consideration Pieter Saenredam's drawing of the same church on 12 July 1636 (fig. 1). In conception they are so similar that Cuyp must have known this drawing or a comparable one by this artist.[2] While Saenredam observed the choir of the church from the first floor at 10 Mariaplaats, Cuyp sketched the church from the street somewhat farther to the right.[3] Cuyp made his drawing a few years later, quite possibly in 1639, and a few differences suggest this passage of time. The pentice for the fire ladders has vanished, as has one of the two millstones set against the wall. The tall chimney of the chapter's office, the annex with the stepped gable, has also disappeared.

Cuyp drew in a more general fashion and was less concerned with details than was Saenredam, as, for instance, in the buttresses on the north side of the choir, which the older artist drew with great sensitivity. Cuyp evidently had less trouble with the perspectival scheme: Saenredam "forgot" to indicate that he saw the tower staircase from below, while Cuyp exaggerated it perhaps just a fraction.[4] Moreover, Cuyp devoted greater attention to elements he deemed important, making, for example, the

square and circular windows of the transept powerful visual accents, whereas Saenredam almost allowed them to vanish in the myriad of details. This difference in approach is also clear in the distinction between the wooden sheds and the stone wall with the little gate giving onto the inner court of the chapter's office, elements that are almost inconspicuous in Saenredam's work. Similarly, Saenredam precisely delineated the painted board above the door to the salesroom of the cabinetmakers' guild, while for Cuyp this architectural element served as a brief yet powerful demonstration of the spatial effects of perspective. The different approach to proportions is also evident in the eastern window (at the left in the drawing). Although both artists depicted the division of the window below the crowning with tracery in two rows of five apertures each, the proportions of the window as a whole are substantially different.

Cuyp depicted the Gothic choir — consecrated in 1421 — and the Romanesque transept of the Mariakerk, which was founded in the eleventh century. The somewhat lower nave and the south tower of the west side are hidden from sight. He also depicted the overgrown ruin of the north tower. The explicit topographical tenor of this drawing is unique in Cuyp's oeuvre. Cuyp undoubtedly drew this work, along with a few other landscape-oriented views of the city (cats. 47 – 49), during a visit he made to Utrecht early in his career. **WK**

47 The Mariakerk in Utrecht from the Northwest

black chalk, gray wash, watercolored in green, yellow, and brown, heightened with white, yellow, and pink, partly brushed with gum arabic, 19.1 × 30.7 (7 ½ × 12 ⅟₁₆). Graphische Sammlung im Städelsches Kunstinstitut, Frankfurt am Main *(Washington, Amsterdam only)*

1 Aelbert Cuyp, **View of Utrecht from the Southwest**, Staatliche Museen zu Berlin, Kupferstichkabinett

· The Mariakerk in Utrecht — so well known from Pieter Saenredam's not fully consistent depictions (namely his paintings in the Thyssen Collection and in the Museum Boijmans Van Beuningen, Rotterdam) — is here presented as if it were a cloister set in a wooded and hilly landscape.

Cuyp characterized the higher elements of the church fairly accurately, with the typical crowning of the transept, the high choir, and the tower staircase at the left and the pseudo transept somewhat more to the right. However, the perspective of the west front with its circular window is not drawn entirely correctly. The tall building visible just past the south tower of the west side (the north tower was shelled by the Spanish troops in the sixteenth century) is probably the choristers' house. This structure, built as a school for choirboys, served as a hidden church for the Catholic congregation of Saint Geerte or Gertrudis in the seventeenth century.

The artist probably drew the building from the city ramparts, presumably the site of the peculiar architectural fragment in the left foreground. On the right side, however, Cuyp abandoned any pretense of topographical accuracy, for neither the water (and, thus, the rowboat) nor the dunes in the distance were visible from this location. One can therefore infer that once back in Dordrecht, Cuyp gave the finishing touches to the drawing, not only accentuating the landscape but also introducing the shadows suggesting that the sun was in the northeast.

The drawing belongs to a group of views of Utrecht that Cuyp made early in his career (cats. 46, 48, 49). On this occasion Cuyp must also have drawn the ambitious profile of Utrecht from the southwest (fig. 1), in which the Dom Tower, the Mariakerk, and the Buurkerk can be distinguished at the left. A comparison between that sheet and far more advanced city views of just a few years later, for example, the view of Amersfoort (cat. 71), makes clear just how great the artist's progress would be.

The rural surroundings Cuyp provided in this drawing play an even greater role in the painting in Salzburg (cat. 5), for which Cuyp used this drawing as well as the *Landscape with Two Groups of Trees,* formerly in Pella (see cat. 5, fig. 1). There the setting of the church — as if on a ridge in the distance — is completely divorced from any urban connection. **WK**

48   The Buurkerk in Utrecht in Rural Surroundings

black chalk, gray wash, watercolored in gray-green, white, and gray-green bodycolor, pen and brown ink, partly brushed with gum arabic, 18.4 × 30.5 (7 ¼ × 12). Mrs. Edward Speelman

· At the left in this sheet Cuyp depicted the Utrecht Buurkerk — the city's first parish church — with its characteristic truncated tower in two sections, surrounded by a great variety of structures. In the middle can be discerned some towers on the city ramparts, while a few mills dot the southwest bulwark of the city. Cuyp, who observed the church from the northwest, created the impression that he drew the tower from the city ramparts. However, in actuality, the Mariakerk would also have been visible from this angle.

Cuyp probably first laid in the composition in chalk and enlivened it with subtle colors back in the workshop. The chalk sketch presumably originated during an early visit to Utrecht, at which time he made the views of the Mariakerk and the Pellekussenpoort (cats. 46, 47, 49). From the city ramparts he also drew the German chapel with the Mariakerk in the distant background.[1] WK

49

**Utrecht with the Vecht River and
the Pellekussenpoort**

black chalk, gray wash, watercolored in green, traces of pen and gray ink and some white bodycolor,
17.6 × 30.7 (6 15/16 × 12 1/8). Staatliche Museen zu Berlin, Kupferstichkabinett *(Washington, Amsterdam only)*

· This early drawing is exceptionally rich, both in technique and in topographical detail. Visible at the left is the profile of Utrecht with the Pellekussenpoort (Pellekussen Gate), the Dom Tower, and in the distance the Sint Jacobskerk. On the opposite side of the Vecht River are the characteristic low-rise buildings of the suburban section of the city and a badly maintained quay. This sheet also depicts numerous moored boats in the bend of the Vecht, as well as a boat, sculled across the water, carrying two women with goods. At the right is a sailboat at anchor with a struck mast, and at the left is a fishing boat with large catch baskets.

Cuyp used many techniques when creating this drawing. First he drew the sketch in black chalk, sometimes heavily accentuated (as in the quay at the right), sometimes with a lively touch (as in the foliage), or with extreme delicacy (as in the mill in the distance). Drawing with the tip of the brush in gray ink, he subtly defined the little figures in the boats and elsewhere. He subsequently applied gray washes for the shadows and the reflections in the water. Over the wash he introduced green watercolor and, finally, some white and red accents in the houses at the right and the roof of the gate. He also reinforced a few passages with the pen, for instance in the boats in the foreground. Initially indicated in chalk, the clouds are also rendered with gray washes that give the impression of being autograph.

The sheet belongs to the group of early drawings of topographical significance that Cuyp made in and around Utrecht shortly before 1640 (see cats. 46 – 48). Related to a painting of 1639, now in Strasbourg, this drawing affords a *datum ante quem* for this group.

Cuyp's depiction of the Pellekussenpoort — a structure that inspired many artists in the seventeenth century — is remarkably accurate.[1] Here, Cuyp has proven that his interest in topographical reality in the drawing stage was not yet hampered by a preference for the picturesque, as is evident in other drawings from this period (cat. 48) and in his use of drawings for paintings (see cat. 5). WK

50 Four Trees near a Fence

black chalk, gray wash, watercolored in brown and green, partly brushed with gum arabic, 18.8 × 30.8 (7 ⅜ × 12 ⅛). The Metropolitan Museum of Art, New York, Rogers Fund, 1907 (*Washington, Amsterdam only*)

· Cuyp almost certainly produced a number of landscape studies during his visit to Utrecht in the late 1630s. Stylistically very close to his Utrecht views (cats. 46–49) are the present sheet and the famous *Landscape with Two Groups of Trees,* formerly in Pella (see cat. 5, fig. 1).[1] The artist would have encountered such uneven terrain to the east of Utrecht, perhaps along a route that took him to Rhenen; see Cuyp's stylistically related *View of Rhenen* in the Teylers Museum in Haarlem (Haverkamp-Begemann essay, fig. 3).[2]

While in the *Landscape with Two Groups of Trees* Cuyp placed emphasis on a few old oak trunks and the human presence (two travelers near a fence pointing to the distant vista), in *Four Trees near a Fence* Cuyp offered a more complex conception of the landscape. The four trees on a rise at the left and the fence across the foreground path constitute a visual screen obstructing the view into the middle ground. Nevertheless, the groves at the right appear to be at the edge of a valley that extends between the foreground elevation and the distant woods.

Technically, Cuyp worked hard on this sheet. In his engaging, crabbed manner of drawing, Cuyp portrayed the fancifulness of the four trees, as well as their transparency. He brought the sheet to life with tiny strokes of watercolor, suggesting the lush overgrowth in the foreground at the right with green and brown. Unfortunately, the drawing is somewhat damaged near the fence and this area has become blurred. WK black chalk, gray wash, 18.6 × 30 (7 $^5/_{16}$ × 11 $^{13}/_{16}$). Museum Boijmans Van Beuningen, Rotterdam

(Amsterdam only)

· In this sheet Cuyp rendered the hilly country-side at the edge of a woods. The landscape is intersected by a few paths, perhaps with a three-forked road at the left. Two travelers, whose upper bodies extend just above a rise in the landscape, have obviously selected the farthest path. They are fully integrated into the landscape and serve primarily to indicate depth. Cuyp made good use of the parallelism of the three elevations rising to the right.

Here, Cuyp wonderfully sustained his fine and lively technique, which found especially beautiful expression in the branches and foliage. This effect is particularly evident in the passage between the swaying grasses in the foreground and the bush at the foot of the tree to the right of center — an unclear bit of land that the artist nevertheless generously elaborated. Clouds in the sky are also nicely detailed with delicate, black-chalk hatching and a light wash.

This drawing belongs to a group of landscape drawings with groves (see also cat. 50). Cuyp must have developed at a rapid pace, and in this sheet, the drawing in Frankfurt (cat. 52), and the highly comparable drawings in Dublin and Saint Petersburg (The Hermitage), he presented a greater refinement, recalling the etchings of Willem Buytewech.[1] **WK**

black chalk, gray wash, brushed with gum arabic, 17.7 × 29.5 (6 ¹⁵/₁₆ × 11 ⅝). Graphische Sammlung im Städelsches Kunstinstitut, Frankfurt am Main *(Washington, Amsterdam only)*

• Although this drawing is consistently called a path through a woods, this description is precluded by the limited number of trees here drawn. To the left of the path in the middle are about six to eight trees, one of which upon closer scrutiny turns out to consist solely of a heavy old trunk

without branches or foliage. At the right several trees are clustered behind an old oak, under whose foliage a few more trunks can be observed; hence the scene is actually nothing more than a grove.

Visible in the distance is the roof of a house. Although the drawing contains no detail of any significance, Cuyp appears to have chosen a vantage point that emphatically invites the viewer to pass by this group of trees and see what the distance has to offer. Cuyp isolated the oak tree at the right and used it in his painting in Melbourne.[1]

The drawing is characteristic of a group of woods and tree studies that Cuyp must have made about 1640, which also includes the drawing in Rotterdam (cat. 51). These sheets correspond with the wooded views that Cuyp made in the vicinity of Utrecht, yet display greater refinement, both in their composition and finish. While he often accentuated the earlier works with a touch of color and white highlights, he limited himself here to black chalk and brush in gray. WK

**53 A Path at the Edge of a Woods
with Two Old Oak Trees**

black chalk, gray wash, watercolored in yellow, partly brushed with gum arabic, 13.8 × 19.3 (5 7/16 × 7 5/8).
The British Museum, London (*London only*)

· Aelbert Cuyp deftly elaborated the tension between breadth and depth in this sheet. The viewer's eye is drawn from the old oak tree in the left foreground to the one at the far right and in the process, discerns the path leading from the right foreground to the edge of the woods screening off the horizon. Cuyp's skillful handling of coulisses, so evident in many of his paintings, is here superbly evident in the dark foreground with its suggestive pattern of curving, partly consonant lines that virtually mirror those at the woods' edge. He cleverly alternated one of these gently undulating lines with short zigzag strokes to indicate low cover. The fanciful old tree branches contrast with the lush, young, fresh, green foliage.

Cuyp's use of black chalk is seen to good advantage in this sheet. He executed the initial phase with a light sketch and subsequently reworked the drawing with a much deeper black chalk. The intensity of the color in the foreground and the left oak was fixed permanently by means of a gum arabic varnish locally applied with the brush.

This drawing, which is related to the sheets formerly in Pella (see cat. 5, fig. 1) and the Metropolitan Museum of Art (cat. 50), but which is smaller and displays less hesitation, must have originated in the early 1640s. **WK**

54 Wide Expanse of Water with Trees in the Right Foreground

black chalk, gray wash, watercolored in yellow and brown, partly brushed with gum arabic, 14.5 × 19 (5 ¹¹/₁₆ × 7 ½). The British Museum, London (*London only*)

• In this sheet, the draftsman looked out over a very broad expanse of water from a relatively high vantage point. A path leads to what must be two dwellings (the artist could see little more than the roofs) just near the water's edge. The elevation is not a dike: the group of trees at the right indicates a naturally uneven terrain. The body of water is also not a river, for the land on the opposite side, vanishing in the far distance, and the two little boats in the middle of the drawing attest to its enormous width. Where in the Netherlands Cuyp could have come across such a combination of hills or dunes, woods, and such a wide stretch of water is not clear.[1]

Most likely dating to about 1640, this drawing is one of the earliest testimonies of Cuyp's interest in panoramic views. As such, the panorama has been connected with early paintings by the master with distant views from an elevation, such as his depiction of Orpheus and the animals (cat. 1) and the river landscape with a shepherd and flock from 1639; both, however, show imaginary scenes.[2] While in these two works Cuyp allotted only limited space to the distant view, in this sheet — albeit summarily indicated — he gave it the necessary latitude. WK

55 A Weather-Beaten Oak Tree

black chalk, gray wash, some graphite, heightened with white and yellow, partly brushed with gum arabic, 15.3 × 19.6 (6 × 7 11/16). Graphische Sammlung im Städelsches Kunstinstitut, Frankfurt am Main

(Washington, Amsterdam only)

· Here, Aelbert Cuyp focused upon a single, weather-beaten oak tree as the primary subject of his drawing. Undoubtedly once struck by lightning, the old trunk survives as little more than a substantial stump. One branch, however, is flourishing and extends out from the middle left to the upper right corner of the drawing. At the left a path is barred by a rickety fence. The landscape opens up on a woods in the left background, in which a few cows stand before a half-hidden dwelling. At the right, a steeple can be seen in the distance between this woods and some trees. The artist indicated the middle ground summarily: only with some effort can a stretch of water with a rowboat be distinguished. Even though largely obscured by a tree, the overcast sky is suggested with wash.

Cuyp probably derived the motif of a windswept old oak from Jan van Goyen, whose famous *Landscape with Two Oaks* in the Rijksmuseum dates from 1641, though his fascination with this subject began in the 1630s.[1] While Van Goyen was inspired by the picturesque possibilities of such old trees, Cuyp, fascinated by the tree's actual appearance, was apparently struck by the contrast between the knotted old trunk and the young foliage fanning out. Aelbert Cuyp addressed the theme of old oak trees in a number of other drawings (see also cat. 53). WK

56 Three Trees in Hilly Terrain

black chalk, gray wash, watercolored in yellow-green, 18.1 × 14.6 (7 ⅛ × 5 ¾).
Staatliche Museen zu Berlin, Kupferstichkabinett (*Amsterdam only*)

• In this sheet, Cuyp paid only cursory attention to the landscape, concentrating instead on the fluttering effect of the foliage. It has become a true "portrait" of a group of trees. At the right two trees bend heavily to the left, largely hiding from sight a third tree — which seems to be propping them up. The widely extending branches with young green foliage fill the largest portion of the sheet. Still, the contrast between the green-yellow dunes on which the trees stand and the gray landscape in the distance effectively suggests great depth. The group of trees gives the impression of having been drawn from life, a captivating motif noticed by the artist and portrayed without much ceremony.

The drawing must have been cropped at the left; thus, the spatial freedom of the trees has been somewhat diminished. WK

57 A Wide Plain, Low Trees in the Foreground

black chalk, gray wash, watercolored in ochre yellow, partly brushed with gum arabic, 19 × 31 (7 ½ × 12 ³/₁₆). The British Museum, London *(London, Amsterdam only)*

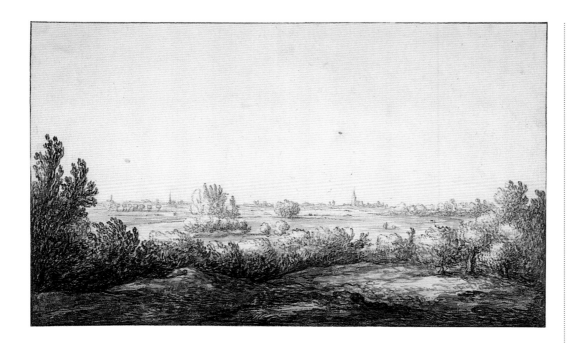

· In this sheet Cuyp opted for a surprising dichotomy in the landscape: a panoramic view is separated from a formless terrain, possibly the foot of a hill, by a screen of low growth. A large part of this grove appears to border the river that leads the eye from the left, past a group of trees, and into the distance. A spire and a mill punctuate the horizon at the left, while to the right of center is a sturdy village church. Small ball-like pollard willows in the distance at the left anticipate the characteristic detailing of the flats that Cuyp would use in his Nijmegen series (cats. 91 – 93).

In technical terms, Cuyp also elaborated the layers of this drawing differently. Despite a certain shapelessness, the foreground is highly varied with nervous strokes in brush and watercolor in a multitude of light yellow, ochre, and gray shades. Cuyp articulated the groves with many delicate strokes from the tip of his brush and darkened the tree at the left, casting its shadow on the ground, with moistened black chalk — an effect Cuyp preserved with some gum arabic. In contrast, the panorama is airy and wide, finely and somewhat vaguely sketched. wk

58 Panorama with a Country Manor

black chalk, gray wash, watercolored in ochre, yellow, and blue, partially brushed with gum arabic, 18.7 × 30.3 (7 ⅜ × 11 ¹⁵⁄₁₆). Graphische Sammlung Albertina, Vienna *(London, Amsterdam only)*

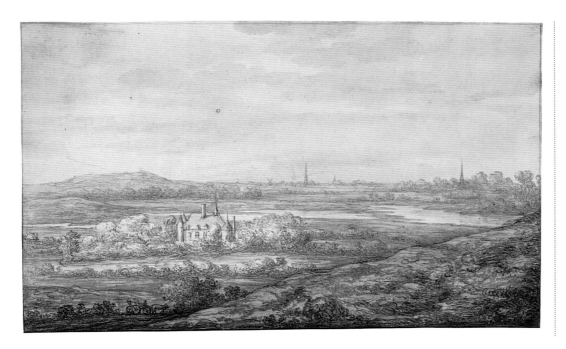

• The artist drew what appears to be the Elterberg, rising beyond a country manor located in the Rhine valley. To the right of center and farther to the right are two churches. In this landscape Cuyp brilliantly indicated the charm of a watery lowland nestled between wooded hills, an effect enhanced by the "rhyme" of the subtle reflections of the manor (as yet unidentified) and the faraway church.

The format of this sheet, which is similar to the London panorama (cat. 57), suggests that Cuyp made this drawing during a trip to the Cleves region in about 1640 – 1642. Cuyp could well have taken along both a sketchbook with very wide sheets (for example, cat. 76), and a more modest album the size of this drawing.

A faithful, eighteenth-century copy of this sheet, in which Cuyp's somewhat later drawing style is aptly imitated, is in Frankfurt.[1] WK

59 A Manor House among Trees, High Hills in the Distance

black chalk, gray wash, watercolored in brown-green, locally brushed with gum arabic, 18.3 × 42.1 (7 3/16 × 16 5/8). Staatliche Museen zu Berlin, Kupferstichkabinett (*Amsterdam only*)

· In this masterful sheet Aelbert Cuyp conceived a broad composition of stunning balance as well as great drama. The powerful effect of light and dark is shown to best advantage in the left foreground and at the right near the tall group of trees. Also exceptional is the way in which the manor, with a pitched roof, chimney, and a single, summarily indicated window, seems to loom up from the trees. Cuyp cleverly used the large tree at the right to emphasize the variety of the afforestation. The strong diagonal of the hill rising up in the background is subtly reiterated by the group of trees advancing in the foreground at the right. The effect of the group of trees at the right projecting just above the diagonal line of the hill is particularly successful. Cuyp varied and further enriched this theme in his magisterial late composition in London (cat. 45).

Using a noticeable subordination of the topographical motif, Cuyp increased the degree of refinement in this drawing to better render the wooded landscape; in its proportions the sheet approximates the sweeping panoramas in which as a rule a city occupies a prominent position. Although the drawing is somewhat damaged by the clouds that were added later and by some brown corroded spots, its quality is nevertheless impressive. WK

60 Peasant Carts near a Farmhouse in a Dune Landscape

black chalk, gray wash, watercolored in yellow and brown, partly brushed with gum arabic, 12.4 × 18.9 (4 ⅞ × 7 ⁷⁄₁₆). Graphische Sammlung Albertina, Vienna *(London, Amsterdam only)*

- In this sheet Cuyp elevated two simple two-wheeled peasant carts, carelessly abandoned in a dunelike landscape, to serve as his main motif. He enhanced the monumentality of the theme by casting the foremost cart in shadows and silhouetting it against the sky and distant dunes. The other cart, set somewhat farther away and tilted from the loss of a wheel, catches the full light instead. This second wagon visually leads to the peasant dwelling and the haystack at the right. The two figures in the right foreground seem to be an afterthought, their static character contributing to the inertia exuded by the carts. The subtle palette contrasts curiously with the shapelessness of the landscape and the simple, archetypal shape of both carts. The motif, which occurs in the subtly watercolored sketches of dilapidated barns by Abraham Bloemaert, also recalls compositions with tumbledown sheds or fences as their main subject by Pieter Molyn, Jan van Goyen, and Salomon van Ruysdael. **WK**

61

The Windmills at Kinderdijk (recto)
The Grote Kerk in Dordrecht from the Southwest (verso)

black chalk, gray wash, watercolored in brown and red, heightened with white, 13.7 × 18.9 (5 ⅜ × 7 ⁷⁄₁₆). Private collection, U.S.A. *(Washington, Amsterdam only)*

recto

verso

• This sheet — which agrees well with others that Cuyp made in the vicinity of Dordrecht about 1640 — was drawn on both sides; therefore, it must have been part of a sketchbook.[1] On one side Cuyp depicted the church of Alblasserdam and, at the left, the windmills at Kinderdijk. This group of windmills, still extant and today an important tourist attraction, was originally set up for the reclamation of a polder in the Alblasserwaard. In the drawing the windmills are visually balanced by a rise surmounted with a wagon near a house amid the trees. In the foreground are a few rowboats near an embankment reinforced with reed matting.

Cuyp used the left part of this drawing for his painting in London (cat. 7), in which the little windmills are less prominently yet very subtly repeated. Although Jan van Goyen is often suggested as the source of inspiration for this painting, the right part of this drawing more closely resembles the work of Salomon van Ruysdael. Two very closely related drawings, used by Cuyp in preparation for the painting, apparently originate from the same sketchbook (see cat. 7, fig. 1).

On the verso is a depiction of Dordrecht with the Grote Kerk seen from the southwest. Here, too, Cuyp privileged rural charm over the city. Beyond some tree trunks in the left foreground and a stretch of water with boats are trees and a farm and haystack, which partly obscure our view of the town. From early in his career, Cuyp drew a number of views of Dordrecht from the landward side, always using different vantage points.[2] **WK**

62 Moored Rowboats on a River, a Church in the Distance

black chalk, gray wash, watercolored in brown, pink, green, and yellow, heightened with white, partly brushed with gum arabic, 14.1 × 19.4 (5 9/16 × 7 5/8). Private collection, The Netherlands

· This drawing undoubtedly depicts a part of the watery area in the vicinity of Dordrecht and was part of a sketchbook made by the young Cuyp in about 1640 (see also cats. 61, 63). Topographical accuracy is entirely subordinated to the artistic effect of a water-rich landscape. Cuyp substantially reinforced the sense of depth by placing a sailboat at the point where the horizon seems to be farthest away. The artist also exploited both the rhythm of the rowboats to suggest depth and — albeit more subtly — that of the two poles in the foreground and the mast of the sailboat. However, the rowboat in the middle ground crossing the width of the water provides a movement parallel to the picture plane and, in its turn, rhymes with the motionless rowboats in the foreground, in one of which is a bent-over fisherman. The reflections suggest a light rippling off the water's surface; however, the weather is chiefly quiet, perhaps even somewhat languid. Cuyp's application of watercolor in exceptionally refined hues greatly enhances the verisimilitude of this Holland landscape.

Cuyp used the composition for his *River View,* a painting in Dulwich that can be dated about 1640.[1] WK

black chalk, gray wash, graphite, pen and brown ink, heightened with white, partly brushed with gum arabic, 14.6 × 19.5 (5 ¾ × 7 ¹¹⁄₁₆). Rijksmuseum, Amsterdam

1 Aelbert Cuyp, **Evening in the Meadows**, The Norton Simon Foundation, Pasadena, Calif.

• Here Cuyp superbly conveyed the atmosphere of a warm, windless afternoon: the water is virtually unruffled; a boat, its sail still unfurled, is pulled ashore between the trees; and two cows seek respite from the heat in the water near the jetty. The entire ensemble at the right, from the man pulling his boat to the jetty with a hook, to the horizontal lines of the boats and the verticals of poles and sails, and finally to the trees at the right, is built up in a stunning rhythm. The representation of depth — with the silhouette of a rowboat at the left extending above the dark water in the foreground, staggered into the distance with sailboats and a windmill — is particularly effective. On the hazy horizon can be discerned a church and a sailboat. Cuyp effectively used some watercolor to enliven this sheet.[1]

Cuyp relied on this sheet for the background of *Evening in the Meadows*, a painting now in the Norton Simon collection and datable shortly after 1650 (fig. 1). In the painting, however, he suppressed a few anecdotal elements, such as the cows drinking, the little rowboat in the foreground, and the moored boat near the jetty.[2] **WK**

64 Country Road with a Cottage alongside a River

black chalk, gray wash, watercolored in green and yellow, 18.8 × 30.3 (7 ⅜ × 11 ¹⁵⁄₁₆).
Kunstsammlungen zu Weimar (*Amsterdam only*)

1 Aelbert Cuyp, **View of 's-Gravendeel**, The State Hermitage Museum, Saint Petersburg

· Cuyp rarely followed a sketch in a painting as closely as he followed this drawing in his *Cattle and Cottage near a River* (cat. 4). Even so, the artist made a number of significant changes. In the painting he allotted greater space to the river, enlivened it with a little boat with a peat rower, and embellished the path in the foreground with a few reclining cows, which in the drawing are sketched on the bank. The dilapidated dwelling, whose most stable element was apparently the chimney, seems to be somewhat more slumped in the painting. Cuyp also faithfully repeated the shadow cast by the tree on the wooden side wall. By widening the composition and raising the sky, Cuyp lowered the horizon of the painted landscape, thus adding substantially to the spaciousness of the scene. Finally, he incorporated action into the painted scene by including a man on the bank (mooring a boat containing peat) and an upturned wheelbarrow in the foreground.

The painting must have originated in 1640 or 1641, and thus the drawing, shortly before. The drawing was undoubtedly made in the vicinity of Dordrecht, as was his *View of 's-Gravendeel* (fig. 1), a drawing similar in composition and lighting. In both drawings, Cuyp used the contrasts of light and shade to define objects as well as the space that surrounds them. WK

**65 A Windmill and Farm Buildings
beyond Meadows**

black chalk, gray wash, partly brushed with gum arabic, 18.3 × 30.4 (7 ³⁄₁₆ × 11 ¹⁵⁄₁₆).
Statens Museum for Kunst, Copenhagen *(Washington, Amsterdam only)*

· In this drawing, Cuyp filled the horizon with farmhouses, a church, a haystack, and a post-mill, while to the right a farmhouse, a tree, and a small, indistinct building are nearer to the viewer. In a remarkable tour de force he gave excitement to the virtually formless land in the foreground and middle ground. The only accent of any significance in this area is a bridge, which also articulates a water channel running parallel to the picture plane. A vast undefined sky unites the landscape.

Cuyp used motifs in this drawing for *Portrait of a Family in a Landscape* (cat. 3) of 1641, a painting in which Jacob Gerritsz Cuyp was responsible for the portraits and Aelbert for the landscape elements. A comparison of the drawing and the painting demonstrates beautifully how Aelbert combined inspiration with practical use. Initially, he must have been excited by the complex problems and possibilities presented by drawing this landscape. Only subsequently would he have understood how to introduce the drawn panorama into a painted landscape background. **WK**

66 A Dike alongside a River, a Bridge, and Trees to the Right

black chalk, gray wash, partly brushed with gum arabic, 18.4 × 30.5 (7 ¼ × 12). The British Museum, London

• In this drawing Aelbert Cuyp depicted a setting typical for Holland: a wide stretch of water, presumably a river, is bordered by a dike or raised embankment with a road — here made visible by a walking figure — while a wooden bridge spans the link between this waterway and a pond or some ditches. A few rowboats — one with a bent-over fisherman, inspected by a figure on the bridge — are moored in a sheltered spot just behind the bridge. This jetty is apparently situated near a farm or an inn surrounded by trees. By including three sailboats and a rowboat, Cuyp underscored both the breadth of the river and its importance for transportation.

The drawing is one of a group of sheets most probably from a sketchbook consisting of both sensitively watercolored drawings (cat. 69) and black chalk drawings with wash applied with brush (cat. 65). Cuyp took great pains to record reality in these drawings made on the spot, but subsequently elaborated them when he returned to his studio.[1] WK

67 A Village near a Bridge

black chalk, gray wash, watercolored in yellow, brown, and green, partly brushed with gum arabic, 18.5 × 30.3 (7 5/16 × 11 15/16). The British Museum, London (*London only*)

· Cuyp viewed this village, with its houses situated on either side of a wooden bridge, from across a pond that spans the entire breadth of the sheet. The dwellings on the left, surrounded by trees, are partially hidden behind fences, while three rowboats are moored in front of them. Beyond the bridge and the houses at the right, set somewhat farther back than those at the left, the sail of a boat is seen, clearly indicating a larger expanse of water up ahead. The pond is bordered in the foreground by long grass on the bank and by a quay with a slightly projecting wooden structure, presumably a dilapidated jetty. At a later stage Cuyp added the two upright poles in front of it to create a greater sense of space in that area.

This sheet shares its provenance with another drawing in the British Museum (cat. 66) and must have come from the same sketchbook (see also cats. 64, 65, 69, 70). These sheets represent villages and marshland in the vicinity of Dordrecht. Cuyp brilliantly characterized the location of the houses, huts, and farms in a landscape abounding with water. With their subtle execution and sensitive use of color, these sketches belong to the best that Dutch seventeenth-century landscape drawing has to offer. WK

68 Farmhouses along Both Sides of a Canal

black chalk, gray wash, watercolored in green-gray, 13.5 × 18.6 (5 ⁵/₁₆ × 7 ⁵/₁₆). The Metropolitan Museum of Art, New York, Bequest of Mrs. H.O. Havemeyer, 1929 *(Washington, Amsterdam only)*

· A striking variety of structures, including thatched huts and a fairly tall stone building, flank a summarily indicated waterway that recedes into the distance. Contributing substantially to this effect is the rowboat that casts its reflection in the water and the illumination of the farmstead at the right. Cuyp masterfully harmonized the compressed roof line of this house with the fence before it. He also elaborated on the various tonal values of the trees at the far right and left. Using a subtle, miniature-like technique, also to be admired in the drawing in Berlin (cat. 69) for example, Cuyp gave this drawing great visual and imaginative appeal.

The drawing was certainly once larger. The wash for the sky, now almost invisible, would have had more significance in the originally wider format. An indentation running parallel to the upper edge raises the suspicion that a farther reduction was once intended. WK

69 View of a Village at Some Distance

black chalk, gray wash, watercolored in green, brown, blue, and ochre, partly brushed with gum arabic, 18.3 × 30.6 (7 ³⁄₁₆ × 12 ¹⁄₁₆). Staatliche Museen zu Berlin, Kupferstichkabinett *(Washington, Amsterdam only)*

• This is one of the richest, most sensitive, and best-preserved of Aelbert Cuyp's colored drawings. Several houses are grouped around a windmill at some distance to the right. Important vertical accents are provided by a few hay barracks with their high stakes. Amid the trees farther back at the left are a couple of dwellings, one of which is almost completely hidden from sight. On the distant horizon Cuyp even suggested a stretch of water by sketching the mast of a sailboat. The foreground is filled with marshland transected by glistening gray water. The artist carefully applied the watercolor in gray, light green, blue green, and brown yellow — it is especially beautiful over the jumble of clumps of earth with grass, some of which he indicated with the tip of the brush and some, with swift chalk strokes, partly moistened. The expansive sky was left empty.

In subject and execution, this drawing is related to sheets in New York, Copenhagen, and London (cats. 65, 67, 68). One may safely assume that Cuyp made them just prior to 1641, the year in which he and his father executed the painting in Jerusalem (cat. 3), a work that includes comparable motifs in the distance. **wk**

70 River Landscape

black chalk, gray wash, watercolored in red-brown, yellow, and green, 18.9 × 30.3 (7 7/16 × 11 15/16).
Musées Royaux des Beaux-Arts de Belgique, Brussels (*Washington, Amsterdam only*)

Aelbert Cuyp has here depicted an exceptionally beautiful, wide, languidly flowing river of a type perceived as characteristic of the lowlands in Holland. The river, which bends in the distant left, winds around somewhat higher land in the middle of the drawing, where a solitary house and the trees that shelter it are distinctly reflected in the water. A series of poles mark the shoals, as do the growth of reeds. One of the two sailboats has already rounded the curve in the river, while a rowboat floats along just right of the center. At the far right, a dwelling nestles amid trees on the bank at a point where a branch in the river is suggested. Cuyp worked out the foreground, an irregular section of the bank, with great feeling for the unevenness of this piece of land, which with the exception of a tree and a few stakes from a dilapidated timbering has no details of any significance. Cuyp's mastery in characterizing such formless land, manifest in many of his landscape drawings, is exceptionally well expressed here. His subtle touch is also evident in the brilliant horizontal accents in the water at the right.[1]

This drawing is similar to a group of meticulously executed sketches of the Dutch countryside, almost surely made in the immediate vicinity of Dordrecht (cats. 64–69). The elaboration of the foreground is reminiscent of the series of larger panoramas, among them *Dordrecht Viewed from the East* (cat. 72). While Cuyp usually depicted a town or a village in the middle ground or in the distance, *River Landscape* lacks any topographical feature identifiable today. WK

71 Amersfoort Viewed from the Southeast

black chalk, gray wash, watercolored in yellow, brown, and green, 19 × 30.4 (7 ½ × 11 ¹⁵/₁₆).
Collection Frits Lugt, Institut Néerlandais, Paris (*Amsterdam only*)

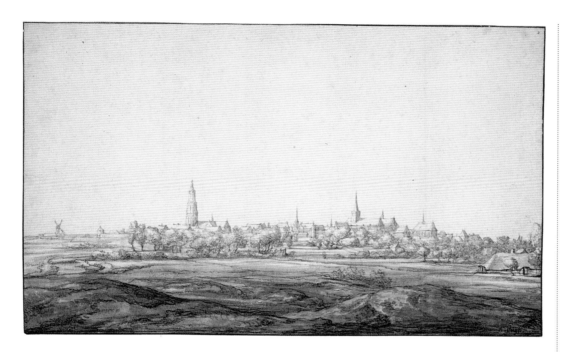

• With a great sense of drama, Aelbert Cuyp presented the town of Amersfoort towering up in a slightly uneven lowland. Some trees in the middle ground indicate the passage of a brook, while to the right is a beautifully characterized farmhouse with a thatched roof. We assume that Cuyp drew the town from the Randenbroek estate and that the Heiligenbergerbeek (a brook) is shown at the left. Rising up at the left is the tower of the Amersfoort Onze Lieve Vrouwekerk, which is almost one hundred meters tall and one of the most famous towers in the Netherlands.[1] The drawing certainly predates the year 1651, when the tower lost its spire, which was rebuilt in 1655. Somewhat farther right is the Sint Joriskerk and to its right, the Agnietenkapel.[2]

The refined execution of the town, particularly evident in the meticulous and precisely placed shadows and in the extensive coloration, almost makes the drawing a completely independent work of art. Though smaller in size, it appears to belong to the group of more broadly laid out panoramas, such as the views of Rhenen and Arnhem (cats. 73, 74), that can be dated to the early 1640s. Cuyp presented two other views of the town in drawings in Chantilly and Edinburgh, the latter one serving as the point of departure for the painting in Wuppertal.[3] WK

72 Dordrecht Viewed from the East

black chalk, gray wash, watercolored in yellow and red, partly brushed in gum arabic, 19 × 44.5 (7 ½ × 17 ½). Rijksmuseum, Amsterdam

· While this drawing is primarily a view of Dordrecht, the leading role is played by the foreground — a bank along the Merwede River — with a border of reeds in the water, some plants in shallow areas, a dike, and the fence wending over it at the far left. The city, easily identifiable by the tower of the Grote Kerk, spreads out on the horizon but is largely concealed behind groves. The Rietdijkspoort and the nearby windmill mark the bend in the river where the city view ends and the Papendrecht skyline on the far shore begins.[1] The clouds were added by a later hand.

Cuyp used this view of Dordrecht as a background motif in several paintings that date from the early 1640s.[2] Consequently, this drawing, in which Cuyp displayed such masterful technical control, must have originated shortly after 1640. One of these paintings (Reiss 1977, 52), moreover, includes a shepherd based on Cuyp's Rotterdam sketch (cat. 105), a combination of motifs that indicates Cuyp's intense drawing activity in these years. **WK**

73 Rhenen Viewed from the Northeast

black chalk, gray wash, watercolored in yellow and brown, partly brushed in gum arabic, 17.9 × 50 (7 1/16 × 19 11/16). Fogg Art Museum, Harvard University Art Museums, Cambridge, Gift of John S. Newberry Jr., given in honor of Paul J. Sachs' 70th birthday *(Washington only)*

· Aelbert Cuyp used the full width of this sheet to give shape to the walled town within its surroundings. Rhenen lies to the right nestled at the base of a foothill of the Amerongseberg. Cuyp drew this scene from the adjacent Grebbeberg. In the distance at the left, past the Rhine River, is the lowland of the Betuwe region. The old, somewhat dilapidated walls of the town merge with the undulating line of the landscape. The Berg or Oostpoort (East Gate) in the middle is the axis around which the composition revolves. Visitors entered Rhenen there through an outer gate, behind which stood the old medieval gate with its two conical roofs. Other than the dominating tower of the Sint Cunerakerk, the town includes only a few buildings of any distinction.

Cuyp corrected the church tower heavily with white bodycolor, and as a consequence this part of the drawing may be considered less successful. The openness of the top section of the tower lacks sophistication, while the characteristic outline hardly shows up well. On the other hand, Cuyp cleverly enhanced the sweep of the river by means of a moored sailboat. He transformed the terrain in the foreground into a natural *repoussoir* with deep, dark passages, some shrubs, and shadows. He gave shape to the land on the other side of the river with a subtle and summary drawing technique, so that the viewer's eye is drawn to the horizon. The lure of the distance, here expressed in an early drawing, would continue to play an important role in Cuyp's conception of the landscape.

Many seventeenth-century artists were fond of portraying Rhenen. Hercules Seghers, Rembrandt, Jan van Goyen, and others recorded the town from the east. Cuyp himself also drew two other views of Rhenen: one is in the Teylers Museum (Haverkamp-Begemann essay, fig. 3) and must have been made during an earlier trip; the other, formerly in the Koenigs Collection, is now in Moscow.[1] **WK**

74 **Arnhem Viewed from the West**

black chalk, gray wash, watercolored in ochre yellow, green, and blue, 18.4 × 50.1 (7 ¼ × 19 ¾).
Graphische Sammlung Albertina, Vienna *(London, Amsterdam only)*

• In the past, this splendid view of Arnhem was divided in two. Fortunately, both sections ended up in the Albertina and have since been rejoined.[1] Together, they approximate the maximum size of panoramas of this nature in Cuyp's oeuvre, namely about fifty centimeters wide.

When Cuyp recorded Arnhem in this sheet, he was closer to the town than he was when working on the Amsterdam drawing (cat. 75), as is clear from the tower of the Grote Kerk (church of Sint Eusebius), here elaborated in greater detail. In both works, the artist seized the opportunity of presenting a rich and varied foreground, here with a few trees and at the right a distant view over a lowland with rows of pollard willows. The south side of the city is marked by the post-mill on the retaining wall, which earlier occupied the center of the right half of the sheet. To the left, before the Grote Kerk, the artist looked down on numerous roofs. This drawing makes a slightly less polished impression than does the Amsterdam sheet. While the latter drawing was provided with a cloudy sky by a later hand, here the sky is a very light blue — probably also added later but before the drawing was divided in two. **WK**

75 Arnhem Viewed from the Northwest

black chalk, gray wash, watercolored in green and ochre yellow, partly brushed with gum arabic, 19 × 48.6 (7 ½ × 19 ⅛). Rijksmuseum, Amsterdam

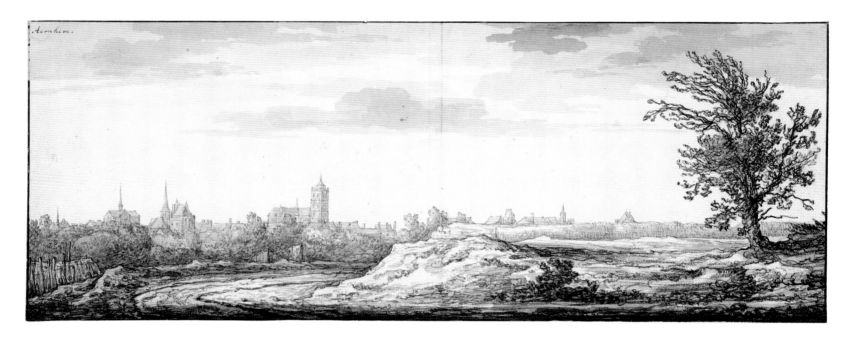

As in his other panoramic views, Cuyp partly concealed the town profile behind an essentially dominating foreground. A path to the left of center winds its way up a rise in the landscape and past a solitary oak tree at the right. An earth embankment or wheat field on this rise largely obscures the view of the town in the right half of the drawing; only a tower and a somewhat taller gable roof protrude. Cuyp, who assumed a low vantage point, must have stood northwest of the town, beyond the Sint Janspoort (Saint John's Gate) near a place formerly called the Tamboersbosje (Drummers grove).

Though largely hidden from view by trees, a few more buildings are just visible at the left. The tower of the Grote Kerk (or Sint Eusebius) determines the city view.[1]

With sensitive handling of the brush and gray, ochre, green, and red-brown watercolor, Cuyp produced a highly polished drawing, marred only by the cloudy sky added in the eighteenth century. The exceptionally consistent execution and the existence of a view of Arnhem from the same angle in the Prentenkabinet in Leiden gave reason to suppose that the sheet under discussion was produced by Cuyp in his workshop.[2] The drawing in Leiden, however, is a copy of the Amsterdam sheet. The initial sketch in black chalk in the present drawing is fully consistent with the drawing in Vienna (cat. 74). Cuyp, however, finished the two views of Arnhem in his workshop in different ways. The Vienna drawing, for instance, was not brushed with gum arabic, while the Amsterdam sheet owes its somewhat polished character to just this treatment.[3] Naturally, the later additions in the sky also engendered a different appearance. **WK**

76 Calcar with Monterberg in the Distance

black chalk, gray wash, watercolored in green and ochre yellow, partly brushed with gum arabic, 18.5 × 49.5 (7 5/16 × 19 ½). The Metropolitan Museum of Art, New York, Promised gift of an anonymous donor *(Washington only)*

· For this view of Calcar and the Monterberg Cuyp took up a position on a high place near a partially leveled rise capped only by a few shrubs deformed by the wind. The foreground here functions as a coulisse behind which the distant vista unfolds. The drawing belongs to a group of broad panoramas, all with a fold in the middle, produced in the early 1640s. In this series, most sheets of which bear witness to a topographical interest, this drawing

and *Hilly Landscape with a River*[1] rank among the freer landscape studies. Cuyp's penchant for the contrasts in elevation of the landscape in the vicinity of Nijmegen, Cleves, and Calcar — contrasts he so lovingly worked out in his paintings — appears to have originated in these drawings. This sheet, too, seems to have aroused Cuyp's interest in depicting panoramas with scattered trees, a theme he would embellish later in his Nijmegen series (cats. 91 – 93).

Later on, in the 1650s, Cuyp used the distant vista in this drawing for the panorama in his painting in the Corcoran Gallery of Art, Washington (cat. 25). Even though he there interpreted the foreground coulisse entirely differently, he never lost sight of the basic artistic principle of creating contrast between the foreground and background. WK

Panorama with a Shepherd Surveying the Landscape

black chalk, gray wash, 18.5 × 48 (7 ⁵⁄₁₆ × 18 ⅞). Rijksmuseum, Amsterdam

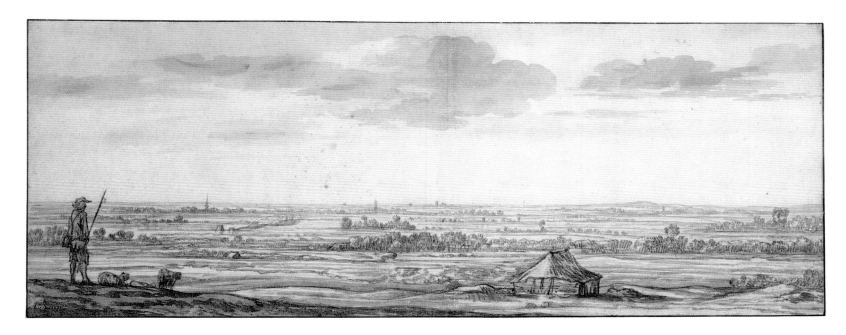

In this wide lowland prospect with a few church spires and a low ridge in the distance, Aelbert Cuyp drew a shepherd with some sheep on a slope at the left. Together with the shepherd, the viewer looks down upon the considerably lower sheep pen. Cuyp, thus, masterfully established a relationship between the viewer, the foreground, and the far-reaching expanse. Although attempts have been made to localize the landscape — the river threading its way through the landscape from left to right is continually identified as the Rhine — no certainty of its location exists.[1] The vista in a painting in Frankfurt, *Shepherd with His Flock*, displays some similarities.[2]

Cuyp sketched the distant view before adding the shepherd and the sheep. Nevertheless, the drawing appears to have been created in a single session. The cloudy sky is evidently by a later hand. Because the technique for defining the trees in the plane is less sophisticated here than in Cuyp's drawings of the early 1650s of the vicinity of Nijmegen (for example, cats. 91 – 93), an earlier date for this drawing, probably between 1640 and 1645, is indicated.

The composition with a shepherd on a height looking out over lowlands is reminiscent of a painting with the same motif by Herman Saftleven in Rotterdam (Wheelock essay, fig. 15). Cuyp was quite possibly influenced by this Utrecht artist, who in his early years worked in the manner of Jan van Goyen and in the 1640s — thus still before Cuyp — discovered the possibilities of the sun-drenched landscape. WK

78 The Hague Viewed from the Northwest

black chalk, gray wash, watercolored in yellow and green, 18.5 × 49.4 (7 5/16 × 19 7/16).
Rijksmuseum, Amsterdam

1 Aelbert Cuyp, **The Hague Viewed from the North with the Grote Kerk or Sint Jacobskerk,** Teylers Museum, Haarlem

• Cuyp portrayed The Hague from the dunes between The Hague and Scheveningen, the fishing village that he recorded in two drawings.[1] From there, the draftsman depicted the Grote Kerk or Sint Jacobskerk of The Hague at the left and in the distance the two churches of Delft. At the far left of this panoramic view is a tall building with a tower, perhaps the Oude Hof (Old Court) at Noordeinde. The four windmills at the right lie on the west side of The Hague.[2] As was his wont, Cuyp joyfully elaborated the foreground: here he used low sand dunes — without any structure but with a lovely recurring pattern — to suggest depth without the aid of any perspectival means worth mentioning. Two tiny figures virtually vanish in the plain. Cuyp probably applied watercolor with bright green and

yellow tints later in his studio. The overcast sky is an eighteenth-century addition.

Cuyp was almost overwhelmed by the great breadth of the panorama: he could never have taken in the dunes at the right in a single glance with the Grote Kerk. He depicted the church from a somewhat different angle than that which he would have seen from the dunes, probably to make it more recognizable.

Cuyp portrayed the Hague Grote Kerk or Sint Jacobskerk yet another time, close by and from the north, in a view determined by groves rather than by buildings, with the exception of the church (fig. 1).[3] Although the Amsterdam drawing displays a more advanced approach, both drawings in all likelihood stem from the same trip, when Cuyp also made his sketches of Scheveningen, Leiden, and Haarlem.[4] The different aspect presently characterizing these drawings is mainly owing to the reworkings Cuyp later introduced.

This drawing most likely dates from shortly after 1640. A source of inspiration for such town profiles with a richly detailed foreground may well have been Rembrandt's *View of Amsterdam,* an etching most likely made in 1641.[5] Should Cuyp have traveled to The Hague in 1643, he would certainly have visited his uncle Benjamin Cuyp, who was recorded as living there in that year. **WK**

79 **Dunes with the Ruins of a Manor in the Distance**

black chalk, gray wash, partly brushed with gum arabic, 19 × 30.2 (7 ½ × 11 ⅞). Rijksmuseum, Amsterdam

• Cart tracks run diagonally through the dunes from the lower right to the left, toward a house whose roof alone is visible. At some distance at the right in the lowlands, the tall remnants of the main tower of a castle rise. This is probably Huis ter Kleef, a manor that was situated just north of Haarlem at the edge of the dunes.[1]

Cuyp allotted the largest share of the drawing to the sky; the line of the horizon gradually merges into the dunes, with only a few buildings or trees. In the dunes, Cuyp paid special attention to the clifflike formations where the sand has steadily been blown away from the vegetation. The line of the path is interrupted only by some growth in the foreground and by the shadow cast on it by a dune.

Stylistically, the drawing is related to both views of Scheveningen, especially the one seen from the east.[2] The drawing, which thus corresponds with the panoramas from the beginning of the 1640s, may have been reduced to its present width by Cuyp himself. Rarely is Jan van Goyen's influence on Aelbert Cuyp so outspoken as in this sheet. **WK**

80 Dordrecht Viewed from the Northeast

black chalk, gray wash, watercolored in brownish yellow, partly brushed with gum arabic, 15.9 × 50.6 (6 ¼ × 19 ⅞). Colnaghi, London *(Washington, Amsterdam only)*

· In this drawing Cuyp depicted Dordrecht stretching out on the other side of the water, with low buildings partially concealed by fortifications. The drawing ends at the right, just where the silhouette of Dordrecht's highly distinctive Grote Kerk would have appeared.[1] Thus, only a few towers, windmills, and some ship masts rise above the buildings: at the far left are the Rietdijkspoort and the nearby mill, and to the right of center, the Groothoofdspoort. The roof of the Nieuwe Kerk and many tall trees, presumably located in the gardens just outside of the Sint Jorispoort, are visible to the left of center. To the right is the tower of the town hall, just to the left of a sailboat's dark silhouette. The windmill at the right is identical to the one on the bulwark in the Lehman Collection drawing (cat. 82). The little gate on the quay to the left of center was known as the Melkpoortje (Small Milk Gate). The vegetation in the foreground serves the important artistic function of a *repoussoir* and enhances the vastness of this panorama, which Cuyp surveyed from the other side of the Noord River, either from the embankment near Papendrecht or from a boat. The artist colored the drawing with subtle gray and brown washes, accents in ochre, and reddish brown in some of the roofs. The combination of the faintly sketched cityscape and the broad washes of water with strong reflections lends this drawing an extraordinary richness enhanced by the simplicity of the profile and the complexity of the details.

Cuyp used the drawing for a few paintings, though always including the Grote Kerk at the right. In the paintings as in this drawing, the city has a somewhat curved skyline, slightly higher in the middle than on the sides. The best-known adaptation of the drawing is the panorama of Dordrecht in two paintings (Los Angeles County Museum of Art; Museum der Bildenden Kunste, Leipzig), which originally may well have been one, larger work,[2] for after all, they are presented as a single entity in a drawing by Aert Schouman from 1759.[3] According to Schouman, the work by Cuyp dates from 1647. Neither painting is dated, but a genesis after 1645 is highly improbable, for they correspond with Cuyp's early style and thus were more likely produced between 1640 and 1643. The most plausible dating for a related painting in the Turin art market, depicting not only a view of the city but also comparable vegetation along the embankment, is about 1644–1645.[4] WK

81

The Groothoofdspoort in Dordrecht from the West

black chalk, gray wash, 18.3 × 31.1 (7 3/16 × 12 1/4). Collection Frits Lugt, Institut Néerlandais, Paris
(Amsterdam only)

· In this drawing Aelbert Cuyp concentrated on the sailboats along the quay by an old section of the city wall; above it various buildings rise, with the graceful tower of the Groothoofdspoort (Gate to the Main Pier) serving as an elegant topographical reference.[1] Cuyp depicted a number of vessels at the far left along the wide quay that extends out from the gate to the west. The entrance to the Wolwevershaven (Wool-Dyers' Harbor) must have been between the boat at the right and the tower on the wall. The drawing presumably originated before 1647, when the palisades near the entrance of the harbor at the right were replaced by a wall. Cuyp probably made it during the same drawing campaign that yielded the sheets in the De Boer Collection, the Lehman Collection, and in the Rijksmuseum, Amsterdam (cats. 82 – 84). This correlation and the vertical fold in the left half of the sheet raise the suspicion that the drawing was initially far larger, most probably with a view of the watery expanse at the left.

Cuyp used the left section of the drawing as his point of departure for a painting from the mid-1650s.[2] **WK**

82 Dordrecht Viewed from the North, with a Windmill in the Foreground

black chalk, gray wash, watercolored with green, some brown chalk, 18.2 × 36.8 (7 ³/₁₆ × 14 ½).
The Metropolitan Museum of Art, New York, Robert Lehman Collection (*Washington only*)

• While in principle this drawing corresponds nicely with the views of Dordrecht in the De Boer Collection and the Rijksmuseum (cats. 83, 84), the differences are not without significance. Given the fold to the right of center, it is not improbable that a section at the right has been lost, along with a bit at the top and bottom. As these reductions could have been executed by the master himself, their significance is minor. Far more important for the comparison with the two other sheets, however, are the lower horizon and the introduction of the strongly silhouetted post-mill on the bank, the poles in the water, and the sailboat—powerful visual accents that almost render the town profile as an interesting background rather than the focus of the artist's attention.

The windmill supposedly stood near the entrance of the Nieuwe Haven (New Harbor), the part now called the Wolwevershaven (Wool-Dyers' Harbor), and is probably the same windmill whose sails are visible at the right in the Amsterdam drawing (cat. 84). Compared to the drawing in the De Boer Collection, the Lehman drawing places Cuyp's vantage point farther away from the Grote Kerk and a little more to the east. The difference in orientation is particularly evident in the transept of the church; in this sheet part of the east roof can be seen, while in the other drawing a bit of the west roof is visible.

Cuyp probably made this drawing in 1647. The quay at the foot of the windmill went up in that year, while the covered gallery near the Papenbolwerk (Papists' Bulwark), which was demolished in that year, seems to have vanished.

This view of Dordrecht recurs in a few paintings from the school of Aelbert Cuyp, namely works in the Museum Boijmans Van Beuningen, Rotterdam, and the Dulwich Picture Gallery, London.[1] WK

83 Dordrecht Viewed from the North, with the Grote Kerk

black chalk, gray wash, 18.6 × 50.4 (7 5/16 × 19 13/16). Stichting Collection P. en N. de Boer, Amsterdam *(Washington, Amsterdam only)*

• Cuyp must have seen this view of Dordrecht from the other side of the Oude Maas, just east of Zwijndrecht. In addition to the Grote Kerk, important landmarks include the round Engelenburch tower on the city wall, and the tall building at the far left near the Blauwpoort (Blue Gate), which flanked the entrance to the Nieuwe Haven (New Harbor). More to the right is the Vuylpoort (Dust Gate), and to its left and somewhat farther into the town is the tower of the Gevangenpoort (Prison Gate); both marked the entrance to the Oude Haven (Old Harbor). Farther right still, the palisades and a sub-

stantial number of masts belonging to the moored boats indicate the opening to the city moat, where not much later the Nieuwe Kalkhaven (New Mortar Harbor) would be constructed.

Of prime importance for dating this drawing is the presence of the Papenbolwerk, the old city wall in front of the Grote Kerk. This defense was demolished in 1647 to make way for the Maartensgat (Martins' Gap) as an outport of the Oude Haven.

Cuyp first quickly laid in the composition in black chalk. While he left a reserve for the sailboat in the trees at the right, he drew the sailboat at the

left over the initial sketch. The reflections in the water were first indicated in chalk and subsequently elaborated with a subtle wash. Cuyp used these reflections to suggest the water's quiet surface. As in so many of Cuyp's panoramas, the overcast sky is a later addition.

In this lovely city view, Cuyp united his topographical interest with his fascination with the countryside, here delicately rendered in the distant prospect at the right. WK

84 Dordrecht Viewed from the North, with the Grote Kerk and the Groothoofdspoort

black chalk, gray wash, 18.7 × 46 (7 ⅜ × 18 ⅛). Rijksmuseum, Amsterdam

Dordrecht.

• Stylistically this drawing is very close to the view of Dordrecht in the De Boer Collection (cat. 83), with which — given their similar inscriptions — it undoubtedly shares a mutual provenance. The artist used the sheet for his views of Dordrecht in Kenwood and Ascott (cats. 35, 36), in which he depicted the city profile partially concealed by a large ocean-going vessel. The composition of the ships along the quay is virtually identical to that in the painting in Kenwood, though the fall of light deviates somewhat. In the painting in Ascott, he made more explicit use of the middle section of

the drawing with the windmill. For these paintings Cuyp also relied on a drawing of a cargo ship and a timber raft (cat. 85). In the Washington painting (cat. 28), Cuyp again derived the city view from the present drawing, though in a more generic way (however, with some details literally adopted).

Here, Cuyp studied Dordrecht from the middle of the water, at the confluence of the Oude Maas, the Merwede, and the Noord Rivers. While the Grote Kerk dominates the city, the main motif is the Groothoofdspoort at the left. To the right of the Grote Kerk, a drawbridge marks the entrance to the

Nieuwe Haven. The view of the Oude Maas is largely blocked by a sailboat[1] crossing in the direction of Zwijndrecht, the village on the opposite bank.

Cuyp initially laid out the drawing very sketchily, probably concentrating on the city profile. At this time he also drew two other parts of the city in the lower left corner: a section of the city wall with houses — presumably the one to the right of the gate hidden behind the sails — and, farther to the left, some more houses, which were partially erased at some point. He finished the drawing later, even down to the reflections in the water. The overcast sky was applied by a later hand.

This and the following sheet (cat. 85) bring into focus the role Cuyp's drawings played in preparing his paintings. As a draftsman, Cuyp created a large stock of visual ideas, which found their way into numerous paintings by the master and from the studio as well.[2] That Cuyp drew rows of houses, which he deemed necessary to complete his image of the city, in the lower left corner of this sheet underscores the topographical importance and the practical purpose he attached to this and similar drawings. His later interventions, however, particularly the application of watercolor and gum arabic observed in so many of his drawings, clearly indicate that Cuyp attempted to give these works a finished quality.[3] WK

85 A Freight Boat and a Timber Raft on Calm Water

black chalk, gray wash, 16.8 × 25.4 (6 ⅝ × 10). The British Museum, London

ship among the raft, the freight boat, and the sloop, but only after introducing a major compositional change. Initially he depicted a ship under sail seen from the side instead of the freight boat. The helmsman at the rudder can still be discerned at the left. While drawing, Cuyp probably altered the direction of this ship first, and only subsequently included the motif of transferring barrels to a rowboat. As this action, naturally, could not take place on a boat under full sail, he omitted the sail in the two paintings. Judging from the wash he applied in the sail to suggest the play of light, the initial composition was in an already fairly advanced stage.[1] Cuyp probably observed the loading of barrels near a quay rather than in the middle of the water, as seen in both paintings. The sloop sailing away, which is lit from the right in the Ascott painting, is shown in the present drawing with an illumination similar to that in a painting at Waddesdon Manor.[2]

In the seventeenth century, Dordrecht played an important role in the lumber trade. Outside of the Sint Jorispoort (Saint George's Gate) on the city's south side were many *houtplaetsen* (lumber yards), sites for the transshipment of wood. The lumber was imported from Germany on rafts and moored in the Merwede River, just south of the Rietdijkspoort.[3] WK

⁌ This sheet and the Amsterdam view of Dordrecht (cat. 84) served as the point of departure for a composition that Cuyp realized in the two impressive paintings in Kenwood and Ascott (cats. 35, 36). In principle, this drawing is closest to the Ascott painting, which includes (as the Kenwood painting does not) a sloop at the right sailing toward the raft. Moreover, the two workmen on the raft at the left in this sheet and in the Ascott painting have similar poses. In both paintings, Cuyp introduced a helmsman at the rafts' rudder. In the drawing, Cuyp established a balanced interrelation-

1 Aelbert Cuyp, **River Landscape with Ferry,** Staatliche Museen zu Berlin, Kupferstichkabinett

2 Aelbert Cuyp, **River Landscape with Ferry,** The Wallace Collection, London

• In this small sheet, Cuyp essentially studied two unrelated crafts: a rowboat in which an oarsman transports some passengers (at least four), and a ferry carrying quite a few people and a wagon with two horses. For the rowboat, Cuyp was seeking an effective way of depicting figures compactly grouped in foreshortening. For the ferry, he was looking for the correct shape for the prow and stern, while also introducing contrasts through diagonal accents such as the large rudder and the ferry rope. He elaborated the boat's reflections with brush and light gray ink, thereby showing just how important he deemed this aspect. Defined with some chalk and a few vigorous brushstrokes, the sky is undoubtedly autograph. Buildings dot the exceptionally subtly drawn horizon, with a town suggested in the distance at the right.[1]

Cuyp used this drawing and a sheet in Berlin (fig. 1) to prepare a painting now in the Wallace Collection in London (fig. 2). Although in the painting the ferry sails in the opposite direction and crosses paths with a large sailboat (creating a confusion of masts and sails), the reflections are very close to those in this drawing. The right foreground of the painting includes the rowboat in the present drawing,[2] while Cuyp used the Berlin drawing to chart the situation on the river in general terms. **WK**

87 Nijmegen with the Valkhof, Viewed from the Northeast

black chalk, gray wash, 15.8 × 24.8 (6 ¼ × 9 ¾). École Nationale Supérieure des Beaux-Arts, Paris
(Washington, Amsterdam only)

• In the foreground of this drawing is the Valkhof, the imposing citadel built by Charlemagne, while beyond it lies the city of Nijmegen with the centrally placed tower of the Sint Stevenskerk. Cuyp, who had either situated himself in a boat in the middle of the Waal River or along the far banks, here combined a disarming directness, a refined application of planes (in the citadel and the city), and suggestive passages (the rapid delineation of many of the houses and boats). The Valkhof's wide main tower with its characteristic pitched roof crowned by a

belfry is so foreshortened that it almost resembles a steeple.[1] To the right of the main tower, the pointed roof of the Sint Nicolaaskapel juts up just above the rampart of the citadel. Today, this chapel is the best preserved remnant of the imposing castle that was largely demolished in 1797 / 1798. To the right of center, the quay is dominated by the Straetemakers-bolwerk (Pavers' Bulwark), the round bulwark that occupies such a prominent place in many views of Nijmegen from the northwest (see cat. 33).

Just beyond the picture plane, to the left of the castle, was the Belvedere, a wall tower heightened with a lookout in 1646; from there Cuyp could have drawn his view of the countryside to the east of Nijmegen (cat. 92).

Cuyp depicted Nijmegen with the Valkhof in other drawings, all probably executed during a trip of about 1652. A drawing now in a German private collection served as the preparatory study for the view of Nijmegen from the northwest known in versions in Woburn Abbey (see cat. 43, fig. 1) and in Indianapolis (cat. 33).[2] Finally, Cuyp again drew the Valkhof from close-up in a sheet in the Pierpont Morgan Library, which served as the point of departure for the painting in Edinburgh (cat. 43).[3] **WK**

black chalk, gray wash, 18 × 27.1 (7 ¹/₁₆ × 10 ¹¹/₁₆). Graphische Sammlung Albertina, Vienna
(London, Amsterdam only)

• Ubbergen castle was located about four kilometers southeast of Nijmegen. With this view of the castle in its ruined state surrounded by water and set before a distinctly demarcated mountain range, Cuyp conjured up one of the most romantic seventeenth-century visions of the lower Rhenish region — a vision he further reinforced in the painting based on the drawing (cat. 31).

In the painting, Cuyp reduced the *repoussoir* motif of the tree to a bush, thereby underscoring the monumentality of the ruins. Moreover, he emphasized the foremost corner tower by making it more slender, illuminating it more forcefully, and stressing its reflection. Cuyp also subtly heightened the mountains in the background so that this tower just barely transects their outline. He introduced a horseman and a shepherd as *repoussoir* elements, thus providing a point of reference for measuring the building's scale. In conceiving the drawing Cuyp must have played with a similar idea, for erased traces of an initial lay-in indicate that he had included two figures at the edge of the moat. The sky at the right in the drawing is filled with ominous clouds primarily done in wash, possibly added in the eighteenth century. In the painting Cuyp reserved this area of the sky for an intense evening light.

By choosing such a low vantage point, Cuyp was able to give the castle and the nearby hills a dramatic appearance — a visual trick followed by many Dutch artists, for example Roelant Roghman (1627–1692) in his impressive series of castle views done in 1646 and 1647.[1] Cuyp's interest in topographical "landmarks," however, differed from Roghman's, who concentrated primarily on buildings. Cuyp's inclination — in which topographical accuracy is wedded to the picturesqueness of the motif — can best be put into perspective by placing the drawing in his series of views near Nijmegen, such as the closely related view of Nijmegen with the Valkhof from the east.[2] **W K**

89 The Rhine Valley with Schenkenschans Fort

black chalk, gray wash, pencil, 17.4 × 24.5 (6 ⅞ × 9 ⅝). The British Museum, London
(London, Amsterdam only)

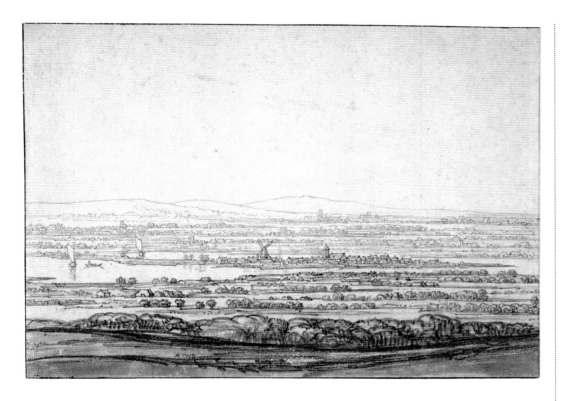

• When making this drawing, the artist looked out from the Sternberg near Cleves over the Rhine river valley to a range of low distant hills, probably the heights near Arnhem. The course of the Rhine is far more regular now than it was in the seventeenth century.[1] At that time, the Rhine forked at an island, on whose eastern point was located the strategically vital Schenkenschans Fort, here mainly indicated as a village with a church and a windmill.[2] Cuyp accentuated the river's course by means of two sailboats and a rowboat on the otherwise smooth water. The slope of the hill where the artist took up his position is sturdily and cursorily delineated. At the foot of the hill a stretch of the woods is robustly indicated in chalk, making a splendid contrast to the fine draftsmanship of the view in the distance.

The powerful and swiftly executed sketch on the back belongs with the Amsterdam *Cleves Viewed from the Galgenberg* (cat. 90). Accordingly, in the original sketchbook this sheet preceded the Amsterdam drawing, and the two views were almost certainly drawn in that order.

Jan van Goyen made a rapid chalk sketch of this view from the same spot in 1650, shortly before Cuyp visited this area.[3] Compared with Van Goyen's deft aide mémoire, Aelbert Cuyp seems to have produced a highly meticulous study. Still, he was not interested solely in topographical accuracy, as is evidenced by his depiction of Schenkenschans Fort; he sketched neither its defenses nor the details of the onion-shaped church tower, which would have been immensely helpful in identifying the location. Cuyp's priority here must have been to give a general impression of the Rhine valley. WK

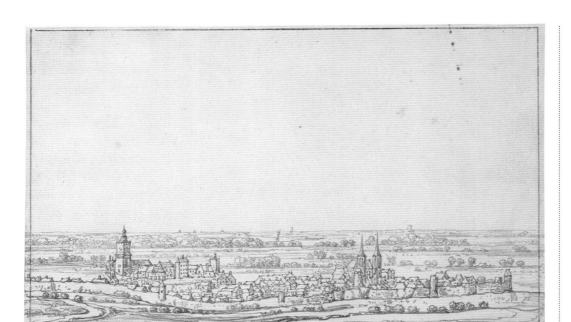

Stretching out beyond the town is a vast pano-ramic landscape with a river and a sailboat. The artistic high point, however, is the undulating line of the town wall that Cuyp repeated in mirror image in the shaded foreground. Cuyp darkened the foreground a deep black with moistened chalk and gray wash, probably after signing his name at the lower left and lower center in the drawing.[2]

A telling comparison may be made between this drawing and a *View of Cleves* by Jacob Esselens in the Hermitage. Esselens chose a vantage point somewhat farther away from the town, probably at the foot of the hill on which Cuyp stood. While Cuyp evinces a subtle yet uniform interest in detail, Esselens devoted far greater attention to the contrasts of light and shade.[3]

A later owner provided a framing line around the main section of the composition, most likely with the intention of framing or reducing the draw-ing accordingly.

Cuyp extended this view onto the verso of the sheet in London (see cat. 89). This affords a good idea of how the artist worked: here he used the back of the previous sheet in his sketchbook when the one he was working on proved too small to contain his vision.[4] **WK**

•   Cuyp drew this view of Cleves from the west-northwest during his trip to the Rhine valley. On the left, the town is dominated by Schwanenburg (Swan castle), the ancient residence of the dukes of Cleves. In Cuyp's time the electors of Brandenburg owned this duchy, and they appointed Johan Maurits van Nassau-Siegen as its stadtholder in 1647. Rising above the town at the right, beyond a wind-

mill, are the two towers of the Stiftskerk. A number of towers dot the town wall, including the Raven-turm (Raven Tower), here still visible in its full glory before the Schwanenburg. The collapse and subsequent demolition of this tower in 1652 provide a *datum ante quem* for this sheet as well as for the entire group of drawings Cuyp made in the vicinity of Nijmegen and Cleves (cats. 87 – 93).[1]

Calcar and the Monterberg Viewed from Cleves

black chalk, gray wash, 15.9 × 23.9 (6 ¼ × 9 ⁷⁄₁₆). Collection Groninger Museum, The Netherlands
(Washington, Amsterdam only)

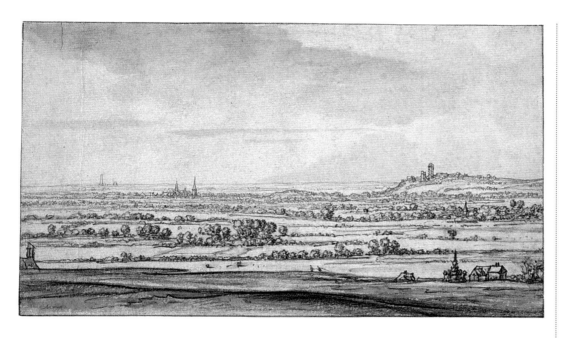

1 Aelbert Cuyp, **River View with Sailboats,** verso

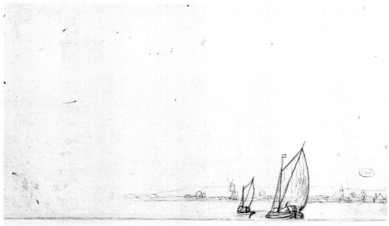

· From the Galgenberg near Cleves, Cuyp surveyed the landscape in the direction of Calcar — looking to the east-southeast. Halfway up the slope in the right foreground was the notable topiary linden tree near the leper house situated on the town's outskirts.[1] Cuyp indicated the distance to the town by rendering a small part of the southern ramparts at the far left. The hill's height prevents us from seeing the full breadth of the water in the Kermisdal, which is reduced to a narrow ribbon, most noticeable at the left. Whether or not the two tiny figures pulling a rope at the lower right are near the water is unclear. The bank on the opposite side is beautifully delineated with a strip of land, trees, and shrubs. Rising in the distance at the right is the Monterberg, the hill on which stood the ruins of the castle of the dukes of Cleves, including a high tower.[2] In the plains at the left can be discerned the towers of Calcar; and in the far distance, the remarkably tall tower could only belong to a church in Wezel.

Cuyp probably incorporated the distant view in a picture that may have been the pendant to a work in Woburn Abbey (see cat. 43, fig. 1), an image known from two workshop paintings.[3]

On the verso (fig. 1), Cuyp sketched two sailing vessels and a little windmill in a summary yet convincing manner. **WK**

92

The Rhine Valley Viewed from Nijmegen toward the Elterberg

black chalk, brush, and gray ink, 15.4 × 24.7 (6 1/16 × 9 ¾). Staatliche Museen zu Berlin, Kupferstichkabinett *(Washington, Amsterdam only)*

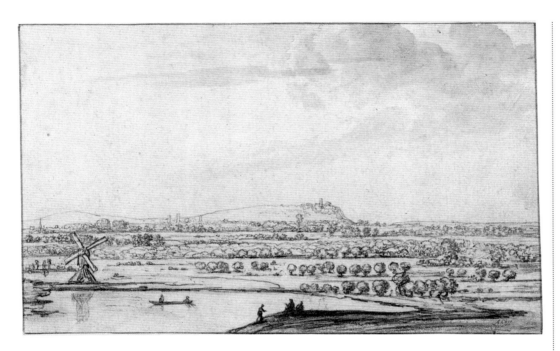

· From a high vantage point in or near Nijmegen —possibly the Belvedere—Cuyp sketched the lowland with the Elterberg in the distance. The foreground is occupied by a lake, before which a few figures, including a seated draftsman, are evidently admiring the view of the lake, a fishing boat, a windmill on the opposite bank, and its reflection in the water. For this panoramic view with emphatically silhouetted figures placed in the darkened foreground, Cuyp relied on principles introduced by the late sixteenth-century landscape artist Paulus Bril, which were widely followed in the Netherlands. The middle ground displays the graceful rhythm of rows of trees so characteristic of the drawings Cuyp made in the vicinity of Nijmegen during the early 1650s (see also cats. 89, 91, 93).

The dominant theme in the drawing is the Elterberg with its steep south flank, a distinguishing topographical feature depicted by many artists. The abbey church of Upper Elten crowned its highest point. Several tall towers, probably belonging to a ruined castle, can be discerned more to the north, at the left in the drawing. The cloudy sky is a later addition. WK

The Rhine Valley Stretching North toward the Elterberg

black chalk, gray wash, pencil, 14.9 × 23.9 (5 ⅞ × 9 ⁷⁄₁₆). Collection Frits Lugt, Institut Néerlandais, Paris *(Washington only)*

· From the Sternberg near Cleves, Cuyp drew the Elterberg with the abbey church and the cloister buildings and, at the left, Lower Elten. In the plain at the left lie the villages of Rindern and, farther to the right, Brienen. Cuyp depicted the Rhine at the foot of the hill, with some sailboats and reflections in the water. With its subtle effect of light and shadow in the groups of trees in the low-lying land at the bottom of the Sternberg, this drawing is more elaborate than the other sketches the artist made in the surroundings of Cleves and Calcar.

The same landscape recurs in the painting in Woburn Abbey (see cat. 29, fig. 1), in which two horsemen have halted near a sleeping shepherd. One of them has taken out a sketchbook to record the panorama. Rarely do a drawing and painting together convey such a sensitive portrayal of the pleasure taken in the sheer beauty of a vista. Whereas the use of this landscape in the Woburn Abbey painting is convincingly realistic, its use in the painting of the young Pompe van Meerdervoort boys (cat. 29) is entirely imaginary. **WK**

94 Study of Leaves, Possibly Rhubarb

pen and brown and gray ink, gray wash, traces of black chalk, 21.7 × 21.4 (8 9/16 × 8 7/16). Museum Boijmans Van Beuningen, Rotterdam *(Washington, Amsterdam only)*

• Even in his earliest work, Aelbert Cuyp avidly depicted waterside vegetation. His predilection for using plants as decorative filler in the foreground of his paintings is evident in early works, such as his 1641 family portrait (cat. 3) and his *A Farm with Cottages and Animals* (cat. 10), as well as in very late works, including the couple on horseback in Washington (cat. 40). He situated the plants in their natural surroundings in one drawing, namely the *Three Cows near a Fence with Butterbur in the Foreground* (cat. 97). Cuyp's distinct interest in and depiction of such plants have led to the (not always decisive) attribution of several detailed studies of plants to this master.[1] Unfortunately, identification of the plants studied by Cuyp is not as easy as it might seem: rhubarb, burdock, sorrel, and butterbur are the names most often forwarded, often without solid justification.

Jacob Gerritsz Cuyp must have introduced his son to the meticulous rendering of plants, as can be deduced from a few of his drawings and the pronounced vegetation in *Diversa animalia*, his series of animal studies.[2] Jacob's interest in vegetation was probably stimulated by Abraham Bloemaert, who not only drew several studies of plants but also included large plants in the foreground of several of his paintings.[3]

In this drawing Cuyp seems to have depicted the leaves of curly rhubarb *(Rheum undulatum)*. Cuyp was not the first to portray this plant: Pieter Saenredam in an earlier sheet dating from 1630 (Staatliche Museen zu Berlin, Kupferstich-kabinett)[4] noted that he had drawn "Dese plant rhabarber…naer 't leeven" (this rhubarb plant… from life). Rhubarb was originally introduced in Europe from Asia, and Saenredam's study is thus primarily botanical in nature. Bearing this in mind, Cuyp made his sketch not along a bank, but rather in a garden. Moreover, Cuyp seems to have been essentially focused on creating light and shadow with the brush in order to approximate the curved and hollow surface of the leaves. WK

95 **Study of Leaves, Possibly Butterbur**

black chalk, gray wash, watercolored in green and yellow, heightened with white, partly brushed with gum arabic, 14 × 19.4 (5 ½ × 7 ⅝). Collection Frits Lugt, Institut Néerlandais, Paris *(Washington only)*

· This sheet is most likely a study of butterbur leaves. Cuyp made it during a drawing campaign in which he produced various detailed studies of nature. In the treatment of the ground, dimensions, and technique — especially the application of color — this and the following drawing are virtually identical. Both undoubtedly came from the same sketchbook, one which the artist was using about 1640 and which may have contained landscape and animal studies as well (see cats. 53, 61 – 63, 96 – 98, 101, 102).

Cuyp must have made these studies for the sake of his paintings. The outlines of the two leaves jutting up occur in his view of cows near a river in Petworth.[1] However, the artist certainly must have used the complete image of this splendid combination of dense vegetation and a few projecting leaves as a *repoussoir* in one of his paintings. **WK**

96 Study of Plants, Possibly Sorrel and Butterbur

black chalk, gray wash, watercolored in red, yellow, and green, heightened with white, partly brushed with gum arabic, 14.6 × 19.3 (5 ¾ × 7 ⅝). The British Museum, London *(London, Amsterdam only)*

• In this drawing, which is very close to the previous sheet, Cuyp depicted several large, broad leaves, presumably butterbur, with curly sorrel rising behind it in the middle and to the left. The artist created a convincing impression of a patch of vegetation growing near a ditch. Cuyp first drew the plants in black chalk and subsequently defined them with the point of the brush, often in very fine lines. He then applied shadows, washing with the brush. Finally, he introduced subtle yellows and greens, while accenting the sorrel at the upper left with a bit of red brown. He finally deepened the dark areas with gum arabic. In terms of technique, the drawing corresponds closely with Cuyp's early work and, like his early, colored landscape drawings, was probably made in about 1639 / 1640.

Cuyp incorporated this delightful and apparently spontaneous study with great accuracy in his landscape painting with cattle and a farmhouse (cat. 10). WK

97 Three Cows near a Fence with Butterbur in the Foreground

black chalk, gray wash, watercolored in yellow and red, heightened with white, partly brushed with gum arabic, 14 × 19 (5 ½ × 7 ½). The British Museum, London *(London, Amsterdam only)*

· This is one of the earliest of Aelbert Cuyp's many drawings of cows. In format, it corresponds with the early landscapes that the artist sketched near Dordrecht.[1]

Although the drawing still exhibits some awkwardness — the two cows at the right are not well proportioned with respect to one another — Cuyp nevertheless demonstrated greater control of the cattle than in his earliest work, the 1639 *Landscape with Cattle* in Besançon.[2] In presentation, the cows and vegetation are very close to those in *A Farm with Cottages and Animals* (cat. 10) dating from the early 1640s.

The depiction of the butterbur in this drawing recalls the work of Abraham Bloemaert, whose predilection for humble farmhouse nooks Cuyp would have known through his father, Jacob Gerritsz Cuyp, who had studied with the Utrecht master. With this drawing Aelbert Cuyp also commented on his father's work — his cows and other cattle, often in artificial poses, were published by Visscher in 1641 in *Diversa animalia*.[3] **WK**

98

A Horse near the Bank of a River with Two Moored Rowboats

black chalk, brush and gray ink, watercolored in brown and green, heightened in gray and white, traces of gum arabic at the lower right, 13.6 × 19.1 (5 ⅜ × 7 ½). Staatliche Museen zu Berlin, Kupferstichkabinett *(Washington, Amsterdam only)*

The artist successfully integrated the horse and the boats into the landscape, which also consists of a wide prospect suggested by the distance to the opposite side of the river and by the far view at the right.

Cuyp derived the motif of the horse half turned to the viewer from his father's engraved series of animal studies, *Diversa animalia*.[1] The entirely natural setting, undoubtedly located in the vicinity of Dordrecht, is Cuyp's own contribution. As a study of cattle along the shore, this early composition dating from about 1640 anticipates Cuyp's impressive paintings of cows near the water (for instance, cats. 21–23), in which, however, all distracting elements are suppressed.

Comparable, though not entirely similar horses occur in a few of Cuyp's paintings. The relationship of the horse to the bank in this drawing corresponds closely to that in Cuyp's painting of a horseman and shepherds with the ruins of the Huis te Merwede in the background (The National Gallery, London).[2]

The sky has been heightened with white, probably to mask a few stains, now again clearly visible. **WK**

· In addition to his careful and concentrated studies of cattle — horses, cows, sheep — Cuyp occasionally depicted animals in their natural surroundings. Here, a horse stands near the water's edge, with trees and a house on the opposite shore. Next to the very irregular quayside, two rowboats are moored near two poles stuck in the riverbed.

· In this sheet Cuyp made two studies of a lean horse. A summary study of a dog at the right, perhaps initially intended to establish the right horse in a setting, was erased by the master himself. The two horses differ not only in the extent of foreshortening, but also in conception. The left one was initially defined in linear terms: one sees the parallel lines so characteristic of Cuyp, for instance, near the ribs and in the neck. Subsequently, the artist smudged the chalk a bit to achieve clearer volume. The subtle handling of the chalk is especially evident in the lines in the stomach region and in the rendering of hair on the legs. Light and shadow are only indicated on the ground, where their sole purpose is to anchor the animal. The study at the right is a classic exercise in foreshortening, similar to those made by other draftsmen at the time, including Pieter van Laer and Karel Dujardin.[1] However, it also represents an attempt to suggest volume and light and dark, particularly in the flank and hindquarters. Cuyp again elaborated the sketch at the right in a drawing in the Collection Frits Lugt, Institut Néerlandais, in Paris (cat. 100), and he included the left horse in a painting in Karlsruhe.[2] WK

black chalk, brush in gray wash, traces of pencil, 8.4 × 12.5 (3 5/16 × 4 15/16). Collection Frits Lugt, Institut Néerlandais, Paris *(Amsterdam only)*

· When Cuyp combined animals in his drawings, he sometimes devised compositions with groups, such as the flocks of sheep or cows in Berlin.[1] In sketching these two animals, however, he utterly disregarded their placement vis-à-vis each other, perhaps because he was intent upon pursuing other aims. With regard to the cow, he carefully and precisely defined its volumes with parallel lines. For the horse, he suggested the effect of light and shadow with a broad wash, placing great emphasis on the shadow on the ground. The same horse, comparable in shape down to the smallest detail, appears in another of Cuyp's drawings (cat. 99). While light and dark receive priority in both sheets, here this effect received even greater emphasis. After jotting down a few pencil lines as orientation, he proceeded to execute the drawing in brush with great bravura.

In slightly altered form, both the cow and the horse reappear in the monumental *River Landscape with Horseman and Peasants* in the National Gallery, London (cat. 45). The cow, with an identical dappled brown marking on its head, is partly concealed by a piebald cow. The horse has a slightly different stance and its head is a bit more raised; however, the left hind flank is the same.[2] With these slight adjustments, Cuyp transformed the weary cart horse in the drawing into the proud gray steed in the painting. WK

IOI A Cow Standing

black chalk, gray wash, 13.6 × 18.9 (5 ⅜ × 7 ⁷⁄₁₆). The British Museum, London

· A fairly large number of Cuyp's drawings of animals, including cows, sheep, horses, and a dog, have been preserved. This group, though, is problematic, for Cuyp has been renowned as one of the foremost specialists in the depiction of livestock since the early nineteenth century, and many animal studies have been wrongly attributed to him. Moreover, a number of his drawings have been worked up, copied, and even forged.

This *Cow Standing* must have been made fairly early in Cuyp's career, a dating indicated by the meticulous delineation of the contours and the still hesitant parallel inner lines, particularly distinct in the animal's neck. Nevertheless, with this direct portrayal, Cuyp clearly distanced himself from his father's animal studies, such as those found in *Diversa animalia*, in which Jacob tried to create interesting, though artificial and somewhat mannered, images.

The *Cow Standing* occurs in virtually the same pose — though the left front leg has been altered to suggest a walking motion — in the *Stable Interior* in Stockholm.[1] A comparison of these works reveals that the illumination from behind was essential to Cuyp, who apparently changed the cow's markings in the painting to create contrast in the dark stable. WK

IO2 A Bullock Standing

black chalk, gray wash, watercolored in brown, 13.6 × 18.1 (5 ⅜ × 7 ⅛). Amsterdams Historisch Museum
(Washington, Amsterdam only)

• While in *A Cow Standing* (cat. 101), the artist primarily delineated form by means of light, in this sheet he focused on rendering the animal's fur. However, the still somewhat hesitant shape of the hoofs and the shadow cast by this young bull are similar to those in the preceding drawing, as is the definition of its outline, which is sporadically interrupted by upright strokes for the hair of the fur. The markings — here in the neck, and on the hindquarters in the cow drawing — are also similarly indicated. Cuyp extensively elaborated the bullock drawing, even adding brown watercolor. In the use of color, the drawing recalls Cuyp's early landscape sketches made in the vicinity of Dordrecht, and therefore probably also dates from about 1640.[1] The application of color brings to mind the work of Cornelis Saftleven, who, perhaps influenced by Abraham Bloemaert, used color in his animal drawings of the 1630s. **WK**

103   A Cow Lying Down

black chalk, gray wash, 7.6 × 13.3 (3 × 5 ¼). Private collection, The Netherlands

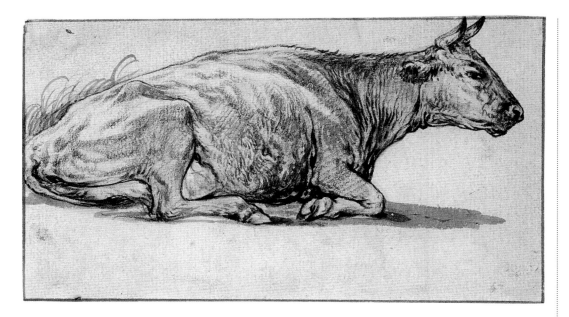

· Here, Cuyp's mastery in depicting cattle at rest is shown at its best. No traces remain of the wavering, nervous drawing style that distinguished the artist's earlier cattle studies. The artist betrayed only a hint of hesitation in searching for the proper contour, particularly along the animal's back. The delineation of the fur and the fall of light over the cow's body, however, demonstrate Cuyp's great accomplishments as a draftsman of cattle. With summarily indicated vegetation and fleetly and convincingly placed shadows, the artist evoked a setting for the animal.

While cows in this position already occur in Cuyp's early work, the drawing's genesis may nevertheless be assumed to be later. The serenity of the cattle in a landscape or near water, such an essential element in Cuyp's more mature paintings, is something he must have discovered through this or similar drawings.[1] Although we have no specific clues, a dating of about 1650 for these more mature studies may be surmised.

The most important reverberation of this study is found in the *River Landscape with Horseman and Peasants* (cat. 45). WK

black chalk, gray wash, watercolored in very light green, 7.1 × 14.3 (2 ¹³/₁₆ × 5 ⅝). Graphische Sammlung Albertina, Vienna *(London, Amsterdam only)*

1 Reinier van Persyn after Jacob Gerritsz Cuyp, **Goats and Horses**, 1641, Rijksmuseum, Amsterdam

· Although Cuyp seemingly drew this dog from life, he nevertheless based its pose on models favored by his father, whose mannered studies of animals (for example, the goat at the left in fig. 1) are often shown from an unusual vantage point.[1] However, this sheet is so naturally elaborated and aptly observed that Aelbert Cuyp probably was unaware of his reliance on a formula inherited from his father's repertoire. In this drawing, Cuyp concentrated on the depiction of the fur — particularly difficult to capture with its short, sturdy curls — and on the effect of light, which he primarily achieved by applying gray to black ink with the brush. Cuyp's rendering of the dog's strained pose is also extremely effective.

Cuyp used this sketch for various paintings, particularly his *Orpheus Making Music for the Animals* in a private collection, which must have been executed about 1645, and a painting with a Moorish page in the Royal Collection, London, from the late 1640s.[2] **WK**

105 Shepherd with a Staff

black chalk, gray wash, traces of gum arabic, 19.4 × 11.8 (7 ⅝ × 4 ⁵⁄₁₆). Museum Boijmans Van Beuningen, Rotterdam (*Washington, Amsterdam only*)

• Cuyp's figure studies represent a problematic group in his oeuvre. Though many of the drawings attributed to the master can be linked to his paintings, some create the impression of having been worked up or provided with rural surroundings by a later hand. Other figure drawings have been associated with Cuyp's early nineteenth-century followers, particularly Jacob and Abraham van Strij.[1] While the sophistication of some of the doubted drawings seems rather nineteenth century, here the almost naive simplicity and the hesitant seeking for proper form pleads for authenticity.

Cuyp used the sketch for a composition from the mid-1640s, in which two shepherds with staffs try to restrain a recalcitrant goat.[2] In this drawing, Cuyp chiefly attempted to capture the movement of a shepherd stepping forward with a compelling gesture of his staff. The sheet is also a study in light and shadow. Only the cheeks and chin of the shepherd's face catch the light. Cuyp emphasized the folds of his clothing and the shadow of his right hand. The exploration of form in this sketch is clearest in the hesitant definition of the boots, beautifully illustrating the creative moment. **WK**

106 Two Resting Shepherds

black chalk, gray wash, brushed with gum arabic in the foreground, 10.9 × 16.8 (4 5/16 × 6 5/8). Collection Frits Lugt, Institut Néerlandais, Paris *(Washington only)*

・ These two figures are unusually positioned in the landscape, with the shepherd at the left seated so that only the upper part of his body is visible to the viewer. Nevertheless, they are depicted with a good sense of balance, their forms related through the parallelism of their staffs. A distant view with a church tower can be seen between them. Cuyp used these figures independently in paintings. He introduced the left figure, submerged in the landscape as it were, in a painting in a private collection.[1] There, too, the shepherd is similarly involved in silent communion with a standing shepherd, a study of whom has also been preserved.[2] He included a comparable figure in a somewhat later painting (cat. 14), though it leans back more and is without a staff. The right figure, too, served as a preliminary study for a shepherd in a cattle painting near Utrecht of about 1645.[3] WK

IO7 A Milkmaid

black chalk, gray wash, some pencil, 12.1 × 14.8 (4 ¾ × 5 ¹³⁄₁₆). The J. Paul Getty Museum, Los Angeles
(Washington, Amsterdam only)

he also accentuated — perhaps unintentionally — the contrast in size between the small girl and the large cow.

Cuyp included the milkmaid in various paintings, the closest and the earliest being the girl in a work in Rotterdam (fig. 1). This painting evinces marked similarities with works from the master's middle period — such as a preference for brown tones and sharply delineated figures — and must therefore be dated shortly after 1645. However, its attribution is not beyond doubt.[1] In other works featuring the milkmaid, the master was already fascinated by the possibilities of late afternoon sunlight.[2]

The drawing originally belonged to a group of figure studies in the Dupper Collection in Dordrecht.[3] The notable influence of some of these drawings on the Van Strij brothers makes it tempting to believe that this group had been accessible to these artists, who played such an important part in the Cuyp revival in about 1800. **WK**

1 Aelbert Cuyp, **The Milkmaid**, Willem van der Vorm Foundation, Museum Boijmans Van Beuningen, Rotterdam

• In this sheet, Cuyp splendidly observed the pose and the fall of light on the folds of the clothing of the seated milkmaid. All one sees of the cow is the outline of its udder, stomach, and legs, a summary indication of the cow's body that Cuyp used to determine the position of the girl. As a result,

108 **Portrait of a Twenty-Nine-Year-Old Man**   1646, pen and brush and gray ink on white prepared parchment, heightened with white, 20.8 × 16.5 (8 3/16 × 6 ½). Staatliche Museen zu Berlin, Kupferstichkabinett *(Washington, Amsterdam only)*

109 **Portrait of a Twenty-Three-Year-Old Woman**   1646, pen and brush and gray ink on white prepared parchment, heightened with white, 20.6 × 16.3 (8 1/8 × 6 7/16). Staatliche Museen zu Berlin, Kupferstichkabinett *(Washington, Amsterdam only)*

Although the compositions of these two miniature-like portraits of a twenty-nine-year-old man and his twenty-three-year-old wife belong to a long tradition, Cuyp nevertheless drew them in a highly personal fashion. Small portraits in an oval stone opening, sometimes with a pronounced trompe l'oeil effect, appeared in Holland as early as 1626 in Frans Hals' portrait of Petrus Scriverius.[1] In 1646, the very year that Cuyp executed these works, Rembrandt created a comparable and even more daring effect in his portrait etching of Jan Cornelis Sylvius.[2]

In the seventeenth century, many artists attempted to draw "little paintings" by using fine penwork on parchment, an art form the Germans call *Federkunststück*. In the Dutch portrait tradition, David Bailly (1584 – 1657) in particular contributed significantly to this manner of working. As a painter of small portraits, he seems to have been important for an unidentified Dordrecht painter, whose set of seven portraits of a family dated 1632 proves that Cuyp's two portraits are closely related to the portrait tradition of his hometown.[3]

Cuyp was able to infuse these two small portraits with the same vigor he gave his painted life-size portraits (see also cats. 26, 27). He himself was twenty-six years old when he recorded these delicate likenesses. The exceptional immediacy of his portrayals, which to some critics indicated that they were Cuyp and his wife, makes it very likely that the artist depicted relatives or good friends.[4] Only one other drawn portrait by Cuyp is known, the portrait of Andreas Colvius, whose execution is somewhat freer but which nevertheless attests to the same direct, personal observation.[5] A print was made of the latter portrait in 1646, suggesting that the drawing also dates from that year. **WK**

46

The Mariakerk in Utrecht from the Northeast

black chalk, gray wash, watercolored in brown, yellow, green, and pink, 22 × 31 (8 ¹¹⁄₁₆ × 12 ³⁄₁₆).[1] The British Museum, London (1836.8.11.95)

Inscription

Lower right, possibly autograph (in pen and brown ink): *A.Cúijp*

Provenance

Possibly D. Versteegh. J. Sheepshanks; The British Museum, 1836

Literature

Hind 1915–1932, 71, no. 18; Bernt 1957–1958, no. 171; Van Gelder and Jost 1969, 102, note 26; Chong 1992, 276; Utrecht 2000, 95–97

Endnotes

1. Strip affixed to the top must be an autograph addition.

2. For instance, Cuyp could have seen the chalk drawing that preceded Saenredam's meticulously worked out sheet, or a copy of it.

3. Arie de Groot in Utrecht 2000, 97.

4. Saenredam corrected this passage in the painting dating from 1659 in the Mauritshuis, The Hague; see Utrecht 2000, no. 3.

47

The Mariakerk in Utrecht from the Northwest

black chalk, gray wash, watercolored in green, yellow, and brown, heightened with white, yellow, and pink, partly brushed with gum arabic, 19.1 × 30.7 (7 ½ × 12 ¹⁄₁₆). Graphische Sammlung im Städelsches Kunstinstitut, Frankfurt am Main (14 356)

Inscription

Lower right (annotated in pen and brown ink): *Á.C.*

Provenance

Possibly D. Versteegh; R.W.P. de Vries; (C.G. Boerner, Düsseldorf, 1913). Graphische Sammlung im Städelsches Kunstinstitut, Frankfurt am Main

Literature

Van Gelder and Jost 1969, 101, 102, fig. 10; Salomonson 1983, 98, 100, fig. 68; Chong 1992, 276, 283

48

The Buurkerk in Utrecht in Rural Surroundings

black chalk, gray wash, watercolored in gray-green, white, and gray-green bodycolor, pen and brown ink, partly brushed with gum arabic, 18.4 × 30.5 (7 ¼ × 12). Mrs. Edward Speelman

Inscription

Upper right (in pen and brown ink): *de Búúrkerk*; lower right (annotated in pen and brown ink): *A.C.*

Provenance

P. Calkoen Wzn; D. baron van Leyden. A.W.M. Mensing; private collection

Exhibitions

London 1937, no. 52; London 1953, no. 339; Washington 1996

Literature

Van Gelder and Jost 1969, 102, no. 26; Salomonson 1983, 98–100, fig. 69; Chong 1992, 276; Washington 1996, n.p., ill.

Endnotes

1. This drawing is in Berlin. See Bock and Rosenberg 1930 (inv. no. 5856).

49

Utrecht with the Vecht River and the Pellekussenpoort

black chalk, gray wash, watercolored in green, traces of pen and gray ink and some white bodycolor, 17.6 × 30.7 (6 ¹⁵⁄₁₆ × 12 ⅛). Staatliche Museen zu Berlin, Kupferstichkabinett (5854)

Inscription

Lower right (annotated in pen and brown ink): *Á.C.*

Provenance

M.D. Collection; A. von Beckerath, Berlin; Staatliche Museen zu Berlin, Kupferstichkabinett, 1902

Literature

Bock and Rosenberg 1930, 1: 113, no. 5854; Van Gelder and Jost 1969, 102, 103, fig. 5; Van Gelder and Jost 1972, 238, note 24; Chong 1992, 276

Endnotes

1. Van Gelder and Jost 1969. They based their theory on a statement by J. Graafhuis. See also Stechow 1938.

50

Four Trees near a Fence

black chalk, gray wash, watercolored in brown and green, partly brushed with gum arabic, 18.8 × 30.8 (7 ⅜ × 12 ⅛). The Metropolitan Museum of Art, New York, Rogers Fund, 1907

Provenance

(Frederik Muller, Amsterdam, by 1907); The Metropolitan Museum of Art, New York, 1907

Exhibitions

Poughkeepsie 1976, no. 47

Literature

Van Gelder and Jost 1969, 102, note 28; Van Gelder and Jost in Washington, Denver, and Fort Worth 1977, 61; Mules 1985, 38–39

Endnotes

1. This drawing was, unfortunately, stolen some years ago. Cuyp used a significant part of the latter sheet as well as a view of the Mariakerk (cat. 47) for his painting in Salzburg (cat. 5).

2. Cuyp used this drawing for the background in a painting by Jacob Gerritsz Cuyp of 1641 (see cat. 3, fig. 1).

51
The Edge of a Woods with Travelers

black chalk, gray wash, 18.6 × 30 (7 5/16 × 11 13/16). Museum Boijmans Van Beuningen, Rotterdam (H. 148)

Provenance

Miss Seymour; F. Koenigs; gift D. G. van Beuningen to the Foundation Museum Boymans, 1940

Exhibitions

Rotterdam 1934, no. 45; Rotterdam 1938, no. 257; Braunschweig 1948, no. 6; Leningrad, Moscow, and Kiev 1974, no. 66; Paris 1974, no. 17; Dordrecht 1977, no. 49.

Endnotes

1. See Brussels, Rotterdam, and Paris 1972–1973, no. 20, pl. 19.

52
Path between Trees

black chalk, gray wash, brushed with gum arabic, 17.7 × 29.5 (6 15/16 × 11 5/8). Graphische Sammlung im Städelsches Kunstinstitut, Frankfurt am Main (3724)

Provenance

Graphische Sammlung im Städelsches Kunstinstitut, Frankfurt am Main, by 1862

Endnotes

1. Chong 1992, no. 69. Illustrated in Reiss 1975, no. 60. Chong dated that work to about 1644.

53
A Path at the Edge of a Woods with Two Old Oak Trees

black chalk, gray wash, watercolored in yellow, partly brushed with gum arabic, 13.8 × 19.3 (5 7/16 × 7 5/8). The British Museum, London (1910.2.18.2)

Inscription

Lower middle: *A C.*[1]

Provenance

Miss M. Hoofman; G. Leembruggen Gzn; Benoit Coster; A. G. de Visser; W. Pitcairn Knowles; Mrs. Robert Low; The British Museum, London, 1910

Exhibitions

London 1912, no. 171

Literature

Hind 1915–1932, no. 3; Chong 1992, 271

Endnotes

1. The date 1640 has been read next to Cuyp's initials. However, this detail seems to be part of the vegetation.

54
Wide Expanse of Water with Trees in the Right Foreground

black chalk, gray wash, watercolored in yellow and brown, partly brushed with gum arabic, 14.5 × 19 (5 11/16 × 7 1/2). The British Museum, London (1912.12.14.11)

Provenance

Sir Benjamin West; Thomas Dimsdale; William Esdaile; C. S. Bale; J. P. Heseltine; Sir Otto Beit; The British Museum, London, 1912

Exhibitions

London 1911, no. 135

Literature

Hind 1915–1932, no. 1; Mellaart 1926, 21, 35; Chong 1992, 254, 262; Broos 1993, 71

Endnotes

1. Cuyp may have seen this view from the westernmost islands in the Holland and Zeeland delta. A drawing by Roelant Roghman, *Panorama with the Fortress of Oostvoorne* (The British Museum, London; ill. in Van der Wyck 1989–1990, 1: no. 146) shows us that this combination of dunes, trees, and majestic panoramas in this area is within the realm of possibility.

2. Illustrated in Dordrecht 1992, no. 15.

55
A Weather-Beaten Oak Tree

black chalk, gray wash, some graphite, heightened with white and yellow, partly brushed with gum arabic, 15.3 × 19.6 (6 × 7 11/16). Graphische Sammlung im Städelsches Kunstinstitut, Frankfurt am Main (3723)

Provenance

Graphische Sammlung im Städelsches Kunstinstitut, Frankfurt am Main, by 1862

Literature

Frankfurt 1994, 140, no. Z60; Frankfurt 2000, 180, no. 78

Endnotes

1. See Leiden 1996, no. 15, 23.

56
Three Trees in Hilly Terrain

black chalk, gray wash, watercolored in yellow-green, 18.1 × 14.6 (7 ⅛ × 5 ¾). Staatliche Museen zu Berlin, Kupferstichkabinett (8505)

Provenance
Probably D. baron van Leyden; C. E. von Liphart; Rudolph P. Goldschmidt. Staatliche Museen zu Berlin, Kupferstich-kabinett (anonymous gift), 1917

Literature
Kunstchronik 1918, 309; Bock and Rosenberg 1930, I: 112; Wegner 1973, 73; Chong 1992, 276

57
A Wide Plain, Low Trees in the Foreground

black chalk, gray wash, watercolored in ochre yellow, partly brushed with gum arabic, 19 × 31 (7 ½ × 12 ³⁄₁₆). The British Museum, London (1880.10.9.28)

Inscription
Lower right (in pen and brown ink): *A:C:*

Provenance
Sir William Worsley, Bt.; The British Museum, London, 1880

Literature
Hind 1915 – 1932, no. 5

58
Panorama with a Country Manor

black chalk, gray wash, watercolored in ochre, yellow, and blue, partially brushed with gum arabic, 18.7 × 30.3 (7 ⅜ × 11 ¹⁵⁄₁₆). Graphische Sammlung Albertina, Vienna (8755)

Inscription
Lower right (annotated in pen and brown ink): *A.C.*

Provenance
Duke Albert of Saxe-Teschen. Graphische Sammlung Albertina, Vienna

Literature
Munich and Bonn 1993, 132, note 9

Endnotes
1. Black chalk, gray wash (14 × 29.2 cm); illustrated in *Stift und Feder* 1927, no. 93.

59
A Manor House among Trees, High Hills in the Distance

black chalk, gray wash, watercolored in brown-green, locally brushed with gum arabic, 18.3 × 42.1 (7 ³⁄₁₆ × 16 ⅝). Staatliche Museen zu Berlin, Kupferstichkabinett (5443)

Inscription
Lower left (annotated in pen and brown ink): *A:Kúip*

Provenance
A. von Beckerath; Staatliche Museen zu Berlin, Kupferstichkabinett, 1902

Exhibitions
Berlin 1974, no. 41

Literature
Bock and Rosenberg 1930, I: 112; Lugt 1931, 44; Wegner 1973, 73

60
Peasant Carts near a Farmhouse in a Dune Landscape

black chalk, gray wash, watercolored in yellow and brown, partly brushed with gum arabic, 12.4 × 18.9 (4 ⅞ × 7 ⁷⁄₁₆). Graphische Sammlung Albertina, Vienna (8694)

Provenance
Duke Albert of Saxe-Teschen. Graphische Sammlung Albertina, Vienna

61
The Windmills at Kinderdijk (recto); The Grote Kerk in Dordrecht from the Southwest (verso)

black chalk, gray wash, watercolored in brown and red, heightened with white, 13.7 × 18.9 (5 ⅜ × 7 ⁷⁄₁₆). Private collection, U.S.A.

Inscription
Verso (in pen): *N.1944* (Goll's inv. no.)

Provenance
Jhr. J. Goll van Franckenstein; Dr. F. Heimsoeth, Bonn; C. Schoeffer; private collection

Exhibitions
Poughkeepsie 1976, no. 45

Literature
Burnett 1969, 372 – 373; Chong 1992, 281

Endnotes
1. In addition to landscapes (cats. 62, 63), a number of sheets with about the same format with other subjects can be mentioned (compare, for instance, cats. 96, 98, 101, 103).

2. The earliest view seems to be the sheet in Munich (Wegner 1973). The drawing in London served as the model for the painting in Rotterdam (see Hind 1915–1932, no. 17, and Reiss 1975, no. 62). Yet another drawing must have been used for the two famous workshop products in London, the so-called *"Small Dort"* and *"Large Dort"*; see Reiss 1975, nos. 79, 83.

62

Moored Rowboats on a River, a Church in the Distance

black chalk, gray wash, watercolored in brown, pink, green, and yellow, heightened with white, partly brushed with gum arabic, 14.1 × 19.4 (5 9⁄16 × 7 5⁄8). Private collection, The Netherlands

Provenance

Jhr. J. Goll van Franckenstein; Jhr. Mr. J. A. Repelaer; Dr. A. Schwarz; private collection

Exhibitions

Amsterdam 1968 (Schwarz Coll.), no. 31, fig. 9; Cambridge and Montreal 1988, no. 20; Dordrecht 1991

Literature

Van Gelder and Jost 1972, 227, 236, note 4; Chong 1992, 285; Broos 1993, 71; Beresford 1998, 81

Endnotes

1. See Beresford 1998, 80.

63

Boats at a Pier on a River

black chalk, gray wash, graphite, pen and brown ink, heightened with white, partly brushed with gum arabic, 14.6 × 19.5 (5 3⁄4 × 7 11⁄16). Rijksmuseum, Amsterdam (RP-T-1967-90)

Provenance

Jhr. J. Goll van Franckenstein; Jhr. Mr. J. A. Repelaer; Rijksmuseum, Amsterdam, 1967

Exhibitions

Dordrecht 1977, no. 45; Amsterdam 1987, no. 37

Literature

Chong 1992, 275, 354; Broos 1993, 71

Endnotes

1. As to the odd line in the water, here Cuyp initially may have had a reflection in mind, similar to that of the long stick resting on the afterdeck of the boat at the right.

2. Cuyp elaborated the motif of the jetty in a second drawing, in which a mill dominates at the right. That drawing served as the point of departure for an early painting, in which the bank in the left background from the drawing under discussion has been incorporated; see Reiss 1975, 49, no. 21, for both drawing and painting.

64

Country Road with a Cottage alongside a River

black chalk, gray wash, watercolored in green and yellow, 18.8 × 30.3 (7 3⁄8 × 11 15⁄16). Kunstsammlungen zu Weimar (KK 4883)

Inscription

Lower right (with the tip of the brush in brown ink): *Á.C.*

Provenance

J. G. baron Verstolk van Soelen; Leembruggen; Dr. F. Heimsoeth; Carl Ruland; Kunstsammlungen zu Weimar

Exhibitions

Weimar 1981, no. 162

Literature

Chong 1992, 280

65

A Windmill and Farm Buildings beyond Meadows

black chalk, gray wash, partly brushed with gum arabic, 18.3 × 30.4 (7 3⁄16 × 11 15⁄16). Statens Museum for Kunst, Copenhagen (II 538)

Inscription

Lower left (with the tip of the brush and brown ink): *Coningsloo*;[1] Earl Spencer's collector's mark

Provenance

Nicola Francesco Haym; Earl Spencer; Jhr. J. Goll van Franckenstein; Isendoorn à Blois; W. van Gogh; V. d. Kock; Weber; W. Pitcairn Knowles; R. P. Goldschmidt; De Robiano; Dr. C. Otto; C. Hofstede de Groot. Ny Carlsbergfondet; Statens Museum for Kunst, Copenhagen, 1931

Exhibitions

Copenhagen 1952, no. 409

Literature

Fisher and Sthyr 1953, 60, 102; Van Gelder and Jost 1969, 100, note 13; Te Rijdt 2000, 152, fig. 221

Endnotes

1. The inscription has also been read as *Tongerloo*. The drawing can in no way be connected to any of the artists from the Coninxloo family. The landscape recalls Holland in all respects and is completely unrelated to the Kempen countryside around Tongerloo in the Southern Netherlands.

66

A Dike alongside a River, a Bridge, and Trees to the Right

black chalk, gray wash, partly brushed with gum arabic, 18.4 × 30.5 (7 1⁄4 × 12). The British Museum, London (1836.8.11.97)

Provenance

J. Sheepshanks; The British Museum, London, 1836

Literature

Hind 1915–1932, 69, no. 9; Burnett 1969, 372; Reiss 1975, 46; Chong 1992, 282

Endnotes

1. This drawing has been connected with Cuyp's painting in Frankfurt (Reiss 1975, no. 18), a painting, however, which follows a drawing now in Hamburg.

67
A Village near a Bridge

black chalk, gray wash, watercolored in yellow, brown, and green, partly brushed with gum arabic, 18.5 × 30.3 (7 5/16 × 11 15/16). The British Museum, London (1836.8.11.96)

Provenance

J. Sheepshanks; The British Museum, London, 1836

Literature

Hind 1915–1932, 69, no. 8

68
Farmhouses along Both Sides of a Canal

black chalk, gray wash, watercolored in green-gray, 13.5 × 18.6 (5 5/16 × 7 5/16). The Metropolitan Museum of Art, New York, Bequest of Mrs. H.O. Havemeyer, 1929 (29.100.931)

Provenance

William Russell; H.O. Havemeyer; Mrs. H.O. Havemeyer; The Metropolitan Museum of Art, New York, 1929

Exhibitions

London 1877b, no. 1138; New York 1992, 65, 286, no. 173

Literature

Havemeyer 1931, 179; Havemeyer 1958, 5, no. 12; Wegner 1973, 1: 73

69
View of a Village at Some Distance

black chalk, gray wash, watercolored in green, brown, blue, and ochre, partly brushed with gum arabic, 18.3 × 30.6 (7 3/16 × 12 1/16). Staatliche Museen zu Berlin, Kupferstichkabinett (5208)

Provenance

A. von Beckerath; Staatliche Museen zu Berlin, Kupferstich-kabinett, 1902

Literature

Bock and Rosenberg 1930, 1: 112, no. 5208; 1: pl. 84; Van Gelder and Jost 1969, 100, note 12; Munich and Bonn 1993, 132, notes 5, 6

70
River Landscape

black chalk, gray wash, watercolored in red-brown, yellow, and green, 18.9 × 30.3 (7 7/16 × 11 15/16). Musées Royaux des Beaux-Arts de Belgique, Brussels (4060 / 974)

Provenance

Probably J.G. baron Verstolk van Soelen; Jacob de Vos Jbzn; De Grez Collection; Musées Royaux des Beaux-Arts de Belgique, Brussels, 1913

Exhibitions

Rotterdam 1954, no. 61; Manchester 1976, no. 63

Literature

De Grez 1913, no. 974; Amsterdam 1999, 51

Endnotes

1. The drawing of the same subject in Weimar (Amsterdam 1999, 50, 51) is evidently a copy.

71
Amersfoort Viewed from the Southeast

black chalk, gray wash, watercolored in yellow, brown, and green, 19 × 30.4 (7 1/2 × 11 15/16). Collection Frits Lugt, Institut Néerlandais, Paris (744)

Inscription

Lower right (annotated in pen and brown ink): *A. Cúijp*

Provenance

John, Lord Northwick; Capt. E. Spencer-Churchill; F. Lugt, 1921; Collection Frits Lugt, Institut Néerlandais, Paris

Exhibitions

London 1929, no. 563; Brussels 1937–1938, no. 55; Paris 1950, no. 114; Brussels, Rotterdam, Paris, and Bern 1968–1969, no. 33

Literature

Van Gelder 1959, 28, fig. 93; Van Hasselt 1964, 374–375

Endnotes

1. The tower continued to stand on its own after the church was demolished in 1787.

2. Other buildings were also identified in Brussels, Rotterdam, Paris, and Bern 1968–1969, 37.

3. Reiss 1975, no. 24.

72
Dordrecht Viewed from the East

black chalk, gray wash, watercolored in yellow and red, partly brushed in gum arabic, 19 × 44.5 (7 1/2 × 17 1/2). Rijksmuseum, Amsterdam (RP-T-1897-A-3393)

Inscription

Lower right (in black chalk): *A.C.*

Provenance

Straatmans; W. Pitcairn Knowles; Rijksmuseum, Amsterdam, 1895

Exhibitions

Washington 1958, no. 86; Dordrecht 1977, no. 48; Cambridge and Montreal 1988, no. 21; Amsterdam 2000b, no. 71

Literature

Reiss 1975, 87, 96; Poughkeepsie 1976, 64; Yapou 1981, 160; Spicer 1989, 135 – 136; Chong 1992, 296 – 298, 429; Plomp 1997, 121

Endnotes

1. The gate and mill were depicted in the same constellation in an early painting (Reiss 1975, no. 22), whose attribution to Cuyp is not entirely secure; see Chong 1992, no. B 17.

2. Reiss 1975, nos. 51, 52, 61.

73
Rhenen Viewed from the Northeast

black chalk, gray wash, watercolored in yellow and brown, partly brushed in gum arabic, 17.9 × 50 (7 ¹⁄₁₆ × 19 ¹¹⁄₁₆). Fogg Art Museum, Harvard University Art Museums, Cambridge, Gift of John S. Newberry Jr., given in honor of Paul J. Sachs' 70th birthday (1949.33)

Provenance

H. Wellesley; Henry Adams; Mrs. Arthur Adams; John S. Newberry Jr.; given to Fogg Art Museum, Harvard University Art Museums, Cambridge, by the latter in commemoration of Paul J. Sachs' 70th birthday, 1949

Exhibitions

Cambridge 1948, no. 40; Poughkeepsie 1976, no. 50; Tokyo 1979, no. 59; Cambridge and Montreal 1988, no. 22

Literature

Lugt 1921, 247; Ford 1930, 124 – 125; Cambridge 1949, 94; Scheyer 1952, 223, 229; Dordrecht 1977, 118; Haverkamp-Begemann 1978, 55; Deys 1981, 37; Plomp 1997, 117

Endnotes

1. Elen 1989, 234, no. 475, not illustrated. The *View of Rhenen* in Berlin (inv. no. 1170, see Bock and Rosenberg 1930), is an autograph repetition of the view in the Teylers Museum.

74
Arnhem Viewed from the West

black chalk, gray wash, watercolored in ochre yellow, green, and blue, 18.4 × 50.1 (7 ¼ × 19 ¾). Graphische Sammlung Albertina, Vienna (8386 / 8756)

Provenance

Duke Albert of Saxe-Teschen. Graphische Sammlung Albertina, Vienna

Exhibitions

Vienna 1936, no. 73; Washington and New York 1984, no. 32 (left half); Vienna 1993, no. 59 (whole); New York 1995, no. 51

Literature

Schönbrunner and Meder 1884 – 1908, nos. 626, 1198; Bernt 1957 – 1958, no. 172; Benesch 1964, r. 195; Paris 1970, under no. 82; Beck 1991, no. 382

Endnotes

1. This drawing was divided before 1818 – 1820, when an inventory was drawn up of Duke Albert's collection. Following Marijn Schapelhouman's identification of the two parts, it was exhibited in its entirety in 1993.

75
Arnhem Viewed from the Northwest

black chalk, gray wash, watercolored in green and ochre yellow, partly brushed with gum arabic, 19 × 48.6 (7 ½ × 19 ⅛). Rijksmuseum, Amsterdam (RP-T-1900-A-4379)

Inscription

Lower left (annotated in pen and brown ink): *A:Kúip*; upper left (in pen and brown ink): *Aernhem*

Provenance

Rijksmuseum, Amsterdam, 1900

Exhibitions

Brussels, Amsterdam, and Hamburg 1961, r. 105; Dordrecht 1977, no. 67; Amsterdam 1987, no. 39

Literature

Boon 1955, 149; Poughkeepsie 1976, 64; Plomp 1997, 121

Endnotes

1. The church tower was fitted out with an octagonal lantern in 1651, an element thus missing in this sheet. For the identification of the buildings, see Dordrecht 1977, 166. There they are identified as follows, from left to right: the peak of the Sint Nicolaaskerk, the church of the Sint Agnietenconvent, the Sint Janskerk, and the Sint Janspoort; behind it are the towers of the Sint Walburgskerk, the Grote Kerk, and then possibly the tower of the Observantenklooster and perhaps the roof of the Sint Pietersgasthuis.

2. Dordrecht 1977, 166.

3. In its finish, this drawing is very close to a view of Harderwijk, also in Amsterdam (inv. RP-T-1950-418).

76

Calcar with Monterberg in the Distance

black chalk, gray wash, watercolored in green and
ochre yellow, partly brushed with gum arabic,
18.5 × 49.5 (7 5/16 × 19 1/2). The Metropolitan Museum of
Art, New York, Promised gift of an anonymous donor

Inscription

Lower right (annotated in pen and brown ink): *A. Kuip*

Provenance

E. Cichorius; Oskar Huldschinsky; Siegfried Kramarsky;
private collection; The Metropolitan Museum of Art, New
York, Promised gift of an anonymous donor

Exhibitions

Brussels 1937–1938, no. 54; Düsseldorf 1953, no. 21; New
York 1959, no. 47; Poughkeepsie 1976, no. 46

Literature

Dattenberg 1941; Henkel 1942, 14; Bolten 1967, 52;
Dattenberg 1967, 80, no. 90; Brown 1979, 6, 7; Amsterdam
and Washington 1981, 120; Schoon and Voorsteegh 1991,
6, 13; Chong 1992, 354, 374

Endnotes

1. Black chalk and watercolor, 18.5 × 48 centimeters, Rijksprentenkabinet, Rijksmuseum, Amsterdam; see Amsterdam
1987, no. 41.

77

Panorama with a Shepherd Surveying the Landscape

black chalk, gray wash, 18.5 × 48 (7 5/16 × 18 7/8).
Rijksmuseum, Amsterdam (RP-T-1961-69)

Inscription

Lower left (annotated in pen and brown ink): *A.Kuip*

Provenance

Palmerston Collection; Sir James Knowles; Henri Duval, by
1910; A. von Beckerath; Edw. Czeczowiszczka; Mr. and Mrs.
I. de Bruijn-van der Leeuw; bequeathed to Rijksmuseum,
Amsterdam, 1949, received 1961

Literature

Jaffé 1944, 41; Trautscholdt 1958, 366; *Bulletin van het
Rijksmuseum* 9 (1961), 83, no. 25; Dattenberg 1967, 80;
Wegner 1973, 73

Endnotes

1. Dattenberg denied that the motif stemmed from the
vicinity of Calcar and Cleves. The distant hills actually also
preclude Rhenen or Wageningen.

2. Reiss 1975, no. 126.

78

The Hague Viewed from the Northwest

black chalk, gray wash, watercolored in yellow and green,
18.5 × 49.4 (7 5/16 × 19 7/16). Rijksmuseum, Amsterdam
(RP-T-1900-A-4379)

Inscription

Upper left (in pen and brown ink): *'s Gravenhaagen*;
lower left (annotated in pen and brown ink): *A. Kuip*

Provenance

Rijksmuseum, Amsterdam, 1900

Literature

Dumas 1991, 142, 144, note 13

Endnotes

1. The two drawings of Scheveningen are in the Gemeente
Archief, Dordrecht, and the Museum Boijmans Van Beu-
ningen, Rotterdam; ill. in Dordrecht 1977, nos. 52 and 57.
See also Dumas 1991, 275–277, 450.

2. On the topography, see Dumas 1991, especially no. 7.

This place was later called *Bij de Westermolens* (near the
Westermolens). These mills are handsomely depicted in
a drawing by Joris van der Haagen in the Gemeent Archief,
The Hague. See Dumas 1991, 141, fig. 1.

3. Smaller than most of Cuyp's panoramas, given the fold
at the right, this drawing may have originally been the same
size. This reduction could have been effected by the artist
himself, even though the cropping at the top is certainly later
in date.

4. The *View of Leiden* is in Amsterdam; see Amsterdam
1987, no. 38. The *View of Haarlem* is in the Teylers Museum,
Haarlem; see Plomp 1997, no. 102.

5. Amsterdam and London 2000, no. 39. The assumption
that this etching along with B. 225 and 226 together consti-
tuted a single panorama (Amsterdam and London 2000, 185,
note 3) makes this comparison even more interesting.

79

Dunes with the Ruins of a Manor in the Distance

black chalk, gray wash, partly brushed with gum arabic,
19 × 30.2 (7 1/2 × 11 7/8). Rijksmuseum, Amsterdam
(RP-T-1966-66)

Provenance

Ustinoff; (P. and D. Colnaghi); private collection, Germany;
(C.G. Boerner, Düsseldorf); Rijksmuseum, Amsterdam,
1966

Exhibition

Dordrecht 1977, no. 53

Endnotes

1. While not contradicting this identification, the many
lovely views of Ter Kleef, including those by Claes Jansz
Visscher, Willem Buytewech, Pieter Saenredam, and Roelant
Roghman, are not sufficiently conclusive.

2. *View of Scheveningen from the East,* Dordrechts Museum, and the *View of Scheveningen from the Southeast,* Museum Boijmans Van Beuningen, Rotterdam (Dordrecht 1977, nos. 52 and 57, respectively).

80

Dordrecht Viewed from the Northeast

black chalk, gray wash, watercolored in brownish yellow, partly brushed with gum arabic, 15.9 × 50.6 (6 ¼ × 19 ⅞). Colnaghi, London

Inscription

Lower right (in brush and gray ink, erased): *A C*; and lower left (in pen and brown ink, erased): *Acuyp*

Provenance

Henry Oppenheimer; S. Larsen-Menzel; H.L. Larsen; Eric H.L. Sexton, Rockport, Maine; private New England trust; Colnaghi, 2001

Exhibitions

London 1929, no. 565; Rotterdam 1938, r. 255; Montreal 1953, no. 141

Literature

HdG 1929, 144; London 1970, no. 38; Van Gelder and Jost 1972, 224 – 228, 234, 238, notes 15 – 18; Reiss 1975, 60; Chong 1992, 287; Turin 2000, no. 12

Endnotes

1. There seems no reason to presume that Cuyp intended the drawing to be larger, as the sheet has not been cut down and the composition is carefully balanced with a *repoussoir* in the middle of the foreground. The drawing has the same width as the largest of Cuyp's panoramas.

2. Van Gelder and Jost 1972.

3. Van Gelder and Jost 1972, fig. 3. This assumption has been doubted for two reasons (Chong 1992): the exceptionally wide painting, a panel more than 160 centimeters wide and twice as wide as high, would constitute an exception in the Dutch painting tradition. Moreover, the Leipzig panel is beveled on the left and right sides (the panel in Los Angeles is cradled). The beveling may also have been done after the painting's possible separation. Another possibility is that the paintings might also have been conceived as pendants.

4. Galleria Luigi Caretto, Turin 2000, quoting the contents of a letter by Alan Chong.

81

The Groothoofdspoort in Dordrecht from the West

black chalk, gray wash, 18.3 × 31.1 (7 ³/₁₆ × 12 ¼). Collection Frits Lugt, Institut Néerlandais, Paris (5258)

Provenance

Probably W. Mitchell, London. Téodor de Wyszewa; A. W. M. Mensing; Frits Lugt, 1937; Collection Frits Lugt, Institut Néerlandais, Paris

Exhibitions

Dordrecht 1977, no. 65; London 1988, no. 1116; Paris 1989, no. 30, pl. 35

Endnotes

1. Cuyp portrayed this part of the town wall from the north in a sketchy section at the lower left in the view of Dordrecht in Amsterdam (cat. 84).

2. Reiss 1975, no. 110.

82

Dordrecht Viewed from the North, with a Windmill in the Foreground

black chalk, gray wash, watercolored with green, some brown chalk, 18.2 × 36.8 (7 ³/₁₆ × 14 ½). The Metropolitan Museum of Art, New York, Robert Lehman Collection (1975.1.768)

Provenance

Misses Alexander, London; Robert Lehman, 1963; The Metropolitan Museum of Art, New York, 1975

Exhibitions

New York 1976, no. 3; New York and Evanston 1988, no. 20

Literature

Van Gelder and Jost 1972, 227, 238, notes 19, 21; Reiss 1975, 117; Murray 1980, 48; Chong 1992, 467; Haverkamp-Begemann 1998, no. 60

Endnotes

1. Museum Boijmans Van Beuningen, Rotterdam, no. 2491. For the painting in Dulwich, see Reiss 1975, no. 80. For other variants, see Haverkamp-Begemann 1998.

83

Dordrecht Viewed from the North, with the Grote Kerk

black chalk, gray wash, 18.6 × 50.4 (7 ⁵/₁₆ × 19 ¹³/₁₆). Stichting Collection P. en N. de Boer, Amsterdam (188)

Inscription

Lower left (annotated in pen and brown ink): *Á:Cúijp fecit.*; at the upper middle (in pen and brown ink): *Dordrecht*

Provenance

Baron W. A. van Ittersum; C. Hofstede de Groot; P. de Boer, 1942; Stichting P. and N. de Boer, Amsterdam

Exhibitions

Leiden 1903, no. 58; Utrecht 1903, no. 44; Leiden 1916, III, no. 20; The Hague 1930, no. 37; Laren 1966, no. 62; Dordrecht 1977, no. 64

Literature

Van Gijn 1908, 1, under no. 309; Van Dalen 1931, 1, fig. 79; Van Gelder and Jost 1972, 229, 238, 239, note 26, fig. 6; Brown 1979, 9, 12, fig. 11; Chong 1992, 417

84

Dordrecht Viewed from the North, with the Grote Kerk and the Groothoofdspoort

black chalk, gray wash, 18.7 × 46 (7 ⅜ × 18 ⅛).
Rijksmuseum, Amsterdam (RP-T-1900-4376)

Inscription

Lower left (annotated in pen and brown ink): *Á:Cúijp fecit.*; upper middle (in pen and brown ink): *Dordrecht*
On the verso, Cuyp drew the top of a mast

Provenance

Rijksmuseum, Amsterdam, 1900

Exhibitions

Amsterdam and Toronto 1977, no. 61; Amsterdam 1987, no. 40

Literature

Van Gelder and Jost 1969, 101, note 23; Van Gelder and Jost 1972, 236, note 5; Chong 1992, 410, 416; Dordrecht 1992, 132, 133; Wheelock 1995, 37, 43, note 10; Plomp 1997, 121

Endnotes

1. Cuyp adopted this boat wholesale in the painting in Kenwood (cat. 36). In the painting in Ascott (cat. 35), it shows up similarly as a pentimento, but he gave the boat a more western course to correspond with the other sailboats. This alteration in the composition also plays a role in the discussion of the chronology of the two paintings in Kenwood and Ascott. See Kloek 1977, 117 – 118.

2. For example, see cats. 91, 100, 106, 107.

3. See also the essay by Haverkamp-Begemann in this catalogue.

85

A Freight Boat and a Timber Raft on Calm Water

black chalk, gray wash, 16.8 × 25.4 (6 ⅝ × 10).
The British Museum, London (1895.9.15.1142)

Provenance

H. van Maarseveen; H. van Eyl Sluyter; Jhr. J. Goll van Franckenstein; J. G. baron Verstolk van Soelen; G. Leembruggen Jzn.; John Malcolm; The British Museum, London, 1895

Literature

Hind 1915 – 1932, no. 14; Van Gelder and Jost 1969, 101, note 23; Van Gelder and Jost 1972, 236, note 5; White 1982, 35; Chong 1992, 416, 418; Dordrecht 1992, 132

Endnotes

1. Van Gelder and Jost 1972 assume that Cuyp later applied the wash in the sail. The attempt to determine the shape of the masts and ropes indicates that Cuyp only later abandoned the idea of a ship under full sail.

2. Cuyp based the lion's share of this composition (*Moored Sailboats,* Waddesdon Manor; Reiss 1975, no. 105) on his drawing, which was sold at Christie's, 26 March 1963, no. 230.

3. Rafts, as depicted here, can be seen in a 1742 map by Isaac Tirion (ill. in Dordrecht 2000, 222). In Adam Willaerts' enormous *View of Dordrecht* of 1629 (Wheelock essay, fig. 8), just such a raft is portrayed, presumably on its way to this destination. See also the drawings by Abraham van Strij (Dordrecht 2000, fig. 239, nos. 133, 134). Cuyp also rendered a lumber port west of Dordrecht in an early painting (Reiss 1975, no. 3).

86

A Rowboat and a Ferry

black chalk, gray wash, 6.5 × 18.9 (2 ⁹⁄₁₆ × 7 ⁷⁄₁₆).
Teylers Museum, Haarlem (P*45)

Inscription

Lower left (in pen and gray ink): *A:C.*

Provenance

J. Danser Nijman; Teylers Museum, Haarlem, 1798

Exhibitions

Washington 1958, no. 85; Dordrecht 1977, no. 68

Literature

Scholten 1904, 173; Chong 1992, 359, 393; Ingamells 1992, 57; Plomp 1997, 122, no. 103

Endnotes

1. There is no reason to doubt that this part of the drawing is by Cuyp.

2. Closely related rowboats occur in other paintings as well (see Reiss 1975, no. 110).

87

Nijmegen with the Valkhof, Viewed from the Northeast

black chalk, gray wash, 15.8 × 24.8 (6 ¼ × 9 ¾).
École Nationale Supérieure des Beaux-Arts, Paris (M 1.601)

Inscription

Lower right: owner's mark; lower left: Jean Masson's mark

Provenance

Jean Masson; gift to the École Nationale Supérieure des Beaux-Arts, Paris, 1925

Exhibitions

Paris 1970, no. 83

Literature

Lugt 1950, 17, no. 142; Stechow 1960b, 10, note 4; Brussels 1983, under no. 43, note 4; Lemmens 1984, 93, 152

Endnotes

1. The well-known Valkhof was not often portrayed from this vantage point probably because it was less recognizable from the northeast than from the northwest.

2. London (Sotheby's), 23 March 1972, no. 17. In a sheet in Nijmegen he portrayed the Valkhof from the southwest, with the windmill on the Hubertustoren (in our sheet at the far right) figuring prominently in the foreground (Dordrecht 1977, no. 72).

3. See Poughkeepsie 1976, no. 49.

88
The Ruins of Ubbergen Castle

black chalk, gray wash, 18 × 27.1 (7 ¹⁄₁₆ × 10 ¹¹⁄₁₆). Graphische Sammlung Albertina, Vienna (8568)

Inscription

Lower middle (in pencil): .*A.Cuyp.*; upper middle (in pencil): *Ubberghe*; upper left (in pencil or black chalk): *Rogman*

Provenance

Charles, prince de Ligne; Duke Albert of Saxe-Teschen. Graphische Sammlung Albertina, Vienna

Exhibitions

Vienna 1993, no. 60; New York 1995, no. 52

Literature

MacLaren 1960, 86; Reiss 1975, 175; Schulte 1983, 293 – 297; Chong 1992, 399; Dordrecht 1992, 131

Endnotes

1. The series is published in Van der Wyck 1989 – 1990.

2. Hind 1915 – 1932, no. 19. Reiss 1975, under no. 129.

89
The Rhine Valley with Schenkenschans Fort

black chalk, gray wash, pencil, 17.4 × 24.5 (6 ⅞ × 9 ⅝). The British Museum, London (1905.11.10.67)

Inscription

Bottom to the left of center (in pencil): *A Cvyp*

Provenance

The British Museum, London, 1905

Exhibitions

London 1912, no. 172

Literature

Hind 1915 – 1932, no. 21; Van Regteren Altena 1948, no. 32; Gorissen 1964, no. 32; Gorissen 1965, 81 – 164; Dattenberg 1967, 76, no. 84; Gorissen 1974, 181; Leiden 1996, 30, 31

Endnotes

1. Presently, the river is largely canalized; the countryside between Cleves and Nijmegen evidences numerous earlier riverbeds.

2. See the painting by Gerrit van Santen (Rijksmuseum, SK-A-3893) depicting the siege of this fort by Frederik Hendrik in 1636. The fort is depicted from the same direction; in portraying the Elterberg, Van Santen was chiefly concerned with the recognizability of this location.

3. See Leiden 1996, 30, fig. 29. An inscription helped Van Goyen to remember the location.

90
Cleves Viewed from the Galgenberg

black chalk, pencil, gray wash, 19 × 27.8 (7 ½ × 10 ¹⁵⁄₁₆). Rijksmuseum, Amsterdam (RP-T-00-106)

Inscription

Lower center (signed in pencil?): *A Cvyp*; lower left (in pencil): *A Cvyp*

Provenance

Rijksmuseum, Amsterdam

Literature

Gorissen 1964, no. 13; Dattenberg 1967, 77, no. 85; Goldner and Hendrix 1992, 224

Endnotes

1. Gorissen 1964, under no. 141.

2. The same manner of signing occurs in other sheets, for instance cat. 93.

3. Brussels, Rotterdam, and Paris 1972 – 1973, no. 32, fig. 33.

4. A copy of this drawing is in Chantilly; see Dattenberg 1967, 78, 79, no. 86.

91
Calcar and the Monterberg Viewed from Cleves

black chalk, gray wash, 15.9 × 23.9 (6 ¼ × 9 ⁷⁄₁₆). Collection Groninger Museum, The Netherlands (1931-146)

Inscription

Lower left (annotated in pen and brown ink): *A. Cuijp*

Provenance

J.P. Heseltine, by 1913; C. Hofstede de Groot Collection, 1913; bequeathed to the Groninger Museum, The Netherlands, 1914

Exhibitions

Dordrecht 1977, no. 70

Literature

Henkel 1916, 341; Dattenberg 1941, 43; Gorissen 1964, no. 20; Bolten 1967, no. 14; Wheelock 1995, 47

Endnotes

1. The complex shape of the linden may be seen to good advantage in a painted "portrait" by Pauwels van Hillegaert and a sketch attributed to Herman Saftleven. See Dattenberg 1967, nos. 263 and 325, respectively.

2. Lambert Doomer drew the ruins from close by, and he also drew Calcar from these ruins: illustrated in Gorissen 1974, 92 and 91, respectively.

3. Brooklyn Museum and Castle Howard; illustrated in Dattenberg 1967, nos. 72, 73.

92
The Rhine Valley Viewed from Nijmegen toward the Elterberg

black chalk, brush, and gray ink, 15.4 × 24.7 (6 1/16 × 9 3/4). Staatliche Museen zu Berlin, Kupferstichkabinett (6661)

Inscription

Lower right, by a later hand in pen and brown ink: *A.Cúyp*

Provenance

J.P. Heseltine; (Amsler & Ruthardt, 1913); acquired for the Staatliche Museen zu Berlin, Kupferstichkabinett, 1913

Literature

Bock and Rosenberg 1930, 1: 113

93
The Rhine Valley Stretching North toward the Elterberg

black chalk, gray wash, pencil, 14.9 × 23.9 (5 7/8 × 9 7/16). Collection Frits Lugt, Institut Néerlandais, Paris (5304)

Inscription

Lower right (annotated in pen and brown ink): *A. cuijp*; to the right: *A*

Provenance

J.P. Heseltine; August Berg; F. Lugt; Collection Frits Lugt, Institut Néerlandais, Paris

Exhibitions

Paris 1950, no. 115; Brussels, Rotterdam, Paris, and Bern 1968–1969, no. 32, pl. 103; Dordrecht 1977, no. 71

Literature

Bolten 1967, 54, note 1; Van Gelder and Jost 1972, 66; Manchester 1976, 35; Chong 1992, 383; Wheelock 1995, 47

94
Study of Leaves, Possibly Rhubarb

pen and brown and gray ink, gray wash, traces of black chalk, 21.7 × 21.4 (8 9/16 × 8 7/16). Museum Boijmans Van Beuningen, Rotterdam (Cuyp 5)

Provenance

Possibly S. Woodburn; G. Leembruggen Jzn; Museum Boijmans Van Beuningen, Rotterdam, 1866

Exhibitions

Washington 1958, no. 87; Rotterdam 1960, no. 19; Brussels, Amsterdam, and Hamburg 1961, no. 103

Literature

New York and Paris 1977–1978, under no. 25; Giltaij 2000, 78

Endnotes

1. Several of these attributions must be rejected, for example, the drawing on blue paper in the British Museum, London (Hind 1915–1932, no. 25, pl. xxxix). The drawing in Dordrecht (Dordrecht 1977, no. 42) is very close to the one under discussion, but has rather atypical hatching in the shadows.

2. For instance, see the drawing in Yale (Haverkamp-Begemann and Logan 1970, no. 369, pl. 205; Reiss 1975, ill. on 27, 83, 87).

3. See Amsterdam 1993c, no. 318, among others. For the paintings, see for instance Roethlisberger and Bok 1993, nos. 444, 445, 448, 455, figs. 617, 618, 620, 629. See also Kloek 1993, 202, 203, note 14; unfortunately, figs. 1 and 7 have been reversed.

4. Schwartz and Bok 1989, 33, fig. 21.

95
Study of Leaves, Possibly Butterbur

black chalk, gray wash, watercolored in green and yellow, heightened with white, partly brushed with gum arabic, 14 × 19.4 (5 1/2 × 7 5/8). Collection Frits Lugt, Institut Néerlandais, Paris (1 1011)

Inscription

Left of lower center (annotated in pencil): *Acvyp*

Provenance

Possibly Ch. Fairfax Murray. (P. and D. Colnaghi, London); Frits Lugt, by 1923; Collection Frits Lugt, Institut Néerlandais, Paris

Exhibitions

New York and Paris 1977–1978, no. 25

Literature

Chong 1992, 302; Giltaij 2000, 78

Endnotes

1. Reiss 1975, no. 63.

96
Study of Plants, Possibly Sorrel and Butterbur

black chalk, gray wash, watercolored in red, yellow, and green, heightened with white, partly brushed with gum arabic, 14.6 × 19.3 (5 ¾ × 7 ⅝). The British Museum, London (1865.1.14.828)

Inscription

Lower left (annotated in pencil): *Acvyp*; upper right (in pen and gray ink): *44*

Provenance

The British Museum, London, 1865

Exhibitions

The Hague and London 1970 – 1971, no. 59

Literature

Hind 1915 – 1932, no. 24; Dordrecht 1977, 64; De Groot 1977, 374; White 1982, 32, 33; Chong 1992, 292, 300 – 302; Giltaij 2000, 78

97
Three Cows near a Fence with Butterbur in the Foreground

black chalk, gray wash, watercolored in yellow and red, heightened with white, partly brushed with gum arabic, 14 × 19 (5 ½ × 7 ½). The British Museum, London (Gg. 2-294)

Provenance

Rev. C. M. Cracherode; bequeathed to The British Museum, London, 1799

Literature

Hind 1915 – 1932, no. 33; Chong 1992, 267, 269, 274

Endnotes

1. The drawing, which was bequeathed to the British Museum along with a *Village Scene* (with virtually identical dimensions), is very close to cat. 64; see Hind 1915 – 1932, no. 10.

2. Reiss 1975, no. 1.

3. *Diversa animalia*, pl. 6. See Wheelock essay, note 15.

98
A Horse near the Bank of a River with Two Moored Rowboats

black chalk, brush and gray ink, watercolored in brown and green, heightened in gray and white, traces of gum arabic at the lower right, 13.6 × 19.1 (5 ⅜ × 7 ½). Staatliche Museen zu Berlin, Kupferstichkabinett (6854)

Inscription

(Annotated in pen and black ink): *Á.C.*

Provenance

J. Goll van Franckenstein; H. van Cranenburgh; Schneider; Staatliche Museen zu Berlin, Kupferstichkabinett, 1913

Literature

Bock and Rosenberg 1930, 1: 113; Wegner 1973, 73; Chong 1992, 379

Endnotes

1. Illustrated in Reiss 1975, 30.

2. See Reiss 1975, 90.

99
Two Studies of a Horse

black chalk, 12.7 × 17.7 (5 × 6 ¹⁵⁄₁₆). Collection of Maida and George Abrams, Boston

Provenance

Verrijn Stuart Family; Maida and George Abrams, Boston, 1996

Literature

Dordrecht 1977, no. 66

Endnotes

1. Bartsch 1803 – 1821, 1: nos. 13, 15.

2. Lauts 1973, 89.

100
Studies of a Cow and a Horse

black chalk, brush in gray wash, traces of pencil, 8.4 × 12.5 (3 ⁵⁄₁₆ × 4 ¹⁵⁄₁₆). Collection Frits Lugt, Institut Néerlandais, Paris (I 458)

Inscription

Lower left (annotated in pencil, AC in ligature): *Acuyp*

Provenance

Hendrik Verschuuring; Simon Fokke; earl of Aylesford; Charles Fairfax Murray; Frits Lugt; Collection Frits Lugt, Institut Néerlandais, Paris

Endnotes

1. Bock and Rosenberg 1930, nos. 6660, KdZ 5314; Dordrecht 1977, no. 63.

2. The cow recurs in paintings in Detroit (Detroit 1929, no. 20) and Prague (Sip 1955, no. 95); both are by followers.

101
A Cow Standing

black chalk, gray wash, 13.6 × 18.9 (5 ⅜ × 7 ⁷⁄₁₆). The British Museum, London (1895.9.15.1141)

Provenance

J. Barnard; Sir Benjamin West; J.C. Robinson; John Malcolm; The British Museum, London, 1895

Literature

Hind 1915 – 1932, no. 28; Amsterdam 1993d, 72

Endnotes

1. Reiss 1975, no. 65. Also related is the cow in the *Milkmaid near a Hay Cart* in the State Hermitage Museum, Saint Petersburg (Reiss 1975, no. 57). However, given the averted head and the entirely different approach, stressing areas of color, the relationship is far less evident.

102
A Bullock Standing

black chalk, gray wash, watercolored in brown,
13.6 × 18.1 (5 ⅜ × 7 ⅛). Amsterdams Historisch Museum
(A 10141)

Provenance

Jhr. J. Goll van Franckenstein; H. van Cranenburgh;
C.J. Fodor; bequest to the City of Amsterdam, 1860;
Amsterdams Historisch Museum

Exhibitions

Amsterdam 1932, no. 17; Cologne 1955, no. 23; Haifa 1959,
no. 16; Brussels, Amsterdam, and Hamburg 1961, no. 106;
Budapest 1962, no. 20; Dordrecht 1977, no. 46

Literature

Broos and Schapelhouman 1993, 72, no. 49

Endnotes

1. The watermark in this sheet, a crowned escutcheon (illustrated in Broos and Schapelhouman 1993, 289; compare Churchill 1935, no. 291), is also encountered in that series.

103
A Cow Lying Down

black chalk, gray wash, 7.6 × 13.3 (3 × 5 ¼). Private collection,
The Netherlands

Provenance

Fürst Von Hohenzollern Sigmaringen; (Galerie Grünwald,
Munich); (C.G. Boerner, Düsseldorf); J.A. Klaver; private
collection, The Netherlands, 1994

Exhibitions

Amsterdam 1993a, no. 55

Literature

Boerner 1981, no. 24

Endnotes

1. A closely related drawing, *A Cow Lying in the Grass Facing Left*, with the same dimensions and identically placed cow, is in the British Museum in London (Hind 1915 – 1932, no. 34).

104
A Dog Lying Down

black chalk, gray wash, watercolored in very light green,
7.1 × 14.3 (2 ¹³/₁₆ × 5 ⅝). Graphische Sammlung Albertina,
Vienna (8388)

Inscription

Upper and lower right, erased

Provenance

Duke Albert of Saxe-Teschen. Graphische Sammlung
Albertina, Vienna

Literature

Chong 1992, 318, 319, 395

Endnotes

1. *Diversa animalia*, published by Nicolaes Visscher, no. 8;
see Wheelock essay, note 15.

2. Reiss 1975, nos. 48, 113, respectively. The dog also occurs
in *Mountain Landscape with a Shepherd and Travelers*, Instituut
Collectie Nederland (NK 1783), a painting attributed to Cuyp.

105
Shepherd with a Staff

black chalk, gray wash, traces of gum arabic,
19.4 × 11.8 (7 ⅝ × 4 ⁵/₁₆). Museum Boijmans Van Beuningen,
Rotterdam (Cuyp 4)

Provenance

G. Leembruggen Jzn; Museum Boijmans Van Beuningen,
Rotterdam, 1866

Literature

Yapou 1981, fig. 29; Chong 1992, 430

Endnotes

1. Doubts have been raised concerning the landscape setting
in the Amsterdam drawing *Three Studies of a Shepherd*
(Amsterdam and Washington 1981, 121, fig. 2), while the
authorship of the very beautiful *Sitting Shepherd Picking
Fleas* (Amsterdam and Washington 1981, 121, fig. 5) has also
been questioned. A drawing in the Museum Boijmans
Van Beuningen, Rotterdam (inv. no. H 131), is certainly by
Jacob van Strij.

2. The painting (Reiss 1975, no. 52; Chong 1992, 429,
no. B 2) may be a copy of an original by Cuyp. The background is based on a view of Dordrecht seen from the east
(cat. 72). The second shepherd, a man shown in profile
with a shepherd's staff, also recurs in Cuyp's painting in
Melbourne (Reiss 1975, no. 60), in which Leiden is depicted
in the background, and is identical to his *View of Leiden* in
the Rijksprentenkabinet; see Amsterdam 1987, no. 38.

106
Two Resting Shepherds

black chalk, gray wash, brushed with gum arabic in the foreground, 10.9 × 16.8 (4 ⁵⁄₁₆ × 6 ⅝). Collection Frits Lugt, Institut Néerlandais, Paris (I 4369)

Inscription

Lower right (annotated in pen and gray wash): *À.C.*

Provenance

H.G.H. Galton; Frits Lugt; Collection Frits Lugt, Institut Néerlandais, Paris

Literature

Bernt 1957–1958, no. 173; Van Gelder and Jost 1969, 3–7, 6; Reiss 1975, 88, 99; Alpers 1983, fig. 33 (ed. 1989, 152); Chong 1992, 305, 314

Endnotes

1. Reiss 1975, no. 53.

2. V. de S. Collection; illustrated in Dordrecht 1977, no. 59.

3. Reiss 1975, no. 64. Chong considered this a workshop product. The German Chapel and the Mariakerk in the background of this painting are based on drawings from Cuyp's Utrecht campaign, shortly before 1640.

107
A Milkmaid

black chalk, gray wash, some pencil, 12.1 × 14.8 (4 ¾ × 5 ¹³⁄₁₆). The J. Paul Getty Museum, Los Angeles (86.GG.672)

Provenance

L. Dupper Wzn; Victor de Stuers; private collection; The J. Paul Getty Museum, Los Angeles, 1986

Literature

Originalabbildungen 1912, pl. 12; Reiss 1975, 90; Potterton

1986, 28–29; New York and Chicago 1988, 15; Chong 1992, 313, 327, 468; Goldner and Hendrix 1992, 222, no. 94; Giltaij 1994, 121, 123

Endnotes

1. The attribution of this painting (formerly Duke of Sutherland Collection, purchased for the Van der Vorm Collection in 1980, and now in the Museum Boijmans Van Beuningen, Rotterdam; Reiss 1975, no. 56; a wide strip at the top was removed shortly before 1980) is questioned in Chong 1992, 468, C 60, and is maintained by Giltaij 1994.

2. Apart from the Rotterdam work, four other paintings include the maid: Dublin (Reiss 1975, no. 55); Saint Petersburg (Reiss 1975, no. 57); Detroit (inv. no. 89.33); and in the art trade in New York in 1942 (HdG 367; Chong 1992, no. C75). The cow being milked in the painting in the Hermitage is very similar to the drawn cow by Cuyp in the British Museum, London (cat. 101).

3. Dordrecht 1977, nos. 58–60.

108
Portrait of a Twenty-Nine-Year-Old Man

1646, pen and brush and gray ink on white prepared parchment, heightened with white, 20.8 × 16.5 (8 ³⁄₁₆ × 6 ½). Staatliche Museen zu Berlin, Kupferstichkabinett (2389)

Inscription

Left center (in pen and gray ink): *AEtatis.29.*; right center, signed: *A.cúijp,*

Provenance

C. Josi; Jhr. J. Goll van Franckenstein; L. Dupper Wzn; Barthold Suermondt; Staatliche Museen zu Berlin, Kupferstichkabinett, 1874

Literature

Bock and Rosenberg 1930, I: 112; Dordrecht 1977, 154; Chong 1991, 612

109
Portrait of a Twenty-Three-Year-Old Woman

1646, pen and brush and gray ink on white prepared parchment, heightened with white, 20.6 × 16.3 (8 ⅛ × 6 ⁷⁄₁₆). Staatliche Museen zu Berlin, Kupferstichkabinett (2390)

Inscription

Left center (in pen and gray ink): *AEtatis.23.1646*; right center, signed: *A.cúijp,*

Provenance

See cat. 108

Literature

See cat. 108

Endnotes

1. The Metropolitan Museum of Art in New York. Slive 1970–1974, I: 58, and Washington, London, and Haarlem 1989, 188, 189 ill.

2. See Amsterdam and London 2000, 227, for further sources for this theme.

3. Rijksmuseum 1976, 449 (nos. SK-A-1747a–g) and Supplement 1992, 104. The sitters are Cornelis Samuelsz van Esch and his wife Josina de Carpentier; see Loughman 1991b. The attribution of these anonymous works to Paulus Lesire is not convincing.

4. According to Josi (in Ploos van Amstel 1821, 108), the portraits were "thought to represent Cuyp and his wife" (qu'on croit être d'Albert Cuyp et son épouse). He also found them "handsome like the portraits by Rembrandt" (beaux comme les portraits de Rembrandt).

5. Gemeentelijke Archiefdienst, Dordrecht (Atlas van Gijn); see Dordrecht 1977, no. 61. The influence of Jacob Gerritsz Cuyp, almost missing in the two oval portraits, is evident in the Colvius portrait drawing. The print after this portrait was used in Matthijs Balen's *Beschryvinge der stad Dordrecht*, 1677.

Bibliography, Exhibitions, and List of Works

Bibliography

Adams 1994
Adams, Ann Jensen. "Competing Communities in the 'Great Bog of Europe.' Identity and Seventeenth-Century Dutch Landscape Painting." In *Landscape and Power*. Ed. W. J. T. Mitchell. Chicago and London, 1994, 35–76.

Alpers 1983
Alpers, Svetlana. *The Art of Describing. Dutch Art in the Seventeenth Century*. Chicago, 1983.

Angel 1642
Angel, Philips. *Lof der schilderkunst*. Leiden, 1642.

Angel 1996
Angel, Philips. "Praise of Painting." Trans. Michael Hoyle with an introduction by Hessel Miedema. *Simiolus* 24 (1996), 227–258.

Anson 1973
Anson, Colin. "The Picture Collection at Stowe." *Apollo* 97 (1973), 595.

Anspach 1892
Anspach, Jacobus. *De Navorsscher, een Middel tot Gedachtenwisseling en Letterkundig Verkeer*. Nijmegen, 1892.

Arkstée 1738
Arkstée, H. K. *Nijmegen, De Oude Hoofdstad der Batavieren*. 's-Gravenhage, 1738.

Art Treasures 1857
Catalogue of the Art Treasures of the United Kingdom. Ed. J. B. Waring. Manchester, 1857.

Ashelford 1996
Ashelford, Jane. *The Art of Dress: Clothes and Society 1500–1914*. London, 1996.

Athenaeum 1877
Athenaeum 2569 (20 January 1877).

Baars 1973
Baars, Cornelis. *De geschiedenis van de landbouw in de Beijerlanden*. Wageningen, 1973.

Baetjer 1995
Baetjer, Katherine. *European Paintings in the Metropolitan Museum of Art by Artists Born before 1865: A Summary Catalogue*. New York, 1995.

Baldwin 1985
Baldwin, Robert. "'On earth we are beggars, as Christ was.'" *Konsthistorisk tidskrift* 54 (1985), 122–135.

Balen 1677
Balen, Matthijs. *Beschrijvinge der stad Dordrecht*. 2 vols. Dordrecht, 1677. (reprint, Dordrecht, 1966)

Balen 1678
Balen, Matthijs. *Dag-lyste*. Dordrecht, 1678.

Balis 1986
Balis, Arnout. *Landscapes and Hunting Scenes*. Vol. 18 of *Corpus Rubenianum Ludwig Burchard*. London, Oxford, and New York, 1986.

Balis 1993
Balis, Arnout et al. *Les Chasses de Maximilien: Les énigmes d'un chef d'oeuvre de la tapisserie*. Paris, 1993.

Bartsch 1803–1821
Bartsch, Adam von. *Le peintre graveur*. 21 vols. Vienna, 1803–1821.

Beal 1984
Beal, Mary. *A Study of Richard Symonds: His Italian Notebooks and Their Relevance to Seventeenth-Century Painting Techniques*. London, 1984.

Beck 1972
Beck, Hans Ulrich. *Jan van Goyen 1596–1656. Ein Oeuvreverzeichnis. I. Einführung. Katalog der Handzeichnungen*. Amsterdam, 1972.

Beck 1973
Beck, Hans Ulrich. *Jan van Goyen: 1586–1656: Ein Oeuvreverzeichnis. II. Katalog der Gemälde*. Amsterdam, 1973.

Beck 1987
Beck, Hans Ulrich. *Jan van Goyen: 1586–1656: Ein Oeuvreverzeichnis. III. Ergänzungen*. Doornspijk, 1987.

Beck 1991
Beck, Hans Ulrich. *Künstler um Jan van Goyen: Maler und Zeichner IV*. Doornspijk, 1991.

Beck 1998
Beck, Hans Ulrich. *Pieter Molyn. 1595–1661. Katalog der Handzeichnungen*. Doornspijk, 1998.

Bedaux 1990
Bedaux, Jan Baptist. *The Reality of Symbols*. The Hague, 1990.

Benesch 1964
Benesch, Otto. *Meisterzeichnungen der Albertina*. Vienna, 1964.

Benesch 1973
Benesch, Otto. *The Drawings of Rembrandt*. 6 vols. Ed. Eva Benesch. London, 1973.

Berenson and Valentiner 1941
Berenson, Bernard, and Wilhelm R. Valentiner. *Dutch Pictures in Public Collections in America*. New York, 1941.

Beresford 1998
Beresford, Richard. *Dulwich Picture Gallery, Complete Illustrated Catalogue*. London, 1998.

Bernt 1957–1958
Bernt, Walther. *Die niederländischen Zeichner des 17. Jahrhunderts*. 2 vols. Munich, 1957–1958.

Blaeu 1649
Blaeu, Joan. *Toonneel der steden van de vereenighde Nederlanden*. Amsterdam, 1649. (reprint, Amsterdam, 1968)

Blanc 1857 – 1858
Blanc, Charles. *Le trésor de la curiosité.* 2 vols. Paris, 1857 – 1858.

Blankert 1982
Blankert, Albert. *Ferdinand Bol (1616 – 1680): Rembrandt's Pupil.* Doornspijk, 1982.

Bock 1996
Bock, Henning, et al. *Gemäldegalerie Berlin, Gesamtverzeichnis.* Berlin, 1996.

Bock and Rosenberg 1930
Bock, Elfried, and Jakob Rosenberg. *Staatliche Museen zu Berlin. Die Zeichnungen alter Meister im Kupferstichkabinett: Die niederländischen Meister.* 2 vols. Frankfurt, 1930.

Bode 1890
Bode, Wilhelm von. "Austellung von Werken der niederländischen Kunst, veranstaltet durch die Kunstgeschichtliche Gesellschaft in Berlin. II Die Gemälde aus Berliner Privatbesitz." *Jahrbuch der königlich preussischen Kunstammlungen* II (1890), 199 – 242.

Bode 1911
Bode, Wilhelm von. *La collection M. Kann.* Paris, 1911.

Bode 1919
Bode, Wilhelm von. *Die Meister der holländische und flämischen Malerschulen.* Leipzig 1919. (rev. ed., E. Plietzsch, ed., Leipzig, 1956)

Bode 1956
see Bode 1919

Boerner 1981
Boerner, C. G. *Kunstantiquariat. Neue Lagerliste 74.* Düsseldorf, 1981.

Bok-van Kammen 1977
Bok-van Kammen, Welmoet. "Stradanus and the Hunt." Ph.D. diss., Johns Hopkins University, 1977.

Bol 1982
Bol, Laurens J. "Francois Ryckhals, een Middelburgse schilder die zijn naam verduisterde." In 'Goede Onbekenden': Hedendaagse herkenning en waardering van verscholen, voorbijgezien en onderschat talent. Utrecht, 1982, 21 – 29.

Bolten 1967
Bolten, Jaap. *Dutch Drawings from the Collection of Dr. C. Hofstede de Groot, Groninger Museum voor Stad en Lande.* Utrecht, 1967.

Boon 1955
Boon, K. G. "De tekenkunst in de zeventiende eeuw." In H. E. van Gelder, *Kunstgeschiedenis der Nederlanden.* Utrecht, 1955, 134 – 151.

Van den Bos 1701
Bos, Lambert van den. *De volmaeckte hovelinck, Van de graef Baldazar de Castiglione.* Dordrecht and Amsterdam, 1701. (originally published, 1662)

Boudewijnse 1959
Boudewijnse, J. H. P. "Bezoek van de Keurvorst van Brandenburg en zijn gemalin aan Nijmegen in 1647." *Numaga* 6 (1959), 177 – 184.

Boxer 1990
Boxer, C. R. *The Dutch Seaborne Empire 1600 – 1800.* London, 1990. (1st ed., 1965)

Boydell 1769
Boydell, John, ed. *A Collection of Prints, Engraved after the Most Capital Paintings in England.* London, 1769.

Boymans-van Beuningen 1972
Old Paintings 1400 – 1900. Museum Boymans-van Beuningen. Rotterdam, 1972.

Braun and Hogenberg 1572 – 1618
Braun, Georg, and Hogenberg, Franz. *Civitates orbis terrarum.* 4 vols. Amsterdam, 1572 – 1618. (facsimile, Amsterdam, 1980)

Breckenridge 1955
Breckenridge, James D. *A Handbook of Dutch and Flemish Paintings in the William Andrews Clark Collection.* Washington, 1955.

Broos 1974
Broos, B. P. J. "Rembrandt's Portrait of a Pole and His Horse." *Simiolus* 7 (1974), 192 – 218.

Broos 1993
Broos, B. P. J. *Rembrandt en de tekenaars uit zijn omgeving: Oude tekeningen in het bezit van de Gemeentemusea van Amsterdam waaronder de collectie Fodor.* Vol. 3. Amsterdam, 1993.

Broos and Schapelhouman 1993
Broos, Ben, and Marijn Schapelhouman. *Nederlandse tekenaars geboren tussen 1600 en 1660.* Zwolle, 1993.

Brown 1979
Brown, Christopher. *Dutch Landscape Painting, Themes and Painters in the National Gallery.* Ser. 2, no. 5. London, 1979.

Brown 1990
Brown, Christopher. "Aelbert Cuyp's River Landscape with Horsemen and Peasants." *National Art Collections Fund: Review* (1990), 87 – 90.

Bruin 1716
Bruin, Claes. *Kleefsche en Zuid-Hollandsche Arkadia.* Amsterdam, 1716.

De Bruyn Kops 1965
Bruyn Kops, C. J. de. "Kanttekeningen bij het nieuw verworven landschap van Aelbert Cuyp." *Bulletin van het Rijksmuseum* 13 (1965), 162 – 176.

Bryant 1990
Bryant, Julius. *The Iveagh Bequest: Kenwood.* London, 1990.

Buchanan 1824
Buchanan, William. *Memoirs of Painting, with a Chronological History of the Importation of Pictures by the Great Masters into England since the French Revolution.* 2 vols. London, 1824.

Buckingham 1838
Stowe, a Description of the House and Gardens of His Grace the Duke of Buckingham and Chandas. London, 1838.

Budapest Szépmüvészeti Múzeum 1968
Pigler, A. *Katalog der Galerie alter Meister.* Szépmüvészeti Múzeum. 2 vols. Tübingen, 1968. (earlier editions, 1937, 1954)

Buffa 1985
Buffa, Sebastian, ed. *Antonio Tempesta.* Vol. 38 of *The Illustrated Bartsch: Italian Masters of the Sixteenth Century.* New York, 1985.

Burlington Magazine 1942
"The Chronology of Aelbert Cuyp." *Burlington Magazine* 81 (1942), 259.

Burn 1984
Burn, Barbara. *Metropolitan Children.* New York, 1984.

Burnett 1969
Burnett, David G. "Landscapes of Aelbert Cuyp." *Apollo* 89 (1969), 372 – 380.

Butlin and Joll 1984
Butlin, Martin, and Evelyn Joll. *The Paintings of J. M. W. Turner.* 2 vols. Rev. ed. New Haven, 1984. (1st ed., 1977)

Buvelot 1998
Buvelot, Quentin, Michel Hilaire, and Olivier Zeder. *Tableaux Flamands et Hollandais du Musée Fabre de Montpellier, Collections flamandes et hollandaises des Musées de Province.* Paris and Montpellier, 1998.

Calvin 1965
Calvin, John. *Calvin's Commentaries: The Acts of the Apostles.* Trans. J. W. Fraser and W. J. G. MacDonald. Edinburgh, 1965.

Cavendish 1657 – 1658
Cavendish, William, the Duke of Newcastle. *La Méthode nouvelle et invention extraordinaire de Dresser les Chevaux.* Antwerp, 1657 – 1658.

Chevalier 1706
Chevalier, Nicolas. *Description de l'Academie à Monter à Cheval.* Utrecht, 1706.

Chong 1987
Chong, Alan. "The Market for Landscape Painting in 17th-Century Holland." In Amsterdam, Boston, and Philadelphia 1987, 104 – 120.

Chong 1988
Chong, Alan. "'In't verbeelden van Slachtdieren.'" In Dordrecht and Leewarden 1988, 56 – 86.

Chong 1991
Chong, Alan. "New Dated Works from Aelbert Cuyp's Early Career." *Burlington Magazine* 133 (September 1991), 606 – 612.

Chong 1992
Chong, Alan. "Aelbert Cuyp and the Meaning of Landscape." Ph.D. diss., New York University, 1992.

Chong 1994a
Chong, Alan. "Arent de Gelder and the Art Scene in Dordrecht." In Van Moltke 1994, 9 – 18.

Chong 1994b
Chong, Alan. "'Very beautiful in all parts….'" *Sotheby's Preview* (July 1994), 30 – 31.

Chong 1996
Chong, Alan. "Aelbert Cuyp." In *Dictionary of Art.* Vol. 8. London, 1996, 293 – 298.

Churchill 1935
Churchill, W. A. *Watermarks in Paper in Holland, England, France, etc. in the XVII and XVIII Centuries and Their Inter-connection.* Amsterdam, 1935.

Cleveland Museum of Art 1942
Catalogue of the John L. Severance Collection. Cleveland Museum of Art, 1942.

Cleveland Museum of Art 1982
European Paintings of the 16th, 17th, and 18th Centuries. Cleveland Museum of Art, 1982.

Coe 1955
Coe, Nancy. "The History of the Collecting of European Paintings and Drawings in the City of Cleveland." Master's thesis, Oberlin College, 1955.

Constable 1970
John Constable's Discourses. Ed. R. B. Beckett. Ipswich, 1970.

Corpus 1982 –
Stichting Foundation Rembrandt Research Project. *A Corpus of Rembrandt Paintings.* 3 vols. The Hague, Boston, and London, 1982 –.

Cundall 1891
Cundall, Frank. *The Landscape and Pastoral Painters of Holland: Ruisdael, Hobbema, Cuijp, Potter.* London, 1891.

Van Dalen 1931
Dalen, J. L. van. *Geschiedenis van Dordrecht.* 2 vols. Dordrecht, 1931 – 1933. (reprint 1987)

Dattenberg 1941
Dattenberg, Heinrich. "Kalkar und der Monterberg; unbekannte Ansichten holländischer Künstler des 17. Jahrhunderts." In *Sonderveröffentlichung des Heimathauses des Niederrheines in Krefeld.* 14 (1941).

Dattenberg 1967
Dattenberg, Heinrich. *Die Niederrheinansichten Holländischer Künstler des 17. Jahrhunderts.* Düsseldorf, 1967.

Delcampe 1658
Delcampe. *L'Art de Monter à Cheval.* Paris, 1658.

Deperthes 1822
Deperthes, Jean Baptiste. *Histoire de l'art du paysage, depuis la renaissance des beaux-arts jusqu'au dix-huitième siècle.*... Paris, 1822.

Descamps 1753–1765
Descamps, Jean Baptiste. *La Vie des Peintures Flamands, Allemands et Hollandais.* 5 vols. Paris, 1753–1765.

Desenfans 1802
Desenfans, Noel. *A Descriptive Catalogue of Some Pictures of the Different Schools, Purchased for H.M. the Late King of Poland.* 2 vols. London, 1802.

Van Deursen 1994
Deursen, Arie Theo van. "England and the Synod of Dort." In *The Exchange of Ideas: Religion, Scholarship and Art in Anglo-Dutch Relations in the Seventeenth Century.* Eds. Simon Groenveld and Michael Wintle. *Britain and The Netherlands.* 11 (1994), 31–41.

Deys 1981
Deys, H.P. *Achter Berg en Rijn. Over boeren, burgers en buitenlui in Rhenen.* Rhenen, 1981.

Drexelius 1627
Drexelius, Hieremias. *Heliotropium.* Munich, 1627. (Dutch ed., *De Sonne-bloem,* Antwerp, 1638).

Drossaers and Lunsingh Scheurleer 1974–1976
Drossaers, S.W.A., and Th. H. Lunsingh Scheurleer. *Inventarissen van de inboedels in de verblijven van de Oranjes.* 3 vols. The Hague 1974–1976.

Dulwich Picture Gallery 1858
A Catalogue of the Dulwich Gallery. Dulwich Picture Gallery Archive, 1858.

Dumas 1991
Dumas, Charles, with Jim van der Meer Mohr. *Haagse stadsgezichten 1550–1800. Topografische schilderijen van het Haags Historisch Museum.* Zwolle, 1991.

Duparc 1980
Duparc, Frederick J., et al. *Mauritshuis, Hollandse schilderkunst: Landschappen 17de eeuw.* The Hague, 1980.

Dutuit 1881–1888
Dutuit, E. *Manuel de l'Amateur d'Estampes.* 6 vols. Paris, 1881–1888.

Edwards 1982
Edwards, JoLynn. "Alexandre Joseph Paillet (1743–1814): Study of a Parisian Art Dealer." Ph.D. diss., University of Washington, St. Louis, 1982.

Van Eikema Hommes 1998
Eikema Hommes, Margriet van. "Painters' Methods to Prevent Colour Changes Described in Sixteenth- to Early Eighteenth-Century Sources on Oil Painting Techniques." *Leids kunsthistorisch jaarboek* 11 (1998), 91–131.

Elen 1989
Elen, Albert J. *Missing Old Master Drawings from the Franz Koenigs Collection, Claimed by the State of The Netherlands.* The Hague, 1989.

Ember 1979
Ember, Idlikó. "Benjamin Gerritsz. Cuyp (1612–1652)." *Acta historiae artium* 25 (1979), 89–141; 26 (1980), 37–73.

Epley 2000
Epley, Brad. "Jan Both's *Italian Landscape.*" *The Hamilton Kerr Institute Bulletin* 3 (2000), 121–128.

Van der Eyck 1628
Eyck, Jan van der. *Corte beschrijvinghe mitsgaders handvesten, priviligien, costumen ende ordonnantien vanden Lande van Zuyt-Hollandt.* Dordrecht, 1628.

Falkenburg 1996
Falkenburg, Reindert L. "'Schilderachtig weer' bij Jan van Goyen." In Leiden 1996, 60–69.

Falkenburg 1997
Falkenburg, Reindert L. "Onweer bij Jan van Goyen. Artistieke wedijver en de markt voor het Hollandse landschap in de 17de eeuw." *Nederlands Kunsthistorisch Jaarboek* 48 (1997), 116–161.

Farington 1978–1984
Farington, Joseph. *The Diary of Joseph Farington.* Ed. K. Garlick et al. 16 vols. New Haven, 1978–1984.

Finberg 1909
Finberg, A.J. *A Complete Inventory of the Drawings of Turner Bequest.* 2 vols. London, 1909.

Fischer 1812
Fischer, Joseph. *Catalogue de la Galerie des tableaux de son altesse le Prince Nicolas Esterhazy de Galantha dans son hôtel de Laxenbourg.* Vienna, 1812.

Fisher and Sthyr 1953
Fisher, Erik, and Jorgen Sthyr. *Seks aarhunderers europaeisk tegnekunst. Udvalgte arbejder fra den Kgl. Kobberstiksamlung [Kobenhavn].* Copenhagen, 1953.

Ford 1930
Ford, Worthington Chauncey, ed. *Letters of Henry Adams (1858–1891).* London, 1930.

Franits 1989
Franits, Wayne. "'Betemt de juegh / sso doet sy deugd': A Pedagogical Metaphor in Seventeenth-Century Dutch Art." *Leids Kunsthistorisch Jaarboek* 8 (1989), 217–226.

Freedberg and De Vries 1991
Freedberg, David, and J. de Vries, eds. *Art In History, History in Art.* Santa Monica, 1991.

Friedländer 1901
Friedländer, Max J. "Niederländische Zeichnungen in der Sammlung des Herrn von Beckerath zu Berlin." *Zeitschrift für bildende Kunst* 11 (1901), 209–220.

Frimmel 1892

Frimmel, Theodor. *Kleine Galeriestudien*. Vol. 1. Bamberg, 1892.

Fuchs 1978

Fuchs, R. H. *Dutch Painting*. New York, 1978.

Gaines 1997

Gaines, Richard V., M. Catherine W. Skinner, Eugene E. Foord, Brian Mason, and Abraham Rosenzweig. *Dana's New Mineralogy*. 8th ed. New York, 1997.

Gaskell and Jonker 1998

Gaskell, Ivan, and Michiel Jonker, eds. *Vermeer Studies*. Studies in the History of Art, vol. 55. Center for Advanced Study in the Visual Arts, Washington, 1998.

Van Gelder 1959

Gelder, H. E. van. *Holland by Dutch Artists in Paintings, Drawings, Woodcuts, Engravings and Etchings*. Amsterdam, 1959.

Van Gelder and Jost 1969

Gelder, Jan G. van, and Ingrid Jost. "Vroeg contact van Aelbert Cuyp met Utrecht." In *Miscellanea I.Q. van Regteren Altena*. Ed. H. Miedema et al. Amsterdam, 1969, 100–103.

Van Gelder and Jost 1972

Gelder, Jan G. van, and Ingrid Jost. "Doorzagen op Aelbert Cuyp." *Nederlands Kunsthistorisch Jaarboek* 23 (1972), 223–239.

Van Gelder and Jost 1973

Gelder, Jan G. van, and Ingrid Jost. In Hartford, Hanover, and Boston 1973, 66.

Gemar-Koeltzsch 1995

Gemar-Koeltzsch, E. *Holländische Stillebenmaler im 17. Jahrhundert*. Vol. 2. Lingen, 1995.

Gerson 1964

Gerson, Horst. "Italy Through Dutch Eyes." *Art Quarterly* 27 (1964), 342–353.

Gervers 1982

Gervers, Veronika. *The Influence of Ottoman Turkish Textiles and Costume in Eastern Europe with Particular Reference to Hungary*. History Technology and Art. Royal Ontario Museum. Monograph 4. Ontario, 1982.

Geyl 1966

Geyl, Pieter. *The Revolt of the Netherlands, 1555–1609*. London, 1966.

Gibson 1928

Gibson, W. "Mr. John Roberts' Collection of Pictures." *Apollo* 8 (1928), 113–119.

Gibson 2000

Gibson, Walter S. *Pleasant Places, The Rustic Landscape from Bruegel to Ruisdael*. Berkeley, Los Angeles, and London, 2000.

Gifford 1996

Gifford, E. Melanie. "Jan van Goyen en de techniek van het naturalistische landschap." In Leiden 1996, 70–81.

Van Gijn 1908

Gijn, Simon van. *Dordracum Illustratum*. 3 vols. Dordrecht, 1908.

Gilpin 1786

Gilpin, William. *Observations, Relative Chiefly to Picturesque Beauty*. London, 1786.

Giltaij 1994

Giltaij, Jeroen. *De verzameling van de Stichting Willem van der Vorm in het Museum Boymans-van Beuningen Rotterdam*. Rotterdam, 1994.

Giltaij 2000

Giltaij, Jeroen. "Aelbert Cuyp. Studie van planten." In Dordrecht 2000, 78–79.

Gimpel 1963

Gimpel, René. *Journal d'un collectionneur*. Paris, 1963.

Goeree 1670

Goeree, Willem. *Inleyding tot de practijek der algemene schilderkonst*. Middelburg, 1670.

Goldner and Hendrix 1992

Goldner, G. R., and L. Hendrix. *European Drawings. J. Paul Getty Museum*. Catalogue of the Collections. Vol. 2. Malibu, 1992.

Goosens 1996

Goosens, Eymert-Jan. *Treasure Wrought by Chisel and Brush: The Town Hall of Amsterdam in the Golden Age*. Zwolle, 1996.

Gordenker 1995

Gordenker, Emilie E. S. "'En rafelkragen, die hy schilderachtig vond': Was Rembrandt een voddenraper?" In *Kostuum verzamelingen in beweging: Twaalf studies over kostuumverzamelingen in Nederland & Inventarisatie van het kostuumbezit in Nederlandse openbare collecties, Nederlandse Kostuumvereeniging voor Mode en Streekdracht*. Ed. H. M. A. Breukink-Peeze et al. Zwolle, 1995, 21–35.

Gorissen 1959

Gorissen, Friedrich. "Die Burgen im Reich Nimwegen außerhalb der Stadt Nimwegen." In *Beiträge zur niederrheinischen Burgenkunde*. Ed. Arnold Mock. *Niederrheinisches Jahrbuch* 4 (1959), 105–168.

Gorissen 1964

Gorissen, Friedrich. *Conspectus Cliviae. Die klevische Residenz in der Kunst des 17. Jahrhunderts*. Cleves, 1964.

Gorissen 1965

Gorissen, Friedrich. *'Rhenus bicornis.' Brückenschlag am Niederrhein*. Düsseldorf, 1965.

Gorissen 1974

Gorissen, Friedrich. *Altklevisches ABC worinnen alle Städte, Dörfer, Bauernschaften, Landesburgen und Herrensitze;… welche von 1816 bis 1974 dem Kreis Kleve angehört haben, in alphabetischer Folge beschrieben….* Cologne, 1974.

Van de Graaf 1958

Van de Graaf, Johannes A. *Het De Mayerne manuscript als bron voor de schildertechniek van de barok.* Utrecht, 1958.

De Grez 1913

L'Inventaire des dessins et aquarelles donnés à l'Etat Belge par Mme la douairière de Grez. Brussels, 1913.

Groen 1988

Groen, Karin. "Scanning Electron Microscopy as an Aid in the Study of Blanching." *The Hamilton Kerr Institute Bulletin* 1 (1988), 48–65.

Groen and Hendrix 1989

Groen, Karin, and Ella Hendriks. "Frans Hals: A Technical Examination." In Washington, London, and Haarlem 1989, 109–128.

De Groot 1977

Groot, J. M. de. "Een vroeg landschap van Aelbert Cuyp (1620–1691) in een Dordtse expositie." *Antiek* 12 (1977), 373–374.

De Groot 1983

Groot, J. M. de. "Kopen voor de eeuwigheid." *Bulletin Dordrechts Museum* 8 (November 1983), 1–5.

De Groot 1992

Groot, J. M. de, et al. *Dordrechts Museum 150 jaar.* Dordrecht, 1992.

Grosse 1925

Grosse, Rolph. *Die holländische Landschaftskunst 1600–1650.* Berlin and Leipzig, 1925.

Grotius 1610

Grotius, Hugo de. *Tractaet vande oudhevt vande Batavische nu Hollandsche republike.* The Hague, 1610. (modern edition, G. C. Molewijk, ed., *De oudheid van de Bataafse nu Hollandse republiek.* Weesp, 1988)

Grotius 1631

Grotius, Hugo de. *Inleidinge tot de Hollandsche rechts-geleerdheid.* The Hague, 1631.

Grotius 1646

Grotius, Hugo de. *Biblio illustrata novi testament.* Vol. 2. Paris, 1646.

Haak 1984

Haak, Bob. *The Golden Age: Dutch Painters of the 17th century.* New York, 1984.

Haitsma Mulier 1994

Haitsma Mulier, E. O. G. "The History of Great Britain as Seen by the Dutch of the Seventeenth Century: A Chapter from the History of Historiography." In *The Exchange of Ideas: Religion, Scholarship and Art in Anglo-Dutch Relations in the Seventeenth Century.* Eds. Simon Groenveld and Michael Wintle. *Britain and The Netherlands.* 11 (1994), 133–149.

Halewood 1982

Halewood, W. *Six Subjects of Reformation Art: A Preface to Rembrandt.* Toronto, 1982.

Harley 1982

Harley, Rosamond D. *Artists' Pigments c. 1600–1835, A Study in English Documentary Sources.* 2d ed. London, 1982.

Van Hasselt 1964

Hasselt, Carlos van. "Old Master Drawings in the Lugt Collection." *Apollo* 80 (1964), 368–378.

Havemeyer 1931

H. O. Havemeyer Collection: Catalogue of Paintings, Prints, Sculpture and Objects of Art. Portland, Maine, 1931.

Havemeyer 1958

H. O. Havemeyer Collection: The Metropolitan Museum of Art. New York, 1958.

Haverkamp-Begemann 1978

Haverkamp-Begemann, Egbert. "Jan van Goyen in the Corcoran: Exemplars of Dutch Naturalism." In *Corcoran Gallery of Art, The William A. Clark Collection.* Washington, 1978, 51–59.

Haverkamp-Begemann 1998

Haverkamp-Begemann, Egbert, Mary Taverner Holmes, et al. *Central Europe, The Netherlands, France, England.* Vol. 6 of *The Robert Lehman Collection. Fifteenth- to Eighteenth-Century European Drawings.* New York and Princeton, 1998.

Haverkamp-Begemann and Logan 1970

Haverkamp-Begemann, Egbert, and Anne-Marie S. Logan. *European Drawings and Watercolors in the Yale University Art Gallery.* 2 vols. New Haven, 1970.

Hazlitt 1824

Hazlitt, William. *Sketches of the Principal Picture-Galleries in England.* London, 1824.

Hazlitt 1942

Hazlitt, William. *Selected Essays of William Hazlitt 1778–1830.* Ed. Geoffrey Keynes. London, 1942.

HdG 1907–1927

Hofstede de Groot, Cornelis. *A Catalogue Raisonné of the Works of the Most Eminent Dutch Painters of the Seventeenth Century.* 8 vols. Trans. E. G. Hawke. London, 1907–1927. (reprint, Cambridge, 1976.)

HdG 1929

Hofstede de Groot, Cornelis. "Éinige Betrachtungen über die Ausstellung holländischer Kunst in London." *Repertorium für Kunstwissenschaft* 50 (1929), 134–146.

Heemskerk 1647

Van Heemskerk, Johan. *Batavische acadia.* Amsterdam, 1647.

Heijbroek 1996
Heijbroek, J. F. "Constantijn Huygens (ii)." In *Dictionary of Art*. Vol. 15. London, 1996, 41–42.

Held 1991
Held, Julius S. *Rembrandt's Aristotle and Other Rembrandt Studies*. Princeton, 1991.

Helicon 1610
Nederduytschen helicon, Eygentlijck wesende der Maetdicht beminders Lust-tooneel. Haarlem, 1610.

Helmus 1991
Helmus, Liesbeth H. "Het altaarstuk met de Sint Elisabethsvloed uit de Grote Kerk van Dordrecht. De oorspronkelijke plaats en de opdrachtgevers." *Oud Holland* 105 (1991), no. 2, 127–139.

Henkel 1916
Henkel, M. D. "Ausstellung von Handzeichnungen Holländischer Meister aus dem Besitze von Dr. C. Hofstede de Groot in der Tuchhalle in Leiden." *Kunstchronik* 27 (1916), 337–343.

Henkel 1942
Henkel, M. D. *Teekeningen van Rembrandt en zijn School*. Vol. 1 of *Catalogus van de Nederlandsche Teekeningen in het Rijksmuseum te Amsterdam*. The Hague, 1942.

Henny 1994
Henny, Xenia. "Hoe kwamen de Rotterdamse schilders aan hun verf?" In Rotterdam 1994, 43–54.

Herbert 1988
Herbert, Robert. *Impressionism: Art, Leisure, and Parisian Society*. New Haven, 1988.

Hermens and Wallert 1998
Hermens, Erma, and Arie Wallert. "The Pekstok Papers, Lake Pigments, Prisons and Paint-mills." *Looking Through Paintings: The Study of Painting Techniques and Materials in Support of Art Historical Research*. Eds. Erma Hermens, Annamiek Ouwerkerk, Nicola Costaras. *Leids Kunsthistorisch Jaarboek* 11 (1998), 269–295.

Herzoglichen Gemäldegalerie Gotha 1858
Catalog der Herzoglichen Gemäldegalerie zu Gotha. Gotha, 1858.

Heyligers 1924
Heyligers, Johan. "Jacob Gerritsz. Cuyp, Porträt-, Genre- und Historienmaler zu Dordrecht." Ph.D. diss., Rostock, 1924.

Hind 1915–1932
Hind, Arthur Mayger. *Catalogue of Drawings by Dutch and Flemish Artists Preserved in the Department of Prints and Drawings in the British Museum*. 5 vols. London, 1915–1932.

Hoet 1752
Hoet, Gerard. *Catalogues of naamlyst van schildereyen, met derzelver pryzen zedert een langen reeks van jaaren zoo in Holland als op andere plaatsen in het openbaar verkogt*. 3 vols. The Hague, 1752. (supplemented by Pieter Terwesten, 1770; reprint, Soest, 1976)

Hogenberg 1983
Hogenberg, Franz. *Geschichteblätter: Kupferwerk über die niederländischen Freiheitskriege*. Ed. F. Hellwig. Nördlingen, 1983.

Hollstein 1949–
Hollstein, F. W. H., *Dutch and Flemish Etchings, Engravings and Woodcuts ca. 1450–1700*. 41 vols. Amsterdam, 1949–.

Holmes 1930
Holmes, Jerrold. "The Cuyps in America." *Art in America and Elsewhere* 18 (June 1930), 165–185.

Holmes 1933
Holmes, Jerrold. "Aelbert Cuyp als Landscaftsmaler." Ph.D. diss., Innsbruck University, 1933.

Van Hoogstraeten 1657
Hoogstraeten, Samuel van. *Den Eerlyken Jongeling, Of de Edele Kunst, Van zich by Groote en Kleyne te doen Eeren en Beminnen*. Dordrecht, 1657.

Van Hoogstraeten 1678
Hoogstraeten, Samuel van. *Inleyding tot de Hooge Schoole der Schilderkonst Anders de Zichtbaere Werelt….* Rotterdam, 1678. (reprint, Utrecht, 1969)

Houbraken 1718–1721
Houbraken, Arnold. *De groote schouburgh der Nederlantsche konstschilders en schilderessen*. 3 vols. Amsterdam 1718–1721. (2d printing, Amsterdam and The Hague, 1753; reprint in 1 vol., Amsterdam 1976, corrected ed. of the 1st printing of 1718–1721)

Howard 1995
Howard, Helen. "Techniques of the Romanesque and Gothic Wall Paintings in the Holy Sepulchre Chapel, Winchester Cathedral." In *Historical Painting Techniques, Materials and Studio Practice*. Eds. Arie Wallert, Erma Hermens, and Marja Peek. Preprints of a Symposium. University of Leiden (Getty Conservation Institute), 1995, 91–104.

Howard 1996
Howard, Helen. "Romanesque and Gothic Wall Paintings in Winchester Cathedral: An Unusual Use and Alteration of Vivianite." *Journal of the Russell Society* 6, 2 (1996), 93–96.

Hutton 1961
Hutton, William. "Aelbert Cuyp: The Riding Lesson." *The Toledo Museum of Art Museum News* 4 (Autumn 1961), 79–85.

Hutton 1995
Hutton, William. *Toledo Treasures: Selections from the Toledo Museum of Art*. Toledo, 1995.

Ingamells 1992
Ingamells, John. *The Wallace Collection: Catalogue of Pictures*. Vol. 4. London, 1992.

Ireland 1790
Ireland, Samuel. *A Picturesque Tour through Holland, Brabant, and Part of France (Autumn 1789)*. London, 1790.

Israel 1995
Israel, Jonathan. *The Dutch Republic: Its Rise, Greatness, and Fall 1477 – 1806*. Oxford, 1995.

Jaffé 1944
Jaffé, H. L. C. "Holländische Meister des 17. Jahrhunderts aus einer Privatsammlung in der Schweiz." *Du. Schweizerisches Monatschrift iv* 12 (December 1944), 35 – 50.

Jameson 1844
Jameson, Mrs. Anna. *Companion to the Most Celebrated Private Galleries of Art in London*. London, 1844.

Janson and Fraser 1980
Janson, Anthony F., and A. Ian Fraser. *100 Masterpieces of Painting*. Indianapolis, 1980.

Janson and Janson 1995
Janson, H. W., and A. F. Janson. *History of Art*. New York, 1995.

Jervis 1854
Jervis, Lady Marian. *Painting and Celebrated Painters Ancient and Modern*. Vol. 2. London, 1854.

De Jong 1990
Jong, Erik de. "For Profit and Ornament: The Function and Meaning of Dutch Garden Art in the Period of William and Mary, 1650 – 1702." In *The Dutch Garden in the Seventeenth Century, Dumbarton Oaks Colloquium on the History of Landscape Architecture, xii.* Ed. John Dixon Hunt. Washington, 1990, 13 – 48.

De Jongh 1968 – 1969
Jongh, Eddy de. "Erotica in vogelperspectief: De dubbelzinnigheid van een reeks 17de eeuwse genrevoorstellingen." *Simiolus* 3 (1968 – 1969), 22 – 74.

De Jongh 1974
Jongh, Eddy de. "Grape Symbolism in Paintings of the 16th and the 17th Centuries." *Simiolus* 7 (1974), 166 – 191.

Kampinga 1917
Kampinga, Herman. *De opvattingen over onze oudere vaderlandse geschiedenis bij de Hollandsche historici der xvie en xviie eeuw*. The Hague, 1917. (reprint, Utrecht, 1980)

Kettering 1983
Kettering, Alison McNeil. *The Dutch Arcadia: Pastoral Art and Its Audience in the Golden Age*. Montclair, N.J., 1983.

Kettering 1997
Kettering, Alison McNeil. "Gender Issues in Seventeenth-Century Dutch Portraiture: A New Look." In *Rembrandt, Rubens, and the Art of Their Time, Papers in Art History from the Pennsylvania State University xi.* Eds. Roland E. Fleischer and Susan Clare Scott. University Park, Penn., 1997, 145 – 175.

Keyes 1984
Keyes, George S. *Esaias van de Velde (1587 – 1630)*. Doornspijk, 1984.

Der Kinderen-Besier 1950
Kinderen-Besier, J. H. der. *Spelevaart der Mode: De kledij onzer voorouders in de zeventiende eeuw*. Amsterdam, 1950.

Kirby and Saunders 1998
Kirby, Jo, and David Saunders. "Sixteenth- to Eighteenth-Century Green Colours in Landscape and Flower Paintings: Composition and Deterioration." In *Painting Techniques: History, Materials and Studio Practice*. Eds. Ashok Roy and Perry Smith. Preprints of the iic Dublin Congress. London, 1998, 155 – 159.

Kloek 1977
Kloek, Wouter Th. Review of London 1976. *Simiolus* 9 (1977), 116 – 118.

Kloek 1993
Kloek, Wouter Th. "Abraham Bloemaert en de 'Prediking van Johannes de Doper.'" *Antiek* 28 (1993), 196 – 203.

Kloek and Niemeijer 1990
Kloek, Wouter Th., and J. W. Niemeijer. *De kasteeltekeningen van Roelandt Roghman*. 2 vols. Alphen aan den Rijn, 1990.

Koslow 1996
Koslow, Susan. "Law and Order in Rubens' *Wolf and Fox Hunt*." *Art Bulletin* 78 (December 1996), 681 – 706.

Krul 1634a
Krul, Jan Hermansz. *Pastorel bly-eyndend-spel van Cloris and Philidia*. Amsterdam, 1634.

Krul 1634b
Krul, Jan Hermansz. *Eerlycke tytkorting bestaende in verscheyde rymen*. Haarlem, 1634.

Kunstchronik 1918
Kunstchronik 29 (3 May 1918).

Lauts 1973
Lauts, J. *Staatliche Kunsthalle Karlsruhe, Neuerwerbungen Alter Meister 1966 – 1972*. Karlsruhe, 1973.

Leeflang 1993

Leeflang, Heigen. "Het landschap in boek en prent: Perceptie en interpretation van vroeg zeventiende-eeuwse Nederlandse landschapsprenten." In Amsterdam 1993b, 18–32.

Lemmens 1984

Lemmens, G. Th. M., ed. *Nijmegen getekend: Aquarellen en tekeningen uit de topografische atlas van het Nijmeegs Museum 'Commanderie van Sint Jan.'* Zutphen, 1984.

Levesque 1994

Levesque, Catherine. *Journey through Landscape in Seventeenth-Century Holland: The Haarlem Print Series and Dutch Identity.* University Park, Penn., 1994.

Levy-Van Halm 1998

Levy-Van Halm, Koos. "Where Did Vermeer Buy His Painting Materials? Theory and Practice." In Gaskell and Jonker 1998, 137–143.

Lewitt 1995

Lewitt, I., ed. *The Israel Museum, Jerusalem.* New York, 1995.

Liedtke 1989

Liedtke, Walter. *The Royal Horse and Rider: Painting, Sculpture, and Horsemanship 1500–1800.* New York, 1989.

Lightfoot 1645

Lightfoot, John. *A Commentary on the Acts of the Apostles.* London, 1645.

Lloyd 1971

Lloyd, J. B. *African Animals in Renaissance Literature and Art.* Oxford, 1971.

Loughman 1991a

Loughman, John. "Aert Teggers, A Seventeenth-Century Dordrecht Collector." *Burlington Magazine* 133 (1991), 532–537.

Loughman 1991b

Loughman, John. "Dordrecht Family Portraits Identified and Attributed to Paulus Lesire." *The Hoogsteder Mercury* 12 (1991), 29–36.

Loughman 1993

Loughman, John. "Paintings in the Public and Private Domain: Collecting and Patronage at Dordrecht 1620–1749." Ph.D. diss., Courtauld Institute, London, 1993.

Lugt 1921

Lugt, Frits. *Marques de Collections (Dessins-Estampes).* Amsterdam, 1921.

Lugt 1931

Lugt, Frits. "Beiträge zu dem Katalog der niederländischen Handzeichnungen in Berlin." *Jahrbuch der Preussischen Kunstsammlungen in Berlin* 52 (1931), 36–280.

Lugt 1938

Lugt, Frits. *Répertoire des catalogues de ventes publiques.* Vol. 1. The Hague, 1938.

Lugt 1950

Lugt, Frits. *École Nationale Supérieure des Beaux-Arts. Inventaire général des dessins des écoles du Nord: école hollandaise.* Paris, 1950.

MacLaren 1960

MacLaren, Neil. *National Gallery Catalogues. The Dutch School.* London, 1960.

MacLaren and Brown 1991

MacLaren, Neil, rev. by Christopher Brown. *National Gallery Catalogues: The Dutch School, 1600–1900.* 2 vols. London, 1991.

Maisak 1981

Maisak, Petra. *Arkadien, Genese und Typologie einer idyllischen Wunschwelt.* Europäische Hochschulschriften 28, Kunstgeschichte 17. Frankfurt am Main and Bern, 1981.

Van Mander 1604

Mander, Karel van. *Het schilderboeck.* Haarlem, 1604. (reprint, Utrecht, 1969)

Van Mander and Miedema 1973

Mander, Karel van. *Den grondt der edel vry schilder-const.* 2 vols. Ed. and trans. Hessel Miedema. Utrecht, 1973.

De Marly 1978

Marly, Diana de. "Undress in the Oeuvre of Peter Lely." *Burlington Magazine* 120 (November 1978), 749–753.

Martone 1977

Martone, Mario Thomas. "The Theme of the Conversion of Paul in Italian Painting." Ph.D. diss., New York University, 1977.

Meder 1919

Meder, Joseph. *Die Handzeichnung. Ihre Technik und Entwicklung.* Vienna, 1919.

Melion 1991

Melion, Walter S. *Shaping the Netherlandish Canon: Karel van Mander's Schilder-Boeck.* Chicago and London, 1991.

Mellaart 1926

Mellaart, J. H. J. *Dutch Drawings of the Seventeenth Century.* London, 1926.

Mellon 1949

National Gallery of Art: Paintings and Sculpture from the Mellon Collection. Washington, 1949. (reprint eds., 1953 and 1958)

The Menil Collection 1987

The Menil Collection: A Selection from the Paleolithic to the Modern Era. New York, 1987, 106–110.

Metropolitan Museum of Art 1995

European Paintings in the Metropolitan Museum of Art: A Summary Catalogue. New York, 1995.

Michel 1892
Michel, Emile. "Une famille d'artistes hollandaise: Les Cuyps." *Gazette des Beaux-Arts* 34 (1892), 5–23, 107–117, 225–238.

Millar 1968
Millar, Oliver, with John Harris and Geoffrey de Bellaigue. *Buckingham Palace.* London, 1968.

Miller 1970
Miller, Dwight. *Catalogue of European Paintings: Indianapolis Museum of Art.* Indianapolis, 1970.

Moiso-Diekamp 1987
Moiso-Diekamp, Cornelia. *Das Pendant in der holländischen Malerei des 17. Jahrhunderts.* Frankfurt, 1987.

Von Moltke 1994
Moltke, J. W. von. *Arent de Gelder. Dordrecht 1645–1727.* Doornspijk, 1994.

Montias 1987
Montias, J. Michael. "Cost and Value in Seventeenth-Century Art." *Art History,* 10 (1987), 455–466.

Montias 1990
Montias, J. Michael. "The Influence of Economic Factors on Style." *De zeventiende eeuw* 6 (1990), 49–57.

Montias 1991
Montias, J. Michael. "Works of Art in Seventeenth-Century Amsterdam." In Freedberg and De Vries 1991, 331–372.

Mules 1985
Mules, Helen B. "Dutch Drawings of the Seventeenth Century in the Metropolitan Museum of Art." *The Metropolitan Museum of Art Bulletin* 42, 4 (1984–1985), 3–56.

Müllenmeister 1973
Müllenmeister, Kurt J. *Meer und Land im Licht des 17. Jahrhunderts.* Bremen, 1973–1980.

Müllenmeister 1988
Müllenmeister, Kurt J. *Roelant Savery: Kortrijk 1576–1639.* Freren, 1988.

Muller 1863
Muller, Frederik. *De Nederlandse historie in platen.* Amsterdam, 1863.

Murray 1980
Murray, P. *Dulwich Picture Gallery, A Catalogue.* London, 1980.

Musée des Beaux-Arts de Bordeaux 1990
Le Bihan, Olivier. *L'or & l'ombre: catalogue critique et raisonné des peintures hollandaises du dix-septième et du dix-huitième siècles, conservées au Musée des beaux-arts de Bordeaux.* Bordeaux, 1990.

Museum van der Hoop 1855
Catalogus der schilderjien van het Museum van der Hoop. Amsterdam, 1855. (new ed., 1872)

National Gallery 1986
National Gallery: Illustrated General Catalogue. London, 1986.

Neal 1828
Neal, John. "Three Days in Boston." *The Yankee and Boston Literary Gazette* 1, 50 (10 December 1828), 398.

Neale 1818
Neale, John Preston. *Views of the Seats of Noblemen and Gentlemen in England, Wales, Scotland, and Ireland.* 6 vols.; 2d ser., 5 vols. London, 1818–1829.

Van Nierop 1993
Nierop, H. F. K. van. *The Nobility of Holland: From Knights to Regents, 1500–1650.* Cambridge, 1993. (Dutch ed., *Van ridders tot regenten: De Hollandse adel in de zestiende en de eerste helft van de zeventiende eeuw.* The Hague, 1984)

Olde Meierink and Bakker 1997
Olde Meierink, Ben, and Angelique Bakker. "The Utrecht Elite as Patrons and Collectors." In Baltimore and San Francisco 1997–1998, 72–85.

Van Oosterzee 1998
Oosterzee, Leonoor van. "Het getekende landschap: een materiaalstudie." In Amsterdam 1998, 27–33.

Originalabbildungen 1912
Aelbert Cuyp: Originalabbildungen nach seinen vorzüglichsten Gemälden und handzeichnungen. 2d. ed. Leipzig, 1912.

Orlers 1610
Orlers, Jan Jansz. *Den Nassau lauren-crans.* Leiden, 1610.

Parsons and Ramsay 1983
Parsons, Melinda B., and William M. Ramsay. "The Scarlet Letter and an Herbal Tradition." *Emerson Society Quarterly* 29 (4th quarter, 1983), 197–207.

Parthey 1863
Parthey, Gustav. *Deutscher Bildersaal: Verzeichnis der in Deutschland vorhandenen Oelbilder verstorbener Maler aller Schulen.* Vol. 1. Berlin, 1863.

Van de Passe 1973
Passe, Crispijn van de. *'t Light der teken en schilderkonst.* Introduction by J. Bolten. Soest, 1973.

Patmore 1824
Patmore, Peter George. *British Galleries of Art.* London, 1824.

Peel 1845
Peel, C. M. "Collection de Sir R. P. Peel." *Le Cabinet de l'Amateur et de l'Antiquaire* 4 (1845–1846), 49–76.

Le Petit 1615
Le Petit, Jean. *Eigentliycks Beschrijvinge Der Vrije Nederlandsche Provincien.* Arnhem, 1615.

Plomp 1986
Plomp, Michiel. "'Een merkwaardige verzameling teekeningen' door Leonaert Bramer." *Oud Holland* 100 (2) (1986), 81–153.

Plomp 1997
Plomp, Michiel C. *The Dutch Drawings in the Teylers Museum. II. Artists Born between 1575 and 1630.* Haarlem, 1997.

Ploos van Amstel 1821
Ploos van Amstel, C. *Collection d'Imitations de Dessins d'après les principaux maîtres hollandais et flamands, commencée par Ploos van Amstel, continuée et portée au nombre de cent morceaux, avec des renseignements historiques et detaillés sur ces maîtres et sur leurs ouvrages.* 2 vols. London, Mannheim, The Hague, and Amsterdam, 1821.

De Pluvinel 1623
Pluvinel, Antoine de. *Maneige royal ou l'on peut remarquer le defaut et la perfection du chevalier en tous les exercises de cet art….* Paris, 1623.

De Pluvinel 1625
Pluvinel, Antoine de. *L'instruction du Roy à l'exercise de monter à cheval.* Paris and Utrecht, 1625.

Pontanus 1614
Pontanus, Johannes. *Historische beschrijvinge der seer wijt, beroemde coopstadt Amsterdam.* Amsterdam, 1614.

Potterton 1986
Potterton, H. *Dutch Seventeenth and Eighteenth Century Paintings in the National Gallery of Ireland.* Dublin, 1986.

Rathgeber 1839
Rathgeber, Georg. *Annalen der niederländischen Malerei und Kupferstichkunst: V. Von Rubens Abreise nach Italien bis auf Rembrandt's Tod.* Gotha, 1839.

Ray 1673
Ray, John. *Observations topographical, Moral, & Physiological; Made in a Journey through Part of the Low-Countries, Germany, Italy, and France.* London, 1673.

Van Regteren Altena 1948
Regteren Altena, J. Q. van. *Holländische Meisterzeichnungen des siebzehnten Jahrhunderts.* Basel, 1948.

Reiss 1953
Reiss, Stephen. "Aelbert Cuyp." *Burlington Magazine* 95 (February 1953), 42–47.

Reiss 1975
Reiss, Stephen. *Aelbert Cuyp.* London and Boston, 1975.

Reitlinger 1961
Reitlinger, Gerald. *The Economics of Taste.* 3 vols. London, 1961.

Repp-Eckert 1989
Repp-Eckert, Anke. *Wallraf-Richartz-Museum. Niederländische Landschaftsmalerei von 1580–1680.* Cologne, 1989.

Reznicek 1961
Reznicek, E. K. J. *Die Zeichnungen von Hendrick Goltzius.* 2 vols. Utrecht, 1961.

Richter 1817
Richter, Henry. *Day-light; A Recent Discovery in the Art of Painting: With Hints on the Philosophy of the Fine Arts, and on that of the Human Mind, as First Dissected by Emanuel Kant.* London, 1817. (previously published in *Repository of Arts*, 2, 2 [November, 1816])

Richter 1988
Richter, Ernst L. "Seltene Pigmente im Mittelaltar." *Zeitschrift für Kunsttechnologie und Konservierung* 2 (1988), 171–176.

Richter and Sparkes 1880
Richter, J. P., and J. Sparkes. *Catalogue of the Pictures in the Dulwich College Gallery with Biographical Notices of the Painters.* London, 1880.

Riezebos and Rappol
Riezebos, P. A., and M. Rappol. "Gravel- to Sand-Sized Vivianite Components in a Saalian Till Layer near Borne (The Netherlands)." *Geologie en Mijnbouw* 66 (1987), 21–34.

Te Rijdt 2000
Te Rijdt, R. J. A. "De tekeningen van Abraham en Jacob van Strij." In Dordrecht 2000, 139–194.

Rijksmuseum 1960
Catalogue of Paintings, Rijksmuseum. Amsterdam, 1960.

Rijksmuseum 1976
Van Thiel, Pieter J. J., et al. *All the Paintings of the Rijksmuseum in Amsterdam: A Complete Illustrated Catalogue.* Amsterdam and Maarsen, 1976.

Roberts 1973
Roberts, Keith. Review of London 1973. *Burlington Magazine* 115 (1973), 132–135.

Robinson 1990
Robinson, M. S. *The Paintings of the Willem van de Veldes.* 2 vols. London, 1990.

Roethlisberger 1968
Roethlisberger, Marcel. *Claude Lorrain. The Drawings.* 2 vols. Berkeley and Los Angeles, 1968.

Roethlisberger and Bok 1993
Roethlisberger, Marcel, and Marten Jan Bok. *Abraham Bloemaert and His Sons: Paintings and Prints.* 2 vols. Doornspijk, 1993.

De Roever 1893
Roever, A. de. *Een tak van het brabantsche geslacht de Roovere.* Helmond, 1893.

Rosand 1969
Rosand, David. "Rubens's Munich *Lion Hunt*: Its Sources and Significance." *Art Bulletin* 51 (1969), 29–40.

Rosenberg, Slive, and Ter Kuile 1966
Rosenberg, Jakob, Seymour Slive, and E. H. ter Kuile. *Dutch Art and Architecture, 1600–1800.* Baltimore, 1966. (rev. ed., London, 1984)

Royalton-Kisch 1988
Royalton-Kisch, Martin. *Adriaen van de Venne's Album in the Department of Prints and Drawings in the British Museum.* London, 1988.

Ruskin 1843
Ruskin, John. *Modern Painters, Their Superiority in the Art of Landscape Painting to All the Ancient Masters.* London, 1843. (subsequent eds., 1844, 1846, 1848, 1851)

Ruskin 1903–1912
Ruskin, John. *The Works of John Ruskin.* 39 vols. Eds. E. T. Cook and A. Wedderburn. London, 1903–1912.

Ruskin 1987
Ruskin, John. *Modern Painters.* Ed. David Barrie. New York, 1987.

Russell 1990
Russell, Margarita A. "Aelbert Cuyp. The Maas at Dordrecht: The Great Assembly of the Dutch Armed Forces, June–July 1646." *Dutch Crossing* 40 (1990), 31–82.

Ruysschaert 1949
Ruysschaert, J. "Juste Lipse et les annales de Tacite." *Receuil de travaux d'histoire et de philologie* 34 (1949).

Salomonson 1983
Salomonson, J. W. 'Op de wal agter St. Marye.' *Topografische aantekeningen bij een onbekend schilderijtje van Herman Saftleven. Koninklijke Nederlandse Akademie van Wetenschappen. Verhandelingen Afdeling Letterkunde, Nieuwe Reeks deel 119.* Amsterdam, Oxford, and New York, 1983.

Sander and Brinkmann 1995
Sander, Jochen, and Bodo Brinkmann. *Niederländische Gemälde vor 1800 im Städel.* Frankfurt am Main, 1995.

Saunders 1955
Saunders, Jason L. *Justus Lipsius: The Philosophy of Renaissance Stoicism.* New York, 1955.

Saunders and Kirby 1994
Saunders, David, and Jo Kirby. "Light-induced Colour Changes in Red and Yellow Lake Pigments." *National Gallery Technical Bulletin* 15 (1994), 79–97.

Schenkenveld 1991
Schenkenveld, Maria A. *Dutch Literature in the Age of Rembrandt: Themes and Ideas.* Amsterdam and Philadelphia, 1991.

Van Schevichaven 1898–1904
Schevichaven, H. D. J. van. *Penschetsen uit Nijmegen's verleden.* 3 vols. N.p., 1898–1904.

Scheyer 1952
Scheyer, Ernst. "Henry Adams as a Collector of Art." *The Art Quarterly* 15 (1952), 223.

Schneebalg-Perelman 1982
Schneebalg-Perelman, Sophie. *Les Chasses de Maximilien: Les énigmes d'un chef d'oeuvre de la tapisserie.* Brussels, 1982.

Schneider 1883
Schneider, H. J. *Katalog der herzoglichen Gemäldegalerie.* Gotha, 1883.

Schöffer 1975
Schöffer, I. "The Batavian Myth during the Sixteenth and Seventeenth Centuries." In *Britain and the Netherlands* 5 (1975), 78–101.

Scholten 1904
Scholten, H. J. *Musée Teyler à Haarlem. Catalogue raisonné des dessins des écoles françaises et hollandaises.* Haarlem, 1904.

Schönbrunner and Meder 1884–1908
Schönbrunner, Jos., and Jos. Meder. *Handzeichnungen Alter Meister aus der Albertina und anderen Sammlungen.* 12 vols. Vienna, 1884–1908.

Schoon and Voorsteegh 1991
Schoon, Peter, and Ineke Voorsteegh. *Aelbert Cuyp (Dordrechts Museum Informatief).* Dordrecht, 1991.

Schulte 1973
Schulte, A. G. "18de-eeuws tuinontwerp voor het huis Ubbergen." *Numaga, Tijdschrift gewijd aan heden en verleden van Nijmegen en omgeving* 20 (1973), 88–102.

Schulte 1983
Schulte, A. G. *Het Rijk van Nijmegen. Oostelijk gedeelte en de Duffelt (De Nederlandse monumenten van geschiedenis en kunst. De provincie Gelderland. Het kwartier Nijmegen).* The Hague and Zeist, 1983.

Schulz 1974
Schulz, Wolfgang. *Lambert Doomer: Sämtliche Zeichnungen.* Berlin, 1974.

Schulz 1982
Schulz, Wolfgang. *Herman Saftleven (1609–1685): Leben und Werke.* Berlin, 1982.

Schwartz 1985
Schwartz, Gary. *Rembrandt, His Life, His Paintings.* New York, 1985.

Schwartz and Bok 1989
Schwartz, Gary, and Marten Jan Bok. *Pieter Saenredam.* The Hague, 1989.

Scriverius 1609
Scriverius, Petrus. *Batavia illustrata.* Leiden, 1609. (rev. ed., *Beschrijvinghe van out Batavien.* Arnhem, 1612)

Sepp 1773
Sepp, Jan Christiaan. *Nieuwe Geographische Nederlandsche Reise- en Zak-Atlas.* Amsterdam, 1773. (facsimile reprint, Alphen aan den Rijn, 1987)

Sip 1955
Sip, J. *Mistri Hollandske.* Prague, 1955.

Slive 1970–1974
Slive, Seymour. *Frans Hals,* 3 vols. New York and London, 1970–1974.

Sluijter 1986
Sluijter, Eric Jan. *De 'Heydensche Fabulen' in de Noordnederlandse schilderkunst circa 1590–1670*. The Hague, 1986. (published dissertation)

Sluijter 1993
Sluijter, Eric Jan. *De lof der schilderkunst, Over schilderijen van Gerrit Dou (1613–1675) en een traktaat von Philips Angel uit 1642*. Hilversum, 1993.

Sluijter 1996
Sluijter, Eric Jan. "Jan van Goyen als marktleider, virtuoos en vernieuwer." In Leiden 1996, 38–59.

Sluijter 1999
Sluijter, Eric Jan. "Over Brabantse vodden, economische concurrentie, artistieke wedijver en de groei van de markt voor schilderijen in de eerste decennia van de zeventiende eeuw." *Nederlands Kunsthistorisch Jaarboek* 50 (1999), 113–143.

Sluijter 2000
Sluijter, Eric Jan. *Seductress of Sight: Studies in Dutch Art of the Golden Age*. Zwolle, 2000.

Smith 1829–1842
Smith, John. *A Catalogue Raisonné of the Works of the Most Eminent Dutch, Flemish, and French Painters*. 9 vols. London, 1829–1842.

Van Someren 1660
Van Someren, Johan. "Wandelingh van Nijmegen op Ubbergen." *Uyt-spanning der vernuften, bestaende in geestelijcke ende wereltlijcke poësy*. Nijmegen, 1660.

Spicer 1983
Spicer, Joaneath. "'De Koe voor d'aerde Statt': The Origin of the Dutch Cattle Piece." In *Essays in Northern European Art Presented to Egbert Haverkamp-Begemann on his 60th Birthday*. Ed. Anne-Marie Logan. Doornspijk, 1983, 251–256.

Spicer 1989
Spicer, Joaneath. Review of Cambridge and Montreal 1988. *Drawing. The International Review Published by the Drawing Society* 10 (1989), 135–136.

Sprey 1953
Sprey, Willem. *Tacitus over de opstand der Bataven*. Groningen, 1953.

Staring 1953
Staring, Adolf. "De ruiterportretgroep van Albert Cuyp in het Metropolitan Museum te New York." *Oud Holland* 68 (1953), 117–118.

Stechow 1938
Stechow, Wolfgang. "Die 'Pellekussenpoort' bei Utrecht auf Bildern von Jan van Goyen und Salomon van Ruysdael." *Oud Holland* 55 (1938), 202.

Stechow 1960a
Stechow, Wolfgang. "Significant Dates on Some Seventeenth Century Landscape Paintings." *Oud-Holland* 75 (1960), 79–92.

Stechow 1960b
Stechow, Wolfgang. "Cuyp's Valkhof at Nijmegen." *Bulletin John Herron Art Institute. The Art Association of Indianapolis, Indiana* 47 (March 1960), 4–11.

Stechow 1966
Stechow, Wolfgang. *Dutch Landscape Painting of the Seventeenth Century*. London, 1966.

Steland Stief 1971
Steland Stief, Anne Charlotte. *Jan Asselijn: nach 1610 bis 1652*. Amsterdam, 1971.

Stephens 1873
Stephens, Frederic George. "Private Collections of England." *Athenaeum* (1873–1887).

Stift und Feder 1927
Stift und Feder. Zeichnungen von Künstler aller Zeiten und Länder in Nachbildungen. Ed. Rudolf Schrey. 7 vols. Frankfurt, 1917–1931.

Stillson 1944
Stillson, Blanche. "The Valkhof at Nijmegen by Aelbert Cuyp." *Bulletin of the Art Association of Indianapolis* 31, no. 1 (April 1944), 7–9.

Van Strien 1998
Strien, Kees van. *Touring the Low Countries, Accounts of British Travellers, 1660–1720*. Amsterdam, 1998.

Sugar 1990
Sugar, Peter F., et al. *A History of Hungary*. London and New York, 1990.

Sullivan 1984
Sullivan, Scott A. *The Dutch Gamepiece*. Montclair, N.J., 1984.

Sumowski 1979
Sumowski, Werner. *Drawings of the Rembrandt School*. Vol. 2. Ed. Walter L. Strauss. New York, 1979.

Sutton 1987
Sutton, Peter C. "The Noblest of Livestock." *The J. Paul Getty Museum Journal* 15 (1987), 97–110.

Sutton 1987–1988
Sutton, Peter C. "Introduction." In Amsterdam, Boston, and Philadelphia 1987, 1–63.

Tacitus
Tacitus, Cornelius. *The Histories*. Trans. Kenneth Wellesley. London, 1995.

Talley 1981
Talley, M. Kirby. *Portrait Painting in England: Studies in the Technical Literature before 1700*. London, 1981.

Temesváry 1982

Temesváry, Ferenc. *Arms and Armor*. Budapest, 1982.

Temple 1740

Temple, Sir William. "An Essay upon the Origin and Nature of Government, Written in the Year 1672." In *Works*. 2 vols. London, 1740.

Ter Raa 1918

Ter Raa, F.J.G. *Her Staatische Leger, 1568 – 1793*. 8 vols. Breda, 1918.

Thoré 1858 – 1860

Thoré, T.E.J. (William Burger). *Musées de la Hollande*. 2 vols. Paris, 1858 – 1860.

Toledo Museum of Art 1976

Toledo Museum of Art. European Paintings. Toledo, 1976.

Tompos 1999

Tompos, Lilla. "Westerse en Oosterse invloeden op de kledij van de Hongaarse aristocratie." In Brussels 1999, 62 – 65.

Trautscholdt 1958

Trautscholdt, Eduard. Review of Bernt 1957 – 1958. *Kunstchronik* (1958), 361 – 371.

Trollope 1832

Trollope, Frances. *Domestic Manners of the Americans*. London, 1832.

Turnau 1991

Turnau, Irena. *History of Dress in Central and Eastern Europe from the Sixteenth to the Eighteenth Century*. Warsaw, 1991.

Valentiner 1929

Valentiner, W. "Dutch Loan Exhibition in Detroit Museum." *Art News* 28 (19 October 1929), 3, 6 – 10, 19 – 21.

Van Veen 1608

Veen, Otto van. *Amorum emblemata*. Antwerp, 1608.

Van Veen 1960

Veen, P.A.F. van. *De soeticheydt des buytenlevens, vergheselschapt met de boucken: Het hofdicht als tak van een georgische litteratuur*. The Hague, 1960.

Veldhuijzen 1988

Veldhuijzen, G. *Nieuwe heeren nieuwe kussen: Het regenten-patriciaat van Dordrecht 1672 – 1685*. Dordrecht, 1988.

Vesey and Norman 1986

Vesey, A., and B. Norman. *Wallace Collection Catalogue: European Arms and Armour Supplement*. London, 1986.

De Vesme 1971

Vesme, Alexandre de, with introduction and additions by Phyllis Dearborn. *Stefano della Bella: Catalogue Raisonné*. New York, 1971.

Vey 1968

Vey, Horst. "Adolf von Carstanjen und seine Gemälde-sammlung." *Wallraf-Richartz-Jahrbuch* 30 (1968), 305 – 344.

Viardot 1844

Viardot, Louis. *Les musées d'Allemagne et de Russie*. Paris, 1844.

Virch 1970

Virch, Claude. *Paintings in the Collection of Charles and Edith Neuman de Végvár*. New York, 1970.

De Vries 1986

Vries, Jan van de. "The Dutch Rural Economy and the Landscape." In London 1986, 79 – 86.

De Vries 1998

De Vries, Willemien B. *Wandeling en verhandeling: de ontwikkeling van het Nederlandse hofdicht in de zeventiende eeuw (1613 – 1710)*. Hilversum, 1998.

Waagen 1838

Waagen, Gustav Friedrich. *Works of Art and Artists in England*. 3 vols. London, 1838.

Waagen 1854

Waagen, Gustave Friedrich. *Treasures of Art in Great Britain: Being an Account of the Chief Collection of Paintings, Drawings, Sculptures, and Illuminated Mss*. 3 vols. London, 1854. Vol. 4. London, 1857. (reprint, London, 1970)

Van de Waal 1974

Van de Waal, H. *Steps towards Rembrandt: Collected Articles 1937 – 1972*. Ed. R.H. Fuchs. Trans. Patricia Wardle and Alan Griffiths. Amsterdam, 1974.

Walker 1976

Walker, John. *National Gallery of Art, Washington*. Foreword by J. Carter Brown. New York, 1976.

Walpole 1927

Walpole, Horace. "Horace Walpole's Journal of Visits to Country Seats." *Walpole Society* 16 (1927 – 1928), 9 – 81.

Walsh 1985

Walsh, Amy. "Paulus Potter: His Works and Their Meaning." Ph.D. diss., Columbia University, 1985.

Waterfield 1988

Waterfield, Giles. *Dulwich Picture Gallery. Rich Summer of Art: A Regency Picture Collection Seen through Victorian Eyes*. London, 1988.

Wegner 1973

Wegner, Wolfgang. *Kataloge der Staatlichen Graphischen Sammlung München, 1, Die niederlandischen Handzeichnungen des 15. – 18. Jahrhunderts*. 2 vols. Munich, 1973.

Wheelock 1984

Wheelock, Arthur K. "History, Politics and the Portrait of a City: Vermeer's *View of Delft*." In *Urban Life in the Renaissance*. Eds. Susan Zimmerman and Ronald F.E. Weissman. Newark and London, 1989, 165 – 184.

Wheelock 1995
Wheelock, Arthur K. *Dutch Paintings of the Seventeenth Century*. The Collections of the National Gallery of Art Systematic Catalogue. Washington and New York, 1995.

White 1982
White, Christopher. *The Dutch Pictures in the Collection of Her Majesty The Queen*. Cambridge, 1982.

Whitley 1928
Whitley, W. T. *Artists and Their Friends in England, 1700–1799*. 2 vols. London and Boston, 1928.

Widener 1885–1900
Catalogue of Paintings Forming the Private Collection of P. A. B. Widener, Ashbourne, near Philadelphia. 2 vols. Paris, 1885–1900.

Widener 1913
Hofstede de Groot, Cornelis. *Early German, Dutch & Flemish Schools. Vol. 1 of Pictures in the Collection of P. A. B. Widener at Lynnewood Hall, Elkins Park, Pennsylvania*. Philadelphia, 1913.

Widener 1931
Pictures in the Collection of Joseph Widener at Lynnewood Hall. Elkins Park, Philadelphia, 1931.

De Winkel 1998
De Winkel, Marieke. "'Eene onbedenklyke vernadering van dragten, en vremde toestellingen omtrent de bekleedingen…,' Het kostuum in het werk van Arent de Gelder." In Dordrecht 1998, 87–97.

De Winkel 1999
De Winkel, Marieke. "Costume in Rembrandt's Self-Portraits." In London and The Hague 1999, 58–74.

Von Wurzbach 1906–1911
Wurzbach, Alfred von. *Niederländisches Künstler-Lexikon*. 3 vols. Leipzig, 1906–1911. (vol. 1, 1906).

Van der Wyck 1989–1990
Wyck, H. M. W. van der, J. W. Niemeijer, and Wouter Th. Kloek. *De kasteeltekeningen van Roelant Roghman*. 2 vols. Alphen aan den Rijn, 1989–1990.

Wyld 1980
Wyld, Martin, John Mills, and Joyce Plesters. "Some Observations on Blanching with Special Reference to the Paintings of Claude." *National Gallery Technical Bulletin* 4 (1980), 48–63.

Yapou 1981
Yapou, Yonna. "A Picture from Aelbert Cuyp's Transitional Period." *Burlington Magazine* 103 (1981), 160–163.

Young 1771
Young, Arthur. *A Farmer's Tour through the East of England*. 4 vols. London, 1771.

Zolnay 1971
Zolnay, László. "Game, Hunting and Hunters in Ancient Hungary." In *Symposium of the History of Hunting*. Budapest, 1971, 6–7.

Zygulski 1965
Zygulski, Zdzisław. "Rembrandt's 'Lisowczyk': A Study of Costume and Weapons." *Bulletin du Musée National de Varsovie* 6, no. 2 / 3 (1965), 43–67.

Exhibitions

Amsterdam 1924
Tentoonstelling van Werken door Dortsche Meesters. Pictura.

Amsterdam 1932
Museum Fodor. Eerste tentoonstelling. Klassieke Hollandse Teekenaars. Museum Fodor (catalogue by J.Q. Van Regteren Altena).

Amsterdam 1936
Tentoonstelling van Oude Kunst. Rijksmuseum.

Amsterdam 1968
De verzameling van A. Schwarz. Rijksprentenkabinet, Rijksmuseum (catalogue by J.W. Niemeijer).

Amsterdam 1981
Rembrandt en tekenaars uit zijn omgeving. Gemeentearchief (catalogue by B.P.J. Broos).

Amsterdam 1982
Met Huygens op reis. Rijksprentenkabinet, Rijksmuseum (catalogue by J.F. Heijbroek et al.).

Amsterdam 1987
Land and Water. Dutch Drawings from the 17th Century in the Rijksmuseum Print Room. Rijksprentenkabinet, Rijksmuseum (catalogue by Marijn Schapelhouman and Pieter Schatborn).

Amsterdam 1992
Episcopius. Jan de Bisschop (1628–1671) advocaat en tekenaar — lawyer and draughtsman. Museum het Rembrandthuis (catalogue by Renske E. Jellema and Michiel Plomp).

Amsterdam 1993a
Tekeningen van oude meesters. De verzameling Jacobus A. Klaver. Rijksprentenkabinet, Rijksmuseum (catalogue by Marijn Schapelhouman and Peter Schatborn).

Amsterdam 1993b
Nederland naar't leven: Landschapsprenten uit de Gouden Eeuw. Museum het Rembrandthuis (catalogue by Boudewijn Bakker and Huigen Leeflang).

Amsterdam 1993c
Dawn of the Golden Age. Northern Netherlandish Art 1580–1620. Rijksmuseum (catalogue by Ger Luijten, Ariane van Suchtelen et al.).

Amsterdam 1998
Buiten tekenen in Rembrandts tijd. Museum het Rembrandthuis (catalogue by Bob van den Boogert et al.).

Amsterdam 1999
Goethe & Rembrandt. Tekeningen uit Weimar. Museum het Rembrandthuis (catalogue by Bob van den Boogert).

Amsterdam 2000a
The Glory of the Golden Age: Painting, Sculpture and Decorative Art. Rijksmuseum (catalogue by Judikje Kiers and Fieke Tissink).

Amsterdam 2000b
The Glory of the Golden Age: Drawings and Prints. Rijksprentenkabinet, Rijksmuseum (catalogue by Epko Runia).

Amsterdam, Berlin, and London 1991–1992
Rembrandt: The Master and His Workshop: Drawings and Etchings. Rijksmuseum, Staatliche Museen Preussischer Kulturbesitz, and The National Gallery (catalogue by Holm Bevers, Peter Schatborn, and Barbara Welzel).

Amsterdam, Boston, and Philadelphia 1987
Masters of 17th-Century Dutch Landscape Painting. Rijksmuseum, Museum of Fine Arts, and Philadelphia Museum of Art (catalogue by Peter C. Sutton et al.).

Amsterdam and Groningen 1983
The Impact of a Genius: Rembrandt, His Pupils and Followers in the Seventeenth Century. Waterman Gallery and Groninger Museum (catalogue by Albert Blankert et al.).

Amsterdam and London 2000
Rembrandt, The Printmaker. Rijksprentenkabinet, Rijksmuseum, and The British Museum (catalogue by Erik Hinterding, Ger Luijten, and Martin Royalton-Kisch).

Amsterdam and Toronto 1977
The Dutch Cityscape in the Seventeenth Century and Its Sources. Amsterdams Historisch Museum and Art Gallery of Ontario (catalogue by R.J. Wattemaker et al.).

Amsterdam, Vienna, New York, and Cambridge 1991
Seventeenth-Century Dutch Drawings. A Selection from the Maida and George Abrams Collection. Rijksprentenkabinet, Rijksmuseum, Graphische Sammlung Albertina, The Pierpont Morgan Library, and the Fogg Art Museum, Harvard University (catalogue by William W. Robinson).

Amsterdam and Washington 1981
Dutch Figure Drawings from the Seventeenth Century. Rijksprentenkabinet, Rijksmuseum, and National Gallery of Art (catalogue by Peter Schatborn).

Ann Arbor 1964
Italy Through Dutch Eyes: Dutch 17th-Century Landscape Artists in Italy. University of Michigan Museum of Art.

Antwerp and London 1999
The Light of Nature: Landscape Drawings and Watercolours by Van Dyck and His Contemporaries. Rubenshuis and The British Museum (catalogue by Martin Royalton-Kisch).

Baltimore and San Francisco 1997–1998
Masters of Light: Dutch Painters in Utrecht During the Golden Age. The Walters Art Gallery and The Fine Arts Museums of San Francisco (catalogue by Joaneath A. Spicer and Lynn Federle Orr).

Berlin 1890
Werken der niederländischen Kunst des 17. Jahrhunderts im Berliner Privatbestiz. Königliche Akademie.

Berlin 1974
Die holländische Landschaftszeichnung 1600–1740. Staatliche Museen Preussischer Kulturbesitz (catalogue by Wolfgang Schülz).

Birmingham 1831

Catalogue of Pictures, Chiefly by the Old Masters of the Italian, Flemish, and Spanish Schools. Society of Arts.

Birmingham 1989

Dutch Paintings of the Seventeenth Century: Images of a Golden Age. Birmingham Museum and Art Gallery (catalogue by Christopher Wright et al.).

Boston 1992

Prized Possessions: European Paintings from Private Collections of Friends of the Museum of Fine Arts, Boston. Museum of Fine Arts (catalogue by Peter Sutton).

Braunschweig 1948

Meisterzeichnungen aus dem Museum Boymans Rotterdam. Herzog Anton Ulrich Museum.

Brussels 1935

Cinq Siècles d'Art. Exposition universelle et internationale.

Brussels 1937–1938

Dessins hollandais de Jerôme Bosch à Rembrandt. Palais des Beaux-Arts.

Brussels 1983

Tekeningen van de 15de tot de 18de eeuw in particuliere verzamelingen van België. Generale Bankmaatschappij.

Brussels 1999

Hungaria Regia: Schittering en strijd 1000–1800. Paleis voor Schone Kunsten.

Brussels, Amsterdam, and Hamburg 1961

Dessins hollandais du siècle d'or. Choix de dessins provenant de collections publiques et particulières néerlandaises. Koninklijke Bibliotheek Albert Ier., Rijksprentenkabinet, Rijksmuseum, and Kunsthalle (catalogue by K. G. Boon et al.).

Brussels, Rotterdam, and Paris 1972–1973

Hollandse en Vlaamse tekeningen uit de zeventiende eeuw. Verzameling van de Hermitage, Leningrad en het Museum Poesjkin, Moskou. Koninklijke Bibliotheek Albert Ier., Museum Boymans-van Beuningen, and Institut Néerlandais.

Brussels, Rotterdam, Paris, and Bern 1968–1969

Dessins de paysagistes hollandais du XVIIe siècle de la Collection particulière conservée à l'Institut Néerlandais de Paris. 2 vols. Koninklijke Bibliotheek Albert Ier., Museum Boymans-van Beuningen, Institut Néerlandais, and Kunstmuseum (catalogue by Carlos van Hasselt and Frits Lugt).

Budapest 1962

XVII. Századi Holland és Flamand Rajzok az Amsterdami Városi Múzeumbói Boedapest. Szépmüveszeti Múzeum.

Cambridge 1948

Seventy Master Drawings. A Loan Exhibition Assembled to Honor Paul J. Sachs on the Occasion of His Seventieth Birthday. Fogg Art Museum.

Cambridge 1949

One Hundred Master Drawings. Fogg Art Museum (catalogue by Agnes Mongan and Jean J. Seznec).

Cambridge and Montreal 1988

Landscape in Perspective. Drawings by Rembrandt and his Contemporaries. Arthur M. Sackler Museum, Harvard University, and The Montreal Museum of Fine Arts (catalogue by Frederik J. Duparc).

Cleveland 1936

Catalogue of the Twentieth Anniversary Exhibition of the Cleveland Museum of Art: The Official Art Exhibit of the Great Lakes Exposition. Cleveland Museum of Art.

Cologne 1876

Kunsthistorische Ausstellung zu Cöln. Wallraf-Richartz-Museum.

Cologne 1946–1947

Meisterwerke der holländischen und flämische Malerei des 17. Jahrhunderts aus dem Besitz des Wallraf-Richartz-Museums. Wallraf-Richartz-Museum.

Cologne 1954

Meisterwerke holländischer Landschaftsmalerei des 17. Jahrhunderts. Wallraf-Richartz-Museum.

Cologne 1955

Rembrandt und seine Zeitgenossen. Handzeichnungen aus dem Museum Fodor Amsterdam. Wallraf-Richartz-Museum (catalogue by Helmut May et al.).

Copenhagen 1922

Udstilling af Aeldre og Nyere Hollandsk Malerkunst og Moderne Anvendt Kunst. Copenhagen.

Copenhagen 1952

Ny Carlsberfondets Jubilaeumsudstilling 1902–1952. Gaver til danske Museer. Charlottenborg.

Detroit 1925

Loan Exhibition of Dutch Paintings of the Seventeenth Century. Detroit Institute of Arts.

Detroit 1926

The Third Loan Exhibition of Old Masters. Detroit Institute of Arts.

Detroit 1927

Old and Modern Masters. Detroit Institute of Arts.

Detroit 1929

Loan Exhibition of Dutch Genre and Landscape Painting. Detroit Institute of Arts.

Detroit 1939

Loan Exhibition of Dutch Landscape Paintings. 20th Loan Exhibition of Old Masters. Detroit Institute of Arts.

Detroit 1949

Masterpieces of Paintings from Detroit Private Collections. Detroit Institute of Arts.

Dordrecht 1924

Tentoonstelling van Werken door Dordtsche Meesters — 17e, 18e, 19e eeuw. Genootschap Pictura.

Dordrecht 1976

Het huis te Merwede. Gemeentearchief.

Dordrecht 1977

Aelbert Cuyp en zijn familie, schilders te Dordrecht. Gerrit Gerritsz Cuyp, Jacob Gerritsz Cuyp, Benjamin Cuyp, Aelbert Cuyp. Dordrechts Museum (catalogue by J. M. De Groot, W. Veerman, J. Giltaij, and J. G. van Gelder).

Dordrecht 1991

Aelbert Cuyp (1620 – 1691): Schilderijen en tekeningen. Dordrechts Museum (catalogue by Peter Schoon).

Dordrecht 1992

De Zichtbaere Werelt: schilderkunst uit de Gouden Eeuw in Hollands oudste stad. Dordrechts Museum (ed. Peter Marijnissen et al.).

Dordrecht 1998

Arent de Gelder (1645 – 1727), Rembrandts laatste leerling. Dordrechts Museum (catalogue by J. W. Von Moltke).

Dordrecht 2000

Kopen voor de eeuwigheid. Verzamelen in het Dordrechts Museum 1975 – 2000. Dordrechts Museum (catalogue by Dick Verheijen, M. H. Peters et al.).

Dordrecht and Enschede 2000

In helder licht. Abraham en Jacob van Strij, Hollandse meesters van landschap en interieur omstreeks 1800. Dordrechts Museum and Rijksmuseum Twenthe (catalogue by Charles Dumas).

Dordrecht and Leeuwarden 1988

Meesterlijk vee: Nederlandse veeschilders 1600 – 1900. Dordrechts Museum and Fries Museum (catalogue by C. Boschma et al.).

Düsseldorf 1953

Niederrheinansichten Holländischer Künstler des 17. Jahrhunderts. Kunstmuseum.

Edinburgh 1826

Ancient Pictures. Royal Institution.

Edinburgh 1883

Works of Old Masters and Scottish National Portraits. Royal Scottish Academy.

Edinburgh 1949

Dutch and Flemish Paintings from the Collection of the Marquess of Bute. National Gallery of Scotland.

Edinburgh 1992

Dutch Art and Scotland: A Reflection of Taste. National Gallery of Scotland (catalogue by Julia Lloyd Williams).

Essen 1938

Holländische Landschaftsmalerei des 17. Jahrhunderts. Museum Folkwang.

Fort Worth 1982

Old Master Paintings, Cranach to Corot: Selected Loans from a Private Collection. Kimbell Art Museum (catalogue by Christopher Wright).

Frankfurt 1994

"Von Kunst und Kennerschaft." Die Graphische Sammlung im Städelschen Kunstinstitut unter Johann David Passavant, 1840 bis 1861. Städelsches Kunstinstitut.

Frankfurt 2000

"Nach dem Leben und aus der Phantasie." Niederländische Zeichnungen von 15. bis 18. Jahrhundert aus dem Städelschen Kunstinstitut. Städelsches Kunstinstitut (catalogue by Annette Strech et al.).

Glasgow 1884

The Bute Collection of Pictures. Corporation Galleries of Glasgow (catalogue by Jean Paul Richter).

Haarlem 1986

Portretten van Echt en Trouw: Huwelijk en gezin in de Nederlandse kunst van de zeventiende eeuw. Frans Halsmuseum (catalogue by Eddy de Jongh).

The Hague 1930

Verzameling Dr. C. Hofstede de Groot, III, Schilderijen, teekeningen en kunstnijverheid. Gemeentemuseum.

The Hague 1933

Genealogisch-Heraldische tentoonstelling. Koninklijk Nederlandsch Genootschap voor Geslacht-en Wapenkunde, Raadsgebouw.

The Hague 1991

The Hoogsteder Exhibition of Dutch Landscapes. Hoogsteder (catalogue by Paul Huys Janssen and Peter C. Sutton).

The Hague 1994

Paulus Potter, Paintings, Drawings and Etchings. Mauritshuis (catalogue by Amy Walsh et al.).

The Hague 1997 – 1998

Princely Patrons: The Collection of Frederick Henry of Orange and Amalia of Solms in The Hague. Mauritshuis (catalogue by Peter van der Ploeg and Carola Vermeeren).

The Hague and London 1970 – 1971

Shock of Recognition. The Landscape of English Romanticism and the Dutch Seventeenth-Century School. Mauritshuis and Tate Gallery (catalogue by A. B. de Vries et al.).

The Hague and San Francisco 1990 – 1991
Great Dutch Paintings from America. Mauritshuis and
The Fine Arts Museums of San Francisco (catalogue by
Ben Broos et al.).

Haifa 1959
Holland's Golden Age — Drawings. Museum of Modern Art.

Hartford, Hanover, and Boston 1973
*One Hundred Master Drawings from New England Private
Collections.* Wadsworth Atheneum, Hopkins Art Center,
Museum of Fine Arts.

Houston 1971 – 1972
Selection from the Menil Collection. Institute for the Arts,
Rice University.

Jerusalem 2000
Landscape of the Bible Sacred Scenes in European Master Paintings.
The Israel Museum (catalogue by Gill Passach).

Kingston-upon-Hull 1981
*Scholars of Nature: The Collection of Dutch Paintings
in Britain 1610 – 1857.* Ferens Art Gallery (catalogue by
Christopher Brown).

Laren 1966
De kunst van het verzamelen. Singer Museum.

Leeuwarden, Den Bosch, and Assen 1979
In het zadel: Het Nederlands ruiterportret van 1550 tot 1900.
Fries Museum, Noordbrabants Museum, and Provinciaal
Museum van Drenthe (catalogue by Charles Dumas).

Leiden 1903
*Vereeniging 'Die Laeckenhalle.' Teekeningen van Oud-Nederlandsche
Meesters.* Stedelijk Museum De Lakenhal.

Leiden 1916
*Tentoonstelling van teekeningen van Oud-Hollandsche Meesters uit
de Verzameling van Dr. C. Hofstede de Groot, I, II, III.* Stedelijk
Museum De Lakenhal.

Leiden 1993
*Between Fantasy and Reality: Seventeenth-Century Dutch Land-
scape Painting.* Stedelijk Museum De Lakenhal (catalogue by
Edwin Buijsen et al.).

Leiden 1996
Jan van Goyen. Stedelijk Museum De Lakenhal
(catalogue by Christiaan Vogelaar et al.).

Leipzig 1889
Ältere Meister aus sächsischem Privatbesitz. Leipziger
Kunstverein.

Leningrad, Moscow, and Kiev 1974
Flamandskiy i Gollandskiy Risunik XVII veka v Ermitazhe.
The Hermitage, The Pushkin Museum, and Museum for
Eastern and Western Art (catalogue by Y. I. Kuznetsov).

Liège 1939
Rétrospective d'art. Palais des Beaux-Arts.

London 1813
*British Institution for Promoting the Fine Arts in the
United Kingdom.* The British Institution.

London 1815
*A Catalogue Raison[n]é of the Pictures Now Exhibiting
at the British Institution.* The British Institution.

London 1818
*British Institution for Promoting the Fine Arts in the
United Kingdom.* The British Institution.

London 1819
*British Institution for Promoting the Fine Arts in the
United Kingdom.* The British Institution.

London 1822
*British Institution for Promoting the Fine Arts in the
United Kingdom.* The British Institution.

London 1824
*British Institution for Promoting the Fine Arts in the
United Kingdom.* The British Institution.

London 1826
*British Institution for Promoting the Fine Arts in the
United Kingdom.* The British Institution.

London 1827
*British Institution for Promoting the Fine Arts in the
United Kingdom.* The British Institution.

London 1828
*British Institution for Promoting the Fine Arts in the
United Kingdom.* The British Institution.

London 1829
*British Institution for Promoting the Fine Arts in the
United Kingdom.* The British Institution.

London 1832
*British Institution for Promoting the Fine Arts in the
United Kingdom.* The British Institution.

London 1837
*British Institution for Promoting the Fine Arts in the
United Kingdom.* The British Institution.

London 1838
*British Institution for Promoting the Fine Arts in the
United Kingdom.* The British Institution.

London 1839
*British Institution for Promoting the Fine Arts in the
United Kingdom.* The British Institution.

London 1841
*British Institution for Promoting the Fine Arts in the
United Kingdom.* The British Institution.

London 1843

British Institution for Promoting the Fine Arts in the United Kingdom. The British Institution.

London 1847

British Institution for Promoting the Fine Arts in the United Kingdom. The British Institution.

London 1849

British Institution for Promoting the Fine Arts in the United Kingdom. The British Institution.

London 1850

British Institution for Promoting the Fine Arts in the United Kingdom. The British Institution.

London 1851

British Institution for Promoting the Fine Arts in the United Kingdom. The British Institution.

London 1852

British Institution for Promoting the Fine Arts in the United Kingdom. The British Institution.

London 1853

British Institution for Promoting the Fine Arts in the United Kingdom. The British Institution.

London 1862

British Institution for Promoting the Fine Arts in the United Kingdom. The British Institution.

London 1866

British Institution for Promoting the Fine Arts in the United Kingdom. The British Institution.

London 1867

British Institution for Promoting the Fine Arts in the United Kingdom. The British Institution.

London 1870

British Institution for Promoting the Fine Arts in the United Kingdom. The British Institution.

London 1875

Exhibition of Works by the Old Masters, and by Deceased Masters from the British School Including a Special Collection from the Works of Sir A. W. Callcott and D. Maclise. Royal Academy.

London 1877a

Royal Academy of Art Exhibition. Royal Academy.

London 1877b

Winter Exhibition of Drawings. The Grosvenor Gallery.

London 1880

Royal Academy of Art Exhibition. Royal Academy.

London 1883

Collection of Paintings Lent for Exhibition by the Marquess of Bute. Bethnal Green Museum (catalogue by Jean Paul Richter).

London 1885

Royal Academy of Art Exhibition. Royal Academy.

London 1887

Royal Academy of Art Exhibition. Royal Academy.

London 1890

Royal Academy of Art Exhibition. Royal Academy.

London 1891

Royal Academy of Art Exhibition. Royal Academy.

London 1892

Loan Collection of Pictures. Art Gallery of the Corporation of London, Guildhall.

London 1894

Loan Collection of Pictures. Art Gallery of the Corporation of London, Guildhall (catalogue by A. G. Temple).

London 1900

Exhibition of Pictures by Dutch Masters of the Seventeenth Century. Burlington Fine Arts Club.

London 1903

Exhibition of Works by the Old Masters and Deceased Masters of the British School, Including a Collection of Paintings by Aelbert Cuyp…. Royal Academy.

London 1911

Exhibition of Old Masters in Aid of the National Art-Collection Fund. The Grafton Galleries (catalogue by Roger E. Fry and M. W. Brockwell).

London 1912

Exhibition of Drawings and Sketches by Old Masters and by Artists of the British School, Principally Acquired Between 1904 and 1912. The British Museum (catalogue by S. Colvin).

London 1922

Royal Academy of Art Exhibition. Royal Academy.

London 1924

Loan Exhibition of Pictures by Old Masters on Behalf of Lord Haig's Appeal for Ex-Service Men. Thos. Agnew & Sons.

London 1928a

Exhibition of Art Treasures. The Grafton Galleries.

London 1928b

Works by a Late Member of the Royal Academy and of the Iveagh Bequest. Royal Academy.

London 1929

Exhibition of Dutch Art 1450–1900. Royal Academy.

London 1936

Pictures, Drawings, etc. Burlington Fine Arts Club.

London 1937

Old Masters. P. and D. Colnaghi and Co.

London 1938
Seventeenth-Century Art in Europe. Royal Academy.

London 1945
Dutch Paintings of the 17th Century. The National Gallery.

London 1946
The King's Pictures. Royal Academy.

London 1947
Some Pictures from the Dulwich Gallery. The National Gallery.

London 1949a
Masterpieces of Dutch and Flemish Painting. Slatter Gallery.

London 1949b
Exhibition of Pictures by Richard Wilson and His Circle.
Tate Gallery.

London 1952
Dutch Pictures 1450–1750. Royal Academy.

London 1953
Drawings by Old Masters. Royal Academy.

London 1957
*European Pictures from an English County in Aid of the British
Red Cross Society, Hampshire Branch.* Thos. Agnew & Sons.

London 1963
Horace Buttery Memorial Exhibition. Thos. Agnew & Sons.

London 1964
The Orange and the Rose. Victoria and Albert Museum.

London 1967
Christie's Bicentenary. Christie's.

London 1970
Drawings from the Teylers Museum, Haarlem. Victoria and
Albert Museum (catalogue by I. Q. van Regteren Altena
and P. W. Ward-Jackson).

London 1971
Dutch Pictures from the Royal Collection. Queen's Gallery
(catalogue by Oliver Millar).

London 1972
The Alexander Gift. The National Gallery.

London 1973
Aelbert Cuyp in British Collections. The National Gallery
(catalogue by Stephen Reiss).

London 1976
Art in Seventeenth-Century Holland. The National Gallery
(catalogue by Christopher Brown).

London 1981
Augustus Wall Calcott. Tate Gallery (catalogue by
David B. Brown).

London 1986
*Dutch Landscape: The Early Years, Haarlem and
Amsterdam 1590–1650.* The National Gallery (catalogue by
Christopher Brown).

London 1988
Art in the Making. Rembrandt. The National Gallery
(catalogue by David Bomford, Christopher Brown, Ashok
Roy et al.).

London 1991
Carlton House: The Past Glories of George IV's Palace.
Queen's Gallery.

London 1994
Turner's Holland. Tate Gallery (catalogue by Alfred Gustave
Herbert Bachrach).

London 1995a
*Conserving Old Masters. Paintings Recently Restored at Dulwich
Picture Gallery.* Dulwich Picture Gallery (catalogue by
Richard Beresford and Giles Waterfield).

London 1995b
In Trust for the Nation, Paintings from National Trust Houses.
The National Gallery (catalogue by Alastair Laing).

London and The Hague 1999
Rembrandt by Himself. The National Gallery and Mauritshuis
(catalogue by Christopher White and Quentin Buvelot).

Los Angeles, Boston, and New York 1981
*A Mirror of Nature: Dutch Paintings from the Collection of Mr. and
Mrs. Edward William Carter.* Los Angeles County Museum
of Art, Museum of Fine Arts, Metropolitan Museum of Art
(catalogue by John Walsh Jr. and Cynthia P. Schneider).

Lugano 1985
Capolavori da musei ungheresi. Thyssen-Bornemisza Collection,
Villa Favorita.

Madrid 1921
*Pintores holandeses dibujos, escultura, lithografia y arte aplicado,
llevados por la cómision del consejo para las artes representativas
de la cómision holandesa en el extranjero.*

Manchester 1857
*Catalogue of the Art Treasures of the United Kingdom. Collected
at Manchester in 1857.* Museum of Ornamental Art.

Manchester 1885
The Bute Collection of Pictures. Queen's Park Museum and
Art Gallery (catalogue by Jean Paul Richter).

Manchester 1928
Old Masters Presented to the Nation by the Late Earl of Iveagh.
City Art Gallery.

Manchester 1976
*Landscape in Flemish and Dutch Drawings of the 17th century
from the Collection of the Musées Royaux des Beaux-Arts de Belgique,
Brussels.* Whitworth Art Gallery, University of Manchester
(catalogue by Eliane de Wilde).

Manchester 1979
Historic Hungarian Costume from Budapest. Whitworth Art Gallery (catalogue by Emöke László).

Minneapolis, Toledo, and Los Angeles 1990
Mirror of Empire, Dutch Marine Art of the Seventeenth Century. Minneapolis Institute of Arts, Toledo Museum of Art, and the Los Angeles County Museum of Art (catalogue by George Keyes).

Montreal 1953
Five Centuries of Drawings. The Montreal Museum of Fine Arts.

Montreal 1990
Italian Recollections: Dutch Painters of the Golden Age. The Montreal Museum of Fine Arts (catalogue by Frederik J. Duparc and Linda L. Graif).

Munich 1869
Ausstellung von Gemälden älterer Meister. Königlichen Kunstausstellungsgebäude.

Munich and Bonn 1993
Das Land am Meer. Holländische Landschaft im 17. Jahrhundert. Staatliche Graphische Sammlung and Rheinisches Landesmuseum (catalogue by Thea Vignau-Wilberg).

Nagasaki 1993
Masters of Dordrecht: 17th-, 18th-, and 19th-Century Paintings from the Collection of the Dordrechts Museum. Palace Huis ten Bosch Museum.

Newcastle-upon-Tyne 1927
Exhibition of Dutch Paintings. Laing Art Gallery.

New York 1939
Masterpieces of Art: Catalogue of European Paintings and Sculpture from 1300–1800. New York's World Fair.

New York 1959
Great Master Drawings of Seven Centuries. A Benefit Exhibition for Columbia University. M. Knoedler and Company.

New York 1976
Tricolour. 17th Century Dutch, 18th Century English, and 19th Century French Drawings from the Robert Lehman Collection. The Metropolitan Museum of Art (catalogue by George Szabo).

New York 1992
Splendid Legacy. The Havemeyer Collection. Metropolitan Museum of Art (catalogue by Alice Cooney Frelinghuysen).

New York 1995
Drawings from the Albertina: Landscape in the Age of Rembrandt. The Drawing Center (catalogue by Marian Bisanz-Prakken).

New York 1998
Master Drawings from the Hermitage and the Pushkin Museums. The Pierpont Morgan Library (catalogue by Alexei Larionov et al.).

New York and Chicago 1988
Dutch and Flemish Paintings from the Hermitage. Metropolitan Museum of Art and The Art Institute of Chicago (catalogue by I. Sokolova).

New York and Evanston 1988
Landscape Drawings of Five Centuries, 1400–1900, from the Robert Lehman Collection. Metropolitan Museum of Art and Mary and Leigh Block Gallery (catalogue by George Szabo et al.).

New York and London 1986
The Northern Landscape: Flemish, Dutch, and British Drawings from the Courtauld Collections. The Drawing Center and Courtauld Institute Galleries (catalogue by Dennis Farr, William Bradford).

New York and Paris 1977–1978
Rembrandt and His Century. Dutch Drawings of the Seventeenth Century. The Pierpont Morgan Library and Institut Néerlandais (catalogue by Carlos Van Hasselt).

New York, Toledo, and Toronto 1954
Dutch Painting: The Golden Age. An Exhibition of Dutch Pictures of the Seventeenth Century. Metropolitan Museum of Art, Toledo Museum of Art, The Art Gallery of Toronto.

Nijmegen 1980
Het Valkhof te Nijmegen. Museum Commanderie van Sint-Jan.

Norwich 1925
Centenary of Norwich Museum: Loan Collection of Pictures. Norwich Castle Museum.

Norwich 1954
East Anglia and the Netherlands. Norwich Castle Museum.

Norwich 1964
Fine Paintings from East Anglia. Norwich Castle Museum.

Nottingham Castle 1878
Pictures and Objects. Midlands Counties Art Museum.

Paris 1921
Exposition hollandaise. Jeu de Paume.

Paris 1946
Les chefs-d'oeuvre des collections françaises retrouvés en Allemagne. Musée de l'Orangerie.

Paris 1950
Le paysage hollandais au XVIIe siècle. Musée de l'Orangerie.

Paris 1952
Chefs d'oeuvre de la collection D.G. van Beuningen. Petit Palais.

Paris 1970
Rembrandt et son temps. Dessins des collections publiques et privées conservées [sic] en France. Musée du Louvre.

Paris 1974
Dessins flamands et hollandais du dix-septième siècle. Collections Musées de Belgique, Musée Boymans-van Beuningen, Rotterdam, Institut Néerlandais, Paris. Institut Néerlandais.

Paris 1989
Éloge de la navigation hollandaise au XVIIe siècle: tableaux, dessins et gravures de la mer et des rivages dans la collection Frits Lugt. Institut Néerlandais (catalogue by Carlos van Hasselt).

Paris and Hamburg 1985–1986
Renaissance des Nordens: Meister Zeichnungen aus der École Nationale Supérieure des Beaux-Arts, Paris. École Nationale Supérieure des Beaux-Arts and Hamburg Kunsthalle.

Philadelphia 1973–1974
Thomas Doughty. Pennsylvania Academy of Fine Arts (catalogue by F. Goodyear).

Poughkeepsie 1976
Seventeenth-Century Dutch Landscape Drawings and Selected Prints from American Collections. Vassar College (catalogue by Curtis Baer et al.).

Rotterdam 1934
Nederlandsche teekeningen uit de 15de, 16de en 17de eeuw (verzameling F. Koenigs). Museum Boymans-van Beuningen.

Rotterdam 1938
Meesterwerken uit vier eeuwen, 1400–1800. Museum Boymans-van Beuningen.

Rotterdam 1949
Meesterwerken uit de verzameling D.G. van Beuningen. Museum Boymans-van Beuningen (catalogue by D. Hannema).

Rotterdam 1954
Tekeningen en aquarellen van Vlaamse en Hollandse meesters uit de verzameling De Grez in de Koninklijke Musea voor Schone Kunsten te Brussel. Museum Boymans-van Beuningen.

Rotterdam 1955
Kunstschatten uit Nederlandse verzamelingen. Museum Boymans-van Beuningen.

Rotterdam 1960
Bloemen, vogels en insecten. Museum Boymans-van Beuningen.

Rotterdam 1994
Rotterdamse Meesters uit de Gouden Eeuw. Historisch Museum (catalogue by Nora Schadee).

Rotterdam and Berlin 1996
Praise of Ships and the Sea, The Dutch Marine Painters of the Seventeenth Century. Museum Boymans-van Beuningen and Staatliche Museen zu Berlin, Gemäldegalerie in Bodemuseum (catalogue by Jeroen Giltaij et al.).

Salzburg 1980
Salzburger Landessammlungen: Residenzgalerie mit Sammlung Czernin und Sammlung Schönborn-Buchheim. Die Galerie (catalogue by Edmund Blechinger).

San Francisco 1939–1940
Seven Centuries of Paintings. California Palace of the Legion of Honor.

Santa Barbara, San Francisco, and Kansas City 1954
The Horse in Art: Paintings—17th to 20th Century. Santa Barbara Museum of Art, California Palace of the Legion of Honor, and William Rockhill Nelson Gallery of Art.

Stoke-on-Trent 1928
Exhibition of Dutch Paintings. Stoke City Museum and Art Gallery.

Tokyo 1979
European Masters Drawings from the Fogg Art Museum. National Museum of Western Art.

Toronto 1926
Inaugural Exhibition. The Art Gallery of Toronto.

Toronto 1940
An Exhibition of Great Paintings in Aid of the Canadian Red Cross. The Art Gallery of Toronto.

Turin 2000
Catalogo. No. 41. Galleria Luigi Caretto.

Utrecht 1903
Tentoonstelling van Tekeningen van Oud-Nederlandsche Meesters. Vereeniging "Voor de Kunst."

Utrecht 1965
Nederlandse 17e eeuwse Italianiserende landschapschilders. Centraal Museum (catalogue by Albert Blankert).

Utrecht 2000
Pieter Saenredam, het Utrechtse werk. Schilderijen en tekeningen van de 17de-eeuwse grootmeester van het perspectief. Centraal Museum (catalogue by L. Helmus et al.).

Utrecht, Frankfurt, and Luxemburg 1993–1994
Het Gedroomde Land: Pastorale schilderkunst in de Gouden Eeuw. Centraal Museum, Schirn Kunsthalle, and the Musée National d'Histoire et d'Art (catalogue by Peter Van den Brink et al.).

Vianen 1999
Johan Wolfert van Brederode 1599–1655: Een Hollands edelman tussen Nassau en Oranje. Historische Vereniging Het land van Brederode (catalogue by A.J.M. Koenhein et al.).

Vienna 1936
Die holländische Landschaft im Zeitalter Rembrandts. Graphische Sammlung Albertina (catalogue by O. Benesch).

Vienna 1993
Die Landschaft im Jahrhundert Rembrandts: Niederländische Zeichnungen des 17. Jahrhunderts aus der Graphischen Sammlung Albertina. Graphische Sammlung Albertina (catalogue by Marian Bisanz-Prakken).

Washington 1958
Dutch Drawings. Masterpieces from Five Centuries. National Gallery of Art (catalogue by J.Q. van Regteren Altena).

Washington 1988
Paintings by Fitz Hugh Lane. National Gallery of Art (catalogue by John Wilmerding).

Washington 1996
Dutch and Flemish Art from the Golden Age. National Gallery of Art.

Washington, Denver, and Fort Worth 1977
Seventeenth-Century Dutch Drawings from American Collections. A Loan Exhibition. National Gallery of Art, Denver Art Museum, and Kimbell Art Museum (catalogue by Franklin W. Robinson).

Washington, Detroit, and Amsterdam 1980
Gods, Saints, & Heroes: Dutch Paintings in the Age of Rembrandt. National Gallery of Art, Detroit Institute of Arts, and Rijksmuseum (catalogue by Albert Blankert et al.).

Washington, London, and Haarlem 1989
Frans Hals. National Gallery of Art, Royal Academy, and Frans Halsmuseum (catalogue by Seymour Slive et al.).

Washington and Los Angeles 1985
Collection for a King: Old Master Paintings from the Dulwich Picture Gallery. National Gallery of Art and Los Angeles County Museum of Art (catalogue by Giles Waterfield, reprint, 1995).

Washington and New York 1984
Old Master Drawings from the Albertina. National Gallery of Art and The Pierpont Morgan Library.

Weimar 1981
Rembrandt seine Zeitgenossen. Handzeichnungen niederländischer und flämischer Meister des 17. Jahrhunderts aus dem Besitz der Kunstsammlungen zu Weimar. Kunsthalle am Theaterplatz (catalogue by R. Barth).

List of Works in the Exhibition

Paintings

The Baptism of the Eunuch (cat. 9) **106**
The Baptism of the Eunuch (cat. 30) **152**
Bulls on a Riverbank (cat. 23) **136**
Cattle and Cottage near a River (cat. 4) **96**
Cattle and Herders, with Mariakerk, Utrecht (cat. 5) **98**
Conversion of Saul (cat. 16) **124**
Cows in a River (cat. 21) **134**
Cows in a River (cat. 22) **136**
Dordrecht from the North (cat. 35) **162**
Dordrecht from the North (cat. 36) **164**
Dordrecht Harbor by Moonlight (cat. 12) **114**
Evening Landscape (cat. 44) **182**
A Farm with Cottages and Animals (cat. 10) **110**
Flight into Egypt (cat. 41) **176**
A Herdsman with Five Cows by a River (cat. 20) **132**
Herdsmen with Cattle (cat. 14) **120**
Horsemen and Herdsmen with Cattle (cat. 38) **168**
Horsemen Resting in a Landscape (cat. 37) **166**
Ice Scene before the Huis te Merwede near Dordrecht
  (cat. 32) **156**
Lady and Gentleman on Horseback (cat. 40) **172**
Landscape with a View of the Valkhof, Nijmegen
  (cat. 43) **180**
Landscape with Herdsmen (cat. 25) **142**
Landscape with Horse Trainers (cat. 39) **170**
Landscape with Shepherds and Shepherdesses (cat. 13) **118**
The Maas at Dordrecht (cat. 28) **146**
The Maas at Dordrecht in a Storm (cat. 18) **128**
Michiel and Cornelis Pompe van Meerdervoort with Their
  Tutor (cat. 29) **150**
Open Countryside with Shepherds and Animals (cat. 2) **92**
Orpheus Charming the Animals (cat. 1) **88**
A Pier in Dordrecht Harbor (cat. 8) **104**
Portrait of a Family in a Landscape (cat. 3) **94**
Portrait of a Man with a Rifle (cat. 27) **144**

Portrait of a Woman Aged Twenty-One, as a Hunter
  (cat. 26) **144**
River Landscape with Bridge (cat. 6) **100**
River Landscape with Cows (cat. 19) **130**
River Landscape with Horseman and Peasants (cat. 45) **184**
River Landscape with Two Horsemen (cat. 42) **178**
A River Scene with Distant Windmills (cat. 7) **102**
Travelers in a Hilly Countryside (cat. 24) **140**
Two Horsemen on a Ridge (cat. 17) **126**
Ubbergen Castle (cat. 31) **154**
The Valkhof at Nijmegen from the East (cat. 34) **158**
The Valkhof at Nijmegen from the Northwest (cat. 33) **158**
Woman in a Stable (cat. 15) **122**
Wooded Landscape with an Artist (cat. 11) **112**

Drawings

Amersfoort Viewed from the Southeast (cat. 71) **239**
Arnhem Viewed from the Northwest (cat. 75) **243**
Arnhem Viewed from the West (cat. 74) **242**
Boats at a Pier on a River (cat. 63) **231**
A Bullock Standing (cat. 102) **270**
The Buurkerk in Utrecht in Rural Surroundings (cat. 48) **216**
Calcar and the Monterberg Viewed from Cleves (cat. 91) **259**
Calcar with Monterberg in the Distance (cat. 76) **244**
Cleves Viewed from the Galgenberg (cat. 90) **258**
Country Road with a Cottage alongside a River (cat. 64) **232**
A Cow Lying Down (cat. 103) **271**
A Cow Standing (cat. 101) **269**
A Dike alongside a River, a Bridge, and Trees to the
  Right (cat. 66) **234**
A Dog Lying Down (cat. 104) **272**
Dordrecht Viewed from the East (cat. 72) **240**
Dordrecht Viewed from the North, with a Windmill
  in the Foreground (cat. 82) **250**
Dordrecht Viewed from the North, with the Grote Kerk
  (cat. 83) **251**

Dordrecht Viewed from the North, with the Grote Kerk
  and the Groothoofdspoort (cat. 84) **252**
Dordrecht Viewed from the Northeast (cat. 80) **248**
Dunes with the Ruins of a Manor in the Distance
  (cat. 79) **247**
The Edge of a Woods with Travelers (cat. 51) **219**
Farmhouses along Both Sides of a Canal (cat. 68) **236**
Four Trees near a Fence (cat. 50) **218**
A Freight Boat and a Timber Raft on Calm Water (cat. 85) **253**
The Groothoofdspoort in Dordrecht from the West
  (cat. 81) **249**
The Grote Kerk in Dordrecht from the Southwest
  (cat. 61, verso) **229**
The Hague Viewed from the Northwest (cat. 78) **246**
A Horse near the Bank of a River with Two Moored
  Rowboats (cat. 98) **266**
A Manor House among Trees, High Hills in the Distance
  (cat. 59) **227**
The Mariakerk in Utrecht from the Northeast (cat. 46) **214**
The Mariakerk in Utrecht from the Northwest (cat. 47) **215**
A Milkmaid (cat. 107) **275**
Moored Rowboats on a River, a Church in the Distance
  (cat. 62) **230**
Nijmegen with the Valkhof, Viewed from the Northeast
  (cat. 87) **255**
Panorama with a Country Manor (cat. 58) **226**
Panorama with a Shepherd Surveying the Landscape
  (cat. 77) **245**
A Path at the Edge of a Woods with Two Old Oak Trees
  (cat. 53) **221**
Path between Trees (cat. 52) **220**
Peasant Carts near a Farmhouse in a Dune Landscape
  (cat. 60) **228**
Portrait of a Twenty-Nine-Year-Old Man (cat. 108) **276**
Portrait of a Twenty-Three-Year-Old Woman (cat. 109) **276**
Rhenen Viewed from the Northeast (cat. 73) **241**

Photographic Credits

Every effort has been made to locate the copyright holders
for the photographs used in this book. Any omissions will be
corrected in subsequent editions.

Gordenker essay

fig. 3: © The British Museum; fig. 4: Photo Bibliothèque
Nationale de France, Paris; fig. 7: Photo Courtesy of
the Bridgeman Art Library; fig. 9: Bildarchiv Foto Marburg

Spring essay

fig. 2: © The Natural History Museum, London

Wheelock essay

fig. 6: © Patrimonio Nacional; fig. 12: Photo Otto Naumann
Ltd., New York, Johnny van Haeften, London

Haverkamp-Begemann essay

fig. 5: © Rijksmuseum, Amsterdam

Catalogue

cat. 2 fig. 1, cat. 15 fig. 1, and cat. 104 fig. 1: © Rijksmuseum,
Amsterdam; cat. 4 fig. 1: © Patrimonio Nacional; cat. 7
fig. 1: © Hamburger Kunsthalle, photographer Elke Walford,
Hamburg; cat. 8 fig. 2: Elke Walford, Hamburg; cat. 9
fig. 1: © Rijksmuseum — Stichting Amsterdam; cat. 28 fig. 1:
© The National Trust, Waddesdon Manor and Photographic
Survey, Courtauld Institute of Art; cat. 29 fig. 1, cat. 32
fig. 2, and cat. 43 fig. 1: © Marquess of Tavistock and the
Trustees of Bedford Estate; cat. 32 fig. 1: © The British
Museum; cat. 47 fig. 1 and cat. 86 fig. 1: © Bildarchiv Preus-
sischer Kulturbesitz, Berlin; cat. 78 fig. 1: © Teylers Museum,
Haarlem; cat. 91 fig. 1: photograph by Piet Boonstra.